A History of
American Labor

2 Litchfield Road
Londonderry, NH 03053
Meetinghouseofnhdems@gmail.com

JOSEPH G. RAYBACK

A History of

American Labor

EXPANDED AND UPDATED

The Free Press, New York
Collier-Macmillan Limited, London

Library of Congress catalog card number: 59–5344

Collier-Macmillan Canada, Ltd., Toronto, Ontario

First Free Press Paperback Edition 1966

printing number
4 5 6 7 8 9 10

to Kay
Who assisted in the preparation
of four versions of this book

Foreword

In preparing the original edition of this book, published by The Macmillan Company in 1959, I had several goals in mind. I wanted to write a history of American labor in which labor was regarded not as a separate entity but as an integral part of American life. Accordingly, and within the limits set by available space, I tried to present the growth of labor against the background of American political, economic, industrial, and social history. Second, I tried to correct the all too common impression that labor as it is known today somehow appeared out of the factory system in some vague period after the Civil War. I therefore gave more than usual attention to earlier developments: the colonial labor systems, the role of labor in the American Revolution, the early labor associations, and the pre-Civil War developments upon which most latter-day labor institutions and traditions and thinking were based. Finally, I tried to indicate the effect of labor upon American institutions. For that reason, without neglecting labor's relationship to employers—in which relationship labor often made economic gains—I also gave more than usual attention to labor's roles in politics and in the legislative process, through which its influence upon American institutions was most often felt.

In this revised edition, my goals have remained the same. Aside from correcting some errors to which my friends and my reviewers have called my attention, I have had one other fundamental aim: I have tried to bring the history of American labor up to date. The original edition ended with the expulsion of the teamsters from the A.F.L.-C.I.O. at the end of 1957; this edition continues the history to the middle of 1965, when much of the political program that labor had developed since the passage of the Taft-Hartley Act was finally being enacted and when an expansive economy appeared to presage a favorable reversal in labor's slowly declining fortunes.

I have not revised the bibliography; instead I have attached an addendum of significant books and articles published since my last writing. I have, however, totally revised the index.

JOSEPH G. RAYBACK

Contents

*A History of
American Labor*

PART ONE

The Colonial and Revolutionary Era

1 ___

The Colonial Economy

Like all pioneer societies the American colonies had an agricultural economy. But while the overwhelming majority of inhabitants in every colony earned their livelihood either as farm owners, tenants, or hired hands, the colonial economy was not exclusively agrarian. From earliest days farmers hired workers to build houses, bedsteads, and to make shoes and other products. The farmer supplied the raw materials to be transformed into finished products; the workers supplied the tools. Under such circumstances the farmer's household became a "manufactory" and the hired men became the first industrial laborers. These laborers were itinerant, moving from farmhouse to farmhouse with their tools and skills; securing lodgings, board, and wages; and departing when the needs of the farmer-employer were satisfied. The itinerant laborer never disappeared from the colonial scene. Throughout the era, farmers continued to hire farm hands and wandering "mechanicks" whenever needs demanded. Even in the nineteenth century the itinerant worker was a common sight in sparsely settled frontier areas.

Itinerant manufacturing did not long dominate the colonial industrial scene. As population increased and thickened, the nonagricultural laborer who had accumulated a little capital settled down in town, erected a home, and opened a workshop. At this point industry entered the "custom-order" stage. A one-man industry, it depended largely at first on individual orders from merchants and farmers who could supply the materials to be transformed. Later, the workshop owner himself began to supply the raw materials of his trade which were transformed at the customer's bidding.

3

While custom-order industry remained widespread throughout most of the colonial era, it gradually gave way to another form of enterprise. The change was occasioned primarily by the transformation of towns into cities and by the growth of a large population within the city environs. As the market expanded, the workshop owner began to employ journeymen to increase production; simultaneously he began to stock up on finished products made by his journeymen for sale to "sojourners" and visitors. Two classes of product were developed: a superior quality for the custom-trade and an inferior quality known as "shop" work for the lower-level trade. The new stage, known as "retail-order" industry, appeared as early as 1715 and reached a climax in the last twenty years of the century.

The change produced America's first industrial classes. In earlier stages there were no distinct employer-employee elements; in the retail-order stage the workshop owner became an employer-merchant. He ceased, except on occasion, to perform manual labor and secured remuneration mainly from his managerial ability and his investments. Relations between him and his journeymen were harmonious. The workshop master was still a skilled worker intimately acquainted with his journeymen's psychology. Moreover, the market was still local: the existing turnpikes were primarily feeders from the city to the near countryside. Since the market was restricted and all masters were confronted with similar conditions, it was simple to equalize competition and to satisfy journeymen's wage demands by shifting any increase in wages to consumers. Journeymen, in turn, recognizing that their wages could best be maintained by cooperating with the masters in suppressing price-cutting competitors, actively supported their employers against those masters who refused to abide by established standards. Evidence of this harmony of interest was revealed by the establishment of "mechanics' societies" during the eighteenth century.

Throughout these developments, manufacturing remained essentially a handicraft enterprise. A considerable portion of it was always conducted, with or without the supervision of an itinerant laborer, in the household, and some was carried on in plantation workshops. But most manufacturing occurred in or near towns and cities. In these the typical workshop of the retail-order stage employed one or two journeymen and an equal number of apprentices. Some shops were larger —notably in the carpentry and cabinet trades, in weaving, and in the tanning and shoe industries. Saw, grist, and flour mills, in which water or wind power supplemented handicraft labor, employed from two to five men. Distilleries, breweries, paper and gunpowder manufacturies, shipyards, and ropewalks achieved greater size, employing generally from five to ten, and sometimes as many as twenty-five laborers. The giant of colonial manufacturing enterprise was the iron industry, established in rural areas where there was an adequate supply of ore, water power, and large quantities of wood to be used for charcoal. An iron plantation averaged twenty-five employees; a number in every colony had more than one hundred workmen.

Manufacturing was only one of the colonial enterprises that developed employer-employee classes. In very earliest times fishing was an individual enterprise, but as a trade in fish with the West Indies developed, owners of fishing boats began to hire labor on a large scale both to help with the catch and to dry and salt the ocean product for export. Whaling went through the same development even more rapidly.

Commerce progressed through similar stages. The first merchants in America, whether trading-company agents or private individuals, were essentially importers; but as soon as surplus agricultural products appeared, they began to develop an export trade as well. Simultaneously the merchants went in search of their own supplies and the enterprise developed several divisions: shipping with its use of ships and its employment of seagoing and longshore labor; wholesaling with its use of warehouses and its employment of factors; retailing with its use of shops and its employment of clerks; and a distributing trade with its use of horses and wagons and its employment of draymen, porters, and carters.

Colonials divided the labor element engaged in their varied enterprises into three kinds: indentured servants, who in exchange for payment of passage to the colonies worked for masters under long-term contracts; free labor which included those hired for wages on farms, those engaged as artisans or as unskilled help in handicraft shops and mills, or in the longshore and distributing trades; and seagoing labor which included fishermen, whalers, and sailors—who were also free labor but were regarded as a special class. Generally, it is concluded that this laboring element formed a relatively minor portion of the colonial population. Actually, the total group constituted a substantial proportion of the population. While there are no reliable statistics upon the subject, a rough figure can be ascertained.

Information concerning the indentured servant class is best. Two census reports made by Maryland in 1707 and 1755, together with certain known trends concerning the rise or decline of indentured servitude in different colonial areas in the seventeenth and eighteenth centuries, and incomplete immigration figures lead to the conclusion that the indentured servant class constituted about 10 per cent of the white population.

More difficult to determine is the size of the free labor population. There are literally no clues to the number of free laborers who hired themselves out to farmers. It is equally difficult to determine the number of free laborers employed in workshop, longshore, and distributing trades. Judging by the amount of enterprise carried on in the colonies and by the ubiquity of colonial manufacturing enterprise, it would seem fair to guess that the total amount of free labor ran between 2 and 4 per cent of the white population. As for seagoing labor, it has been estimated, and the figure is generally accepted, that there were 33,000 seamen employed in the colonies on the eve of the Revolution—about 2½ per cent of the white population. This proportion of seagoing laborers to the rest of the population probably remained fairly constant throughout the colonial era.

The total labor supply of the colonies can thus be reckoned as somewhere between 14 and 17 per cent of the whole white population. Of this portion about two-thirds were indentured servants, and the remainder belonged to the ranks of free labor. Similarly, about two-thirds of the whole labor element was employed in agricultural callings and the remaining third in manufacturing, fishing, and commerce.

2 ——

Colonial Labor

Of the three kinds of colonial labor, indentured servitude was in many ways the most important. Created originally by the London Company to fill the acute need for manpower in its Virginia settlements, it was thence transferred to all other American colonies. No less than 50 per cent of the total white population came to the colonies as servants. In the seventeenth century they came chiefly from England; in the eighteenth century so many Scots, Scotch-Irish, Irish, Germans, Swiss, and other nationalities came into the country as servants that by the time of the Revolution 50 per cent of the population south of New England was of non-English stock. The institution was one of the greatest colonizing agencies of history.

The overwhelming majority of servants migrated to the colonies voluntarily. Contrary to general opinion, they were not the traditionally poor, but came from the class made homeless and jobless by current economic developments—by enclosures and by the decline of the guilds. A prime force of encouragement to their migration was the persuasions of those who saw profit in the trade. Merchants early recognized that indentured servants made a fine cargo. Accordingly, they circulated printed handbills and pamphlets throughout Britain and the Continent setting forth the opportunities afforded in the American colonies in language that was the forerunner of modern advertising. This paper-and-ink campaign was supplemented by agents who worked upon the longings of the gullible and persuaded them to sign up for the long voyage.

Along with those who came freely there was another group: the convicts. Crime greatly increased in Britain, along with economic instability, after 1500. For a time the effort to suppress it took the form of a brutal code which punished some three hundred felonies with death. But in 1615 some leniency was introduced into the system by

substituting exile for the death penalty. Very few convicts were sent
to the American colonies in the first half of the seventeenth century,
but after 1655 the numbers increased steadily. In all about 35,000
convicts were transported with Maryland and Virginia together receiving the largest bloc. Despite efforts to glamourize this element,
the convicts thus bestowed on the colonies were a sorry lot; most of
them were outright criminals, and probably one-fifth were guilty
of serious crimes.

Not all servants were imported; a substantial amount of servant
labor was recruited in the colonies. Colonial authorities regularly
sentenced to servitude persons guilty of criminal actions on the
ground that servitude would be a corrective. Imposition of servitude
for crime was applied both to servants and to free persons. Applied
to servants, the penalty did not create new labor; it merely lengthened the term of indenture. It was imposed for a number of offenses,
chief of which was unlawful absence. A sentence of servitude upon
free persons was imposed for most felonies. A more important colonial source of labor was the judgment debtor. The colonies originally
adopted the practice of imprisoning debtors, but the need for labor
led to the passage of legislation releasing the debtor from prison to
serve the creditor for a period of time sufficient to satisfy the debt.
The institution, despite its inequities, worked fairly satisfactorily.
Debtors often petitioned the court to sell them and advertised themselves in the press to the same purpose. In the eighteenth century,
with the development of an indigent poor element in colonial
society, the judgment debtor became a common character.

The times and conditions under which servants were employed
and lived were severe. Typical indentures—those imported from
Europe—generally reached an American port in miserable condition,
undernourished and disease-weakened by the voyage across the
Atlantic. Upon arrival their outward appearance was refurbished
and they were marched ashore where their terms of service were
promptly auctioned to the highest bidder. Once sold, the indentured
servant found himself bound to labor for a master at whatever tasks
appointed for the period of time stipulated in his contract, if he had
brought one with him, or according to the "custom of the country"
if no written indenture had been made. The term of service varied
from as little as one year to seven years or more. The bulk of the

contracts averaged about four years. Compensation for the indentured servant consisted of food, clothing, and shelter during the term of servitude.

The colonies for the most part regarded and treated a servant, or more correctly his term of service, as private property. A servant was bought and sold at will and could be leased or hired out with almost no restrictions. He was likewise regarded as the property of a deceased person's estate to be passed on by will, distributed by an administrator, or attached to satisfy debts.

The law gave masters authority to administer corporal punishment as a corrective to a servant for neglect of duty, abusive conduct, or general insubordination, which in practice meant refusal to work in accordance with the master's direction or wishes. It provided for and permitted masters to extend the term of a servant who took French leave for a few days' dissipation or who attempted to run away from his contract. The law—particularly in the southern colonies—provided severe penalties for servants who in combination refused to work or who deserted in a group. Whipping, branding, and laboring in irons were imposed upon the comparatively mild conspiracy of refusing to work; imprisonment and hanging were common punishments for the greater crime of desertion.

The disciplinary measures imposed upon the indentured servant indicate that his lot was not a happy one. Yet no accurate generalization can be made. An analysis of court records shows that cruelty and oppression of servants was not typical of New England or New York, where servants were but a small part of the population and were more frequently artisans than field hands. South of the Hudson the lot of the servant was worse. In Pennsylvania maltreatment was common. In the "tobacco colonies," where many of the masters led drunken and dissolute lives, treatment was often brutal and sadistic.

But the temper of a master was not the only cause of misery. Those who came to America as servants were accustomed to obedience and suffering. They were not, however, accustomed to the American climate or the American working conditions. In the South the heat of the sun was fearful and exacted a heavy toll of migrants both in illness and in death until experience taught the colonists that rest during the heat of the day, on Saturday afternoon, and upon the Sabbath was more profitable. Work in the field—the lot of most servants—was more exhausting than in Europe because it included the task of preparing new land for planting. Trees had to be felled, trimmed, and dragged away; brush had to be cleared, stumps removed, and the soil turned for the first time in the history of the earth without good tools and sometimes even without the help of animals. It was a back-breaking task; even seasoned European farmers suffered under the load.

While the colonies for the most part treated the indentured servant as property, they also recognized him as a human being, different only because his mobility, his freedom of occupational choice, and certain liberties were curbed for a term of years; his children did not inherit his condition. In all other respects his rights remained unimpaired.

The factor which confirmed the servant's status as a person was his right to a day in court. In general his appearance there revolved around enforcement of the conditions of his contract against his master. He came to pray for relief on grounds of undue discipline or insufficient food and clothing, and to sue for his freedom when his term ended. On the whole the courts were sympathetic to his plight. New England judges were especially eager to curb physical maltreatment of servants, even occasionally calling in the church to aid them. New York courts had a record unsurpassed in according relief to servants abused by their masters; in every single case of maltreatment brought before the judicial authorities of that colony before 1774 the servant was given his freedom. New Jersey and Pennsylvania courts could also boast fine records. Though they seldom discharged an abused servant, they often granted relief by transferring the servant to another employer or by admonishing the master to better performance on pain of future loss of his servant. The records of the southern colonies, however, were marred by palpable injustices. The laws of Maryland, Virginia, and the Carolinas specifically provided against abusive or negligent treatment, but it was no easy task to convict a master of wrongdoing in the South where the bench was invariably occupied by members of the master class and where there was a tendency to look upon servants as brute beasts. Nevertheless the courts granted redress, usually admonition to the master, in about two-thirds of the cases brought to their attention.

In addition to the right of redress in court the servants also had limited property rights. A servant who brought goods to the colonies had absolute right of property in them and full right of disposal. He had the right to receive gifts, bequests, and inheritances, and to lend money. He had the right to engage in trade and to work for himself, with his master's permission. A term of servitude in the colonies, miserable as it was on occasion, was not wasted time. It seasoned the servant to colonial climate, accustomed him to new modes of living and working, and taught him the best methods of farming and the colonial system of marketing. It gave him acquaintances which might become useful at the end of his term; if he was an artisan his skills became known and he might acquire customers in advance for the days of his freedom. Once freed of his contractual obligations the former servant was readily accepted as a free man with the same opportunities as others. Scarcity of labor meant that he could readily acquire independence.

How many servants took advantage of their opportunities is unknown. In the southern colonies it appears that only about one in ten survived his seasoning, worked out his time, took up land, and became prosperous; probably a like number joined the ranks of the artisans, living comfortably without owning any land. The remainder died by the way, or returned to England, or became "poor whites" owning a little land, living as tenants, or earning a precarious living as hired farm labor. Outside the South the record of success was better. The indentured class of the North, more carefully culled and more liberally treated, had a much better chance to achieve an average standard of living. Taking the element in its entirety, its success in later days was probably not too far behind the record established by those who came to the colonies as free men.

Important as the institution of indentured servitude was to the colonies, it had little influence upon the condition of other forms of colonial labor and no influence upon the history of American labor as a whole. Far more significant were the condition and development of free and seagoing labor. The free-labor supply of the colonies was recruited from three sources: immigrants who paid their own way and brought with them their tools and skills, indentured servants who became free to use their skills after their term of bondage had ended, and the children of these groups, who learned their trades in America.

The condition of free labor rested upon two factors: the condition of the economy and the Tudor Industrial Code. In Britain the Code sought to assure a profit to the agricultural or industrial proprietor by guaranteeing him an adequate low-wage labor supply and, at the same time, to safeguard the worker against undue and unrestrained exploitation. The principles of the code were extensive:

1. With few exceptions it provided for the compulsory labor of all able-bodied persons;

2. To protect the workingman and to check unemployment, it restrained wrongful dismissal of employees;

3. It provided for the fixing of maximum wages by justices of the peace "according to the plenty or scarcity of the times";

4. It declared illegal any combination of workmen to secure higher wages;

5. It provided that no workman was to depart before the end of his agreed term, and then he was required to produce letters testimonial to show that he was free to hire himself out;

6. To assure an adequate supply of skilled workmen and good quality in the manufactured product it set a term of apprenticeship of seven years; eighteenth century amendments to the code further attempted to maintain the skilled labor supply by restricting the emigration of artisans.

Every American colony made some attempt to apply the principles of the Tudor Industrial Code in whole or in part in both the seventeenth and eighteenth centuries. While the application was neither complete nor entirely successful in practice, it made a recognizable impression upon the condition of labor.

All colonies adopted the principle of compulsory labor. As pioneer societies, short on manpower, they resented idleness and denounced it as the parent of all vices. The earliest laws punished idleness by whipping or fines; eighteenth century enactments provided for forced labor or commitment to the workhouse and for deportation of newly arrived unemployed individuals to the colony from which they came. All colonies, moreover, required that men between the ages of sixteen and sixty work at certain times during the year on public works projects—usually roads and highways. In time of war male inhabitants were often conscripted to carry on the agricultural pursuits of men in the militia. Since there was generally more work to be done than labor to accomplish it, the problem of finding work in the colonies was seldom acute until the eighteenth century when world economic cycles occasionally influenced employment conditions and groups of idle men appeared in the seacoast towns. It was then that workhouses were developed as corrective institutions for "beggars, Servants running away or otherwise misbehaving themselves, Trespassers, Rogues, Vagabonds, and other people refusing to work." As the Revolution approached, colonial towns also began to set up manufacturing establishments which provided jobs for the unemployed and for children whose parents were unable to maintain them. Both the workhouse and the public manufactory upheld the principle that labor was required of all inhabitants.

Colonial authorities also enacted legislation dealing with restraints upon dismissal. Neither indentured servants nor free workmen under contract could be dismissed without reasonable and sufficient cause. Incurable illness was generally not sufficient cause. Masters were sometimes fined for breach of such law and frequently were required to provide medical attention for one injured or taken sick during employment. Although the colonists' attitude was based upon a desire to save the local treasury the cost of relief, the principle provided definite protection to workingmen.

All colonies gave attention to the problem of wages. The most significant experiment took place in Massachusetts Bay where the early colonial leaders held strongly to the prevailing mercantilistic views concerning the obedience and honest carriage of the "lower orders." Their first piece of legislation, enacted in 1630, was directed at the building trades in which skilled workers were limited to two shillings a day. Three years later when complaints became loud of "great extortion used by diverse persons of little conscience" because skilled tradesmen were demanding three shillings a day, the colony promulgated a comprehensive wage law. Skilled labor was limited to a daily wage rate of two shillings and the "beste sorte of labourers" to eighteen pence; the normal working day was established as running from 5:00 A.M. to 8:00 P.M. for the summer months and from the "spring of the day until night" for the winter. Two and one-half hours were allowed for breakfast, dinner, and drinking. The colony also set prices on commodities "necessary for life and comfort," which were to be sold at a figure not more than 30 per cent higher than that which prevailed in Britain.

From the start the law was ineffective: current wages exceeded the legal levels by 50 per cent. In 1636 the authorities, recognizing their failure, turned the regulation of wages over to the freemen of the towns, vesting the right of imposing discretionary punishments in the courts. Initially, Bay Colony towns made full use of their authority, even reducing wage levels below those laid down in general legislation. After 1675, however, the system of wage and price fixing quietly disintegrated; the codes remained on the statute books, but the court's enforcement became desultory and eventually ceased completely.

The pattern set by Massachusetts was followed to a lesser degree in Plymouth, New Haven, and Connecticut. Each enacted general codes in the early years of their history but abandoned them in the 1640's and replaced them with laws against "oppression." Connecticut's law was typical: those taking "excessive" wages or "unreasonable" prices were to be punished by fines or imprisonment "according to the Quality of the offenses." In deciding such complaints the court was required to use the opinion of "two or three of the same Occupation or Trade" as the defendant as the basis of judgment. By the eighteenth century, however, these laws were forgotten.

Wage codes outside New England were less thorough. In the middle colonies regulations were established by local authorities and in most cases applied only to specific callings. In the Dutch period of New York's history the most common regulation concerned wages and hours of weighhouse and beer porters—both monopolistic callings; occasionally towns and counties placed limitations upon other trades, but during the English period the number of such regulations decreased. Only Pennsylvania among the middle colonies ever seriously considered the establishment of a general wage code; in 1684 it enacted a law empowering the justices of each county to set wages of workmen and to provide penalties for violation, but there is no evidence that the law was ever invoked.

Southern colonies revealed some favor for wage legislation in their formative years, but their experiments were short-lived. Maryland, in 1640, passed an act empowering the county courts to set "wages and rates of artificers, labourers and chirurgeons according to the most current rate of tobacco"; the law was never executed. In Virginia the governor and council of the London Company fixed wage rates in 1621—at about twice the amount granted to skilled workers in Massachusetts. Several counties on the Eastern Shore enforced the code during the early seventeenth century, but in general the regulations were ignored everywhere after 1640. In South Carolina interest in wage regulation appeared in the colony's earliest years, as evidenced by the appointment of committees to draft bills of "rates," but no legislation was enacted and interest in the problem quickly waned.

The pattern of wage legislation throughout most of the colonies was thus markedly similar during most of the period. Initially the commonly held principle that wages and prices should be fixed produced colony-wide legislation. But almost immediately authorities in colonies with a general code recognized the failure of their efforts and either by direct enactment or by tacit consent turned the problem over to local jurisdictions—where it always rested in the middle colonies. Although local authorities in some areas made a strong effort to set and enforce regulations, by the eighteenth century the wage codes were forgotten everywhere.

There was one major reason for this development. The period was one of labor scarcity in which the laborer held the whip hand. If his wage demands were not met, he could depart for other regions where he received his price without question or he could give up his trade and turn to the soil. The great need for the services of skilled and unskilled alike meant that their wage demands were paid with little legal complaining.

The principle of regulation did not die out entirely. Long after the codes were abandoned, colonial towns continued to set the fees of persons considered to be quasi-public functionaries: porters, cartmen, draymen, millers, smiths, chimney sweeps, gravediggers, and pilots. They fixed fees for such services as slaughtering, sawing wood, or grinding corn, in addition to fares on ferries, rates for wharfage and storage, prices of meat and other commodities, and charges for lodgings, food, and drink in taverns. Many colonies, particularly in the South, also laid down standards of quality and measure for certain manufactured goods, and passed laws impeding free traffic and curbing production. While such legislation affected workmen only indirectly, it did have a tendency to limit wages which employers in some fields were able to pay.

Unlike other provisions of the Tudor Industrial Code, the doctrine concerning combinations—whether created by masters to secure a monopoly of business operations or whether created by journeymen workers to secure better wages and working conditions—was not accepted by the colonies.

The craft guild, the one type of combination which was legal in Britain, did not take root in the colonies. In 1648 Massachusetts—over the vigorous protests of the country artisans who denied the colony's right to "hinder a free trade"—chartered a shoemakers' guild and a coopers' guild in Boston for three years. Neither charter was renewed. New York permitted formation of a weavers' guild, and Philadelphia chartered cordwainers' and tailors' guilds. None lasted more than a generation.

While the guild system was rare, attempts were made to enforce some guild regulations. Boston forbade any person who had not completed a term of apprenticeship to open a workshop, and limited the crafts to those who had been admitted as inhabitants. New York based the right to engage in a trade upon the Dutch "burgher-right"; the English translated this to mean that only freemen of the city could ply their callings—a measure enforced particularly against "foreigners" from New Jersey. A number of colonies sought to limit tradesmen to one craft. Most often such legislation was aimed at the leather industry in which butchers, curriers, tanners, and shoemakers were strictly enjoined from poaching on the territory of any allied crafts. Various cities also tried to keep farmers from engaging in trades during "off" seasons. Originally such regulations did have the effect of curbing occupational choice, but during the eighteenth century, when the laissez faire trend became stronger than the statutes, enforcement was relaxed. By the time of the Revolution these aspects of the British Code had given way to the prevailing demand for a free labor market.

The colonies' treatment of combinations in the licensed trades likewise failed to conform to the Code. American authorities, like the British, regarded the licensed trades as public utilities—setting them up as monopolies and providing for strict regulations. But there the parallel stopped. While the British punished any action in concert by the licensed tradesmen as a criminal combination and imposed severe penalties, the colonies were more tolerant. Colonial tradesmen frequently acted in concert, petitioning the government or even striking for higher fees and prices. Colonial authorities sometimes met such acts by levying small fines or by depriving individuals of their licenses; just as frequently, however, they granted the strikers' demands. On only one occasion, the New York City bakers' strike of 1741, was a licensed group prosecuted as a criminal conspiracy, and conviction was not obtained even in that isolated instance. At no time was any attempt made to dissolve combinations that were at odds with the government.

Another type of combination unhindered by the law was the mechanics' society, an organization developed in most cities along the coast after 1725. Often mistaken for guilds, they were actually "benevolent and protective" associations open to both masters and journeymen. As benevolent societies they were legal. During the decade before the Revolution they often acted in collaboration with the Sons of Liberty; the societies thereby became quasi-political bodies and could have been prosecuted under the common law. No action was ever taken.

Also unmolested were combinations of journeymen. While such combinations were comparatively rare, evidence of their existence in the form of strikes, slowdowns, and conspiracies to desert can be found from the earliest days of settlement. John Winter, overseer on Richmond Island off the coast of Maine, began complaining as early as 1636 about workers who struck in "Consortship" because he withheld a year's wages. Boston caulkers formed some sort of combination in 1741 when they agreed among themselves not to accept paper money or due bills as wages from their employers. Some twenty tailors refused to work in New York City in 1768 because of a "late Reduction of the Wages of journeymen Taylors," and set up their own "House of Call" to compete with their former masters. Peter Hasenclever, eighteenth century ironmonger, was constantly harassed by slowdowns among his artisans and was forced to raise wages. Carpenters at the Hibernia Iron Works in New Jersey went on strike in 1774 because their wages were not promptly paid. All such concerted activities were illegal in that they were contrary both to the Tudor Industrial Code, which the common law courts might

have enforced, and to statutes setting criminal penalties for the refusal of laborers in stated occupations to work. Except in one instance, colonial authorities took no action. In 1746 a number of house
carpenters in Savannah went on strike; Georgia trustees, living in
Britain, announced that the act was outlawed by Parliament and imposed fines as punishment. It was significant that the initiative was
not taken by local officials—colonial custom ran too strongly to the
contrary.

The requirement that a contract be observed by masters and laborers alike was one provision of the Tudor Code generally accepted
in the colonies. Many enacted specific laws. Rhode Island's labor
code of 1647 provided that any artificers or laborers who agreed to
finish any specific task should "not depart from the same . . . until it
be finished." Penalty for noncompliance was forfeiture of five pounds.
Maryland enacted a law in 1661 which declared that all servants
"hired for wages" were liable to be taken up as runaways if found
ten miles from home without written permission from their masters
and provided a penalty of ten days' service for every day of absence.
A Virginia act of 1726 was similar. Whether statutes existed or not,
the courts of all colonies enforced specific performances of contract
and granted damages for failure to fulfill an agreement. They also
awarded judgment where workmen failed to perform a task in a
"workmanlike manner." Although both types of decision became
less and less frequent in the eighteenth century, colonial judges
never wholly ceased enforcement.

The final principle of the Tudor Code, which called for the development and maintenance of an adequate labor supply, was so
wholeheartedly adopted by the colonies that it worked to the disadvantage of Britain. The colonists' attitude on this point was colored
by their own labor needs, which meant that they tried by various
means to create and preserve a skilled labor supply of their own and
simultaneously sought to attract labor from abroad, a practice which
ran contrary to British efforts to preserve a skilled labor supply in the
mother country.

With some modification almost all colonies adopted the traditional
British apprenticeship system. Most colonies required that the apprenticeship contract be written and recorded. None imposed any
property qualifications upon the parents of children "bound out"; it

was not unusual, however, for a master in professions like law or medicine, or in commerce, to demand "premiums"—a tuition fee—from a parent. Although terms of service varied, apprenticeship was normally terminated at the age of twenty-one (sixteen or eighteen for girls) regardless of how many years had been served. Once bound out, apprentices came under the discipline of the master and his household. Masters obligated themselves to provide "sufficient Meat, Drink, Apparel, Lodging and washing," to employ the apprentice in his trade, and to teach him its "mysteries." In turn the apprentice promised not to reveal his master's secrets. Northern colonies required that apprentices be afforded time to acquire formal schooling. Except on rare occasions an apprentice received no wages, though it was common to give him a lump sum at the end of his term.

The apprenticeship system never proved fully adequate in meeting colonial needs for skilled workers. Accordingly masters tried several other expedients. Efforts were made to attract artisans from other colonies through advertisements in the press; these efforts were assisted by colonial authorities who offered men with particular skills exemption from taxation for a term of years, exemption from labor on roads and highways, and exemption from militia service. In addition, the colonies adopted practices which ran contrary to British industrial needs. In the early years of settlement the British Government had sought to encourage migration because it believed that Britain was overpopulated. But when Britain's industrial and commercial needs expanded, the official attitude changed. Restrictions upon emigration of skilled artisans were imposed; in time even the emigration of vagabonds and the unemployed was limited, a development culminating in the Act of 1774 which placed a prohibitive capital tax on all emigrants from the British Isles.

The colonies made no attempt to conform with the obvious aims of such legislation. They imported craftsmen from England, Wales, and Scotland contrary to law; they imported sawyers from Holland; naval store workers from Poland; glassworkers from the south of France, Italy, and the Rhineland; miners, forgers, colliers, carpenters, masons, and laborers from Germany; flax workers from the north of Ireland; salt and indigo workers from Huguenot France; silk workers from Italy; pottery makers, brickmakers, limeburners, cabinetmakers, shoemakers, and tanners from Sweden. Colonial ability to attract the skilled was so successful that many a British official, concerned with the future of British industry, began to suggest that emigration of skilled Europeans through British ports be prohibited.

Despite this noteworthy success the colonies' supply of labor remained inadequate. Part of the shortage was made up by the use of women and children—particularly in unskilled trades and in household crafts. The South—where towns were lacking, markets were far apart, and wages were paid in tobacco and only at yearly intervals —ultimately turned to the training of slaves. Although white artisans bitterly opposed this encroachment upon their preserves and sought legislation to check it, the training program developed rapidly. By the time of the Revolution the South's supply of skilled labor, though still low, was probably as adequate as that of the North.

Taken as a whole the lot of the free laborers of the colonial period was comparatively enviable. Living as they did in a noncompetitive handicraft economy, their relations with employers harmonious and their working conditions leisurely, they enjoyed—because of the laws restraining dismissal and providing for apprenticeship as a prerequisite to employment, and because labor was scarce—a high degree of job security. Unhampered by rules that limited the crafts to specific classes or by guild regulations, their freedom of occupational choice was complete. Although laws concerning specific performance limited the right of laborers under contract to quit their jobs at will and code provisions prohibited combinations of workingmen to improve their conditions, it is doubtful that these regulations worked any real hardship. While the courts enforced specific performance contracts against individuals—particularly in the South—laborers learned to avoid any trouble by demanding short-term, even daily, contracts. The effect of provisions concerning concerted action and the formation of combinations was also slight. Existence of the laws may have been a psychological deterrent to concerted action, but the evidence indicates that neither tradesmen nor journeymen hesitated to act in combination when their grievances were strong; they revealed little fear of the law. In the seventeenth century wage and fee-fixing provisions, when enforced, placed a limitation upon the laborer's ability to charge whatever the traffic would bear, but the need for labor quickly undermined the wage codes. By the eighteenth century, except in those trades where fees were still enforced, laborers were receiving wages 100 per cent above the legal rates. Wages were so high that they gave rise to the oft-repeated statement that payment would make masters out of servants and servants out of masters. It was generally recognized that wages in the colonies were three times as high as in Britain; some reported that they were six times as high as in the Scandinavian countries. While statistical evidence is scanty, there is enough to estimate that free laborers earned real wages from 30 to 100 per cent higher than British workingmen.

The comparatively high wages thus provided the colonial laborer with a living standard far higher than that obtainable in Britain or in Europe. Poverty among the free labor element was virtually unknown in the seventeenth century and was but a minor incident in the eighteenth. A Maryland report of 1699 was rather descriptive of the whole colonial era: "Here are no beggars, and they that are superannuated are reasonably well provided for by the country."

Nothing so well illustrates the position of the free laborers in the colonies as the comparatively great respect that was accorded them. In Britain during the same period there was a sharp class differentiation. Labor on the whole was regarded as the "lower order," more in need of discipline than of employment. While British officials in America and some of the gentry reflected the same attitude, the settlers generally were inclined to hail the "virtuous" mechanic and to treat artisans with esteem. One almanac editor described the prevailing attitude neatly when he urged his countrymen "to prevent the execution of that detestable maxim of *European* policy amongst us, viz: That the common people, who are three quarters of the world, must be kept in ignorance, that they may be slaves to the other quarter who live in magnificence. . . . He that will not work neither shall he eat," he declared, should be the American standard. To a great extent it was, and the workingman profited.

Seagoing labor of the colonial period was regarded as free labor, but the seaman's condition was more thoroughly determined by tradition and law than that of other free-labor elements. On the high seas his lot was governed by a tradition that ran back to the maritime code of the ancient Greeks which the colonists, well versed in the customs of the sea, incorporated into their own laws.

The colonial seaman's contracts of employment, unlike labor contracts of landsmen were almost invariably in writing. Whether individual or collective, the agreements usually specified wages, the amount of provisions and liquor to be supplied, the nature and length of the voyage, the date on which duties would start, and the capacity in which the seaman was to be engaged.

Wages of seamen were generally in money. In fishing, whaling, or privateering the mariner was also frequently given a share in the net proceeds of the voyage—a type of accommodation highly favored by owners of vessels since it "made every man more careful for the good of the voyage"; in addition a seaman customarily had the right to ship aboard a small amount of cargo for himself. Colonial practice permitted seamen to demand a third or a half of the amount of wages earned up to the time a vessel reached any port at which cargo was discharged.

Theoretically, seagoing labor was given special legal protection. Seamen were entitled to relief from, or a discharge from, their contracts if any punishment meted out was excessive or inhumane, if the food and living conditions were bad, if illness were contracted on a voyage, if the ship were unsafe, if the ship deviated from its specified course, or in case of wrongful dismissal. That such protection was accorded in practice is doubtful. Punishment was a part of discipline at sea, and the courts were inclined to look upon it not in relation to its moderation but in relation to its reasonableness. While murder or the drawing of blood was frowned upon, as was the administration of corporal punishment to a sick mariner, or short rations to a quarrelsome one, flogging with the "cat," confinement, docking of provisions, and hazing were recognized as a necessary part of strict discipline. Bad food, particularly a long diet of salt pork without fresh provisions, and unfit living conditions in the small, poorly ventilated, vermin-ridden forecastles were common. Only when the food and living conditions were inadequate in addition to being bad was a seaman given relief. A seaman taken ill on a voyage could readily receive his discharge, if he did not die, for medical facilities aboard ship and in port were notoriously inadequate. Although seamen were able to compel the repair of an unseaworthy ship, they seldom secured a discharge for even serious deviations in course. They were, however, rather fully protected against wrongful dismissal, particularly overseas. Payment of full wages, or restoration in good standing, and return to home port was the usual decision enforced in such cases.

What set seagoing labor most thoroughly apart from the land-lubber was the crimes of insubordination and mutiny. Refusal to work under orders, particularly in concert with others, was a much more serious offense at sea than ashore. This not only could be punished aboard ship but could be and was prosecuted ashore. Penalties ranged from whipping and heavy fines to imprisonment and death by hanging. Inability thus to protest without fear against his conditions at sea made the seaman's lot most unenviable. Those who embarked upon a seagoing life, however, recognized it as a hard and hazardous service. Cruel and abusive masters, scurvy and pox, storms, piracy, bad food, cramped and unhealthful living conditions, and monotony were accepted as part of a seaman's condition. Men exchanged it for companionship and chance adventure, for the hope of striking it rich, and for the not infrequent opportunity of promotion to a master's berth.

3 ——

Colonial Politics: Labor's Role

Before the French and Indian War labor, whether free or indentured, skilled or unskilled, played a very minor role in colonial politics. The right to vote in colony elections was granted only to persons who owned specified amounts and types of income-producing property, a qualification which few laborers could meet. Labor, however, was not totally disfranchised. From time to time and from one locality to another the laws were interpreted to permit participation of laborers in local elections. In Connecticut towns "hired servants" were admitted to the polls when the majority of townsfolk deemed them to be persons of "honest conversation." New York City and Albany both granted voting rights to freemen: those who were given the "freedom of the city." This freedom, needed also to carry on a trade, was purchased by workmen for a moderate fee; New York City, moreover, gave many a laborer his freedom "Gratis, being a poor man." Artificers and common laborers could purchase freedom of the city in Philadelphia, Annapolis, Baltimore, and Charleston; and artisans who had served a five-year apprenticeship were granted voting privileges in Williamsburg and Norfolk, Virginia.

But if labor did have a share in town voting, its influence upon colonial affairs was slight. There is a record of only one significant activity: during the late 1730's Deacon Adams, father of the revolutionary propagandist, developed a political machine in Boston. Known as the "Caucus," consisting primarily of North End shipyard workers but including other artisans and shopkeepers, the organization for a time secured a firm grip on town offices. In the 1740's, when Massachusetts was suffering from a severe currency stringency that lowered the earnings of Boston workingmen, the Caucus allied itself with Elisha Cooke's debtor farmers—who called themselves the Country party—to demand relief through a land bank designed to issue paper money backed by real estate. The alliance won control of the Massachusetts General Court and established its bank, which was later destroyed by the Board of Trade.

For most of the colonial period labor was content with its small part in political affairs, but in the middle of the eighteenth century its attitude changed. Recognizing that most of the colonists regarded workingmen with high esteem, artisans and seamen began to develop the attitude that such esteem entitled them to a greater share in public affairs. The attitude was revealed in many ways. Labor grumbled about its inability to vote in county and colony elections; it complained because cities were under-represented in the colonial legislature; it muttered about inequalities in the tax structure; in some colonies like New York it complained because the land was granted too freely to governors' favorites; it growled about what remained of regulations concerning manufacturing and trade which held down wages; it revealed resentment over tithes paid to established churches; and it grumbled about sumptuary legislation which kept the laborer and his family publicly in their places. In brief, labor was developing an objection to privilege and a demand for equality.

In the 1760's—in some cases earlier—political clubs designed to protect civil and religious liberties appeared in a number of coastal cities. Led by a handful of liberal-minded merchants and lawyers, they also included storekeepers, masters, artisans, and day laborers. They adopted many names: in New York City the Whig Club, in Philadelphia the "Volunteer Heart and Hand Fire Company," in Baltimore the "Ancient and Honorable Mechanical Company." What role they may have played is impossible to say; before they undertook any action they became embroiled in the pre-Revolutionary contest with Britain.

That contest began after the French and Indian War when Britain issued a series of orders and laws designed to tighten imperial trade and to provide for imperial defense. The colonists showed little alarm over the first measures intended to accomplish these ends: the Order and the Proclamation of 1763, the Sugar and Currency acts of 1764. But a pall of depression settled upon the colonies in 1765: trade became dull, money scarce, and unemployment developed in the seaport towns. Amid the general disgruntlement news of the passage of the Stamp Act arrived in the colonies. Almost instantaneously the colonists reacted. They concluded that the depression had been caused by the Sugar Act which had destroyed trade with the West Indies and which drew money out of the colonies and by the Currency Act which prohibited the issue of paper money. The Stamp Act would make matters worse; it would increase the cost of doing business, drain more specie out of the colonies, and might even paralyze trade entirely. In addition, the act struck at two cherished political institutions: the right of self-taxation and the right to trial by jury. Those whose pocketbooks were unaffected by the act were angered by the curb on their political liberties.

The merchant gentry, injured economically, acted first. Denouncing the year-old Sugar Act as burdensome and the new Stamp Act as unconstitutional, they instituted a boycott of British goods in the northern seaports. Other elements also joined the contest. In Connecticut an organization known as the Sons of Liberty appeared. Almost immediately bodies with similar names developed in other seacoast towns. The exact origins of the various Sons of Liberty groups are obscure. In Boston, the Caucus, now captained by Sam Adams, was responsible; in other cities the new political clubs provided leadership; elsewhere, the Liberty Boys seem to have sprung from the streets. Like the political clubs the Sons of Liberty were led by a few merchants and lawyers; the main body, however, consisted of an admixture of workingmen—masters, mechanics, day laborers, and seamen. Wherever they appeared, they threw their strength into the campaign to nullify the Stamp Act. In Boston a Sons of Liberty mob hanged the local stampmaster in effigy; then, led by Andrew Mac-Intosh, a cobbler, it attacked and gutted his house. Later the same mob tore down the customhouse offices and attacked the home of Lieutenant Governor Thomas Hutchinson, a symbol of the aristocratic ruling clique of Massachusetts. When Hutchinson fled, the Sons of Liberty assumed control of the town. The mob was reorganized: servants, Negroes, and sailors were placed under the command of the carpenters; the Sons of Liberty were organized as the "Mohawks"; and an élite corps of 150 men was turned over to Cobbler MacIntosh. Courts and economic enterprise resumed normal operations without stamps. Meanwhile, in New York City a mob of mechanics and artisans, sailors, and the "rough element" of the city hanged Lieutenant Governor Cadwallader Colden in effigy and sacked the home of an army major who had threatened to cram the stamps down the public throat with bayonets. The stamps were then stored in the city hall and never used. Similar, though less violent, action occurred in Newburyport, Providence, Philadelphia, and Charleston.

When the initial controversy with Britain ended, the Sons of Liberty could look back upon their actions with considerable satisfaction. Although their conduct had not been exemplary, tending too much toward rioting and destruction of property, they could claim a share in defeating the detested measure which violated colonial rights. In addition they had learned that power could be exerted, without the vote, through the medium of mass demonstration.

The second contest with Britain was precipitated by the Townshend Act which levied a tax upon tea, lead, paint, glass, and paper imported into the colonies and was intended to raise revenue which would be used to pay the salaries of colonial officials, thus freeing them from dependence upon colonial legislatures; and by an act suspending the New York Assembly until such time as it complied with the provisions of the Quartering Act.

Organizations with which workmen were associated reacted first.

In Boston the Caucus denounced the Townshend Act both as an un-constitutional tax intended to drain money from the colonies and as an act to place the governor and his minions out of reach of the public where they could suppress popular liberties. Late in 1767 the town meeting—to which the "lowest mechanics" swarmed in a body—demanded a boycott of British goods. When nearby towns echoed the demand, Boston merchants drew up a one-year nonim-portation agreement to become effective when New York and Phila-delphia approved. Although New York merchants complied, Phila-delphians, recognizing that they could readily pass the new duties on to the consumers, played laggards. The initial effort at reprisal collapsed.

The Caucus continued its campaign; through a heavily attended town meeting it persuaded Boston merchants to adopt their own nonimportation measures in August, 1768. Mercantile groups in other New England towns quickly subscribed to the new effort. In New York City merchants adopted a similar compact; tradesmen and artisans adding their support with a separate agreement that pledged boycott of British goods until all obnoxious acts and duties were re-pealed. In Philadelphia, meanwhile, several mass meetings of "inhabi-tants" persuaded the Quaker merchants to join the campaign. The movement then spread to the South. In North Carolina the Sons of Liberty of Wilmington and Brunswick made their own agreement, and the colonial assembly extended it to the province. In Charleston the "mechanicks" finished the task begun by their Boston counter-parts. In October, 1768, they elected half of their own city ticket for the colonial assembly; with their influence at high mark they allied themselves with a planter group and pressed local merchants to pledge nonimportation. When the pressure failed, they formed their own agreement and announced that they would boycott the mer-chants who did not sign it. South Carolina soon lined up with the other colonies.

Although workingmen were partially responsible for the institu-tion of the nonimportation agreement of 1768, they had only a minor share in its enforcement. Boston mechanics and day laborers devel-oped a boycott against merchants who failed to sign the nonimporta-tion compact; in New York City, where the Sons of Liberty appar-ently dissolved temporarily, its former members occasionally imposed a tar-and-feather treatment upon persons deemed guilty of grossly "unpatriotic" behavior. But generally the task of enforcement was left to the merchants themselves.

Workingmen, on the other hand, became embroiled with the British military forces which descended upon the colonies. Troops arrived in New York City in 1767. Although their appearance reminded the city's inhabitants that their assembly had been dissolved for failure to provide for the troops, no incident marred their arrival. Within the next year, however, as the city sank more deeply into an economically depressed condition, laborers began to charge that their distress was caused by the soldiery which, according to British custom, had been allowed to accept civilian employment on their off-duty hours. Accordingly, when the bill providing British soldiers with fuel, candles, and a liquor ration was introduced into the colonial assembly in December, 1768, the "inhabitants" of New York proceeded to agitate and parade against it. The pressure failed; the bill passed.

During 1769 economic conditions in the city and colony reached a stage of crisis as prisons filled up with insolvent debtors, and it became necessary to pass laws for their relief. When the provision bill was introduced for renewal in December, 1769, the city burst forth in wrath. A group of former Liberty Boys published a handbill charging that the assembly had betrayed the colony in passing the previous provision bill; a huge mass meeting of mechanics and seamen adopted resolutions urging the assembly to refuse all funds to the soldiery. When these incidents were followed by the arrest of Alexander McDougall as the author of the incendiary handbill, a large crowd of artisans and laborers vented their feelings by attacking a group of British soldiers who had cut down the Liberty Pole on Golden Hill, erected to commemorate the repeal of the Stamp Act.

Meanwhile, British troops also arrived in Boston. Almost immediately a hot feud sprang up between them and the laborers along the wharfs, for in Boston, too, the soldiers were permitted to accept off-duty employment, thus taking the bread out of the mouths of the "honest and sober citizenry and their families." Head cracking between the two elements became a daily occurrence in taverns, in alleys, and even in the streets. Incident piled upon incident, culminating in the Boston Massacre early in March, 1770, when five Bostonians were killed.

The Battle of Golden Hill and the Boston Massacre had wide significance. Well publicized, the incidents bred a marked feeling of hostility throughout the colonies against the British Government; they raised the thought that Britain was treating the colonies like stepchildren. Whether fair or not, relations between Britain and her colonies were poisoned. Among seacoast laborers the effect was permanent; thereafter they refused almost to a man to work for the British Army, even when the wages offered were above those current.

In the spring of 1770 Parliament repealed all the Townshend duties except that on tea. The news placed the colonists on the twin horns of a dilemma. Except for the merchants of Boston, whose prosperity was based on unrestricted trade, mercantile interests along the seaboard agreed that they had won their point; they were ready to repeal the boycott. The Sons of Liberty objected. During the course of the second controversy with Britain, many towns had made a strong effort to develop domestic manufactures to replace the goods regularly imported. While some of the larger projects failed, those that succeeded created a large demand for both skilled and unskilled labor. Workingmen readily recognized that a breach of the nonimportation agreement would produce a flood of British-made goods to the jeopardy of their jobs. In addition laborers had developed ideologies. Through association with liberal merchants and lawyers they had become believers in the principle that Parliament had no right either to levy taxes upon them or to dissolve colonial assemblies. Their quarrel with Britain had become one of principle; repeal of some duties without repealing all did not satisfy their conception of what was due them.

With these factors as spurs, the Caucus in Boston and a mass meeting of "manufacturers and mechanics" in Philadelphia announced their determination to make the nonimportation agreement permanent. In New York City the one-time Sons of Liberty warned that they would "brand with public infamy and public punishment, the miscreants who, while the odious Power of Taxation by Parliamentary authority, is in one single instance exercised, even dare to speak of the least infraction of the nonimportation agreement."

While these announcements persuaded merchants to postpone repeal, their desire to resume their profitable trade with Britain soon grew stronger than their fear of mob action. In July, 1770, New York merchants announced that they would begin importing all products except tea. Former Sons of Liberty denounced the statement in violent language and paraded the streets in an effort to uphold nonimportation, but a poll of the city's electors revealed that the majority favored the resumption of trade in all articles except tea. Although scathing criticism descended upon the New York merchants from every point of the compass, the poll broke the impasse. Soon after, the merchants of all cities and towns along the coast resumed trade with Britain.

While the second controversy with Britain ended somewhat unsatisfactorily, the Sons of Liberty had learned several valuable lessons. They had discovered once again that they could influence political affairs; they had learned that there was a definite conflict in principle between the merchants' concept of the controversy and their own; that the merchant class had its eyes fixed on the profit-and-loss columns of its accounting ledgers and not on colonial liberty; and that their organization was still not a thoroughgoing one.

The three years that followed repeal of the Townshend duties were years of prosperity and quiet in the colonies. The tradesmen and mechanics of Philadelphia continued their political activities, placing several of their nominees on the assembly ticket in the elections of 1770 and 1771 and creating a "Patriotic Society" for the purpose of voting *en bloc* at elections. But elsewhere, even in Boston, the shopkeepers, mechanics, and laborers retired into everyday living.

But these years of peace were also years of development. Beneath the placid surface of colonial life men were preparing for the next contest. The leader of the movement was Sam Adams, who was determined to keep the local machines functioning and to weld them somehow into an intercolonial unit; and at the same time he was determined to spread the spirit of liberty, which had been awakened in the seaport towns, among the farmers of the interior. Two events gave him his opportunity. In 1771 Britain provided for payment of the salary of the governor of Massachusetts from crown funds; shortly afterward it made the same provision for the governor of New York. While neither act aroused the colonies out of their sense of well-being, Adams used them to create a Boston "Committee of Correspondence," designed to keep other localities informed of what new steps Britain was taking toward establishing "tyranny" in the colonies. The Committee, which was nothing more than the leaders of the Sons of Liberty, proved inspired. Shortly it began to flood the rural areas of Massachusetts with propaganda setting forth the rights of man and urging all believers in natural law to establish committees of correspondence which would guard the liberties of the colonial peoples against further encroachments. Among the elements who had constituted the Sons of Liberty and who had become impressed with their previous defenses of colonial liberties the propaganda quickly took hold. In three years local committees of correspondence had appeared in a multitude of seacoast and interior towns stretching from Casco, Maine, to Savannah, Georgia.

The value of the intercolonial organization that was developed in these years of quiet became apparent after 1773. In that year Britain passed the Tea Act, authorizing the East India Company to export its tea directly to the American colonies; all tea thus shipped was to be free of British duties, but consumers would have to pay the threepenny Townshend duty still in effect in the colonies. The Tea Act thoroughly alarmed the merchants: in one stroke it destroyed their tea trade, for even the smuggler could not hope to compete against the lower cost of the East India house; in addition it granted the company a monopoly. The act also alarmed the old Sons of Liberty, since importation of East India tea would compel all colonists to pay the unconstitutional tea tax. Merchants and Liberty Boys agreed that enforcement of the act had to be prevented.

As before, Boston assumed the leadership of the colonial cause. Led by the Committee of Correspondence, the Sons of Liberty reformed and demanded that the tea consignees resign their commissions. When the consignees refused, a mob attacked the store of one of them; the attack was repulsed. While the failure brought a sharp drop in Boston's reputation as a patriotic stronghold, the city's Liberty Boys soon restored their position. When the tea ships arrived, merchants, artisans, shipyard workers, and shipmasters from the North End descended upon the vessels tied up at the docks and quietly dumped their cargoes of choice Bohea into the bay.

News of the Tea Party streaked down the seacoast; the nation was charmed by the sublimity of the act. Everywhere Sons of Liberty set out to emulate Boston's example. In New York City, where a huge mass meeting of inhabitants had persuaded the tea consignees to resign their agencies, and where the reconstituted Sons of Liberty had circulated a document threatening all who dealt in dutied tea with a severe social and economic boycott, the patriots waited for three months until a ship arrived in port with a private cargo of tea. Without attempting to negotiate, the city's "cobblers and tailors" threw the tea overboard. In Philadelphia "the inhabitants," who had given notice that any one who attempted to bring tea ashore would be treated as a public enemy, turned back the first ship to arrive with a single question: "What think you, Captain, of a Halter round your neck, Ten gallons of liquid tar decanted on your Pate, with the Feathers of a dozen wild Geese laid over that to enliven your Appearance?"

The rejoicing of the Sons of Liberty over the defeat of the Tea Act was loud and gleeful. They recognized that they were establishing a point which they had failed to establish three years earlier when the merchants had resumed imports from Britain before all legislation which the colonies regarded as unconstitutional had been repealed. Among the gentry, however, the destruction of private property produced a shocked and remorseful silence; they recognized that punishment was certain.

First news of the expected punishment, in the form of the Boston Port Act, reached the colonies in May, 1774. In the succeeding weeks notice arrived of other punitive legislation: the Massachusetts Government Act, the Administration of Justice Act, a new Quartering Act, and the Quebec Act. The five laws changed completely the nature of the contest with Britain. The merchants and their desire for trade reforms had dominated the earlier controversies; the Sons of Liberty and the issues of taxation without representation and trial without jury—which shopkeepers and mechanics regarded as paramount problems—had played subordinate roles. The Intolerable Acts eliminated all commercial principles from the contest; all that remained was the starkly simple political question of the right of Parliament to punish Boston and to expurgate the Constitution of Massachusetts.

In this situation the merchants instinctively sided with Britain.

Belatedly recognizing that their welfare was closely tied with the British mercantilistic system, they could see no commercial advantage to be gained in fighting over constitutions and natural rights. But the Committees of Correspondence and the Sons of Liberty now suddenly came into their own. Here was a dispute untainted by a profit motive, a dispute in which their own concepts of colonial rights were at stake.

The struggle to assert the colonial position began in Boston. Early in May a town meeting, dominated by the Caucus, appealed to the colonies to impose a complete boycott on trade with Britain till the blockade of Boston was lifted. Simultaneously the local Committee of Correspondence drafted a "Solemn League and Covenant," pledging signers to suspend all commercial intercourse with Britain until the laws "tending to the entire subversion of our natural and charter rights" were repealed. Enforcement of the pledge was to rest entirely in the hands of those "two Venerable orders of Men stiled Mechanicks and husbandmen, the strength of every Community."

But the campaign of the Caucus met with obstacles. Merchants, even in Boston, objected to the precipitate haste, pointing out that this was not a struggle against American merchants who would be ruined by another nonimportation agreement, and suggesting resort to "moderate prudent measures" before use of economic warfare. New York City's merchants urged that a Continental Congress be called to discuss the problem. Although the Sons of Liberty denounced the suggestion as dilatory, they accepted it and promptly began an intensive campaign to win control of the Congress.

In New England they had little trouble. Led by the well organized Committees of Correspondence they easily captured a majority of the section's delegates. But their task was much harder in the two great colonies of the Middle Atlantic States where the conservative merchants held a firm grip upon the machinery of government and publicity. The Sons of Liberty, nevertheless, scored a partial victory. In New York they accomplished their aim through a "Committee of Mechanics," named by a mass meeting, which by demanding that any delegates selected be given popular approval, finally forced the merchants into a compromise whereby the city named conservative delegates who announced that they were of the opinion "that a general nonimportation agreement, faithfully observed, would prove the most efficient means to procure redress of . . . grievances." In Philadelphia the "inhabitants"—a mass meeting heavily attended by all kinds of workingmen—gained their objective by calling a convention which demanded that the colonial assembly name delegates with unrestricted power to suspend trade relations with Britain. The legislature, which recognized that its power of decision was being threatened, promptly chose a slate of conservative delegates and granted them the widest authority to adopt measures for redress and the establishment of union and harmony with Britain. South of Pennsylvania workingmen influenced the selection of delegates only in South Carolina where Charleston mechanics, participating almost as a unit in the elections, helped name three of their ticket of five to represent the colony.

The Sons of Liberty were more than satisfied with the results of the First Continental Congress. When the delegates gathered at Philadelphia, a majority revealed a tendency toward moderation and negotiation of differences. Yet for several reasons the Congress ultimately adopted a radical program. At the time of the election of delegates only the provisions of the Boston Port Act had been generally known, and many felt that the measure was just. But the publication of the other four Intolerable Acts which appeared to be unnecessary and arbitrary served to reenforce the radical contention that Britain was bent on imposing tyranny upon the colonies. The demand for drastic colonial retaliation accordingly increased. The Sons of Liberty, moreover, had a program of action in the Resolves which had been drawn up by a convention of Committees of Correspondence in Suffolk County, Massachusetts. The Resolves denounced the coercive acts as a gross violation of the British Constitution to which no obedience was due; they recommended an absolute nonimportation agreement; and they called upon all inhabitants to arm themselves in defense of their liberties. Presentation of these Resolves to the Congress placed the delegates in a difficult position. Conservatives regarded them as rash and impolitic, but even they found it difficult to disapprove because such action would divide the colonies' solid front, and almost all delegates recognized that unity was essential. Accordingly, a majority of the state delegations approved, an action tantamount to making the Resolves into the program of the Congress.

After swallowing the camel presented by the open rebellion in the lines of the Suffolk Resolves, the Congress could hardly strain at the gnat of nonintercourse. By their subsequent actions the delegates wrote the program of the Sons of Liberty into a platform for all the colonies. In the "Declaration and Resolves" they protested against Britain's imposition of taxes without their consent, against deprivation of trial by jury and the imposition of standing armies in time of peace, against dissolution of colonial assemblies, and against the attempt to coerce them with five measures "most dangerous and destructive of American rights." In the Continental Association they made provision for redress through a nonimportation, nonexportation, nonconsumption agreement. Enforcement was to be carried out by committees elected in each city, town, and county. Pledges were given that there would be no withdrawal until all the obnoxious and unconstitutional acts previously mentioned had been repealed.

When the First Continental Congress adjourned, it was the liberal merchants and professional men, the shopkeepers, master craftsmen, artisans, and free laborers—the Sons of Liberty—who rejoiced. They had finally placed the contest with Britain on their own terms. A Newport newspaper well expressed the spirit when it proclaimed that the action of the Continental Congress had revealed that "mechanics and country clowns (infamously so called) are the real and absolute masters of kings, lords, commons and priests."

The statement had to be proved. Many of the conservative gentry, aghast over the presumption of Congress that it had a right to legislate for the colonies, resolved not to obey the regulations. Had these conservatives united, they might have checked the radicals; but their organization quickly disintegrated, torn between those who would give no allegiance to the extralegal activities of the Congress and those who hoped to guide the colonies toward a more temperate course. The small tradesmen, shopkeepers, and "many who could not get credit for twenty shillings" manned the committees named to enforce the boycott, forcing all persons to choose between loyalty to the crown and allegiance to the Continental Congress. Because those who most conspicuously chose loyalty to the king were of the gentry class, who had surrendered principles before, the committees' determination to defend colonial rights grew more rigid. Out of this determination the war was born. In New England enforcement of

the Continental Association was accompanied by "farther regulations" which were deemed necessary to execute the instrument. Those
additional regulations consisted of the gathering of military supplies
and the drilling of troops which would be ready to defend colonial
rights by arms. Governor Thomas Gage's attempt to seize the cache
of arms so gathered at Concord was the event that precipitated the
war. The platform of the Sons of Liberty had plunged the colonies
into an armed defense of their rights within the empire.

In the whole process from verbal resistance to war workingmen
had played an important role. Although they had supplied little, if
any, of the leadership and polemics for the contest, they had provided—through participation in the activities of the Sons of Liberty
and a myriad of committees, through mass meetings, mob action,
and public demonstrations—the supporting force which leaders of
the resistance needed to make their goals achievable.

4 ——

Revolutionary War Developments

During the fifteen months between the battle of Lexington and
the Declaration of Independence workingmen continued to participate in political events. Two issues secured their attention: organization of the infant war and the problem of severing the tie with
the empire.

When the war began, the colonists were not totally unprepared.
Assemblies and provincial congresses of New England had named
Committees of Safety to supervise the drilling of militiamen and the
gathering of supplies and munitions in October, 1774. These colonial
committees had used the local committees of inspection, heavily
weighted with mechanics, to fulfill their obligations. With the opening
of the war this organization moved smoothly and unspectacularly.
The committees of inspection merely transformed themselves into

committees of defense and stepped up the tempo of their activities. South of New England, however, preparations for war had proceeded much more slowly. In New York little thought was given the problem until news of Lexington reached the city. The situation then changed rapidly; a mob, led by the old Sons of Liberty, seized control of the city, forced the arsenal, and distributed war supplies. A new committee of defense was named to take over the government. Using the city's artisans and laborers as deputies, the committee opened the port, established a night watch, secured arms and ammunition, and began military drill. Philadelphia and Charleston workingmen engaged in the same activity, carrying out the necessary task of mobilizing for war in the months before the colonies of Pennsylvania and South Carolina could officially organize resistance.

The question of severing imperial bonds, which had been hidden in the minds of some men from the opening days of the war, did not become an openly discussed issue until the end of the year 1775. From the first, artisans and laborers apparently welcomed the idea as a logical conclusion to the long struggle to establish colonial rights; in addition it held forth an opportunity to destroy gentry domination. In New England, where the movement for independence was inherent in the whole program of pre-Revolutionary resistance and where the attitude prevailed that Britain had cast off its colonies by opening the war at Lexington, there was no great struggle over the issue. A few important individuals hesitated, but the prevailing tide was too strong.

The story was different in the colonies of the Middle Atlantic States. New York, even after the war began, was dominated by moderate elements. The first provisional assembly that governed the colony was controlled by conservative back-country agrarians. Their caution was clearly revealed by their refusal to acknowledge the authority of the Continental Congress and to break off relations with the royal governor, William Tryon. When New York City's "radicals" began to agitate the question of independence late in 1775, the assembly studiously ignored the clamor, even refusing to name delegates to the Third Continental Congress which was expected to act on the issue. But the radicals were not to be denied so easily. Acting through a "mechanics' committee" chosen at a mass meeting, they threatened to name their own delegation to the Continental

Congress. The threat alarmed moderates who were beginning to recognize that severance of the tie with Britain was needed both to produce a revival of the colony's stagnated commerce and to bring about the consummation of a foreign alliance without which successful resistance was doubtful. To forestall any hasty action they consented to the election of new assemblymen from the city—fifteen of whom favored independence. Although this action brought no immediate results, the radicals' continued agitation, through demonstrations in which workingmen participated in large numbers, made the question of severing the tie with Britain the chief issue of the election of June, 1776. The provisional assembly chosen at that time declared the bond between Britain and New York dissolved on July 9, 1776.

In Pennsylvania the contest over the issue of independence was also protracted. The attitude of the colonial assembly, which contained a western minority inclined toward radical measures, was revealed by its rejection of suggestions for reconciliation with Britain and by its disarming of those "notoriously disaffected to the Cause of America." Nevertheless, the assembly was conservative enough to instruct its delegates to the Continental Congress to reject any proposition leading to separation from the mother country. The leading radicals of Philadelphia, accordingly, began to lay plans for erecting a government more responsive to their wishes. The strategy worked. After a mass meeting of the "inhabitants"—largely workingmen—of Philadelphia suggested the calling of a convention to reconstruct the government, the assembly's conservatives, fearing the loss of their century-old control of affairs, changed their instructions to the colony's delegates, authorizing them to vote on the question of severing ties with Britain. Thus, when the Congress finally declared the independence of the United Colonies, workingmen of the northern cities could claim a small share of the credit for the act.

Because of the lack of historical evidence labor's role in the Revolutionary War after the nation's declaration of independence is obscure. That labor—both indentured and free—enrolled in the American armies is clear. Enlistment of indentured servants, an issue complicated by the master's property interest in the services of his servant, presented the states with some of their knottiest problems. In the colonial period New England had disregarded this interest, providing for compulsory military service of all servants, while Pennsylvania and the tobacco colonies forbade enlistments and compensated masters where servants enlisted without consent. During the Revolution no consistent practice was followed. The Continental Congress encouraged recruitment of servants. Rhode Island, New Jersey, and Maryland declared them eligible for enlistments without their masters' consent. New York permitted enlistment with consent of masters, but without compensation to masters. Pennsylvania and the southern states specifically exempted servants, but Pennsylvania found it necessary to compensate masters because a large number of servants enlisted anyway and the southern states changed their attitude after the war spread into the South.

Enlistment of free labor was less complicated. Conscription for militia duty had been a universal practice in the colonial period; exemption from military service for workers in essential or favored industries had also been universal. During the Revolution the Continental Congress, state governments, and Committees of Safety followed colonial practices. Congress recommended exemptions for workers in powder mills and munitions factories. The states in general exempted a portion of the artisans employed in flour and grist mills, shipyards, foundries, ropewalks, and upon ferries.

What part conscripts and volunteers from the ranks of labor played in the armed forces is not clear. While the army needed and used the services of many kinds of artisans ranging from military engineers (posts often filled by carpenters) to tailors, and while the muster rolls of every company contained the names of men identified as artisans, laborers, or servants (lieutenants and sergeants were commonly skilled laborers) their services as a group are unrecorded.

The war had little direct effect upon indentured servitude. Ideologically, many men became convinced that servitude was "contrary to the idea of liberty this country has so happily established," but the institution remained intact during the whole war, weakened only by the fact that there was no importation of servants. While there were only a handful of persons still under contract at the end of the war, this situation was quickly remedied in the 1780's. Importation of servants, particularly from Germany and Ireland, was resumed on a scale every bit as large as in the pre-Revolutionary years. The postwar migration was different: it contained no convicts and it was

channeled almost exclusively into the area between the Hudson and
Potomac rivers—a change which in no way affected the vigor of the
system.

But the Revolution was an indirect cause for the eventual disappearance of servitude. The war gave the more humanely inclined
element in America an opportunity to enact legislation correcting the
horrors of the trip across the Atlantic. These new laws regulating
conditions aboard ships, providing for quarantine and registration,
greatly reduced the profits earned in the trade, and the number of
indentured servants coming to America gradually declined. Northern
attacks upon slavery helped destroy the system. The Quock Walker
case in Massachusetts (1783) which ruled that slavery was contrary
to the state constitution was applied to indentured servants. Mary
Clarke's case in Indiana (1812) which ruled that indentured servants
were held in involuntary servitude which was contrary to the Northwest Ordinance struck at the institution over a wide area. In 1817 the
system still existed in almost every state in the union; by 1831 it had
disappeared.

The Revolution had slight effect upon most of the normal activities
of free laborers who continued their peacetime callings. Only one
effort was made to abridge labor's freedom during the war—in the
form of a program of wage-and-price regulation north of the Mason-
Dixon line. The Second Continental Congress provided the impetus
for the action when it ordered the army to pay no more for military
goods than "the first cost of them and five percent for charges," and
called upon the states to aid in getting goods for the army at suitable
prices. Local committees of inspection, accordingly, began setting
the prices of numerous commodities.

It soon became evident that such efforts were insufficient: the de-
preciating continental and state currencies made it almost impossible
to maintain prices on a stable level. Early in 1776 Connecticut took
off the shelves its old statute against oppression and added amendments to make it more effective; in the meantime Massachusetts and
New Hampshire towns began to petition their legislatures for relief
from high prices. The widespread agitation resulted in a convention
of four New England states at Providence late in 1776. The convention suggested adoption of a wage schedule in which skilled labor
was limited to 5 to 7 shillings a day, about 50 per cent higher than in

1774, and a scale of prices for some twenty-seven domestic commodities. While New England legislatures immediately adopted the proposals, the program quickly disintegrated. As the value of currency continued to decline, farmers began to withhold their produce from town and city markets, and the pressure for lifting ceilings became intense. Less than a month after the plan became effective Massachusetts revised all schedules upward. Although other states protested, they, too, made revisions and the whole program fell into contempt.

In November, 1777, the Continental Congress recommended that further efforts be made "to regulate the prices of labour, manufacturing, [and] internal produce." A convention at New Haven, attended by delegates from New England, New York, New Jersey, and Pennsylvania, suggested the enactment of schedules which in general placed wages and prices 75 per cent above those current in 1774. Four states—Connecticut, New York, New Jersey, and Pennsylvania—responded, but their laws proved ineffective. When Congress recommended repeal in the summer of 1778, the states quickly suspended their regulations.

The catastrophic decline in the value of paper currency during the following year led to one more effort at wage and price control. District conventions in Massachusetts and Rhode Island, and citizens' committees in various counties and towns of New York, New Jersey, Pennsylvania and Delaware, set up wage scales limiting the skilled laborer to a daily rate of 75 shillings, a figure about fifteen times higher than wages current in 1774. These local efforts came to a climax when New England and New York combined in a call to the states as far south as Virginia to attend a wage- and price-fixing convention at Philadelphia. But opposition to wage and price limitations had grown too strong: such controls were denounced as futile, as unconstitutional, and as a violation of property rights because they compelled a person to accept less in exchange for his goods than he could obtain in an uncontrolled market. The Philadelphia convention of January, 1780, accomplished nothing.

While the revival of wage and price controls during the war was unsuccessful, it had a direct effect upon labor's condition. Workingmen, generally, supported the restrictive measures; they were interested in keeping down prices and were willing to hold down their wages to keep the cost of living at prewar levels. When they learned that prices were advancing beyond the schedules set, they raised their own demands—for which they were severely censured. The evidence, however, tends to confirm labor's argument that it was merely trying to keep pace with rising costs. In 1778, for example, a Massachusetts farm laborer, accustomed to receiving the equivalent of one bushel of corn for a day's work, was receiving a wage equal to only three pecks. In 1779, Philadelphia's master craftsmen estimated that prices of food and other commodities had risen twenty times while wages had increased only fourteen times over the prewar figures. The net result of the whole desultory system of controls was adverse to labor; it served to check the rise of wages while it failed to check the rise in the price of commodities.

Politically, the Revolutionary War period should have been one of major significance to labor. A time of constitution making and social reform, it offered workingmen an opportunity to solve old grievances, which had caused some of them to join pre-Revolutionary political clubs. Pushed into the background during the decade between 1765 and 1775, these grievances nevertheless had remained alive and had even solidified into simple demands for an extension of the suffrage by lowering or abolishing property qualifications for voting—workingmen would have been satisfied with a system which granted voting rights to all males who paid taxes, or who were eligible for militia service—and for a more equitable distribution of representation in the legislature which would have given a much larger influence to the seaboard cities where labor was concentrated.

The response of constitution makers and legislators to this platform was disappointing. Between 1776 and 1784 the franchise was broadened in virtually every state, but few lowered qualifications enough to permit labor to vote. New Hampshire extended the franchise to all taxpayers. New York granted voting rights to all who had been freemen in Albany and New York City as of 1775, but not to those who became freemen at a later time. Pennsylvania, where the constitution was produced by radicals, granted the vote to all adult males who paid taxes. Virginia gave the vote "to certain artisans residing in Norfolk and Williamsburg." All other states continued to maintain a freehold qualification, making it necessary to own land or large amounts of productive property as the prerequisite for enjoyment of the franchise.

Most states set up a more equitable system of representation. But while city delegations were enlarged, labor reaped little benefit. Boston's representation in the Massachusetts Assembly was increased, but the mechanics and laborers had no vote. New York City had its seats in the state legislature increased from four out of thirty-five to nine out of sixty-four; but the labor vote was confined to those who had been freemen in 1775, and the increased representation could hardly reflect the will of the laboring element. Philadelphia, on the other hand, had its representation reduced from four out of forty-one to six out of seventy-two votes—an act which partially nullified the new franchise gained by the city's artisans and laborers.

Considering the strong supporting role which labor had played in pre-Revolutionary developments this failure seems strange. Yet the explanation is simple. Once the Revolution began it secured support from two elements: a comparatively small, conservative property-owning group and the old Sons of Liberty. The conservative elements were still the voters; only a minority of the Sons of Liberty was enfranchised. In almost all the colonies the conservative electors remained in control of the agencies of government, even the revolutionary conventions and provisional congresses. This conservative element was neither democratic nor inclined to give up the control it had so long enjoyed. Moreover, it feared the propensity of the propertyless laboring element for mob action. It could not be expected to extend the franchise to those whom it regarded as an irresponsible rabble.

In addition the Sons of Liberty disintegrated. Many of the leaders, professional and propertied for the most part, became "respectable" and conservative. Sam Adams was an example: extremist among revolutionaries, he was concerned primarily with the tyranny of rulers and not with the broadening of the basis of government. He was willing to accept "the people" as they existed in 1776; suffrage extension was no part of his program. John Morin Scott, Alexander McDougall, and Marinus Willett, leaders of New York City's mechanics, represented the same sort of thinking.

The attention of the members of the old Sons of Liberty, furthermore, shifted from the problem of political rights to the more elemental problems of keeping alive and winning the war. The task of earning a daily wage and of producing ships, arms, and munitions, to say nothing of additional civilian goods once imported from Britain, became more important than political privileges. In addition, the four largest labor centers of the nation—Boston, New York, Philadelphia, and Charleston—were occupied by enemy forces for varying periods of the war; it could hardly be expected that the workingmen of these cities would have much opportunity to exert an influence upon the assemblies that drew up the laws.

Finally there was the agrarian influence. Traditionally regarded as radical, the farmers were essentially a conservative landowning group, not very favorably inclined toward city labor. In Massachusetts, where they had long been suspicious of the headlong impetuosity of the Caucus, they were inclined to side with the merchants. In New York they formed only a small part of the constituent assembly, but here too their innate conservatism caused them to side with the merchant-landlord class. In Pennsylvania the convention which created the constitution of 1776 contained an influential radical delegation from Philadelphia which wrote a liberal suffrage law into the document. But the western agrarians, who held a majority in the convention, motivated in part by their desire to revenge themselves upon the three southeastern counties which had so long dominated the colonial assembly and eager to establish their own control of the government, partially nullified these gains by reducing Philadelphia's voice in the legislature.

Deprived thus of any direct share in the deliberations of most of the assemblies that drew up new governments during the Revolution, or forced to share control with elements unfriendly to them; deprived of leadership which turned conservative, occupied with the problems of inflated living costs, of producing war materials, and of living in occupied territory, it was not strange that labor gained few of the political privileges it requested.

PART TWO

The Transitional Era

5 —

The Transformation of
Economic Enterprise

At the close of the Revolution, American economic enterprise was in various stages of development. Itinerant industry dominated the sparsely settled frontier areas; custom-order industry existed in every city and village; and retail-order industry reached its fullest growth. In the twenty years that followed the war, relations between industrial classes reached their highest level of harmony. The old mechanics' societies were revived and broadened into city-wide associations with expanded functions. In addition to providing payment of sick, accident, and death benefits and supervising the education of children of deceased members, the societies sought to promote "inventions and improvements in their art," giving prizes for ingenuity displayed by apprentices and journeymen. Some set aside funds "to assist young mechanics with loans" to enable them to become independent producers. They acted as trade courts to resolve differences between members and to prevent expensive litigation; they undertook to collect money owing to members, and they lent money to members in need.

This relationship, which in some trades lasted well into the nineteenth century, soon began to break down. Expansion of the market provided the background for the change. In the colonial period Americans had looked abroad for much of their market which they reached in wooden sailing vessels; their internal commerce, carried on horseback, by carts, and in wagons, was generally localized. But the war made Americans profoundly aware of other areas besides their own; in the post-Revolutionary period they made a vigorous effort to increase their knowledge of the entire nation and to take advantage of its limitless opportunities. Although few changes were made in the means of transportation, the wave of enthusiasm for internal improvements which spread through the country turned the old turnpikes into interstate arteries and filled the intercoastal trade with new shipping. The retail-order shopkeeper began to receive orders from the country storekeeper. At first he received requests for his products from the region near the city, but his market quickly expanded southward and westward. Industry entered the wholesale-order stage.

The change made a difference in the shopkeeper's attitudes and functions. His goods were now sold in large lots; he found it necessary to increase his supply of raw materials, to increase his stock of finished goods, and to increase storage space. Since his goods were sold to country storekeepers who must in turn sell them before payment could be expected, he had to extend long-term credit. The shopowner ceased to be a workman with close knowledge of his employees' problems; he became an executive and a merchant interested fundamentally in costs and markets.

The wholesale-order stage did not last long. In the early nineteenth century it became evident that manufacturers were handicapped in their efforts to supply the nation's increasing demand for their products by inadequate financial and marketing facilities. Several expedients were tried to offset these disadvantages. Patriotic individuals, eager to develop industrial self-sufficiency, created associations to secure funds for manufacturers from private investors and state legislatures. Most famous of these was Tench Cox's "Pennsylvania Society for the encouragement of manufacturers and the useful arts." Others sponsored collective warehouses, known as "commission stores," to attract business. None of these efforts proved successful. At this point the merchant-capitalist appeared to take advantage of the opportunities afforded.

The merchant-capitalist was a man who had already succeeded in making money in some other enterprise such as land speculation or overseas shipping. Because of his previous successes he had easy access to credit. Equally important, he was a keen analyst of markets. With little or no knowledge of the technical processes of a trade, he entered the manufacturing field by the back door with the purchase of raw materials in large lots, securing thereby a local or regional monopoly of unfinished goods. Then, using his own warehouse, or "manufactory" as it was called, he employed skilled workers to prepare the raw material. This in turn he handed over to a master with a small shop engaged in manufacturing for wholesale, retail, or custom orders, or to a journeyman working in his own home, to work into finished products. The next step was to collect and sell the finished goods to retailers who in turn disposed of it to consumers.

The merchant-capitalist, who first appeared around 1800, was an almost inevitable success. Even under stable economic conditions wholesale-order and retail-order shopowners were unable to compete against him. Without credit facilities they could not hope to buy raw materials as cheaply; with crude marketing methods they could not hope to reach as many customers. The early years of the nineteenth century were not economically stable. The embargo of 1807, the boycotts of England and France, the War of 1812, and the postwar depression created financial, production, and merchandising problems that the shopowners could not solve. Growth of transportation facilities after the War of 1812—the building of roads and canals and the development of steam-driven riverboats—which enormously expanded and simultaneously intensified competition for the market increased the complexity of their problems. Gradually they lost their initiative, ceased to buy and sell, and became contractors. By 1830 the merchant-capitalist emerged as the undisputed master of workshop enterprise—a position which he held as long as handicraft remained an important segment of the economy.

The merchant-capitalist did not confine his activities to handicraft manufacturing. He also became the organizer and owner of the American factory system. Factories in the modern sense require a composite of four ingredients: a large capital outlay, a concentration of labor, use of mechanical power in place of muscle power, and use of machinery in place of skills. Some of the ingredients of the factory system had appeared in the colonial period. Relatively large amounts of capital had been invested in iron plantations; concentrations of labor had developed in the shipbuilding, ropewalk, and iron industries; water power had been used in place of muscle power in some of the operations of the grist, flour, and fulling mills. But no factory had existed, for no machinery had been introduced to replace skills.

After the adoption of the Constitution a metamorphosis began. It started when Samuel Slater, arriving in America from Britain, put together, after a few years' labor, a cotton-spinning machine driven by water power. A mill, using this machinery, set up at Pawtucket, Rhode Island, in 1791, is generally regarded as the first American factory. It was a factory, but only the first step toward the transformation of the cotton textile industry. Progress was slow until 1815 when a power loom for weaving was perfected and a group of Massachusetts merchant-capitalists established the first integrated American textile factory at Waltham where the cotton fiber brought from the South was carded, spun, and woven into cloth under one roof. Thereafter, the factory system expanded rapidly along the Merrimac, Piscataqua, and Saco rivers north of Boston, around the edges of Narragansett Bay, in the lower Mohawk Valley, and in the Paterson-Philadelphia area. By 1850 cotton textile production had become wholly mechanized. The woolen textile industry, into which power-driven machinery to take care of all processes of manufacturing was introduced by 1815, began its changeover in 1830. Carding, spinning, and fulling mills were erected in large numbers after that date, particularly in Massachusetts; weaving, which required prohibitively expensive machinery, remained a handicraft operation. By 1860 over one-half of the product was manufactured in factories. Mechanization of the boot and shoe industry began after 1840 when the McKay sewing machine was introduced; machines for splitting, soling, buffing, and dyeing followed. By 1860 the industry had experienced a significant shift.

In the iron industry and its corollaries, the iron plantations remained dominant. But new fuels, new blast-furnace techniques, and new refining techniques were introduced after 1840 and made the industry more efficient. The industry also moved its center away from New England, New Jersey, and the Delaware coast and began to concentrate in the northern river valleys: along the Hudson, Lehigh, Delaware, Schuylkill, Susquehanna, Alleghany, Monongehela, and Ohio rivers. There were changes also in the manufacture of secondary and finished iron products after 1840. The shaping of metals into finished products continued to be dominated by the blacksmith and the forge, but foundry operations for making castings began to mechanize. After 1840 steam engines, factory machinery, stoves, hardware, and household utensils were generally cast; by 1860 power-driven machinery was used almost exclusively in the production of nails, tacks, screws, spikes, bolts, files, chains, wire, and rifles.

The Civil War with its tremendous demand for uniforms, munitions, and military supplies gave a strong boost to the American factory system. Woolen textiles and boots and shoes underwent the final transformation to power-driven, mechanized, and heavily capitalized industries; the metal, agricultural machinery, cigar, and printing industries were heavily mechanized. The greatest expansion of the factory system occurred during the twenty-five years after the war. A number of forces influenced and encouraged this development. These were years when the nation's railway lines, which had begun to make transportation more rapid and efficient even in the fifties, built 150,-000 miles of roadbed, crossed and recrossed the continent, penetrating into every village in the nation; years when the nation's population increased from thirty to sixty million, creating one of the world's most insatiable markets. These were years when the war-born banking, currency, and debt structure produced a vast amount of fluid capital available for financing factory enterprise; years when the Federal Government opened a vast amount of natural resources to private exploitation without restriction; when the government adopted a tariff policy which reduced or destroyed foreign competition, enabled inefficient industries to remain in business, provided a foundation for the development of new industries, and earned the nation's manufacturing interests incalculable increments which were often thrown back into the business to enlarge and more fully mechanize the whole of the nation's industrial fabric.

They were also years when the number of inventions and technological improvements multiplied and remultiplied. The technique of transporting heavy and bulky products like coal, iron, and ore to the mills was greatly improved. Steam-driven elevators and inclined planes, improved ships and railroad cars, loading and unloading machinery aided the process. The iron industry became the iron and steel industry with the introduction of the Bessemer converter and the Siemens-Martin open-hearth process. With steel came new power-driven machinery for rolling, drawing, and forging. Numerous inventions increased the efficiency of the textile industry—culminating in the Northrop loom in cotton manufacture. In the food industry the roller process for grinding wheat into flour was introduced. Even

motive power improved: the old-fashioned water wheel all but disappeared; the steam engine became the steam turbine, and a coal
gas engine appeared.

The growth and effect of the factory system can be revealed in a
few, simple statistics:

DATE	PER CAPITA PRODUCTION	No. OF MFG. UNITS	VALUE OF PRODUCT PER UNIT	VALUE OF PRODUCT PER EMPLOYEE
1810	$ 26	–	–	–
1840	29	–	–	$ 600
1850	44	123,000	$ 8,300	1,050
1860	61	140,000	13,400	1,430
1870	90	252,000	13,500	1,650
1880	108	254,000	21,000	2,000
1890	150	355,000	26,500	2,200

The slow increase in per capita production between 1810 and 1840
indicates that the handicraft system still dominated manufacturing
throughout that period. The handicraft workshop in fact produced
about 70 per cent of manufactured goods in 1850 and was still producing around 50 per cent of the goods in 1870. But a sharp increase
in per capita production, in the value of product per manufacturing
unit, and the value of product per employee after 1840 reveals both
the increased productive capacity of the machine and the growing
domination of the factory. By 1890 factories were producing 80 per
cent of the nation's manufactured goods.

The twenty-five years after the Civil War was not only a period
when the factory took over control of American industry but also
an era in which industry spread from its base along the North Atlantic Coast into the nation's interior. In 1850 New England and the
Middle Atlantic States were the center of American industry. They
produced practically every variety of goods manufactured in the
nation; they employed 71 per cent of the wage earners engaged in
manufacturing. By 1890 a large number of changes had occurred. Although the cotton, woolen, hosiery, hardware, and machine-tool industries remained in eastern cities, and an iron and steel industry
maintained itself along the Delaware and Susquehanna rivers, the
section's proportion of manufacturing dropped to 58 per cent. Mean-

while, the Midwest areas assumed a new importance. The juxtaposition of bituminous coal in the Transappalachia, of iron in the Lake Superior area, and of the waterways of the Great Lakes quickly made the Pittsburgh-Youngstown-Cleveland region, with outlying points at Buffalo, Detroit, Chicago, and St. Louis, the center of a gigantic steel industry. The meat-packing, flour-milling, agricultural machinery, and chemical industries also centered in the area. By 1890 the Midwest accounted for 22 per cent of the nation's industrial products.

The factory system even penetrated the South. In 1850 southern manufacturing was concentrated in tobacco, wheat, and lumber products. After the Civil War the South expanded its tobacco and lumber industries, but the more significant developments came in iron and cotton textiles. A large-sized foundry-iron industry was established in the Richmond and Chattanooga-Birmingham areas; a small-mill cotton textile industry appeared over a wide area in the uplands of the Carolinas and Georgia. In 1890 the South accounted for 10 per cent of the nation's manufacturing.

The number of laborers, skilled and unskilled, used by the nation's growing commercial and manufacturing enterprises during the transitional era grew very rapidly. The size of the labor population at the beginning of the era is unknown; the free labor element was probably about the same as it had been in the colonial era—5 per cent of the whole. By 1840 it had undoubtedly increased. Census figures for that date reveal nearly 800,000 men, women, and children employed by manufacturing units alone—about 4.5 per cent of the whole population; the number engaged in farming, the sea trades, and commerce would increase this amount to about 6 per cent, and if families were added, to about 18 per cent of the population.

After 1840 the census figures reveal a constantly increasing number of employees in manufacturing establishments: 1,300,000 by 1860, 2,000,000 by 1870, 2,700,000 by 1880, 4,250,000 by 1890. Employees in agriculture, fishing, and commerce would swell the last figure to about 5,500,000—nearly 9 per cent, and if families were added, to about 30 per cent of the whole population.

6 ——

The First Trade Unions and Labor Parties

The transformation of economic enterprise that began after the Revolution was the major cause for the development of labor's most significant institution: "permanent" trade unions. Labor combinations created before the Revolution and those established during the Revolution—most notable of which were those of the printers employed by James Rivington on the *Royal Gazette* of New York who went on strike in 1778, and of the Philadelphia seamen who struck in 1779— were intentionally temporary. During the Confederation period New York cordwainers and Philadelphia printers also established organizations and went on strike for higher wages, but in neither case was there any effort to make the strike organization permanent.

This situation changed abruptly after the adoption of the Constitution when wholesale-order employers began to take control of industry. The wholesale-order shopkeeper operated in a different economy from his predecessors; his market was highly competitive and he found it impossible to pass increased costs to consumers in the form of increased prices. Instead he found it necessary to reduce his costs. At first he met this problem by asking his journeymen to produce wholesale-order work more cheaply than shopwork. Realizing that their employer had to meet competition, they agreed. But when demands for decreases continued and the nation entered a period of inflation—cost of living increasing 30 per cent between 1791 and 1800 —their turnouts became frequent. While most workingmen created temporary organizations to conduct their struggles, some tried to establish permanent "associations" and "societies"—the terms usually adopted—for the same end.

Philadelphia shoemakers made the first attempt in 1792. Though their organization lasted less than a year, it was organized anew in 1794 and was still in existence in 1806. New York printers organized a permanent "Typographical Society" in 1794. Between that date and 1818, shoemakers established fairly permanent organizations in New York, Philadelphia, Baltimore, and Pittsburgh; printers organized in Boston, New York, Albany, Philadelphia, Baltimore, Washington, and New Orleans. Carpenters, cabinetmakers, masons, coopers, and tailors organized in New York City; carpenters and cabinetmakers organized in Philadelphia, and tailors in Baltimore.

These organizations were local in nature, and their membership was confined to journeymen of a single craft. Upon becoming a member a mechanic paid an initiation fee of fifty cents and monthly dues of six to ten cents; he was required to attend monthly meetings on pain of fine and to conduct himself in a decent and orderly manner.

The biggest problem faced by skilled laborers was the competition they met from inferior workmen—"runaway apprentices"—whom employers in the wholesale-order stage hired in order to reduce their costs. The locals, accordingly, sought to create strict rules concerning the number of apprentices to be employed in a shop and to establish a minimum wage; adoption of such a wage would force the employer to pay the same rates for both good and bad workmanship and, it was hoped, would eliminate the poor worker.

Labor's tactics at this stage were relatively simple. Membership of the organization would agree on a wage scale and pledge to cease working for any employers who would not pay the amount. Although bargaining with the employer was generally an individual affair, instances of collective bargaining occurred as early as 1799 when a deputation of Philadelphia cordwainers met with master shoemakers and formed a trade agreement. Refusal to meet the demands of workers usually resulted in a strike. In addition labor sought to create the "closed shop" by compelling employers to hire none but association men and by driving scabs from employment. The weapon used most effectively was the social boycott; association members even refused to live in the same boardinghouse or to eat at the same table with nonassociators.

The success of these early trade associations in achieving their simple aims is not clear. From a study of strikes it would appear that the cordwainers were generally able to secure what they wanted. Baltimore tailors also had their demands met on several occasions. But direct evidence concerning other trades is lacking. One indication that workingmen did make gains was the appearance of employers' associations. Master house carpenters, masons, shoemakers, and printers organized societies in all principal industrial centers in the 1790's for the purpose of holding down wages and destroying labor combinations "root and branch." Equally significant was employer resort to the courts to protect their interests, an action which gave rise to the trials known as the Cordwainers Conspiracy Cases.

There were six cases involving the cordwainers in the period 1806-1815, but only three are recorded: those in Philadelphia (1806), New York (1809), and Pittsburgh (1815). The cases, which climaxed the wholesale-order stage of industry, developed when journeymen shoemakers, squeezed between hard-pressed employers and rising living costs, demanded a minimum wage. Employers, turning to the courts for aid, charged that the cordwainers' organizations were conspiracies in restraint of trade under the common law.

The trials that followed were a district departure from past American practices. While the doctrine of criminal conspiracy had been a part of the Tudor Industrial Code, it had never been applied to combinations of free laborers in America. In each case, therefore, the main point at issue was the applicability of the law. The Philadelphia court set the pattern when it ruled that the common law of criminal conspiracy was the law of the American nation. The law, however, assumed that some illegal act had been committed. It was on this point that the three cases differed.

In the Philadelphia case the court declared: "A combination of workmen to raise their wages may be considered in a two-fold point of view; One is to benefit themselves . . . the other is to injure those who do not join the society. The rule of law condemns both." In brief, a mere combination of workers who intended to raise wages was an illegal act and punishable. The Philadelphia decision was roundly denounced by the shoemakers and the Jeffersonian press because it was "incompatible with the existence of freedom, and prostrates every right which distinguishes the citizen from the slave."

The outcry probably affected later decisions. In the New York case (*People* v. *Melvin*) the question of the illegality of a combination to raise wages was dismissed; the issue was whether the journeymen on strike had combined to raise wages by unlawful means. The journeymen, the court declared, had equal rights with other members of the community, but they could not use means "of a nature too arbitrary and coercive, and which went to deprive their fellow citizens of rights as precious as any they contended for." In the Pittsburgh case the issue of unlawful means was more thoroughly defined. "Where diverse persons confederate together by direct means," the court declared, "to impoverish or prejudice a third person, or to do acts prejudicial to the community," they were engaged in unlawful conspiracy. Concretely, it was unlawful to conspire "to compel an employer to hire a certain description of persons," or to conspire "to prevent a man from freely exercising his trade in a particular place," or to conspire "to compel men to become members of a particular society, or to contribute toward it," or to conspire "to compel men to work at certain prices."

The Cordwainers Conspiracy Cases proved disastrous to many of the nation's early labor organizations. While most of the decisions did not condemn mere combinations to raise wages as illegal per se, they declared that almost every action that labor could take to increase wages might be criminal. Labor could not use coercive or arbitrary means; it could not demand a closed shop; it could not do anything to the injury of third persons or the public. The cases, in effect, destroyed the efficacy of the early labor organizations by strangling their activities.

What remained of labor's associations after the conspiracy cases was destroyed in the depression that followed the War of 1812. It was the normal type of postwar depression. During the period of embargo and war, industrial enterprise had grown large in an effort to fill the vacuum created by the lack of European manufactures. When the war ended, however, British industrialists, who either could produce more cheaply or could dump goods at a loss, once more invaded the American market. Unable to compete, many native enterprises were compelled to close their factories and workshops.

Large numbers of laborers were thrown out of work. Contemporaries estimated that there were twenty thousand persons seeking employment in both New York and Philadelphia in 1819, and ten thousand in Baltimore. The hard-pressed journeymen either dissolved their societies or subordinated their economic activities. Of all locals established in the country, the records reveal that only one survived intact, its economic activities unimpaired: the Columbia

Typographical Society, located at Washington, where the volume of government printing was hardly affected by hard times.

The postwar depression not only destroyed early labor organizations, but also ended the domination of the wholesale-order manufacturer. By 1820 the merchant-capitalist had assumed a commanding position in the house-building, printing, and shoe-making trades, and in the textile workshops. During the twenties he gradually secured control of the nation's whole industrial fabric. The result was another change in the condition of labor. The merchant-capitalist operated in a market where competition for the goodwill and trade of retail storekeepers was intense. It was to his advantage to produce as cheaply as possible. While his ability to purchase raw materials in large lots helped, he likewise found it necessary to squeeze manufacturing costs by contracting for production at the lowest possible rates. This in turn affected workshop proprietors whose incomes became dependent upon their ability to hold down labor costs. Accordingly they resorted to every possible expedient to keep wages down. They hired unskilled labor, women, and children; they pitted skilled against unskilled, increased exertion, and reduced wages. In the process they unknowingly began to destroy the importance of skills; in addition they depressed labor's standard of living.

The full impact of the merchant-capitalist system descended upon labor during a period of prosperity between 1821 and 1828, a period in which the expanding market created an abnormally strong demand for labor. Workingmen, recognizing the situation, reacted as they were going to react ever afterward during periods of inflation. Once more they began to form trade associations, and the struggle between capital and labor begun in the wholesale-order stage was renewed. It was a much larger struggle and much more bitter.

The movement to organize began in 1821 and continued all through the decade. It extended over a wider area than before—to all coastal cities and to smaller interior towns along the nation's highways of travel. It involved a larger number of trades; stable organizations were formed among shoemakers and printers, hatters, tailors, house and ship carpenters, house painters, stonecutters, and cabinetmakers. Associations, which first used the term "union" to designate a labor organization, appeared among factory workers. Women in the weaving and tailoring trades joined the movement.

The organizations formed in the twenties were duplicates of those formed earlier. As before, they were associations of skilled workers —even in the factories; their chief problem was wages; their chief weapon remained the "turn-out." While the records do not reveal the outcome of the movement to increase wages, labor must have had some success. That may be deduced from the fact that employers again resorted to the courts to destroy labor organizations.

There were six conspiracy trials aimed at labor in the twenties of which records exist for only three: New York Hatters case (1823), the Philadelphia Tailors case (1827), and the Philadelphia Spinners case (1829). The three together were a refinement of earlier decisions. In all three the court refused to consider the issue of the illegality of a labor combination to raise wages; in the Tailors trial the presiding judge specifically ruled out the proposition as bad law. In all cases therefore, the trial revolved around the question of the legality of the means used. The Tailors case was the most complete. It involved the shop of Robb and Winebrenner and the manufacture of women's riding clothes of pongee—a type of work for which there was no fixed wage scale. Five workmen insisted on the rate paid for heavier materials; when they were discharged the shop's journeymen went on strike. The shop was picketed; scabs who were employed were hounded; other masters were persuaded not to work for Robb and Winebrenner. All these activities were adjudged illegal—being both coercive and injurious to third persons. The cases were another heavy blow to labor associations. Although indirectly their right to combine to raise wages was recognized, some of their most vital weapons— picketing, circulation of scab lists, and the sympathetic strike—were outlawed.

Significant as these cases were, the question of hours which arose during the period was to prove equally important. While the "sunrise to sunset" system was acceptable in most of the trades during the twenties, some workers began to consider the long stretch unbearable and to suggest that the working day should be limited to the hours from six to six with two hours off for eating—what came to be called the ten-hour day. In 1825 Boston house carpenters precipitated the first great struggle over the issue. The contest was conducted on one side by the merchant-capitalists who financed building enterprise in alliance with contractors, and on the other side by organized journeymen. In an era when the sun-to-sun system was still normal for the vast majority of the population, the carpenters could not find much sympathy; they lost the strike.

Failure in Boston did not mean abandonment of the movement. In New York City trade associations made the ten-hour day a part of their program. Almost invariably, whenever a demand for reduction of hours was made, employers granted it with little opposition, for labor in New York City was exceedingly scarce in these years when the Erie Canal had just been completed and had opened a vast new market to New York's manufacturers. By 1828 it could be said that New York was a "ten-hour town" as far as skilled labor was concerned.

The movement also had important, though unexpected, results in Philadelphia where in June, 1827, some six hundred carpenters began a ten-hour drive. Although their campaign proved a failure, it suggested that wider organization and more adequate strike funds might produce victory. Late in the year the suggestion was implemented when some fifteen societies formed the Philadelphia Mechanics' Union of Trade Associations, thereby creating the nation's first city federation of labor. The Mechanics' Union, designed to lead a ten-hour drive in Philadelphia, never conducted a strike; in the spring of 1828 it converted itself into a political party. The metamorphosis, strange on the surface, was the product of a long series of events.

In the period between the Revolutionary War and the late twenties, labor played only a minor role in politics. Limited voting rights was one reason, but there were others. During the Confederation period workingmen were not united politically. In their attitude and activities some reflected a close identity of interest with their employers. At the time, foreign industrial products being imported into the United States were threatening to destroy American industrial enterprises. Anxious to save the source of their livelihood, shopowners and some of their journeymen often cooperated in a movement to strengthen the American industrial fabric. The mechanics' societies of this period originated the slogan "Patronize home industry"; they also organized movements to secure tariffs from state governments.

When these proved ineffective, many of the societies joined in the growing agitation for strengthening the Confederation government's power over trade and commerce—which resulted in the meeting of the Constitutional Convention. Although no workingmen attended the convention, the representatives of manufacturing interests who were present probably voiced the desires of a portion of the journeymen. The powers granted to Congress "to lay and collect Taxes, Duties, Imposts and Excises," and "to regulate Commerce with foreign Nations, and among the several States," represented the wishes of this labor element.

Workingmen also were involved in the campaign to ratify the Constitution. In Boston, tradesmen and mechanics, some of whom had once constituted the rank and file of the Caucus, adopted lengthy resolutions announcing their support. In New York, the city-wide Mechanics Society announced that it looked to "the patronage and protection of the General Government" for its "most flattering hope of success." In both cities mechanics were conspicuous in the processions commemorating the adoption of the new Constitution.

On the other hand there were workingmen who disregarded their identity of economic interest with employers. Some were members of organizations similar to the pre-Revolutionary Sons of Liberty. Known as the Whig Club in Boston and Baltimore, as the Constitutional Society in Philadelphia, as the Society for the Preservation of Liberty in Virginia, these bodies all had the same aim: the safeguarding of popular rights. Occasionally during the period workingmen who were members of these groups or who held similar attitudes entered a political campaign. In 1785 New York City mechanics petitioned the legislature for incorporation; their request encountered stubborn resistance from the Senate which ultimately defeated the measure because it would give the workingmen "too much political importance." The rebuffed mechanics promptly reacted by nominating their own assembly ticket and in the following campaign elected all but two of their candidates—including a blacksmith and a shoemaker.

It was this element among the laboring classes which revealed dissatisfaction with the Constitution that emerged from Philadelphia. They criticized it because the legislative bodies were not annually elected, because the judiciary and the Senate were not responsive to popular will, and above all because it lacked a bill of rights. During the ratification period they joined or cooperated with "Societies of Federal Republicans," designed to defeat ratification. The action of these societies was too slow; not until nine states had ratified were they organized in sufficient numbers to make their voices felt. At that point they changed their aim; they became a nation-wide pressure group demanding a bill-of-rights amendment—some societies also advanced the name of George Clinton as a candidate for Vice President because he could be relied upon to support the amendment.

For a time after the inauguration of the Federal Government and the adoption of the first ten amendments there was a drop in labor's political interest. During this period, however, news of the storm and strife in France swept across the Atlantic. The appearance of a crusading French Republic made the old champions of popular rights realize that they had become lethargic in their effort to preserve the liberties for which they had fought during the Revolutionary War. Scrutinizing the political scene anew, they saw much to alarm them. They suspected that the Federalists, if not inclined to monarchy, were intent on establishing some sort of aristocratical equivalent—a government of the rich, able, and well born. They could discern monarchial tendencies in the funding and assumption systems which had produced an enormous debt structure and increased taxes which would inevitably weigh heavily on the farmers and mechanics and keep them in their lowly places. An example of such taxes could be readily perceived in the onerous excise tax on whisky, a tax on the drink of the common man. They mistrusted the Washington administration's friendly attitude toward the arch foe of republicanism, Britain, and concluded that Washington was conniving with Britain in its war on France in a gigantic conspiracy to crush democracy and republicanism everywhere.

These alarms and suspicions came to a head in 1793 and resulted in the establishment of about forty societies which quickly formed a network of organizations along the Atlantic Coast and spread even into the hinterland of Kentucky. Called by many names, these organizations have been generally known as the Democratic-Republican societies. Membership was rather diverse. A handful in each society were government officials; 25 to 40 per cent were professional men and merchants. These constituted the leadership. In rural areas the rank and file was made up of landowners, small farmers, and renters; in cities the majority of members were artisans and sea-going laborers. So numerous, in fact, were the mechanics and mari-time workmen that one Bostonian suggested that the organizations unite themselves into a "Labouring Society." The essential aim of the Democratic-Republican societies was to make the opinion of the people known to the government so that its actions would be truly representative of popular will. They fostered town meetings, county associations, and state federations of Democratic-Republican so-cieties. In addition they sponsored newspapers, which became their favorite and most effective forum.

The societies took a prominent share in all the activities of the years 1793–1794. They welcomed Edmond Genêt with open arms as the representative of a sister republic; many of them lent their support to Genêt's plans to recruit American troops to attack British and Spanish possessions in North America. While they were cautious in criticizing Washington, they became furious over the appointment of John Jay as envoy to Britain while he was still Chief Justice. Such an act they regarded as an effort to place power in the hands of a few men. The fury they spent on Jay's appointment turned to apoplexy over the treaty which Jay brought home. They also criticized the Whisky Tax in fulsome phrases and condemned the use of the army to suppress the Whisky Rebels as "tyranny worse than that of George III." The societies also engaged directly in election contests. They entered the campaign of 1794 in New York City and Baltimore; in the latter city they joined with the Carpenter and Mechanical societies to name their own legislative ticket. Elsewhere in the same election they pledged their support to state and Federal representatives who in their opinion had reflected the popular will.

In 1795 the Democratic-Republican societies began to disintegrate as independent organizations. In part this was because the Federal Government had quieted some of the discontent which had incited merchants and Westerners to join the clubs; it had demanded com-pensation of Britain for ships which had been seized in the West Indies; it had negotiated the Pinckney treaty giving Americans the right to navigate the Mississippi River; and it had secured British evacuation of western forts. More important, however, was the fact that the societies merged with Jefferson's Republican party.

The Jeffersonian movement was based upon the planter and the small farmer; it was essentially agrarian. The fact that the city laborer became an integral part of the movement seems very strange, for on several occasions Jefferson declared that he regarded "the . . . artificers as the panders of vice, and the instruments by which the liberties of the country are generally overturned." His mistrust of workingmen probably stemmed from his fear that the laboring classes of the city, dependent for their livelihood upon commercial, financial, and manufacturing interests, would become the minions of those interests—to the eternal hurt of the virtuous agrarian class.

In spite of this suspicion Jefferson made no attempt to repel the artisans; his urban lieutenants, moreover, were usually members of the Democratic-Republican societies who knew the workingmen and assiduously courted their support. Many laboring men responded. While there were some who felt that their best interests lay with the Federalist party and stronger tariffs, a large number, perhaps a majority, became Jeffersonians; they did not recognize Jefferson's mistrust, and they were attracted by his championship of their own ideals.

Workingmen were well satisfied by their alliance with the Republican party. They were particularly gratified with the conduct of the Jeffersonians in the Cordwainers Conspiracy Cases. The attorneys who defended the cordwainers in Philadelphia and in New York were members of the Republican party, as were the newspaper editors who took up the cudgels in defense of the cordwainers' rights. They were also satisfied with the Republicans' handling of economic matters. The period from 1801 to 1807 was one of general prosperity; labor, sharing in that prosperity, was content. International events and Jefferson-Madison policies after 1807, which seriously curtailed and depressed commercial activity, did not change the workingmen's attitude.

Although unemployment appeared in the seacoast towns after the enactment of the Embargo of 1807 and the Federalists became solicitous for their welfare, laboring men remained loyal to the Republican party. In New York City unemployed seamen and ship carpenters demanded some relief for their condition from the municipality, which they received in the form of a public works program, but they were chary in their denunciations of the embargo itself. Nor did the second war with Britain transform the workingmen's attitude. In New York City, Newark, Philadelphia, Norfolk, and Charleston laboring men were quick to enlist and in some cases formed companies made up entirely of mechanics. In New York, Brooklyn, and Philadelphia several trade associations donated weeks of their time without pay to construction of forts for the defense of those cities. No voice of labor denouncing "President Madison's War" is on record.

But a change occurred after the war. It was a period when a new generation, born after the Revolution, reached maturity and power. Restless, impelled by a sense of urgency and the need for change, it groped for new goals which generally included some vague desire to advance the interests of the common man—a striving toward greater dignity, equality, and democracy. Workingmen who were of this new generation were caught up in the trend. With their living standards lowered by depression and the merchant-capitalist system, they became conscious of a sense of inferiority and inequality. As one workman expressed it, "The laboring classes in our country, in consequence of inroads and usurpations of the wealthy and powerful, have for years been gradually sinking in the scale of public estimation." Manual labor had ceased to be respectable. Laboring men, particularly the skilled, began to develop a "Workingmen's Platform," intended to establish or restore the equality of esteem which had once been theirs. It included:

1. A ten-hour day. Under the prevailing sun-to-sun system the average time worked by labor was twelve hours and thirty minutes—a seventy-five-hour week. This system, workingmen argued, was not conducive to good citizenship. It afforded the laborer almost no time for consideration of public questions; it kept him ignorant, and ignorance spelled inferiority.

2. Universal male suffrage in order that labor's interest in society would be recognized by politicians and officeholders.

3. Abolition of imprisonment for debt. The practice of imprisonment was not mandatory; local judges were permitted to use their discretion in assigning debtors to prison. But a survey made in 1829 revealed that of the 75,000 persons annually imprisoned for debt, one-half had debts of less than $20. The burden fell upon the poorer classes. Labor condemned the practice as degrading; it put the poor man in jail and made of him a criminal.

4. Abolition of the militia system. The laws provided that there should be periodical militia drills at which all citizens of the proper age must appear. Failure to attend was punished by fine or imprisonment. Men who could, paid the fine. But the laboring man who had to work as much as ten days to earn the fine was forced to attend the drills, losing several days' wages, or go to jail. This was another indication of degradation, of inferiority.

5. A mechanics' lien law. Since laboring men lost thousands of dollars annually by reason of the death or bankruptcy of their employers, they demanded that their wages be protected by liens which would make them privileged creditors. Thus they could cease to live in fear of penury, cease to feel that they had to cringe and whine to secure their just due.

6. Abolition of all chartered monopolies. This was the time when incorporation was granted to those whom the state legislature wished to encourage or to those who owned the favor of its members; it was the merchant-capitalist who most often was able to secure such franchises and through them create monopolies. Worst of all were the banking monopolies. Since banks issued paper currency which the laborer received at face value as wages but which he could use only at a discount in buying commodities, he was constantly defrauded of a part of his livelihood and kept moreover in a state of inferiority. Banks also extended credit. Since credit followed the successful marketeer, neither the small master nor the workingman could secure it. The banks, in short, stifled freedom of enterprise and prevented the laboring man from developing his potentialities. Almost as bad, however, were the chartered manufacturing enterprises. The small tradesman or journeyman who hoped to set up a shop in areas close to these enterprises found the competition too strong; he found himself forced to work for the merchant-capitalist who owned the enterprise and to remain in an inferior position.

7. Equal and universal education. Of all labor's demands this was the most persistent. In most of New England the principle of a tax-supported school system had been firmly established, but school attendance was not compulsory. In Rhode Island, New York, and Pennsylvania, private schools for children of parents who could pay tuition and charity schools which required the parents to take the degrading pauper oath made up the educational system. The result

was that about half of the children between five and fifteen were not attending school. Workingmen, recognizing that they were often scorned because of their ignorance, accordingly demanded free and universal education so as to win an equal place in society.

The Workingmen's Platform took definite shape only gradually. Since it was essentially a political program, labor turned to its allies in the Republican party to secure its enactment. For a time the party responded. In 1818 Connecticut Republicans granted the right to vote to all who paid taxes and did militia duty. Two years later Massachusetts Republicans abolished the state's freehold franchise and gave the vote to all adult males who paid taxes. In 1821 the constitutional assembly of New York, controlled by Republicans, granted voting rights to all adult white males who had paid taxes, had performed work upon the public roads, or had been enrolled in the militia. Four years later New York became the first industrial state to grant universal white manhood suffrage. But the response soon ended. During the 1820's control of the Republican party was gradually assumed by the advocates of the American system, men whose constituency was the banker, the manufacturer, the domestic trader —in short, the merchant-capitalist who had no sympathy for the workingmen's objectives.

Thus, as the decade advanced, labor found its existence threatened by a new wave of conspiracy cases, its ten-hour movement making few gains, and its demands for political and social equality frustrated by its own party. In the midst of this situation the nation dipped into a depression. The suffering of labor in the winter of 1828–1829 was intense; a correspondent of the *New York Times* reported: "Thousands of industrious mechanics who never before solicited alms, were brought to the humiliating condition of applying for assistance." It was against this background that the workingmen of the seaboard turned to independent politics for relief.

The first labor party appeared early in the spring of 1828 when the Mechanics' Union transformed itself into the "Republican Political Association of the Workingmen of the City of Philadelphia." The political situation in the Quaker City at the time was confused. There was still a strong Federalist party, and the Republican party was split into Adamites and Jacksonians. The Federalist-Adamite groups were merging into a single political coalition which called itself the

Federal-Republican party; in 1828 they controlled the city of Philadelphia. The Jacksonians controlled the county of Philadelphia.

In the summer of 1828 the Workingmen's party nominated an
assembly ticket for the county and a council ticket for the city. Of
all the candidates nominated only eight were on the Workingmen's
ticket alone; the rest were either Federalists or Jacksonians, pledged
"to support the intérests and claims of the Working Classes." The
Workingmen's party made a strenuous campaign. It acquired a journalistic spokesman in the *Mechanics' Free Press* and appointed committees to secure pledges of support. The result was encouraging.
While no straight "Worky" received enough votes for election, all
Federalist and Jackson nominees in both the county and the city
who were also on the Workingmen's ticket received from 300 to
600 more votes than candidates not on the ticket.

In 1829 the laboring elements intensified their activities, organizing clubs and pressing all laboring men to "have themselves duly
assessed" in order to be able to vote. To avoid commitments to either
Federalists or Jacksonians, they made their nominations early. Although the opposition worked assiduously to break up the apparent
unity of the workingmen by endorsing twenty-one of the fifty-four
Worky candidates, the election results were very heartening. Twenty
of the party candidates, each of them endorsed by one or the other
of the major parties, were elected.

During the next year Philadelphia Workies again named full county
and city tickets; the major parties countered with endorsements and
with a bitter attack upon labor as antireligious atheists and infidels, as
agrarians who believed in the equal division of property, and as
disciples of the free-love preachments of Fanny Wright. The charges
made a deep impression. Although the party's voting strength increased, the number of the party nominees elected dropped. In the
city the Workies elected only the eight councilmen endorsed by Jacksonians; in the county the Jacksonians took all offices against the
combined opposition of Workingmen and Federalists. In 1831 the
party disappeared.

A year after Philadelphia labor went into politics New York City
workingmen took the same step. At the time New York mechanics
had already acquired the ten-hour day. In the spring of 1829, however, some employers, taking advantage of the depression, hinted

that a restoration of a longer working day was desirable. Led by Thomas Skidmore, a machinist, the city's workingmen held several huge mass meetings, announced their determination to maintain the ten-hour day, and appointed a Committee of Fifty to assist mechanics in maintaining it. Of itself the meeting ended employer attempts to increase hours.

The Committee of Fifty, with little to do, turned its attention to other labor grievances and to politics. Skidmore—who was writing a book to prove that all the evils of society stemmed from unequal ownership of property—was the leader of the movement. The Committee of Fifty drew up a labor platform which incorporated Skidmore's ideas and laid it before another mass meeting of mechanics in October, along with a recommendation to take independent action to gain their ends. Although the meeting revealed little enthusiasm for Skidmore's ideas, it heartily endorsed the recommendation to take political action.

The political situation in New York City was in a state of transition. Federalism had all but disappeared, and the Republican party had split into two factions. There was a regular Tammany Hall organization, its allegiance at this stage wavering between Henry Clay and Andrew Jackson; there was also a Masonic Hall party, which was inclined to support Clay but contained some Jacksonians. The two factions had broken over spoils of office. Late in October the New York Working Men's party added to the confusion with the nomination of candidates for the State Assembly—all but two were journeymen. The campaign lasted two weeks and was bitterly fought. Tammany and Masonic Hall newspapers poured a steady stream of invective upon the Workies, denouncing them as agrarians, atheists, and infidels. But when the votes were counted, workingmen had good cause to cheer. One Worky, a carpenter named Ebenezer Ford, was elected to the assembly, and every candidate on the ticket received at least 6,000 of the 21,000 votes cast.

With high hopes, labor began to prepare for the next campaign. But several intraparty quarrels developed. One revolved around Skidmore's agrarianism which most workmen disliked; they were not looking for panaceas but for immediate amelioration of their own condition of inferiority. Accordingly, Skidmore and a handful of men seceded and formed the Equal Rights party. A second quarrel revolved around labor's education plank. One faction led by George Henry Evans and Robert Dale Owen championed a plank calling for the establishment of state boarding schools where all children would receive not only equal instruction but equal food and clothing at public expense. Another faction led by Noah Cook and Henry G. Guyon preferred a simple public school system to which they could send their children without breaking up their homes. While vigorous efforts were made to prevent it, a breach developed.

In the meantime, organizations of "farmers, mechanics, and workingmen" had appeared in upstate New York. Mechanics' tickets swept to local victories at Albany, Troy, Syracuse, and Canandaigua in the spring of 1830; parties developed at Schenectady, Rochester, Geneva, Ithaca, Auburn, Batavia, Palmyra, Kingsbury, Lansingburg, and Glens Falls. Appearance of the movement over so wide an area made the next step inevitable: a state convention of workingmen met at Syracuse in August, 1830. The meeting recognized the Cook-Guyon faction as the official branch of the party in New York City, and then nominated Erastus Root, a Democrat, as their gubernatorial candidate. Root was temporarily out of favor with the state machine and Tammany.

Shortly after the Working Men's convention adjourned the Democrats named Enos Throop as their candidate for governor. Meanwhile the Owen-Evans faction held its own convention and nominated Ezekiel Williams, an Auburn leather manufacturer; the Anti-Masonic party also placed a candidate in the race. In New York City the Workies, Tammany, the Owens-Evans faction, and Skidmore's agrarians named local tickets.

The election spelled the beginning of the end for the workingmen's parties. Root withdrew from the race, leaving the regular Working Men's party without a gubernatorial candidate. Both the Regency, the State Democratic machine, and Tammany made strong efforts to win over the rebellious workmen. Their candidates pledged their wholehearted support for the labor program and pointed out that they had not only secured enactment of a mechanics' lien law for New York City during the previous session of the legislature but had also pushed the passage of legislation designed to restore "specie money in place of paper rags." The campaign proved highly effective. Although Cook and Guyon tried to swing the party's support to the

Anti-Masonic candidate for governor in return for Anti-Masonic sup·
port of the Workies' city ticket, it appears that the majority of
workingmen upstate and in the city gave their vote to Democratic
candidates. In New York City the total vote cast for workingmen's
tickets dropped more than 60 per cent, about equal to the increase
in Tammany's vote.

In the next two years the Workies disappeared completely from
the political scene. In the fall of 1831 the Owen-Evans wing named
its own ticket, but its vote dwindled to less than a thousand. In
1832 George Henry Evans suggested that the party support the
Tammany candidates for President, Vice President, for Congress and
Assembly because they were opponents of the United States Bank,
and because they were "much more favorable to the measures of the
workingmen than their opponents." The advice marked the end of
the party.

Workingmen's parties were not confined to Philadelphia and New
York. Although less numerous elsewhere, laboring men in other parts
of the nation also turned to independent political action in the early
thirties. The most widespread appeared in New England. At New
London, Connecticut, the three candidates of the "mechanics and
workingmen" were elected to the state legislature in 1830, and the
mechanics put their entire slate of town candidates into office the
following year. Parties were also formed in Boston and Plymouth, in
most Massachusetts counties, in Burlington, Middlebury, and Wood-
stock, Vermont. At Newark, New Jersey, the workingmen's candidates carried the town election in the spring of 1830. Labor parties
appeared in a number of Pennsylvania towns: Lancaster, Harrisburg, Carlisle, Pottsville, Philipsburg, Milesburg, Pittsburgh, and
Erie. Political movements also developed at Wilmington, Delaware,
where workingmen captured thirteen of the eighteen charter offices
of the city, and at Canton and Zanesville, Ohio.

All the workingmen's parties disappeared for much the same reasons. One cause was the denunciation and revilement heaped upon
labor parties by the "respectable" politicians and their journalistic
spokesmen. While many workingmen could shrug off such names as
"levelers," "mob," "Dirty Shirt party," "rag, tag and bobtail," "ring-
streaked and speckled rabble," there were just as many who feared
the pointing finger of scorn. Such individuals returned quickly to the

ranks of the more orthodox parties. Also important was the return
of prosperity. As jobs became more plentiful laboring men lost something of their sense of injustice, some of their sense of inferiority.
They became interested now in wages and living standards—in economic matters which could be better taken care of through trade
associations.

But there were other, perhaps more significant, causes for the disappearance of the workingmen's parties. The composition of the parties themselves, the activities of major party politicians, and the
influence of the bank issue in the election of 1832 are also involved.
Exactly what effect these factors had, however, is a moot point which
revolves around the question, "Did labor vote for Jackson?"

Older historians interested in the role of labor and some contem-
porary historians have concluded, primarily on the basis of opinions
of editors and labor leaders who lived in the 1830's, that workingmen's parties were organized and operated by workingmen who had
deserted the party of Jefferson. In their opinion these workingmen
returned to their old party, now led by Jackson. Various factors were
involved in this return: workingmen recognized the Jacksonian Democracy as the party of the common man; they were attracted by the
promises of Jacksonian politicians and by the fact that the Jacksonians began to fulfill their promises—in New York, for example, the
Democrats enacted a part of the workingmen's platform by passing
a mechanics' lien law in 1830, by abolishing imprisonment for debt,
and by reforming the militia system in 1832. Finally, they were attracted by the fact that Jackson was an enemy of the Bank of the
United States, which workingmen hated. The old-school historians
conclude that labor voted for Jackson in 1832 and became an integral
part of the Democratic party.

In recent years other historians have cast doubt on these conclusions. Their research into the period, while recognizing contempo-
rary opinion, is based primarily upon an analysis of the occupations
of members of Worky committees and conventions and Worky candidates, and upon an analysis of election returns. Concerning the
composition of the workingmen's parties they have come to the
following conclusions: In Boston the party, from its origin, was
largely led by manufacturers and shopkeepers. In New York the
skilled artisans created and ran the party during its first campaign,

but skilled artisans held only forty-two seats on the seventy-man Executive Committee established to run the party after the split with Skidmore in 1830; most of the remaining members were "manufacturers." In the city of Philadelphia the party was also organized by skilled artisans, but beginning in 1829 its leadership was strongly infiltrated by anti-Jacksonians. In other Pennsylvania cities—Harrisburg, Lewiston, and Pittsburgh—the workingmen's parties were only remotely connected with labor; they were developed by anti-Jacksonians to split the labor vote. The implication in these conclusions is that the manufacturers and anti-Jacksonians were able to lure workingmen into the camp of the Jacksonian opposition, at this period known generally as the National Republicans or Anti-Masons.

Analysis of the election returns, with the most careful and thorough work on the cities of Boston and Philadelphia, appears to substantiate the implication. Although the Democratic vote increased in Boston, the city was overwhelmingly anti-Jackson in 1828 and 1832, and against Van Buren in 1836. The Philadelphia situation was more complex. The city voted for Jackson in 1828; most of the wards where workingmen lived were strongly Jacksonian that year. Thereafter, however, the Jackson and Democratic vote dropped from a high of 56 per cent in 1828 to 37 per cent in 1832 and 34 per cent in 1836. There was a slight rise in 1840. Further analysis of election returns from the rest of the state leads to the conclusion that, except for the county of Philadelphia, "the wage earners were the first to drop from the Jackson bandwagon." In short, the workingmen went over to the Jackson opposition. In general it appears that the new-school historians would agree with this conclusion.

The historian who tries to weigh these contradictory conclusions is faced with many problems. Admittedly, the conclusion of the old-school historians is based on less "scientific" evidence than that of the new school. But does that mean their conclusions should be lightly cast aside? The old-school historians have strong supporting evidence for their conclusion that workingmen became Democrats: in the period after 1833 agitation regarding workingmen's demands was very strong in the Democratic party; no comparable agitation developed within the Whig party. This could mean that the Democratic party was indeed the party of the workingmen, or at least the more articulate and politically conscious workingmen, and that the Whig party was not.

In addition the historian must examine carefully the scientific evidence of the new-school historians. One statistical study of the Boston returns which uses correlative coefficients reveals that, in spite of the election results, the majority of workingmen were pro-Jackson. In short, the scientific evidence concerning Boston has been contradicted by a scientific technique using the same evidence.

There are other weaknesses. It cannot be assumed that all "manufacturers" or wealthy men were anti-Jacksonians; such an assumption would be carrying the doctrine of economic determinism too far. It cannot be assumed, moreover, that anti-Jacksonians in the workingmen's parties successfully lured workingmen into the anti-Jackson camp; they might have repelled workingmen. It cannot be assumed that the obvious decline of the Democratic vote in Philadelphia was caused only by the desertion of workingmen; it might as readily be assumed that the decline was due in whole or in part to the desertion of Jackson and his party by other elements living in the city, elements which had been attracted to Jackson when they did not know his philosophy and deserted him when they came to know him better. Finally, even if the conclusions concerning Pennsylvania labor are correct, it cannot be assumed that these conclusions apply elsewhere. Among the industrial states of the union, Pennsylvania has seldom followed the prevailing or typical political trend.

The historian can safely conclude only the following: the workingmen's parties of the early Jackson period disappeared because the parties were not "respectable," which made workingmen who were members feel inferior; because workingmen turned once more to trade unionism in order to achieve economic ends; and because they in one way or another were persuaded to join the Democratic or Whig parties or both to gain political ends.

7 —

The Jackson Period—Locofocoism

Very few labor organizations created in the twenties survived the effect of the Conspiracy Cases and the depression of 1828–1831, and little effort was made to revive them for several years. Labor's energies, as has been indicated, were directed toward politics. Nevertheless, before the Workingmen's parties disappeared trade associations sprang up again. The revival was brought about, in part, by the expansion of the activities of the merchant-capitalist. So complete did his domination become in the 1830's that he forced his subcontractors to destroy many of the institutions with which labor had protected its living standards. Trades were split up; the apprentice who had once served five years was now taught only part of a trade which he learned in a few months—a practice that worked a hardship on the skilled worker who found shop after shop operating efficiently with halfway mechanics who worked for low wages. Women who were employed at lower wages than skilled men were brought into the workshops in huge numbers; by 1837 they were found in one hundred different industries. The contractor dug even lower into the economic scale; he employed convict labor, a practice which enabled merchant-capitalists to sell goods at from "40 to 60 per cent below what the honest mechanic . . . can afford them for."

Equally important was the return of prosperity and its accompanying rise in prices. With the removal of deposits from the Bank of the United States in 1833, there followed a spectacular increase in the nation's money and credit supply and an equally spectacular rise in prices and the cost of living. Flour which sold for $5 a barrel in 1834 was selling at $12 by 1837; real-estate values advanced more than 220 per cent, and rents increased proportionately. The nature of the circulating medium aggravated the hardship. Before 1834 gold and silver had been coined at a ratio of 15 to 1, which undervalued gold and drove it out of circulation; after that date the ratio was changed to 16 to 1, which undervalued silver and drove it out of circulation in turn. All that was left was paper of doubtful value. Workingmen who were paid in notes at face value frequently found it necessary to use the notes at a discount. The combination of factors led to a "luxuriant" revival of trade associations.

The revival began on a small scale in 1831, increased in 1833, and became a near crusade in 1835-1836. All the once-organized trades resuscitated their old organizations; dozens more organized for the first time—most notably the workers, men and women, in the cotton and woolen factories along the Merrimac and the Delaware rivers. In all, at least two hundred trade associations were formed in those years, with a membership that has been estimated to run from 100,-000 to 300,000. The new associations were substantially the same as those which had been created in the 1790's and the early 1820's. They were organizations of skilled labor, with much the same rules and regulations, and much the same problems: competition from cheaper labor, apprenticeship, the closed shop, and wages adequate to maintain a decent standard of living. At the same time several new trends appeared.

The most widespread of the new developments was the movement to organize city federations. The basis for the movement was the recognition by laboring men that their associations were far too weak to cope with employers alone; experience with political parties suggested that a city-wide organization could be more effective. The movement in this direction, begun at New York City in 1833, spread to Boston, Philadelphia, Baltimore, Washington, New Brunswick, Newark, Albany, Troy, Schenectady, Pittsburgh, Cincinnati, and Louisville within the next three years.

One of the first acts of these federations was to establish a newspaper; through it they informed the public that their aims included maintenance of wages to provide a decent standard of living and reduction of hours to provide workingmen with adequate leisure for self-improvement. They intended to be moderate; no strikes concerning wages and hours were to be supported until investigated and judged by the federation. Approved strikes would be supported by dues collected from all members and by a boycott of the commodities of the employers at whom the strike was directed.

In spite of a determination toward reasonableness, support of strikes became the chief activity of the city federations. In the period from 1833 to 1837 a wave of strikes swept through the cities along the seaboard. Sometimes they began before the federations were organized, but there can be little doubt that the existence of the relatively powerful assemblies encouraged action. Almost all the strikes that occurred in 1833–1834 revolved around the question of wages. But the issue which dominated the year 1835 and the whole era was the ten-hour day. The demand for institution of the six-to-six system was heard in all industries. The arguments advanced for its adoption varied. Often heard was the claim that long hours were injurious to health. More frequently workmen argued that shorter hours would make them better and more sober citizens: leisure would give them opportunity for mental cultivation and improvement. Workmen also argued that the ten-hour day would bring no drop in production because a rested and cheerful man could produce more goods in ten hours than an exhausted and discontented man could produce in fifteen.

The climax to the movement came in the campaign of seventeen Philadelphia trade associations in the summer of 1835. Securing support from professional men, merchants, and politicians, it paralyzed the city and swept to a complete victory. Even the public employees were granted a ten-hour day. The victory was so overwhelming and was given so much publicity that strikes to secure the ten-hour day immediately swept through Salem, Hartford, Batavia, Seneca Falls, New Brunswick, and Paterson. All were successful. Ten-hour days were granted without a struggle in Albany, Troy, Schenectady, Newark, Wilmington, and in many Baltimore trades. By the close of the year the ten-hour day had become standard for skilled labor throughout the Middle Atlantic States.

Nothing indicates the success of the ten-hour movement so much as the fact that almost no strikes for a shorter day occurred during the next two years. Demand for higher wages was the dominant theme in 1836–1837, and for the most part the demand was met. Current wages for skilled workers in the period rose from a level of $1.00–$1.12 to a level of $1.50–$2.00 a day.

A second development among laboring men was the organization of specific trades along national lines. The immediate reason for this trend was found in the extension and development of the nation's system of transportation. Canals, improved rivers, and railroads (which totaled 2,300 miles by the end of the decade) drew industrial centers closer and threw them into competition with one another. Not only did goods move more freely but passengers, including strikebreakers, could be transported long distances. Strikers found their employers fulfilling contracts with goods bought in other areas and advertising for workers from one hundred to five hundred miles distant. The need for national organization became painfully apparent.

Best known of all nationals established during the decade was the printers' association. The printing industry was undergoing a thorough transformation at the time. It was a period when the practical printer who produced newspapers and books began to disappear; organizations with an interest to propagate—political parties, agricultural and industrial societies—became newspaper publishers and merchant-capitalists became book publishers. The ability to print ceased to count; ability to reach subscribers, voters, customers, and subsidizers became important. The effect on the printers was disastrous. With publishers in control, the shopowner became a mere employer of labor, his profits dependent upon his ability to keep down cost of production, which he did by using apprentices.

The notorious use of apprentices by Duff Green, editor of the *United States Telegraph,* friend of John C. Calhoun and printer for the Federal Government, led to the creation of the printers' association. In 1834 Green set up the Washington institute to train printers; his announced intention was to take in about two hundred boys and use them in his plant at a wage of $2.00 a week for seven years. His proposal, condemned as a clever stratagem to reduce the wages of journeymen printers, caused a strike. Because of the issues involved, a convention of printers from eastern cities met at Washington in March, 1835, organized the National Typographical Society, drew up an elaborate set of apprenticeship rules, and proposed the adoption of a "union card." The effect of the society on the trade is unrecorded. Shoemakers, comb makers, carpenters, and hand-loom weavers also created national organizations during the period. All of them disappeared during the depression of 1837.

Another of the new trends to appear in the decade was found in the organization created at Providence, Rhode Island, in December, 1831. It grew out of a determination of the skilled laborers of the city to establish the ten-hour day. To strengthen their campaign they called a meeting of delegates from all over New England. The convention adopted the name "New England Association of Farmers, Mechanics and Other Workingmen." As established, the association was designed to be a union of all producing classes. Not only artisans and unskilled laborers, but master workmen who were exposed to the "ruinous competition" of the merchant-capitalists, farmers whose interests were "indissolubly" connected with the welfare of "mechanics and other classes of labor," and the factory operatives, who had hitherto played but the slightest role in labor movements, were invited to join. The organization, in short, anticipated the Knights of Labor and the industrial union movement of later years.

The first convention resolved that its membership would limit itself to a ten-hour working day, and it provided for the payment of an annual "tax" of fifty-five cents per member as a "war chest" to relieve the distress of those members who lost their jobs because of their efforts to enforce the association resolution. It recommended that auxiliary branches be established in every town and that committees be established in every state "to collect and publish facts respecting the working conditions of labouring men, women, and children, and abuses practised on them by their employers," and to prepare memorials to state legislatures urging the adoption of a ten-hour day by law.

Almost immediately Boston ship carpenters, engaged in the second largest industry in New England, attempted to put the ten-hour day into practice. Their effort led to a lockout and defeat. The failure undoubtedly influenced the second convention, which boasted delegates from every New England state, to release its members from their pledge to work no more than ten hours. At the third convention, in 1833, the failure of the association to achieve its aims became evident. Although resolutions to send delegates to a national convention of workingmen were adopted, the greatest attention was given to a proposal calling upon the association to take measures "to redress

the wrongs of the producing classes, by recourse to the Ballot Box."
The New England Association was turning to political action.

The final and in some ways most significant development of the
period was the formation of a national organization of city federations. The size of the labor movement—more than 100,000 members, presumably with the same objectives but with little communication between them—provided the impulse. The New York General
Trades' Union took the lead in creating the organization when it invited delegates from all city federations to meet in the city in 1834.
The meeting adopted the name National Trades' Union. Throughout
its three-year existence it included among its officers some of the
most important local labor leaders of the nation: Ely Moore, Robert
Townshend, John Commerford, and Levi D. Slamm of New York;
Thomas Hogan, William English, and John Farrell of Philadelphia;
B. H. Hammond, J. L. Parsons, and Dr. Charles Douglas of Boston;
Amaziah Whitney of Albany; James Murray of Pittsburgh; and A. J.
W. Jackson of Baltimore.

At the start the National Trades' Union assumed that its function
was to be one of exhortation. It urged the creation of more trade
associations and issued arguments to advance the labor platform of
the twenties—giving particular notice to the faulty educational system. It also added new, or once minor, issues to the Workingmen's
platform. At its first meeting it roundly condemned the "deplorable
condition" of women and children in the cotton and woolen factories; later it denounced the sale of public land and proposed—since
few laborers had sufficient funds to purchase land—that it be given
away to actual settlers. It excoriated the convict labor system as a
practice which took bread from the mouths of honest citizens, and
demanded its abolition.

In spite of its original assumption the National Trades' Union did
not remain an advisory body. In 1835 it made the ten-hour day for
mechanics employed by the Federal Government its own special
concern when it took up the appeal of the mechanics of the Brooklyn and New York Navy yards and drew up a memorial on the subject to Congress. Ely Moore presented the petition which was referred
to a committee and buried. Meanwhile mechanics at the Philadelphia Navy Yard appealed directly to the President for a reduction
of hours; the N.T.U. added its own pleas. Jackson responded with

a proclamation establishing the ten-hour day in the Philadelphia yard. The act convinced the National Trades' Union that thereafter it would best secure its objectives through the Chief Executive, and that the way to reach him was through the ballot box. In its address to the workingmen of the nation in 1836 the N.T.U. urged all laborers to cast their vote for President with care. The suggestion was appropriate, for by that year the whole labor movement had turned political again.

As in earlier years the growth and success of trade associations in the thirties had its inevitable by-product in the formation of a large number of employers' associations. Appearing in all cities in which trade unions were organized, even as far west as St. Louis, they had only one purpose: the destruction of labor organizations which fostered "oppression, tyranny, and misrule" and obstructed "the free course of trade."

While the blacklist became the employers' most used weapon— particularly in factories—the courts became their most effective weapon. Between 1834 and 1836 five different cases were tried. Most significant were the Geneva Shoemakers and the New York Tailors cases, which were based not upon common but upon statute law. In the recodification of New York's law of 1829 the statute defining "champerty" designated as criminals all persons who confederated by oath or otherwise "to commit an act injurious to public morals or to trade and commerce." Although the provision, taken directly from the common-law definition of conspiracy, was not specifically directed against wage earners, it was used in both New York cases.

Precedent for its use was set up in the Geneva case of 1835 which involved a society of shoemakers, who forced the discharge of a man working for less than society wages, and were indicted under the statute. The case was carried to the state's supreme court where the chief justice announced that the action was "injurious to trade and commerce," on the ground that Geneva shoemakers had so enhanced the price of boots made in Geneva as to permit boots made elsewhere to be sold cheaper, and because they had driven an honest man out of employment, diminishing both the quantity of productive labor and internal trade. The decision was immediately recognized as a threat to labor's entire campaign to maintain living standards.

The following year some twenty tailors of New York City, who had been black-listed by an employers' association, began picketing employers' shops and were arrested for conspiracy. When the tailors were found guilty, the anxiety of New York City workingmen turned to fury. In the week that elapsed between the court's decision and its sentence preparations for a storm of protest were made. The courtroom was thronged on the day the sentence was delivered. The fines imposed were heavy, but more important to labor was the court's reasoning: "In this favoured land of law and liberty," the judge declared, "the road to advancement is open to all, and the journeymen may by their skill and industry, and moral worth, soon become flourishing master mechanics. Every American knows . . . that he has no better friend than the laws and that he needs no artificial combination for his protection. They are of foreign origin and I am led to believe mainly upheld by—Foreigners." The dictum aroused bitter replies in all parts of the nation; everywhere workingmen shrieked "slavery." In New York's City Hall Park a gigantic meeting of 27,000 laborers shouted fiercely for a revival of political action. Since legislators and judges were men "whose situation in life" would not permit them to sympathize with the working people, the only remedy was resort to the ballot box.

The explosion of New York workingmen over the Tailors case did not create a political movement; for a number of reasons a trend in that direction had been developing for several years. In the period immediately after the disappearance of the first workingmen's parties laboring men had expected that politicians who had promised to advance their welfare would move with reasonable speed. They had moved too slowly, or not at all. In 1833 the Workingmen's Platform still needed enactment. The failure provided the impulse for renewal of political activity in Massachusetts in 1833 where workingmen in Charleston and Lowell nominated Samuel C. Allen, a Democrat, as their candidate for governor. In the election that followed, Allen received a mere 1,900 votes, one-fourth from Boston, but ten candidates for the state legislature who had been endorsed by workingmen were elected.

In 1834 the New England Association converted itself into a political party and renominated Allen on a program which advocated hard money, attacked bank monopolies, demanded factory legislation, condemned the evils of child labor, and called for the establishment of "republican education." The campaign proved discouraging; the number of votes which Allen received were hardly worth counting. But failure was due in part to the fact that in 1834 labor's attention had focused upon the struggle over the issue of chartered monopolies in the Democratic party. The problem of banking monopolies and their operations was the most important reason for the revival of workingmen's political activity.

Labor leaders and many workingmen supported Andrew Jackson because they recognized him as the enemy of bank monopolies. In 1832 they had hailed his veto of the bill to recharter the second Bank of the United States as a step in the right direction. In 1834 Jackson took a second step toward destruction of the Bank by ordering the removal of $6,000,000 of government deposits, which were then placed in the "Pet Banks." This act started a fearful controversy among the enemies of the Bank. Agrarian and local banking interests commended the move: it opened up credit and made bigger profits possible. Labor leaders were openly dismayed. In their opinion the act was no solution: it merely transferred Federal money from one monopoly to another. Moreover, they were convinced that it would create an inflationary spiral which would bring disaster upon the nation. They had another solution—one that had been provided for them by William Gouge, editor of the *Philadelphia Gazette* and a member of a committee named by the Workingmen's party of Philadelphia to draw up a report on the banking system of the nation.

Gouge did not call for total annihilation of banks; he proposed to restrict their operations by making them into institutions of deposit and exchange which would take away their right to issue paper money. Hard money would thus become the normal circulating medium, and workingmen could not be defrauded if their wages were paid in specie. In addition Gouge proposed that the existing system of chartering banks by special acts of legislature should be abolished and that a "free banking" system be erected in its place. Free banking would permit any person who could meet state requirements for safe operations to open a bank. Adoption of such a principle would destroy monopolies with their favored customers and advance free enterprise which would give workingmen a chance to become independent tradesmen.

In 1834 labor elements in the northeastern states suggested that

Gouge's policy be incorporated into the Democratic platform. When their proposal was vigorously rebuffed by the agrarian and local banking interests, they began a campaign to secure control of the party. Action centered in Massachusetts, Pennsylvania, and New York.

In Massachusetts the campaign was headed by such labor leaders as Dr. Charles Douglas, first president of the New England Association; Seth Luther, secretary of the Boston General Trades' Union; and Theophilus Fisk, editor of the *New England Artisan*. In 1835 public figures like George Bancroft, Marcus Morton, and Frederick Robinson, who had recently spearheaded a successful drive to abolish imprisonment for debt, joined the campaign. A bitter intraparty battle followed as Massachusetts Democrats divided into the Custom House wing and the Hard Hands. In 1836 the Hard Hands took control and wrote a platform which, one newspaper declared, made the workingmen's program "part and parcel" of Democratic policy.

A different pattern of events developed in Pennsylvania where the Democratic party was controlled by forces closely tied to the Bank of the United States. Nevertheless, Philadelphia workingmen—or at least the articulate portion—proposed not only total destruction of the Bank but complete reform of the state banking system along hard-money lines. As the first step toward this objective they demanded the abolition of all paper money printed in denominations of ten dollars or less—the kind of money used to pay wages. The test came during the election of 1835. When the incumbent governor, George Wolfe, who had revealed himself as a "monopoly man," was nominated for reelection by the party machine, the laboring element of Philadelphia named Henry A. Muhlenburg, a bitter enemy of the Bank, as its candidate on a third ticket. Muhlenburg received 37,800 votes, more than 35 per cent of the Democratic total, but the split in the party gave the state to the Whigs.

Even more significant developments occurred in New York. The state's Democracy was headed by a small group of men known as the Regency, described by one of their most bitter opponents as "men of great ability, great industry, indomitable courage, and strict personal integrity." Its captain was Martin Van Buren. Other things being equal, the Regency favored reform. It had never rejected workingmen's ideals. Van Buren himself had worked for years to abolish imprisonment for debt and had been a champion of universal suffrage. Between 1831 and 1834 the legislature, which the Regency controlled, had adopted a mechanics' lien law, abolished imprisonment for debt, and reformed the militia system.

In New York City the Regency's ally was Tammany, which many workingmen had joined since the collapse of their own parties. They were fairly well satisfied with Tammany until 1834 when an investigation into the affairs of the Seventh Ward Bank revealed that its founders had given shares of stock to more than one hundred state and city officials—including every Tammany senator. Workingmen, accordingly, began to suspect that Tammany's opposition to the Bank of the United States was based on the fact that it was a rival of the state banks in which Tammany leaders had an interest. Late in 1834 a group of labor leaders within the Tammany organization created the Working Men's General Committee. Among its members were George Henry Evans, Ebenezer Ford, Levi D. Slamm, John Commerford, Alexander Ming, Robert Townshend, and Ely Moore. The committee warned Tammany that it would support no candidate for national or state office who would not pledge opposition to all monopolies and all charters of incorporation which granted exclusive privileges. Tammany accepted the ultimatum, and its ticket was triumphant in the fall elections.

Democratic workingmen soon discovered that Tammany would not fulfill its pledges. The legislature which met in the winter of 1834–1835 was controlled by a wing of the Regency which favored state banks. Adopting a policy of "judicious opposition to Whig Monopoly," it proceeded to charter a large number of Democratic state banks. When Tammany representatives joined the movement, New York City workingmen, furious over the betrayal, became determined to force trustworthy candidates upon the organization.

Their opportunity came in October, 1835, at which time the rank and file appeared at Tammany to pass judgment upon the candidates whom the leaders had chosen to bear the party banner in the coming municipal election. When the organization ticket was announced, it was met by a chorus of hisses, hoots, and catcalls, for many of the nominees had been false to their antimonopoly pledges. But before any formal protests were made, the chairman declared the ticket approved, and Tammany leaders retired. A moment later the gas lights flickered and died—an old method of quelling mutiny at Tammany Hall. The workingmen were prepared; extracting candles and some new matches, popularly known as "loco focos," from their pockets they lined the stage with tapers, named their own candidates, and then proceeded to rouse the city with a huge torchlight parade. Newspapers promptly dubbed their slate the "Locofoco ticket." Tammany carried the election, but by a very narrow margin.

For several months after the election the Locofocos, eschewing schism, tried to regain control of Tammany Hall, but their efforts met with failure. In 1836 they began setting up their own organization. At this juncture the workingmen of the city exploded over the Tailors case.

Encouraged by the strong political impulse which the case unleashed, Locofoco leaders adopted tactics intended to punish Tammany. They endorsed two Democratic candidates and one Whig candidate for Congress; they also endorsed a Whig candidate for the state senate in return for Whig endorsement of two Locofoco candidates for the state assembly. The result was most gratifying: all Locofoco-endorsed candidates were elected, and Tammany lost control of the city delegation in the state legislature.

In the midst of these state campaigns workingmen turned their attention to the presidential campaign. Their first choice for the Democratic presidential nomination was a Kentucky senator, Colonel Richard M. Johnson, champion of a Federal measure to abolish imprisonment for debt and bitter foe of the Bank. When the Democrats nominated Martin Van Buren with Johnson as his running mate, labor leaders in most industrial centers extended a hearty endorsement. Only the New York Locofocos remained officially cold, primarily because they held Van Buren responsible, as titular head of the Regency, for the large number of banks which the Regency-Tammany forces had chartered in the winter of 1834–1835, and because Van Buren, who had not made up his mind, refused to pledge himself to maintain a consistent stand against paper money and monopolies. The Locofocos, accordingly, had dismissed all presidential candidates as "second rate men." Their refusal to endorse Van Buren, however, did not lessen his vote in New York City, which he carried triumphantly.

Meanwhile the nation moved toward economic catastrophe.

Throughout 1836 the inflationary spiral which had inspired a wave of strikes for higher wages continued to mount. The proportion of paper to specie increased; speculation in bank stocks, internal improvements, and public lands grew wilder. Extensive crop failures made it difficult for farmers to pay their debts to merchants and land speculators, who in turn failed to meet their obligations to banks; crop failures also cut down agricultural exports and made it necessary to export specie. Jackson's Specie Circular requiring that public lands should thereafter be purchased in gold and silver forced a contraction of credit. Clay's Distribution Act, which provided for the distribution of the Federal surplus among the states, brought a withdrawal of public funds from the Pet Banks and a further contraction in the money market. A depression began to set in. The winter of 1836–1837 brought hardship to the cities. Unemployment appeared. Prices of essential foods took a sharp upward turn, placing them out of reach of the poor. Then, in May, 1837, New York City banks suspended specie payments. As other banks closed their doors a wave of panic swept through the country, and all eyes turned to the White House.

Van Buren had been under ceaseless pressure to do something about the approaching collapse ever since his inauguration. Whigs and conservative Democrats had been urging him to repeal the Specie Circular and turn his back upon the hard-money program. But Van Buren refused to be moved. Instead he gave his attention to a plan, conceived by Gouge and endorsed by Locofocos, for a divorce of the government from banks. When he learned that eastern Democrats approved, Van Buren laid the plan before Congress. It called for the erection of an Independent Treasury System which would remove public funds from the banks, end the use of bank notes in the payment of obligations to the Federal Government, and require payment in legal tender. It was an apt interpretation of the hard-money program: by removing the public funds from the banks it reduced the amount of specie on which paper could be issued and thus had a stabilizing effect upon the nation's economy; by rejecting bank notes in payment of revenue it restricted the power of the banks over currency; by confining banks to the needs of commerce it limited their ability to redistribute wealth in favor of a single class.

Van Buren's endorsement of the hard-money program precipitated the final contest of the workingmen for control of the Democratic party. Backed by Federal patronage, Massachusetts Hard Hands fastened their grip on the party more firmly; in 1839, with Marcus Morton as their candidate, they won the governorship. In New York, after defeats by Whigs in the elections of 1837–1838, primarily because of the loss of labor support, the Regency surrendered. In New York City Locofoco leaders persuaded Tammany to name a ticket composed of "politically and morally satisfactory" candidates and to adopt a "Declaration of Rights" satisfactory to labor. Hard-money advocates also took control of the Democratic organizations in Maine, New Hampshire, and Connecticut; congressional candidates of the party in New Jersey, Pennsylvania, and Ohio avowed hard-money principles.

In the meantime the battle to enact the Independent Treasury bill raged in Congress. As originally drawn the bill was furiously opposed by Whigs, Democrats who were allied with local banking interests, and western agrarians who had no love for the hard-money policy. It failed to pass. But after the election of 1838 and a second suspension of specie payments in 1839—which convinced many Westerners and Southerners of both parties that reform was necessary—the bill was reintroduced and became law in July, 1840. Almost simultaneously Van Buren issued an executive order limiting the working day of Federal employees to ten hours without any reduction of wages. Widely condemned because it infringed upon the right to work, the act, which Van Buren acknowledged had been "devised by the mechanics and laborers themselves," was a symbolic indication of the influence of the workingmen in the councils of the Democratic party.

The workingmen's program, translated into Locofoco principles, dominated the Democratic party until the Civil War. As the war approached, those principles were often transcended by the interests of southern cotton growers and western agrarians, but the Democratic party and particularly its northeastern wing never entirely lost the views injected into it by the workingmen.

The workingmen's program also made a deep impression on the Whigs. As the research of the new school of labor historians indicates, local conservatives had pledged themselves to work for portions of the laboring men's demands during the period when the workingmen's parties were springing up in the industrial centers of the East. While it is impossible to say whether or not these pledges attracted workingmen into the ranks of the Jackson opposition, it is clear that the political power of workingmen influenced the anti-Jacksonians who in 1834–1835 became the Whig party. When the workingmen's principles were translated into Locofocoism, the Whig effort to hold or attract a labor vote became a national policy. After 1840 Whigs, who had once voiced the view that property owners were a distinct class, the natural leaders of mankind to whom all political power should be given, denied the existence of any class conflict in America and denied even the existence of classes. They also became ardent defenders of "democracy." They denied advocating rule by an aristocracy of wealth. There was no danger of a single class tyrannizing over the American people; there was only danger that the Chief Executive, through his power over patronage and through the veto, would submerge American liberties. They thus became defenders of the popular will, as expressed by Congress, against executive usurpation of power. Whigs in the East also adopted many of the principles of the workingmen. In Massachusetts they began to "descend from the public forum and take the voters by the hand." In New York and Pennsylvania they became the supporters of "republican education."

With both major parties adopting Locofoco principles, the workingmen's platform was written into law in the northeastern states after 1836. The franchise was extended: Rhode Island and Connecticut adopted universal male suffrage in the forties; only Massachusetts and Pennsylvania of the industrial states maintained the taxpayers' qualification until 1861. Other corollary laws, urged by both farmers and workingmen, were enacted, providing for abolition or reduction of property qualifications for holding office, for apportionment of legislatures according to population rather than to property, and for popular election of all state officials.

The practice of imprisoning debtors was swept out of existence in most northeastern states. Vermont and Ohio abolished the practice in 1838; New Hampshire and Massachusetts in 1839; Connecticut, New Jersey, and Pennsylvania in 1842. Abolition of the militia system, which secured the support of employers, proceeded more slowly. The general trend in the northeastern states after 1836 was to follow the example of New York, which reduced the fine for nonappearance at drill to a very nominal sum and then canceled the fine. By the opening of the Civil War militia drill was confined to volunteers in almost all the northern states. Enactment of mechanics' lien laws also proceeded slowly, but New Hampshire, Connecticut, New Jersey, Pennsylvania, and Ohio enacted such laws by 1861.

The demand that paper money and the chartered monopoly banking system be replaced with a hard-money and free banking system met with considerable success. Jackson's Specie Circular and the Independent Treasury Acts of 1840 and 1846 went a long way toward establishing a hard-money policy. Abolition of the circulation of small notes by various states, including Maine, New Hampshire, Connecticut, New York, New Jersey, and Pennsylvania, between 1835 and 1837 aided the principle. The most significant development in the field was the reform in banking. The movement began in New York in 1838 when Governor Marcy asked a Whig-controlled legislature to enact a Free Banking Law. Though Whigs and conservative Democrats protested, both soon recognized that such a law would not interfere with business if it did not impose the severe limitations upon the issue of paper money which the Locofocos demanded. Whigs seized the opportunity. The Free Banking Act, as passed, provided for free incorporation and the maintenance of a specie reserve of 12½ per cent. It permitted banks to issue notes up to the full value of all 5 per cent Federal and state bonds and up to one-half the value of 6 per cent mortgages which were deposited with the state comptroller. If a bank failed to redeem, the state comptroller could close the bank at discretion and force a public auction of the assets to redeem the notes. Hard-money advocates found the law faulty and voted against it. Nevertheless, it was a triumph for the workingmen who had clamored for such a law for ten years.

Once New York's Free Banking Law was in effect and had proved its worth—to financiers, merchants, manufacturers, and farmers—it was copied by Vermont, Massachusetts, Connecticut, New Jersey, and Pennsylvania in the East, and by all the states in the Old Northwest. Not all these acts were written as labor would have desired, nor did they always prove successful in operation. But with all their weaknesses they made the free banking system an established principle of the nation in the period before the Civil War. A corollary of the demand for a reform of banking was the adoption by many states of constitutional provisions forbidding special charters for any corporations and the enactment of General Incorporation Laws. The movement, led in the East by New York, swept through most of the nation by the Civil War. Thus workingmen had begun a movement which freed industry of many of its legislative shackles and advanced free enterprise.

A republican system of education became a reality in the industrial areas of the nation by the Civil War. In New England the states of New Hampshire, Massachusetts, and Connecticut thoroughly refurbished their common school laws between 1834 and 1848. State supervision, compulsory erection of schools, adequate support from public monies, lengthening of the school term, and compulsory attendance once more made New England schools the model for the nation. Rhode Island followed the pattern in the next decade. In New York the Whigs erected a tax-supported, compulsory common school system for New York City in 1842, a state system in 1849. New Jersey's free school system was erected in 1839. In Pennsylvania the Whigs provided for a voluntary tax-supported school system in 1834; the Democrats made it compulsory in all counties in 1854.

Locofocoism also had an affect on the courts as revealed in the case of *Commonwealth* v. *Hunt*. The trial grew out of the refusal of several members of the Boston Journeymen Bootmakers Society to work alongside nonsociety members—a clear case of an attempt to impose a closed shop. When the Boston Municipal Court adjudged society members guilty of conspiracy, they appealed. Chief Justice Lemuel Shaw handed down the decision which clearly followed election returns. Shaw ruled that the case contained two issues: the legality of the combination and the legality of its method. He declared that combinations of workingmen were lawful even though their object was to adopt measures "that may have a tendency to impoverish another, that is, to diminish his gains and profits." Far from being criminal such object might be "highly meritorious and public spirited." As far as the methods in the case were concerned, Shaw likewise judged them legal. "We cannot perceive, that it is criminal for men to agree together to exercise their acknowledged rights, in such manner as best to subserve their own interests."

Commonwealth v. *Hunt* was a landmark in labor history. Shaw's decision concerning the legality of labor combinations was widely accepted; it thereby ended the application of the common law of criminal conspiracy to trade unions—though not the possibility that new statutes based on the common law might be applied—and became the foundation for recognition of labor's right to organize. Shaw's decision on the legality of labor methods was not so widely adopted. But between his decision and the Civil War labor was never seriously worried about judicial hostility to its combinations and methods.

8 —

The Ten-Hour Day and Social Reform

The depression which settled upon the nation in 1837 almost completely destroyed the labor organizations which had developed in Jackson's administration. By January, 1838, one-third of the nation's workingmen were jobless and the majority of the remainder were employed only on a part-time basis; by 1839 wages had dropped from 30 to 50 per cent. Unable, because of this condition, to secure financial support most trade associations, all the city federations and national trade associations, and the National Trades' Union disintegrated.

Hard times lasted with only slight ameliorations until 1842 when a slow, economically healthy recovery, accompanied by a slight increase in the cost of living, began. Almost immediately a labor movement revolving around the ten-hour day developed. It began in New England where mechanics and factory operatives had made fewer advances during the thirties than workingmen elsewhere. Late in 1842 a new organization calling itself the Ten-Hour Republican Association was established in several Massachusetts towns. Almost simultaneously it began to petition the legislature to establish a ten-hour day by law, on the ground that the sunrise-to-sunset system was far too demoralizing to permit the average worker to give his energies to anything but labor. The petitions resulted in the introduction of a ten-hour bill, but the measure was defeated. The failure checked developments only briefly. In 1844 the Fall River Mechanics' and Laborers' Association, an organization of skilled shop workers and unskilled factory operatives, determined upon a wider campaign. It issued a call for a convention of all New England labor and appointed S. C. Hewitt to tour the industrial areas of the section to arouse workingmen to the necessity of organizing and attending the convention. Hewitt's tour was a signal success; when it ended, southern New England teemed with new labor organizations.

In the fall of 1844 more than two hundred delegates met at Boston, adopted the name New England Working Men's Association, and recommended a concerted ten-hour drive. Almost immediately, however, the campaign was submerged. The convention had not only attracted workingmen but Fourierites and land reformers, and the persuasive eloquence of these delegates shifted the attention of the convention from the ten-hour day to utopianism and homesteads. The same group dominated the proceedings of the association until the fifth meeting held at Lowell in the spring of 1846.

Meanwhile another movement had developed among New England's female operatives. During the twenties and thirties women in factories had played a minor role in the labor movement; female operatives had been farm girls who could "go home to Pa" if conditions in the factories became too miserable to endure. But the depression of 1837 and the competition of cheap western agricultural products wiped out thousands of New England farmers, most of whom became town laborers; their daughters, who worked in the factories along the Merrimac and Piscataqua rivers, became a permanent factory population dependent upon their wages for survival.

In 1841 there had appeared in Massachusetts the Lowell *Offering,* a magazine dedicated to the principle that the lot of the factory girls was a veritable heaven on earth. Recognizing the palpable falseness of the publication, groups of girls at Lowell and Exeter established their own periodicals, the *Factory Girl* and the *Factory Girl's Album.* These publications, crudely produced as they were, soon demolished the myth concerning the bucolic beauties of factory life. They revealed that the working day ran from fourteen to sixteen hours for which a wage of $1.56 a week was paid, that wages were so low many girls were "forced to abandon their virtue" to live. They told of managers who worked them to dispel the "languor" induced by fatigue, of store-order wage payments which cut their earnings in half, and of the speed-up system introduced with new machinery. The magazines also provided the stimulus for the organization of a number of associations among women. The first was the Female Labor Reform Association of Lowell, organized by Sarah Bagley, a former operative turned schoolteacher. Its aim was the establishment of the ten-hour day in place of the "unmitigated labor" which prevailed in the factories to the destruction of the health and the "injury of the constitutions of future generations." Similar associations soon appeared at Manchester, Dover, and Fall River. Their delegates appeared in force at the fifth meeting of the New England Working Men's Association.

The association, freed for the first time from the distractions of reformers, drew up a diverse campaign to secure the ten-hour day. Its first step was to call a joint conference of delegates from the association and from the textile manufactures—an attempt at industry-wide bargaining. When factory owners refused to attend the conference, the association turned to political pressure, undertaking a campaign not only for the ten-hour day but—here the influence of the female operatives was visible—also for the amelioration of the lot of children in factories. Hundreds of petitions praying for the establishment of a ten-hour day and for a limitation upon the labor of children were sent to New England's industrial areas for circulation and signatures; they were then forwarded to the various state legislatures. By 1847 the petition campaign became a veritable deluge, and the legislatures began to respond. In New Hampshire, controlled by Democrats, the legislature fixed ten hours as the legal working day unless workingmen contracted to work longer, and prohibited the labor of children under fifteen for more than ten hours without the written consent of their parents. In 1848 Maine, likewise controlled by Democrats, adopted similar laws. Unfortunately this early legis-lation proved ineffective. While small workshop employers were inclined to accept the spirit of the law, the factory owners presented their working forces with contracts for longer hours and demands to permit children to work beyond legal limits. Although laboring men in many communities pledged themselves to sign no such contracts, their determination quickly broke down in the face of black lists and starvation.

Meanwhile control of the New England Working Men's Association was once more assumed by social reformers, and the workingmen deserted it. In March, 1848, it disintegrated. But the ten-hour movement was not dead in New England. Demands for a shorter working day for both adults and children were renewed in Massachusetts in the early fifties, and when Lowell workers elected Benjamin F. Butler on a ten-hour platform in the face of corporation threats to discharge all who voted for him, the association, renamed the New England Industrial League, was revived. In 1852 the league organized a vigorous campaign for the ten-hour day in the mill towns of Massachusetts and secured the election of a large number of ten-hour advocates. No legislation was enacted, but the agitation was not without effect. During 1852 a large number of millowners in five towns of the Merrimac region "voluntarily" lowered the working day of men to eleven hours; in 1853 Lowell, Lawrence, and Salem textile factories likewise conceded the eleven-hour day, and Worcester became a ten-hour town. Continued campaigns by various labor associations also had an effect upon Rhode Island and Connecticut. In 1851 Rhode Island named a commissioner to investigate labor conditions. His report resulted in the enactment of a law establishing ten hours as the legal day for all factory operatives and mechanics, except where special contracts were signed, and of a law prohibiting the employment of children under twelve. Connecticut followed with similar legislation in 1855.

Agitation for the establishment of the ten-hour day in New England ultimately spread to other areas. Skilled labor in the cities and larger towns of the Middle Atlantic States was relatively content with its lot in the mid-forties. As the depression lifted and unemployment disappeared, the mechanic entered a period of comparative prosperity. Wages in general kept pace with the cost of living in most trades. There were, accordingly, few efforts to renew trade association activities until 1847 when a sharp rise in the cost of living produced a rebirth of trade associations throughout the whole mid-Atlantic and Ohio Valley regions. By the end of 1850 city federations, which usually adopted the name of Industrial Council, had been organized in all the important manufacturing centers from the Hudson to the Miami River. The reappearance of these assemblies in turn contributed to the creation of state industrial congresses which were established to put pressure upon legislatures for the enactment of labor laws. Both the councils and the congresses were short-lived. Wages soon caught up with the cost of living, and most mechanics remained satisfied with their lot. In addition both the councils and congresses were joined by a host of intellectuals: Fourierites, co-operationists, and land reformers; many laboring men remained members but the majority turned their attention elsewhere.

In spite of their short lives the revived city federations and mechanics' conventions played a valuable role in the ten-hour movement in the mid-Atlantic area. In New York, where the trades had enjoyed shorter hours since the late twenties, the councils conducted a movement on behalf of the factory hands. Tammany representatives introduced legislation as early as 1847. When the Whig majority buried it, the State Industrial Congress continued its efforts and ultimately secured a ten-hour law for labor employed on public works —the first state law of its kind. In New Jersey the Workingmen's Association of Trenton began a campaign on behalf of factory operatives in 1848 with the announcement that it would not support legislative candidates who would not pledge themselves to work for a ten-hour law. When the legislature gave the demands no attention, the Trenton workers organized a State Industrial Congress in preparation for further action. Both the Democrats and Whigs adopted the workingmen's demands as their own. In 1851 New Jersey enacted a ten-hour law for all factories and mills and forbade employment of children under ten. Pennsylvania enacted a ten-hour law, except where special contracts were signed, for all "cotton, woolen, silk, paper, bagging and flax factories" in 1848; employment of children under twelve in these factories was prohibited. Ohio, pressed by a State Industrial Congress, enacted the customary ten-hour law in 1852; it also forbade the employment of children under fourteen.

The net result of the ten-hour drive begun by New England mechanics is indicated in the meager statistics of the period. In 1840 of sixty-nine establishments reported by the Bureau of the Census, 52 per cent worked eight to eleven hours, 36 per cent worked eleven to thirteen hours, and nearly 12 per cent worked more than thirteen hours; by 1860 of 350 establishments reported, 67 per cent worked eight to eleven hours, 31 per cent worked eleven to thirteen hours, and only 2 per cent still worked a longer day.

While the ten-hour movement of the forties was running its course, using up the energies of most workingmen, there were other movements designed to cure the ills of labor and society which also attracted labor interest. One of the most important of these was a movement to reform capitalism by making production into a cooperative enterprise. The idea was not new to American workingmen. In 1791 Philadelphia carpenters, on strike, had set up a producers' cooperative; in 1806 the Philadelphia cordwainers had established a boot and shoe manufactory after their disastrous conspiracy trial. During the thirties a number of trade associations, unable to resolve differences with employers over wages and hours, had set up producers' cooperatives which disappeared as soon as their strikes were settled. In Philadelphia the movement became so widespread in 1836 that the *National Laborer* had suggested that all the trades go into business for themselves; the Philadelphia General Trades' Union had approved the idea, but the panic had checked the movement.

The impulse for renewal of such enterprises may have come from men like Horace Greeley and from news of the establishment of National Workshops in France during the Revolution of 1848. Greeley often urged workmen on strike to set up cooperatives and gave enthusiastic publicity to those enterprises which were created. Labor journals in the East gave much attention to the establishment of National Workshops in France. Whatever the cause, a producers' cooperative movement developed at midcentury, at a time when trade associations began to revive. The first important cooperative was established by the iron molders of Cincinnati during the winter of 1847–1848 to support themselves during a strike. In 1850 several dozen similar enterprises were begun. Coopers, hat finishers, shade painters, cabinetmakers, and tailors in New York; seamstresses in Boston, Providence, and Philadelphia; molders, glass blowers, and silver platers in Pittsburgh; foundry workers in Sharon, Wheeling, and Steubenville set up cooperatives. Although few of these enterprises lasted more than a year or two, they attracted widespread attention. Many laboring men came to regard them as the hope of the future.

Some workingmen became involved in a consumers' cooperative

movement, based on the theory that workingmen could improve their standards by reducing living costs. The movement was begun by Boston mechanics who created the "Protective Union" in 1845. Members were required to pay an initiation fee of $3.00 and a small monthly assessment which would entitle them to purchase groceries, fuel, and other goods at the union store. A member would receive $3.00 a week when sick and a weekly pension of $7.50 after sixty-five. By the end of 1847 the Protective Union had forty divisions, most of them in eastern Massachusetts, with a membership of three thousand. The peak was reached in 1854 when nearly eight hundred divisions had been organized in New England, New York, Michigan, Illinois, Wisconsin, and Canada. In 1855 the number of co-ops began to decline; by the opening of the Civil War they had disappeared, victims of insufficient capital and price wars.

During the forties workingmen also became interested in a plan to cure their ills and those of society by giving away the public lands to actual settlers. Although the National Trades' Union had advocated the program, it was not until 1844, when George Henry Evans refurbished the idea, called it "Land Reform," and began a campaign to secure enactment of legislation to grant every citizen a portion of the public lands as his "rightful heritage," that it became important. Evans's campaign was aimed primarily at labor. Land reform would drain excess workers from the eastern manufacturing areas— trade associations could aid the movement by transporting the penniless. Their removal in turn would create both a labor scarcity and an excess of housing in the East. Workers who remained behind would be rewarded by higher wages, better working conditions, and lower rents.

Evans recognized that his program could be secured only by forcing politicians to pledge themselves to support the measure or run the risk of losing office. Accordingly, he organized the National Reform Association. Its object was to secure the signatures of voters— workingmen in particular—to a pledge, whereby they would agree to vote for no man who would not pledge himself in writing "to use all the influence of his station, if elected, to prevent all further traffic in the Public Lands of the United States, and to cause them to be laid out in Farms and Lots for the free and exclusive use of actual settlers." Those who signed such a pledge were to be mobilized to cast their votes for candidates who supported land reform.

Labor leaders were attracted from the start; a dozen working mechanics sat on the first central committee of the association. The labor press, ranging from the Lowell *Operative* to Lucius A. Hines's Cincinnati *Nonpareil*, also backed the movement. It is doubtful that many laboring men expected to take advantage of any land-reform law. They were urban dwellers out of contact with the soil; even if they had wanted to move westward they would have found it difficult since the cost of migrating and outfitting a farm was too great. They supported the movement because it would benefit them indirectly. Free lands in the West would attract those eastern farmers who found their soil too poor to compete with the richer western lands and who might, therefore, flood the cities in search of work. Free lands might also attract the immigrants pouring into the country and keep them from congregating in the industrial centers where they would drive down wages. Labor's aim was to create a labor scarcity in the eastern cities, a scarcity which would redound to its benefit in the form of shorter hours and higher wages.

Workingmen's support of the campaign was revealed primarily through the industrial councils which appeared after 1847. Petitions requesting Congress to pass laws granting "free farms for the workingmen" and interrogation of congressional candidates upon the issue became a regular feature of their activities. In most cities the Democratic organizations willingly adopted the program in return for votes. The strength of this labor pressure, together with that of farmers, was quickly seen. In the election of 1848 Martin Van Buren, Free Soil candidate for President, and Gerrit Smith, Liberty League standard bearer, both endorsed the land-reform program. In the same election nearly a hundred congressional candidates pledged themselves to vote for "free land." In 1852 a majority of northern congressional candidates who won office had taken the pledge. Labor's influence upon the movement reached its peak in that year. Thereafter the land-reform campaign became the homestead movement with Westerners in control and a farm philosophy dominant. In 1856 the pressure of farm voters made the Republican party the champion of the homestead movement, and six years later the Republicans placed a homestead law on the statute books.

The most significant of the reform movements of the period before

the Civil War which attracted labor was the antislavery crusade.
Begun in the early thirties, it was originally a movement designed
to abolish the "peculiar institution." Workingmen did not support
it; they revealed indifference, even hostility, to the movement. The
sentiment may have had its origin in the repeated attacks made by
William Lloyd Garrison, the nation's leading abolitionist, against
the New England Association as an organization which preached the
"pernicious doctrine" that taught the "poor and vulgar . . . to consider the opulent as the natural enemies of the laboring classes."
Such charges raised the suspicion among laboring men that the
abolitionist crusade was motivated by a desire to reduce "both Northern workers and Southern slaves to the lowest level of wage dependence, and to anarchical competition with each other, for the privilege of doing the drudgery of capital."

There were other reasons for labor's attitude. Workingmen recognized that the condition of the Negro in a state of chattel slavery
might be abominable, but the condition of the northern white man
in a state of wage slavery was equally abominable. If, they pointed
out, slaveholders could declare that "free laborers" did not have
"the thousandth part of the rights and liberties of Negro slaves," it
was obviously the duty of the laboring man to consider himself
first, to secure the right to dispose of his own labor "at his own price,
and to make the price just and equivalent to his toil" before he did
anything for the black man. Workingmen also feared the effects of
emancipation upon their own living standards. They recognized
that abolition would bring thousands of black laborers into the nation's industrial centers to compete for jobs that unskilled white
laborers wanted, and that the wages of the whole working class
would be driven down. They could not work for their own destruction.

The question of annexing Texas and the introduction of the Wil-
mot Proviso in 1846 changed the nature of the antislavery crusade;
thereafter it became a movement to check the further advance of
slavery into the western territories. The change altered the attitude
of some workingmen. Officially, organizations and leaders continued
to reveal an indifference to the whole movement. Almost no workingmen's organization included any resolutions upon the subject in
its platform. To a degree laboring men continued to be dominated by

the attitude revealed by the "Workingmen of Massachusetts," who condemned the abolitionists' "pretended love for slaves thousands of miles away" as "hypocrisy," and a "cloak for their insidious designs."

In spite of this official attitude, a number of labor leaders and labor newspapers spoke out upon the subject. Several labor societies, among them the New England Working Men's Association, became vociferous opponents of the annexation of Texas and the extension of slavery into the territories. The Cincinnati *Daily Unionist* aptly summarized the attitude: "We are no abolitionists in the popular sense of the term, but we would belie our convictions of democracy did we not oppose slavery's extension over new lands."

There were a number of reasons for this change. While abolitionism had contained an economic threat to the white laborer, checking the extension of slavery did not. Equally important were the arguments of the nation's antiextensionists. In 1848 the Free Soil party pointed out that slavery extension was a threat to free labor. Their argument upon that subject was simple. The existence of slavery in any given area degraded and demeaned all labor. If proof was necessary one needed only to examine the haughty attitude of southern slaveowners toward laboring men or to compare wages and hours in the free North with those of the slave South. To permit the extension of slavery into the territories, then, was tantamount to excluding free labor from those territories, for what free laborer would go willingly to any region where he could be placed politically and socially and perhaps economically upon a level with slaves? If slavery were permitted in the western territories, it was logical to conclude that these territories would become slave territories—barred forever to the self-respecting free laborer. What then would become of the condition of free labor in the North? Already the attacks upon the freedom of labor were becoming frequent. In the South slave labor was rapidly replacing free labor in the factories; in the North employers were telling their labor force that they had to work as long and as cheaply as the slaves of the South in order to compete with the southern manufacturer. How much worse would the situation become if the western territories were turned over to the slaveocracy? This element regarded "slavery as the natural and normal condition of the laboring man." It insisted that free society was not only a delusion but a danger in which "greasy mechanics" and "filthy opera-tives" were able to organize trade associations, engage in strikes, vote, and attend schools. All this foretold the day when northern states would have to enslave their free workers. That day would come when the western territories were turned over to slavery.

While such arguments did not persuade more than a minority of workingmen to vote for Free Soil candidates in 1848, they made a deep impression—particularly since they were usually uttered by politicians who had supported Locofoco principles. In the next six years the impression grew that slavery was a menace to free labor. By the time of the introduction of the Nebraska bill many mechanics had become so thoroughly conscious of the issue that they openly and frequently branded any effort to extend slavery as an attempt to "degrade free labor." Between 1854 and 1860 the Republican party assumed leadership of the antislavery crusade. Several founders of the party were former labor leaders, and they exerted strenuous efforts to win the allegiance of the nation's laboring elements. They re-minded workingmen that the extension of slavery threatened their freedom and economic welfare; they revealed themselves as cham-pions of civil liberties and the equality of men. Many a workingman accordingly joined the party in 1856, marched in its torchlight pro-cessions, and voted for Frémont. Four years later an even larger number supported Lincoln, giving him a heavy vote in New England, Pennsylvania, Ohio, Illinois, and Missouri.

The Republicans did not win the support of all workingmen. A large segment remained within the Democratic fold. While many of this group were opposed to the extension of slavery, they were convinced that the Douglas wing of the party was able to handle the problem as effectively as the Republicans were. They were suspi-cious, moreover, of a party which talked about free labor and yet contained a large industrial element which had never been known for its friendliness to labor objectives. Many reasoned that Repub-lican victory would bring secession and war. A large number feared that Republicans would bring abolition and competition for jobs with four million emancipated blacks; Irish workers were particularly concerned with this last problem. As a result labor gave the Demo-crats a large vote in the Narragansett Bay region, New York City, Newark, Baltimore, and Pittsburgh.

In the final analysis, therefore, labor did not combine as a unit in the antislavery crusade. Whether it remained divided upon the issue of slavery during the war is impossible to determine. Although many labor organizations and newspapers indicated at the start of the war that they were fighting only to preserve the union, and occasionally mass meetings of laboring men announced that they would not tolerate competition of free Negro workers, it would appear that as the war progressed northern labor in common with the rest of the population was more and more inclined to support emancipation. Many labor groups approved John C. Frémont's order freeing slaves of rebels in Missouri; reports from northern industrial centers in 1862 indicated a growing conviction among laborers that the war should be fought until slavery was wiped out. At any rate there is no protest on record made by laboring men against Lincoln's preliminary proc-lamation of emancipation, nor against the adoption of the Thirteenth Amendment at the end of the war.

9 —

"Pure and Simple" Unionism—Steps Toward Nationalization

While the social reform movement, which had begun with labor's help in the forties, was running its course through the fifties, workingmen began a new labor movement. Discovery of gold in California and a spurt in railroad construction in the East, which produced a sudden upswing in industry and trade early in 1850 and brought a sharp rise in the cost of living, provided the impulse for the new organizing campaign. The movement developed with phenomenal speed. By mid-1850 workingmen of all trades were busily engaged in organizational activities in most industrial centers even as far west as San Francisco. Late in 1851 a drop in business activity accompanied by a decline in cost of living brought the movement to a mo-

mentary halt, but with the recovery of prices in 1852 and a new and
even steeper rise in living costs activity was once more renewed. During 1853 and 1854 trade associations reached new heights. Practically
every trade in every industrial center of the North and West was
organized locally; membership reached 200,000.

On the surface the trade unions—as they were now called—which
were formed in these years bore a strong resemblance to earlier
societies. Essentially craft organizations, their chief aim was to secure
an increase in wages to match the rising living costs. Their method of
securing increases changed slightly. As before, the locals first agreed
upon a price list, but then appointed a committee to visit each employer on behalf of all his mechanics. Failure to secure approval of
the new scale gave the committee the right to call a strike in the
shop. The effort to increase wages—which produced more than four
hundred strikes in 1853–1854—was fairly successful. By 1854 the average mechanic was earning 25 per cent more than he had earned in
1850. The locals also made strong efforts to limit the number of apprentices hired in each shop and to fix their length of service and
wage scales. In some trades efforts were made to bar women. Less
attention was given the closed shop. Most trades reasoned that they
could enroll practically all journeymen in their associations, and they
expected to raise their lot without resort to the closed shop.

The trade unions of the early fifties also revealed some marked
differences in comparison to the past. On the whole, organization
was tighter and more efficient; dues were collected systematically and
attempts were made to accumulate strike funds. Efforts were made
by many trades to develop labor exchanges to provide jobs for
strikers and unemployed mechanics. Collective bargaining was used
more extensively. Employers were invited to attend union meetings
to discuss wages, prices, and hours. The trade agreement was introduced. In several trades, notably among printers and tailors, committees of employers and trade unionists met to discuss price lists
for the entire industry. Cooperation among associations of the same
trade in various localities became fairly common. New York City's
organizations were frequently called upon to supply organizers for
other cities; constitutions and bylaws were frequently exchanged
and copied; efforts were made to prevent mechanics from going to
a city where a strike was in progress; occasional donations or loans

of money were made to aid striking workers of the same trade in another city.

The most significant difference between the labor organization of the fifties and those of the past was one of attitude. Trade associations of the twenties, thirties, and forties were anything but single-minded. Essentially economic organizations, they were nevertheless easily persuaded to turn from economic to political activity. Although strongly interested in wages and hours, they were equally concerned with broader political and social problems which affected not only their status and condition but also the whole nation. The trade unions of the fifties were dominated by men who had been impressed by the dissention that developed among workingmen because a political program could not be agreed upon, by the tendency of labor candidates once in office to forget the welfare of workingmen, or by the fact that legislation was often ineffective because it contained loopholes. To them economic action appeared to have fewer pitfalls; trade unions, accordingly, became "pure and simple."

The labor organizations formed in the early fifties were remarkably short-lived. The sharp recession of the winter of 1854–1855 dealt workingmen a severe blow. An unusually large number of journeymen lost their jobs in the fall of 1854; during the winter the number of unemployed increased steadily until more than one-half of the nation's skilled laborers were out of work. In the face of mass unemployment the trade unions collapsed. When business revived in the summer of 1855, the survivors of the recession took the lead in a new organizational drive. Not all the previously established associations were able to re-create themselves. Many remained dormant; many more failed to regain the ground they had lost. The events of these lean years taught the trade unions some valuable lessons. They learned that they needed funds to support members during times of unemployment or during times of idleness because of strikes; they came to recognize, moreover, that since all trades were affected during depressions, each had to rely on its own membership to build up its funds. A number began to build their coffers by investing in industrial and railroad stocks.

The panic of 1857 gave labor another setback. By October at least 200,000 were unemployed. Although the lessons learned earlier enabled more local organizations to survive, the trade-union movement came to a temporary stop. Phenomena of this depression, not unknown in the past but which now appeared on a more extensive scale, were the unemployment demonstrations. In New York, Newark, and Philadelphia mass meetings of unemployed petitioned municipal authorities for the institution of programs of public works. In New York City a large crowd broke into the shops of flour merchants in search of food. Little relief in any form was granted.

Trade unions ultimately recovered from the panic of 1857. As business conditions began to improve in 1859, as men returned to work and costs of living began to climb again, locals came back to life. An extraordinary number of strikes broke out. Most important, largely because it was the most extensive in American history before the Civil War, was the New England shoemakers' strike of 1860. Beginning in Lynn when factory workers were refused an increase in their $3.00 a week wage, it soon spread through Maine, New Hampshire, and Massachusetts. Twenty thousand boot and shoe makers turned out. Lynn employers capitulated, and the settlement they made was extended to the whole boot and shoe region. Similar victories followed in other trades, victories which brought large increases in membership during the summer and fall of 1860.

Revival of locals and adoption of "pure and simple" unionism was only one labor development in the fifties. Equally significant was the reappearance of labor organizations on a national scale. The basis for the movement was the widespread extension of the nation's transportation facilities—including railroads—which not only expanded the market but produced nation-wide competition among industries and among labor. In short, workingmen more and more found themselves in competition with cheaper labor areas to their own detriment. National trade associations were created to help equalize wages and working conditions.

As before, the printers took the lead. In 1850 a national convention of printers urged locals throughout the nation to adopt the wage scales and apprenticeship regulations current in New York, to issue traveling certificates, to draw up and exchange lists of "rats," and to raise strike funds. The address stimulated the organization of printers in several cities, and led to a second convention in 1852 when delegates from twelve cities formed the National Typographic Union. Between that first organization and the panic of 1857 ten more nationals were established. These included the upholsterers, hat finishers, plumbers, railroad engineers, stonecutters, lithographers, cigarmakers, silver platers; a National Union of Building Trades made up of house painters, stonecutters, plasterers, carpenters, bricklayers, plumbers, and masons; and a Mechanics' Trade Association about which nothing is known. Only three—the typographers, hat finishers, and stonecutters—survived the panic of 1857.

Between the panic and the election of 1860 five other trades organized nationally. These included the cotton mule spinners, painters, and cordwainers. Most significant were the associations established by the iron molders and by the machinists and blacksmiths. Periodic reduction in wages whenever prices of raw materials in the foundry industry rose, the requirement that workers supply their own tools, and the introduction of "helpers" who slowly destroyed the value of skilled labor brought about the formation of the first molders' union in Philadelphia in 1855. Desperate competitive conditions led to the organization of the Moulders' International four years later with William H. Sylvis as head and with fifty-six locals as affiliates. Mechanization, which transformed the machinist from "a compound of handiwork, a kind of dross between millwright and whitesmith, a fitter, finisher, [and] locksmith" into a builder and repairer of machinery, with the blacksmith as his chief assistant; and discharge of skilled workers while apprentices were continued in employment during depressions led to the formation of the first machinists and blacksmiths' local in Philadelphia in 1858. The National Union of Machinists and Blacksmiths, with Jonathan Fincher as head and with fifty-seven affiliates, was organized a year later.

The five nationals formed between 1857 and 1860 were, like earlier organizations, all "craft" unions. But three of them—mule spinners, molders, and machinists—were something else. They were part of the factory system. As such they were a revelation of the long process, begun in the wholesale-order stage, whereby labor's skills had been destroyed or divided. In short, they were organizations representing not skills but parts of skills—"operations." They were representative of the future. Two of them, molders and machinists, provided labor with much of its leadership in the next decade.

Lincoln's election and the secession movement which followed gave the nation's economy and the labor movement a severe shock

Much of American enterprise was based upon an interchange of raw materials and finished products between North and South. As the southern states left the Union, northern businessmen, recognizing the possible loss of $300,000,000 of investments and credits, became paralyzed with fright. Trade slowed; factories and workshops cut production, and large-scale unemployment developed. Workingmen, hit hard by the crisis, reacted with a spontaneous denunciation of the whole secession movement. Leadership was assumed by the trade unions of the border area. A mass meeting of workingmen in Louisville, held in December, 1860, laid the blame for the crisis on the politicians of both sides and called for a convention of workingmen to decide on what concerted action should be taken to preserve the union. The meeting stimulated a large number of similar gatherings throughout the border area and the North, and culminated in a "national" convention at Philadelphia in February, 1861. While the convention represented only eight states from areas closely associated with the South, it probably well expressed the attitude of labor. It attacked secession as dangerous to the welfare of labor and announced its opposition to "any measures that will evoke Civil War." In addition it revealed a willingness to compromise the whole slavery issue on terms favorable to the South in order to maintain economic prosperity.

This attitude was quickly dispelled after the firing upon Fort Sumter. The excitement which eternally accompanies the opening of war seized the entire nation. Volunteers from the ranks of labor, many of them unemployed, flocked to the colors. Among them were whole locals who entered the army to fight as a unit. Hundreds of labor leaders were commissioned in various state regiments. Investigations conducted after the war revealed that northern armies were made up in large part of laborers. At the end of the war a Senate report estimated that between 500,000 and 750,000 of the men employed in industry had seen service during the war. Since there were about 1,300,000 employed in manufacturing enterprises in 1860, and an unknown number in trade and commerce, it is not unlikely that about one-third of the North's labor supply was enlisted in the northern armies. A second investigation made in 1869 revealed that out of every 1,000 northern soldiers, 421 were mechanics or laborers. Since only 16 per cent of the nation's population lived in urban communities at the time, it is evident that labor supplied a far greater proportion of northern troops than its total numbers warranted.

While labor's contribution to Union armies was a tremendous one, it was not always willingly given. The chief obstacle to cooperation was the wartime draft policy. Labor's antagonism to the Conscription Act of 1863 was similar to the objections of other elements. They objected either because it was discriminatory or because they regarded it as an invasion of their personal liberties. The Conscription Act contained a clause which made it legally possible to evade service by providing a substitute or by paying a $300 commutation fee. Trade-union leaders and the labor press sought to counteract labor's resentment against this provision. Although they admitted the law was faulty, they urged compliance until it could be amended. But such preachments often fell upon deaf ears. Aided by Copperhead propaganda a large portion of labor became convinced that the whole war was being fought "to enable abolitionist Capitalists to transport Negroes into the northern cities to replace . . . workers who were striking for higher wages," and they denounced the conflict as " a rich man's war and a poor man's fight."

Resentment over conscription eventually incited several bloody and destructive draft riots. Most important was the three-day riot in New York City in mid-July, 1863, where a mob wrecked the main recruiting station, destroyed shipyards, railroads, and streetcar lines, closed factories and machine shops, attacked homes of leading Republicans, and killed a number of Negroes. Rioting also occurred in Troy, New York; in the anthracite regions of Pennsylvania; in Hartford, Indiana; and in Port Washington, Wisconsin. Workingmen played a prominent part in all of them.

There were other reasons for labor's attitude. The draft dodging of men acting as dummy settlers for speculators who took advantage of the loosely drawn Homestead Law; the fortunes accumulated by a comparatively few men—some by supplying the government with shoddy materials—while at the same time living standards of workingmen took a sharp drop; the Contract Labor Law of 1864 permitting employers to import European labor under contract which increased competition on the labor market—all these caused much labor resentment.

A final and significant reason for labor's unfavorable attitude was the handling of strikes by military officials. Strikes during the war were frequent, caused primarily by labor's effort to keep its wages on a par with the standard of living. In striking, however, labor ran into the public attitude that strikes injured production and retarded the war effort. Many employers, harassed by striking workmen, appealed to the government for aid—suggesting laws to prohibit strikes in wartime and the use of the army to enforce such laws. Although no legislation prohibiting strikes was passed, the army was used to break strikes. Troops were employed against gun workers at Cold Springs, New York, against engineers on the Reading Railroad, and against miners in Tioga County, Pennsylvania. General Thomas ordered the arrest and deportation northward of two hundred mechanics on strike in Tennessee. The most notorious use of troops occurred in Missouri in April, 1864, when Major General William Rosecrans issued General Order No. 65 which prohibited the organization of men engaged in war production, forbade picketing, and assured military protection for strikebreakers. The order was used several times against striking coal miners, machinists, printers, and tailors.

In spite of the feeling that it was being ill treated, labor continued to support the war, partly because of a natural loyalty, and partly in response to the attitude of President Lincoln toward their problems. On several occasions Lincoln "requested" that increases in wages be given to Navy Yard workers; he ordered Rosecrans to stop interfering with the "legitimate demands of labor," and tactfully aided a strike by machinists against a Federal contractor. While such action was slight enough, it made labor feel that it had a friend in the White House. Labor responded in kind. Although they tried to avoid politics during the war, trade unions, nevertheless, conscientiously supported prowar candidates. In 1861 the New York Typographical Union's newspaper, the *Iron Platform*, was instrumental in securing labor support for Republicans and War Democrats in the New York State elections. In 1864 a Workingmen's Democratic-Republican Association was formed in New York, Boston, Philadelphia, and Chicago to campaign for Unionist candidates of both parties. Lincoln was their candidate for President. A large number of local trade unions temporarily surrendered their objections to political activity and joined with the association to urge Lincoln's reelection. A "Workingmen's United Political Association" was also formed by Tammany Democrats to work for McClellan's election. None of New York's trade unions gave it any support; indeed, there is no evidence that any trade union anywhere in the country endorsed McClellan's candidacy. Labor, in short, supported Lincoln for reelection, and because of that action the generality of labor, which had been about equally divided between Democrats and Republicans in 1860, became Republican by the end of the war.

The Civil War did not destroy the labor movement of the fifties. In the early months of 1861 business, as has been indicated, had slowed and unemployment rolls had begun to grow. With the outbreak of the war business became paralyzed and unemployment figures swelled into the hundred thousand. The depression which settled upon the country and the demand for military personnel dealt trade unionism a severe blow. Yet, a large number of locals managed to hold meetings and to keep their organizations intact, and three of the nationals—printers, molders, and machinists—were able to stagger through the year. The continuity of trade unionism was never broken.

The depression lifted by the middle of 1862; unemployment disappeared, and the cost of living which had stood at 100 in 1860 reached 115. The cost of living continued to rise during the rest of the war, reaching 143 by mid-1863, 170 by mid-1864, and 176 by mid-1865. Labor, as it had in all previous periods of prosperity, promptly renewed its activity. The resurgence began on a local level and progressed rapidly. There were twenty trades organized with seventy-nine locals by December, 1863; the number increased to fifty-three trades with 203 locals by December, 1864, and to sixty-nine trades with 300 locals by November, 1865. Seventy per cent of the locals were established in Massachusetts, New York, and Pennsylvania; 20 per cent in the Middle West. The largest organizations were those of the molders, machinists, carpenters, and printers. Total union membership in 1864–1865 was estimated at 200,000.

The revival of trade unionism was accompanied by the reappearance of city federations. Rochester tradesmen organized the first of these bodies in March, 1863; by the end of the war they existed in every important industrial center in the nation. Designed to have only advisory powers, their influence was soon felt throughout the labor world. They assumed the job of organizing trades and boycotts, became publicity agencies during strikes, and worked to prevent the importation of strikebreakers. They also became the parents of a large labor press—among the most influential were *Fincher's Trade Review* of Philadelphia, the *Evening Voice* of Boston, the *Workingman's Advocate* published at Cincinnati and Chicago by Andrew C. Cameron, and the Belleville (Illinois) *Weekly Miner* edited by John Hinchcliffe. City federations also assumed leadership of a campaign to establish consumers' cooperatives, a movement motivated by a desire to escape the full effect of rising prices. The first of the cooperatives was set up in Philadelphia by Thomas Phillips, ex-Chartist and a shoemaker. City federations took up the movement in 1863 and aided in the establishment of cooperative stores in thirty-six cities and towns between Biddeford, Maine, and San Francisco.

The national trade association movement was also renewed during the war. Several forces were involved: competition of the same products from widely different localities in the same market; competition for employment between locally organized mechanics and migratory out-of-town journeymen; organization of employers; and the introduction of machinery which split up the old established trades and laid industry open to the invasion of "green hands." First of the nationals formed after the outbreak of the war was that of the anthracite miners who established the American Miners Association, an industrial union, under the leadership of Daniel Weaver in 1861. Its successor, the Workingmen's Benevolent Association, established in 1868, had some thirty locals with an estimated membership of at least 30,000 by the end of the decade. Between 1862 and 1865 eleven others were organized. These included the Sons of Vulcan (iron puddlers), locomotive engineers, plasterers, cigarmakers, ship carpenters, coachmakers, house carpenters, bricklayers and masons, tailors, painters, and heaters.

Like their predecessors, the nationals established during the war were loose organizations with little or no power over locals. Yet they had greater significance. They provided labor with its first national leaders: Sylvis of the molders; Fincher and Ira Steward of the machinists; Cameron, J. C. C. Whaley, Alexander Troup, and John Collins of the printers; Richard Trevellick of the ship carpenters; John Siney of the anthracite miners. They began the development of a feeling of national trade solidarity and of the idea that local conflicts were the concern of all men in the trade. Some created small national treasuries; printers perfected the traveling certificate.

The rapid growth of labor unionism on a local and national scale during the war did not produce an entirely successful labor movement. Although locals and city federations exerted strong efforts to keep abreast of the rising cost of living, they never succeeded; at the end of the war wages were still 15 per cent behind prices. Labor, nevertheless, was successful enough to cause employers to revive their own organizations.

Employer associations, most of them founded in the late war years, were of many kinds. Typical was the organization of a single trade on a local basis. In addition city federations and regional organizations like the Northwestern Publishers Association were developed; even one national organization was created—the American National Steel Manufacturers' and Iron Founders' Association. Whatever the type, the policy of these organizations was the same. They deplored the "general and persistent interference" of trade unions in the affairs of business which would ultimately "result in wide-spread beggary, with all its attending evils—suffering, bread riots, pillage and taxation." It was to prevent these evils, to preserve freedom of labor, and to promote the welfare of their employees that the employer associations were organized. In short it was their aim to destroy trade unions.

During the war employer associations confined their attacks upon labor primarily to campaigns for state laws preventing "intimidation" or interference with workingmen and curbing the right to strike. A number of states enacted anti-intimidation legislation, most famous of which was Illinois' La Salle Black laws, which declared any person who by threat, intimidation, or otherwise sought to prevent another person from working, guilty of crime. Several states also passed laws permitting the ejection of strikers from company-owned houses.

The employers' campaign for antilabor legislation forced some trade unions to abandon their "pure and simple" principles. In New York, where employers secured consideration for an anti-intimidation bill in 1864, the city federations of New York City, Troy, Albany, Rochester, and Buffalo undertook a state-wide pressure and lobbying campaign in order to defeat the measure. In Massachusetts labor mass meetings and lobbying by trade unions of Boston, Worcester, and the Merrimac mill towns forestalled enactment of a similar bill.

Because of the extraordinary demand for labor, employer associations were unable to destroy or even seriously to check the growth and activity of trade unionism during the war. But within eighteen months after Appomattox the nation plunged into a sharp postwar recession, and the situation changed. As unemployment developed and membership in locals, city federations, and nationals dropped, employers promptly assumed the offensive. Using the black list, the lockout, and the yellow-dog contract as their major weapons, they crushed local after local. Where such tactics did not succeed, they turned for aid to the state legislatures. Their pressure usually brought about the enactment of new legislation based upon the common law of criminal conspiracy. A number of conspiracy cases followed. Most famous, and one which thoroughly agitated a large segment of labor, was the Kingston (New York) cigarmakers case, which arose from the fact that a local had designated one of its members as a "rat" and had denied him the privileges of the union. Suit was brought against the individual members of the local as conspirators, and the court found them guilty.

In the midst of the economic decline two nationals tried to assume leadership of their trades and met with disaster. The molders supported a nine-month struggle of foundry workers in Cincinnati against the Iron Founders' Association; defeat pushed them out of the labor world's limelight. The Locomotive Engineers fought a long, losing contest with the Michigan Southern and Indiana Railroad and then changed into a "moral uplift" society.

Several nationals tried to counter the trend with producers' cooperatives. Molders led the movement with the establishment of a stove foundry at Troy in 1866. After the disastrous Cincinnati strike, the whole organization turned toward cooperation for relief from the "wages system." Eleven more foundries were set up in 1868. The coopers established seven successful and relatively permanent cooperative factories to supply barrels to the flour millers in Minnesota; by so doing, however, they gradually removed themselves from the labor world and became proprietors. The Crispins were likewise assiduous in their attempts to set up producers' co-ops. None of their efforts succeeded.

Despite the obvious decline of their movement during the recession of 1866–1868, workingmen did not surrender. In fact the decline led them to create a new and highly significant organization—the National Labor Union. A movement to create a national federation had been attempted several times after the disappearance of the National Trades' Union. On the eve of the Civil War both the molders and the machinists had suggested creation of a federation of trades. The outbreak of the war had pushed the idea into the background, but labor took it up once more when the Louisville Trade Assembly invited the officers and delegates of all city federations to a meeting in September, 1864. Twelve delegates from eight cities responded and established the International Industrial Assembly of North America. They recommended that all trades work for laws which would abolish the convict labor system and the store-order system of paying wages, and they commended consumers' cooperatives. The I.I.A.N.A. never met again, primarily because there was yet no issue around which labor might rally.

Nevertheless such an issue was already in the making. This was the demand for an eight-hour day. The demand had been raised before. In the midst of the ten-hour movement in 1836 there had been labor spokesmen who indicated that workingmen would not be satisfied until their work day had been reduced to eight hours. During the fifties the New York City and Philadelphia industrial councils and a number of locals incorporated the idea into their programs; few, however, actually achieved the objective.

In 1863 Ira Steward of Boston, who in the course of his life became known as "the eight-hour monomaniac," became the leader of a new eight-hour movement when he persuaded a convention of machinists to adopt the eight-hour day as their cardinal plank. Steward's theory was that wages depended upon the habits, customs, and desires of the workingmen. A man who worked ten, twelve, or fourteen hours a day had neither the energy nor the imagination to develop more than the simplest demands. If, however, his hours of labor were reduced and he had time for leisure and reflection, the workingman would quickly develop new desires and demand more pay. Since industry was daily revealing its capacity to expand its production through the use of machinery, it could readily meet the demands of the increased market and, because it would sell more goods, it could readily pay the higher wages.

Steward, who belonged philosophically to the labor movement of the thirties and forties, did not believe that the eight-hour day could be secured through trade-union action. Skilled workers might be able to force the system upon isolated employers, but the mass of unskilled workers would gain nothing. To make the movement common to all labor it was necessary for laboring men to combine into organizations which they could use to "vote themselves an eight-hour day." Accordingly, in 1865 he created the Grand Eight Hour League of Massachusetts, made up primarily of machinists and blacksmiths, to agitate the issue. The league entered politics in Massachusetts in 1865 and forced the Republican party to adopt an eight-hour plank, but no law was enacted. In the meantime eight-hour leagues sprang up in other industrial centers, as far west as California. But no concerted campaign for adoption of the eight-hour day developed until 1866. At this point trade unionists, harassed by unemployment and the employers' antilabor campaign, turned almost simultaneously to the eight-hour day as the best way out of their difficulties. They turned to it, however, not in the spirit that Steward conceived it, but as a "make-work" measure. Several trades began a simultaneous agitation for a national organization to unify the movement. Friction over the kind of labor bodies such an organization should represent delayed action until the summer of 1866 when the Baltimore Trades Assembly and delegates from fourteen nationals united to call a "congress" of all labor organizations at Baltimore.

Of the seventy-seven delegates who met together in August, 1866, fifty represented locals, seventeen were from city federations, seven from eight-hour leagues, and three from nationals. These represented some 60,000 workingmen in thirteen states. The Baltimore congress formed the National Labor Union, the first "permanent" organization of labor in America on a national scale; named a president, J. C. C. Whaley of Washington; and provided for a regular annual meeting at which each "Trades' Union, Workingmen's Association and Eight-Hour League" would be entitled to one delegate for each five hundred members and each national would be entitled to one delegate.

Although the congress did not announce a platform, its various committee reports constituted an excellent reflection of the problems

agitating labor. It recognized that "all reforms in the labour movement" could best be directed through "trade organizations"; at the
same time it recommended the organization of the unskilled into a
"general workingmen's association" affiliated with the National Labor
Union. It demanded rigorous enforcement of apprenticeship regulations, condemned strikes as productive of great injury to the laboring
class, and recommended the substitution of arbitration. The objectives of the new organization were few. It insisted that the public
domain should be granted to settlers only, revealing that the organization was in some respects a child of earlier days in that it still regarded the public domain as a "safety valve" for economic discontent.
It demanded the abolition of the convict labor system, gave its approval to cooperative stores and workshops, and announced that its
main aim would be the establishment of eight hours as the legal day's
work. The second congress added a demand for the repeal of the
Contract Labor Act of 1864.

The formation of the National Labor Union did not check the decline of trade unionism; for reasons already indicated locals continued
to disappear and membership continued to drop through 1867 and
1868. At the third congress of the N.L.U. plans were made to reverse
the trend. William H. Sylvis was elected president with instructions
"to take the field and canvass the principal cities and towns . . . for
the purpose of discussing and disseminating the principles of the
National Labor Union, and forming branch Unions to co-operate
therewith." Sylvis began his organizing campaign with a three-month
tour of the South, where he organized twenty-six "labor unions," as
the locals created by the N.L.U. were named.

In 1869–1870 Richard Trevellick led a five-month organizing campaign that covered most of the area east of the Mississippi River. His
tour added 127 locals to the organization. At that point N.L.U. efforts
ended, for in the meantime the nation had entered a period of fren-
zied prosperity, and the trade unions, local and national, had assumed
leadership of the organizing movement. A vast expansion followed,
best indicated by the formation of national associations. Between
1868 and 1873 fourteen new nationals were organized. In order of
appearance they included the spinners, Knights of St. Crispin (shoemakers), the railway conductors, the wool hat finishers, Daughters
of St. Crispin, the Morocco dressers, the telegraphers, the coopers.

the woodworking mechanics, the Brotherhood of Iron and Steel Heaters, Rollers and Roughers, the iron and steel rollers, the furniture makers, the Miners' National Association (bituminous), and the locomotive firemen. By 1873 there were twenty-five national associations in existence with a membership of 170,000; total trade-union membership probably reached 300,000.

The organizing drive used up only a part of the N.L.U.'s initial energy. The organization also developed a nation-wide campaign for the eight-hour day and secured repeal of the Contract Labor Law. First results in the eight-hour campaign were disappointing. Urged on by the N.L.U., labor organizations throughout the East and Midwest poured memorials into state capitals. A dozen bills were introduced, and six legislatures responded in 1867: Connecticut, New York, Illinois, Missouri, Wisconsin, and California. But all the laws enacted had faults. Connecticut, Illinois, Missouri, and California statutes provided for an eight-hour day, except when longer hours were stipulated by contract. The Wisconsin law applied only to women and children. In New York, where the law contained no loophole, Governor Reuben Fenton publicly refused to enforce it on the ground that a proclamation requiring observance of the statute would be an act of "unwarranted assumption."

The initial campaign for a Federal eight-hour law was also frustrated. The Baltimore congress appointed a committee headed by John Hinchcliffe to secure President Andrew Johnson's support for an eight-hour day for Federal employees. Johnson had already revealed himself friendly to labor's objectives when he ordered the establishment of an eight-hour day in the Government Printing Office, but he would not pledge himself to further action. The N.L.U. did not give up. Pressure on Congress, applied primarily by Richard Trevellick, who constituted himself a lobbyist for the measure, brought the enactment in June, 1868, of a measure introduced by Senator B. Gratz Brown of Missouri and providing an eight-hour day for mechanics and laborers employed by the government. Labor cheered the law to the echo. It contained no jokers and was expected to provide a precedent for legislation throughout the nation.

It was four more years, however, before the law was enforced to labor's satisfaction. While all Federal departments reduced hours, they at the same time reduced wages 20 per cent. A committee of

Washington workingmen protested, but Johnson's attorney-general, William M. Evarts, upheld the reduction. When Ulysses S. Grant became President, the National Labor Union requested a new opinion upon the subject. Grant's attorney-general, Ebenezer R. Hoar, took the same attitude as Evarts. N.L.U. leaders protested vociferously. Ten weeks after he took office Grant issued a proclamation prohibiting reductions of pay, but the order was flagrantly ignored. Grant was forced to repeat the proclamation three years later, in May, 1872. At the same time, Congress enacted a law compensating all Federal employees for cuts in wages since the establishment of the eight-hour day. Both the order and the law were obvious political moves. Grant and the Radical Republicans who controlled the administration were concerned about the rapidly developing Liberal Republican and Labor Reform movements. Nevertheless, the eight-hour day was finally established for all mechanics and laborers of the Federal Government.

In the meantime leadership of the eight-hour campaign had been assumed by locals and nationals. As prosperity returned and the demand for labor increased, revived trade unions adopted the eight-hour program as their own, using it both as an organizing issue and as a demand to be made upon employers. A number of notable conflicts resulted, among them the strike of 25,000 anthracite miners in the Schuylkill area in 1868, and a strike of 100,000 building tradesmen in New York City in 1872. Although one national, the Crispins, met with disaster over the issue—successive losses in San Francisco, Philadelphia, Worcester, and Lynn in 1869–1871 forcing them to disband—most of the eight-hour strikes were successful. On the eve of the depression of 1873 it appeared that the eight-hour day was well on its way to becoming the national standard.

The National Labor Union's campaign to repeal the Contract Labor Act of 1864 was comparatively short. The act, which had been intended to fill the need for a greater labor supply during the war, provided for importation of alien workmen who would pledge not more than twelve months of their wages to repay the cost of transportation to the United States. Immediately after its enactment an American Emigrant Company was formed to import labor "for . . . manufacturers, railroad companies and other employers." Immigrants who came to America were induced to sign contracts which pledged their first year's wages to pay the cost of transportation and pledged further years of wages to pay the cost of maintenance during the first year's residence in the United States. Labor of this nature was highly inefficient and unskilled, but it was so cheap that employers readily resorted to it—particularly in those industries where machinery was replacing skills or where sheer muscle power was important. Labor was inclined to blame much of its employment problems in 1866–1868 upon this cheap labor supply. Since aliens were also regularly imported to break strikes, labor's bitterness over the practice during the recession years steadily grew deeper. The N.L.U. began to pressure Congress for abolition of the practice in 1867, and in the following year Congress responded with a bill repealing the act.

Leadership of an organizing campaign, initiation of the eight-hour drive, and the conclusion of the movement to repeal the Contract Labor Act constituted the N.L.U.'s achievements. The rest of its history consisted of a series of quarrels over policy. One of the most important arguments arose over the question of admitting women to full membership in the trade-union movement. The war brought a marked increase in the number of laboring women; and the number remained high afterward because, as one government employer declared, women did "more and better work for $900 per annum, than many male clerks who were paid double that amount." But this philosophy made the wages and the condition of women in industry extremely poor. Surveys made during the war revealed that umbrella sewers received wages as low as three dollars a week, tassel makers earned four dollars a week, shirtwaist makers received twenty-four cents for a fifteen-hour day. Various efforts had been made to ameliorate such conditions. Most notable was that inaugurated by Moses Beach, editor of the New York *Sun,* who began action that led to the organization of the Working Women's Protective Union. The organization trained women in new occupations in order to keep them out of overcrowded older trades; it ran a placement bureau and offered legal services to women who were often bilked of their wages for "imperfect" workmanship. Similar protective unions appeared in Boston, Philadelphia, Indianapolis, Chicago, and St. Louis. Women also organized trade associations. A number of these conducted successful strikes for higher wages which in turn induced organization and strikes in other trades.

The influx of women into industry produced a varied reaction from male labor. The natural tendency was to regard women solely as competition: accordingly, men alternately deplored, condemned, and bitterly opposed their use by employers. This attitude remained dominant in the labor world in the postwar era. It was one of the reasons for the appearance of separate organizations of women in trades where they often worked side by side with men. Many workingmen, however, recognized that women were in industry to stay. They argued that the logical answer to the problem was to organize women and secure for them the same wages and hours granted men. It was this element which aided working women on strike, which helped women set up their own organizations in trades where the hostility of men against women in industry ran high and in trades where the social association of men and women was considered immoral, and which in some cases invited women into their own unions.

In 1868 the problem of women was presented to the National Labor Union. After a bitter wrangle, the congress admitted Susan B. Anthony, Mary Kellogg Putnam, and Mary MacDonald, all representing protective unions, as delegates, and thereby endorsed the women's labor movement. But relations between the N.L.U. and the feminists remained cordial for only a short time. At the fourth congress the credentials of Susan B. Anthony were challenged on the ground that she had used the Protective Union as a strikebreaking organization. When Miss Anthony admitted the charge, justifying her action on the ground that the only way the woman's rights movement could advance was to give women experience in industry, the National Labor Union rejected her credentials.

The incident soured relations between the N.L.U. and the suffragettes. It uncovered some of the hidden opposition to woman suffrage in the labor world; it increased the enmity of those already hostile to women in industry. Although the National Labor Union continued to seat delegates from bona fide women's labor organizations, continued to advocate equal pay for equal work and to demand an eight-hour day for women as well as men, its suspicion of the objectives of the woman's rights movement was easily noted. Male support for women's trade unions fell off; by 1872 most of the women's labor organizations had disappeared.

More disruptive than the problem of women was the issue of the laboring Negro. Labor's general attitude toward the free Negro in the postwar period was well illustrated in its comments upon Negro suffrage. A few labor newspapers like the Boston *Evening Voice* argued that enfranchisement of the Negroes was necessary to "elevate" their intelligence, so they would then cooperate with white labor in raising the conditions of all labor. But the *Voice* cried in a wilderness of indifference and opposition. Most workingmen were suspicious of the movement which was led by men who were former abolitionists and were hostile to the eight-hour day. They charged that the subject of Negro suffrage had been introduced to divert the attention of the public from the "struggle between labor and capital"; that the issue would be used as a cover for an attempt to enslave the "white mechanics of the North." This attitude was undoubtedly intensified by the appearance of Negroes in northern industries. The freedmen with their low living standards and a willingness to accept lower wages came northward during the recession of 1866–1868, and violent clashes between white and Negro laborers became frequent in the northern industrial centers.

Between 1867 and 1869 Negro labor began to create separate organizations. Negro dock workers in Baltimore, Charleston, Savannah, and Mobile paced the movement which spread to all trades throughout the chief industrial centers of the South. In 1869 delegates from nine Negro associations, led by Isaac Myers, a Baltimore calker, asked for admission to the National Labor Union. The issue of Negro recognition was thus squarely presented to white labor. After a bitter argument, the congress not only seated all nine delegates but also urged the formation of colored labor organizations throughout the nation, promising them equality at the next congress. It also established a special committee to "organize the colored men of Pennsylvania into labor unions."

Some labor leaders, among them William Jessup, president of the New York State Workingmen's Assembly, and Alfred W. Phelps, head of the carpenters, accepted the example of the National Labor Union and called upon nationals to remove the bars against admission of Negro mechanics. But almost all trades revealed unsurmountable prejudices. The color of the Negro's skin and his former state of servitude, which made the white laborer look upon him as an inferior species of mankind; the feeling that the Negro would not sustain union wage rates, or that he would be false to unionism and become a strikebreaker in times of crisis, formed the foundation of the prejudice. There was also a genuine difference of objective between the two races. Many white laborers were turning toward Greenbackism as a solution of their problems; their program was a condemnation of the Republican party. Negroes on the other hand were primarily concerned with opportunities to secure equal education and a liberal homestead policy in the South; they looked to the Republican party for their salvation.

For about a year Negro labor did not recognize this situation. In December, 1869, Negro trade unionists and intellectuals created the National Colored Labor Union. The platform concentrated upon the problem of discrimination which was stigmatized as "an insult to God, an injury to us, and a disgrace to humanity," and recommended the formation of cooperative Negro workshops as a remedy against the exclusion "of our people from other workshops on account of color." The National Colored Labor Union expected to affiliate itself with the white man's movement at the fifth N.L.U. Congress. During 1870 Isaac Myers spearheaded an organizing drive throughout the South. His object was twofold: to prevent the arrival of the day when Negroes would be totally ousted from the skilled trades and left as "the sweepers of shavings, the scrapers of pitch, and the carriers of mortar," and to prove to white labor that the Negro would take seriously his responsibilities to trade unionism. But Myers's high hope of complete affiliation with the N.L.U. was given a rude setback. The fifth congress announced itself in favor of the creation of an independent labor party. The National Colored Labor Union promptly severed relations and proclaimed the allegiance of the Negro laborer to the Republican party. Solution of the Negro issue was postponed to another day.

Most disruptive of the policy issues which the N.L.U. encountered was known in the nineteenth century as Greenbackism. Edward Kellogg, a New York merchant, was the philosophical father of the movement. In 1848 he published a book on the subject of money and credit in which he argued that the nation's monetary laws were oppressive to labor. They allowed bankers to create and loan money and, by permitting them to withhold capital, allowed bankers to create a monetary scarcity that produced high interest rates which were disastrous to the general public. He proposed that the Federal Government issue paper money based on real estate and bearing 1 per cent interest. This would force banks to lower their interest rates and enable farmers, manufacturers, planters, and mechanics to secure the money they needed at a rate they could afford. This reform would permit trade unions to secure cheap capital and lead to the abolition of the wage system.

Kellogg's theories made little impression upon labor in the fifties, which was still wary of all paper-money schemes. After the Civil War, the situation changed. This was a period when financiers and farmers were locked in a struggle over the proper method of redeeming government bonds; business demanded redemption in gold, farmers in greenbacks. Talk about bonds and greenbacks was on everyone's lips. It was also the period when several national trade associations were thinking seriously of producers' cooperatives. Several labor leaders, among them Sylvis, Trevellick, and Cameron, became advocates of Kellogg's theories. In 1867 they persuaded the National Labor Union to adopt a monetary reform platform based upon but not identical with Kellogg's proposals. Their plan, known as "interconvertibility," called for the abolition of the national banking system and the fixing of interest rates by the government instead of by banks. It called upon the government to reduce the interest on its bonds to 3 per cent and to make them convertible into greenbacks at the option of the owner. The government would lend paper money—greenbacks—directly to its citizens at about 1 per cent interest. This would accomplish two things: it would enable cooperatives to obtain capital at a reasonable rate of interest and would permit small businessmen to secure funds to enlarge their enterprises and provide more employment.

It is doubtful that the leaders of the N.L.U. recognized the importance of the issue when it was introduced. There was in it a measure of inflation which labor traditionally opposed, but in the period following the Civil War many workingmen felt that inflation could do the economy no harm. Moreover, they were mainly interested in the provision for government loans at 1 per cent interest, which would enable trade unions to set up producers' cooperatives. During the recession and for a short while after—when the trades were concerned with falling membership, declining wages, and the eight-hour movement—producers' cooperatives seemed to provide a logical escape from a dire situation. The fact that interconvertibility could be secured only by political action did not prove bothersome. As long as the "pure and simple" trade unionists dominated the organization, no serious movement in that direction was authorized.

Events gradually changed the situation. As the trade-union movement revived, and as the interest of labor leaders turned more and more toward problems involved in organizing and in securing the eight-hour day, their control of the N.L.U. loosened. Meanwhile, political movements of labor had developed in Massachusetts and Pennsylvania.

The Crispins, who were in the midst of a political pressure campaign to secure incorporation in order that they might set up cooperative shoe shops, led the movement in Massachusetts. Their failure to secure passage of the needed legislation in the 1869 session induced them to form the Independent party with E. M. Chamberlin as their gubernatorial candidate. Their platform called for incorporation of trade unions, establishment of a bureau of labor statistics, adoption of a legal eight-hour day, and abolition of the convict labor system which was making inroads upon the shoemakers at the time. The election proved astonishing to both labor and its opponents. The Independent party, polling some 13,000 votes, elected a senator and twenty-two assemblymen. With high hopes the organization changed its name to Labor Reform party and entered the campaign of 1870. To win over a large intellectual element which was supporting the eight-hour day, it nominated Wendell Phillips for governor and announced itself favorable to monetary reform. Although it failed to secure any measurable increase in its vote and lost most of its seats in the state legislature, it achieved one triumph: Massachusetts created the nation's first Bureau of Labor Statistics.

In Pennsylvania the political movement was led by the anthracite miners, organized as the Workingmen's Benevolent Association, under the leadership of John Siney. The W.B.A. entered politics as a pressure group—threatening to vote against candidates who would not pledge themselves to vote for legislation favorable to labor—and secured passage of a law in 1869 which provided for the appointment of an inspector of mines and a law for inspection of ventilation and safety devices in Schuylkill County. A few months later a disastrous explosion in a mine at Avondale in Luzerne County which cost the lives of 109 men brought enactment of a bill for mine inspection in the whole anthracite area.

While these state activities did not revolve around the Greenback issue, they suggested that a political movement by labor on a national scale would be successful. Greenbackers in the National Labor Union quickly took advantage of the situation at the 1870 congress. Brushing aside the objections of the "pure and simple" trade unionists, they proceeded to divide the organization into two parts: industrial and political. The congress—no longer based upon local and national associations but upon state federations—became an advisory body, a forum in which measures would be formulated for action by a political party. These actions destroyed the trade-unionist nature of the National Labor Union. While many of the old leaders—Trevellick, Hinchcliffe, Cameron, and Siney—supported the change, no national, except the Crispins who had been shattered by successive strike losses, sent delegates to the sixth congress held in 1871. That body was attended only by politically conscious labor leaders and intellectuals. Their sole action was to approve the division of the National Labor Union into industrial and political branches.

Early in 1872 the first "political" convention of the N.L.U. met at Columbus with one hundred delegates from fourteen states in attendance. The convention adopted the name Labor Reform party and a platform which dealt with monetary reform, land, convict labor, cooperatives, the eight-hour day, Chinese exclusion, and the tariff, which it wanted to reduce "so as to admit free such articles of common use as we can neither produce nor grow." Then the convention turned to the problem of a presidential candidate. The time was propitious. The Republican party had split into two wings—Radicals and Liberals; the Democrats, out of power for fourteen years, were eager to make concessions. A host of politicians who recognized that a nomination by a labor party would increase their chances for a nomination by Liberal Republicans or Democrats descended upon Columbus to pull wires. The convention nominated David Davis of

Illinois, associate justice of the United States Supreme Court, and John Parker, governor of New Jersey, as its candidates.

Davis's nomination was not greeted with joy. Several delegates to the convention announced that they would not support him; a number of local workingmen's committees demanded a new nomination. Davis accepted the nomination, but after the Liberal Republicans nominated Horace Greeley as their presidential candidate he withdrew from the race. The executive committee of the Labor Reform party promptly called a meeting of the Columbus delegates. Thirty-five answered the call. But when one group announced that it was "inexpedient at this late date" to make new nominations, the remainder joined those dissident Democrats who had refused to accept Horace Greeley as their party candidate and endorsed Charles O'Conor, Tammany Hall wheelhorse, as Labor Reform candidate for the Presidency. O'Conor received less than 30,000 votes. At the next "industrial" convention of the National Labor Union held in 1872, only seven delegates appeared. The first postwar attempt to form a national labor movement had ended.

It is usually concluded that the National Labor Union disappeared because it turned political. The judgment is too simple. The National Labor Union was inherently weak from its origin because its membership held two conflicting philosophies which were never resolved: one was the politically conscious, humanitarian, and reform philosophy inherited from the thirties and forties; the other was the "pure and simple" trade-unionist philosophy of the fifties. During the N.L.U.'s early years, coincidental with the recession of 1866–1868, trade unionists dominated the organization. Their interest centered in membership, the eight-hour day, and elimination of cheap labor competition. They were willing to endorse any expedient to achieve these goals. Accordingly they supported the reformers' suggestions for legislation to establish the eight-hour day and legislation to eliminate the competition of labor imported from Europe under contract. After the recession, when trade unionism revived and the economic campaign for the eight-hour day began to show success and the cheap labor competition from Europe appeared to have been eliminated, the trade unionists in general drew back from any political, humanitarian, and reform policies. It was at this point that the National Labor Union began to disintegrate. When reformers urged cooperation with women and Negroes in industry, trade unionists who were inclined to look upon both groups as cheap labor competition became incensed. During the postwar recession trade unionists accepted Greenbackism as a means of establishing cooperatives which would eliminate "wage slavery" and alleviate the "miserable condition of workingmen." After 1870, however, when labor began to share in business recovery, the same trade unionists found Greenbackism "highly amusing," a description which in turn angered the reformers. The clashes over these issues were hardly conducive to unity; they bred mistrust and a tendency toward fragmentation.

By 1870 the National Labor Union had become a house divided, half trade and half political. It could not survive in that condition. It became political, and the transformation destroyed it. Trade unionists withdrew their support. A large proportion of them were loyal to one or the other major parties; another portion looked upon the leaders of the Labor Reform party as hopeless visionaries—hardly to be followed into the tortuous maze of politics. Even those who were willing to support a labor party were disappointed. The nomination of David Davis, who had previously revealed no sympathy for the labor movement, alienated many. Davis's subsequent withdrawal produced a feeling of hopelessness and despair in others. The nomination of O'Conor further splintered the politically minded. Therefore, the whole movement collapsed.

In spite of its short life the National Labor Union played a significant part in the history of labor. It was a strong effort to unite labor into a single national organization; as such it paved the way for future efforts. It served to spotlight the chief labor problems of the period. But most important, it represented the transition between the democratic, egalitarian, politically-conscious, humanitarian, and reformist labor movement of the antebellum period, and the self-centered, wage-conscious, trade-unionist labor movement of the late nineteenth century.

10 ____

The Depression of 1873

The National Labor Union disintegrated a year before one of the nation's worst depressions. Reckless speculation and wholesale stock watering, practices which destroyed the widespread purchasing power needed to ensure prosperity, together with hard times in Europe which forced European investors to withdraw their funds from the United States and which reduced the demand for American agricultural products, were the main causes. The depression began with the failure of the banking house of Jay Cooke and Company in September, 1873, and quickly spread through the whole economy. For labor the depression was disastrous. By 1877 it was estimated that one-fifth of the nation's workingmen were completely unemployed, two-fifths worked no more than six or seven months a year, and only one-fifth worked regularly. By the winter of 1877–1878 the total unemployed had reached three million. Along with unemployment came lower wages and longer hours. In the New York City building trades where artisans had been paid $2.50–$3.00 for an eight-hour day in 1872, they could secure only $1.50–$2.00 for a ten-hour day in 1875. Wages in the textile industry dropped 45 per cent; wages of railway workers dropped 30 to 40 per cent; wages of furniture workers dropped 40 to 60 per cent.

One of the first labor organizations to succumb to the depression was the Industrial Brotherhood which the national trade associations had set up to replace the National Labor Union in July, 1873, with the pledge that it would not "deteriorate into a political party, or a refuge for played out politicians." The organization never had a chance to develop. Its second meeting, which convened after the depression began, was well attended and cheerful, but its third meeting was attended by only a handful of woebegone individuals. Its disappearance in 1875 was a reflection of the situation throughout the whole labor world. Out of all the nationals in existence in 1872 only seven survived; those that did lost much of their membership: the cigarmakers lost more than 80 per cent, the coopers 75 per cent, the machinists 66 per cent, and the printers 50 per cent. Locals experienced the same decline. In New York City trade-union membership dropped from 45,000 to 5,000; strongly unionized Cincinnati had only 1,000 union members by 1878; Cleveland became a nonunion city. On the eve of the depression there had been 300,000 trade unionists in the nation; Samuel Gompers estimated that there were only 50,000 by 1878.

To a great extent organized labor activities ceased. Staying alive became the most important consideration. Thousands descended into a stage of abject misery—a condition known in previous depressions but never on so large or so wide a scale. In New York City alone about 90,000 laborers lost their homes. Communities built of discarded lumber and junk sprang up in all industrial centers. The number of tramps became an alarming problem. Raiding of garbage cans for food became a common sight in the cities and towns across the nation. Unemployment demonstrations occurred in New York and Chicago. In New York the unemployed culminated their demand for a public works program with a gigantic parade which was attacked by the police. Conditions were relieved slightly when Tammany stepped in and began to distribute food and fuel—a measure which was to give it a strong grip on the labor vote of the city for several decades. In Chicago 20,000 unemployed paraded the streets in the early winter of 1873–1874 to demand "bread for the needy, clothing for the naked, and houses for the homeless." The city did nothing, but the mayor persuaded the Relief and Aid Society, which had some $700,000 left over from the fund collected for the victims of the Chicago fire, to open its coffers.

One early effect of the depression upon labor was to turn its attention to an old panacea for miserable conditions—consumer cooperatives. The movement centered in New England where, in 1874, William H. Earle, an organizer for the Grange, created the National Council of the Order of Sovereigns of Industry designed to unite all persons "engaged in industrial pursuits" into local councils that would set up cooperative stores which would eliminate middlemen and which would sell "pure goods at low prices" to members. By

1875 the total membership, most of it in New England, was estimated at 40,000; there were forty-six stores in operation, and their annual trade was estimated at $3,000,000. The Sovereigns of Industry did not survive very long. Members without jobs dropped out when they found themselves unable to buy on credit; private enterprises won back old customers with lower prices. The jealousy of die-hard trade unionists contributed. Their chief organ, the Pittsburgh *National Labor Tribune,* began a systematic attack upon the order late in 1875. It warned labor to stay away from the Sovereigns because their "only object" was to "buy cheap" even if they had "to reduce wages a dollar a day to do it." Such attacks undoubtedly prevented an extensive expansion of the order outside New England. By 1880 the Sovereigns had been reduced to a mere handful of members.

Despite misery and unemployment normal labor activities did not stop entirely during the depression. In 1873 John Siney, who resigned as head of the anthracite miners, was able to combine the weak local and state bituminous mining associations in western Pennsylvania, Ohio, and Illinois into the Miners' National Association. By 1875 the organization had 35,000 members and had secured a standard wage rate in the Tuscarawas Valley in Ohio. In 1876 the Sons of Vulcan (puddlers), the Iron and Steel Heaters (roughers, rollers, and catchers), the Iron and Steel Roll Hands, and the Nailers united to form the Amalgamated Iron and Steel Workers. Most labor activities, some of which attracted nation-wide attention, ended in defeat. New York City's cigarmakers lost a strike to maintain their wages in 1873, and another strike to abolish the tenement-house system of manufacturing in 1877. Fall River mule spinners engaged in an eight-week strike—the "Long Vacation"—against four successive wage cuts in the summer of 1875. Although every mill in the city was closed, the strike was broken with French-Canadian immigrants, and Fall River became a nonunion town for more than a half-century.

More highly spectacular and more significant than the Long Vacation were the events in the anthracite coal fields. Although organization of anthracite labor had been tried in the 1850's and in the early months of the Civil War, it was not until the formation of the Workingmen's Benevolent Association in 1868 that the miners had any success. In one year the W.B.A., or the Miners' and Laborers' Benevolent Association as it was renamed, organized 85 per cent of the miners; in 1869 it forced mineowners to recognize the union as a bargaining agent, to grant a minimum wage, and to provide for a sliding scale of wages above that minimum whenever the price of coal increased. The agreement lasted until 1874 when the anthracite mineowners, led by Franklin B. Gowen, president of the Philadelphia and Reading Railroad, refused categorically to renew it. A strike began in January, 1875—the "Long Strike" in coal history—led by John F. Walsh. It lasted until June, 1875, when hunger forced the miners to yield and to accept a 20 per cent cut in wages. Walsh and other leaders of the M. & L.B.A. were forced to leave the area, and the "weak and tottery" locals ceased to function.

The Long Strike of 1875 was closely followed by the so-called "Molly Maguire Riots." As reported by the newspapers, the "riots" —directed by the Molly Maguires—consisted of a series of murders, murderous assaults, robberies, and acts of arson. The general impression made by these reports in the years 1875–1876 was that mine foremen and mine officials were the general victims, and that mine property was alone singled out for destruction. The purpose was to strike terror into the hearts of mineowners who would then give all miners the kind of jobs they wanted and restore wage levels to predepression figures.

The identity of the Molly Maguires has never been proved. In 1876–1877 they were described as the "secret ring" that controlled the lodges of the Ancient Order of Hibernians in the anthracite field. The order was described in turn as a group organized in Ireland to oppose the encroachments of landlords. It was incorporated in Pennsylvania in 1871 as a "humane, charitable, and benevolent organization." But according to the "members" who testified at the trial of the Mollies in 1876, the organization acted primarily in politics seeking election to those offices that handled public money. The "members" also testified that the order had 6,000 lodges throughout the nation and that the entire organization was "criminal in character." Its purpose was punishment of mineowners or bosses not on general principles, but because the victims had offended some member of the order. The evidence is difficult to accept. The "members" who testified as to the purposes of the order were either Pinkerton detectives or criminals who had joined the order after 1875. The districts where the Mollies entered politics were never revealed. The number of lodges in the order was fantastically large, and no evidence of their existence anywhere else in the nation was ever produced.

The charge has been made that the Molly Maguire episode was deliberately manufactured by the coal operators with the express purpose of destroying all vestiges of unionism in the area after the Long Strike of 1875. There is some evidence to support the charge. It is known that the Philadelphia and Reading Railroad hired Pinkertons for some unknown purpose before or during the Long Strike, that the "crime wave" that appeared in the anthracite fields came after the appearance of the Pinkertons, and that many of the victims of the crimes were union leaders and ordinary miners. It is known also that the men prosecuted for crimes were closely associated with the labor movement in the anthracite region and were obnoxious to the interests of the employers.

Whoever was responsible for the Molly Maguire Riots, labor was their victim. Late in the fall of 1875 twenty-four men, most of them members of the Miners' and Laborers' Benevolent Association, were arrested in the anthracite area and charged with a large number of criminal offenses. They were brought to trial early the following year. The evidence against them, supplied by James McParlan, a Pinkerton, and corroborated by men who were granted immunity for their own crimes, was tortuous and contradictory, but the net effect was damning. All twenty-four were convicted; ten were executed. The trial temporarily destroyed the last vestiges of labor unionism in the anthracite area. More important, it gave the public the impression that miners in general were inclined to riot, sabotage, arson, pillage, assault, robbery, and murder; and that miners were by nature criminal in character and were to be condemned and disciplined by the more respectable element in society. The impression became the foundation of the antilabor attitude held by a large portion of the nation to the present day.

A year after the trial of the Mollies, the nation sank to the depths of the depression. It was a year in which the New York *Commercial and Financial Chronicle* could declare: "Labor is under control for the first time since the war." But it was also the year of what has been described as the most violent and most significant labor upheaval in the nineteenth century—the Railway Strike of 1877. The event had long preparation. A 35 per cent cut in wage rates in three years, irregular employment, high living expenses in railway hotels away from home, black listing of members of the three nonmilitant brotherhoods—locomotive engineers, firemen, and conductors—forceful dissolution of the engineers' lodges by the Reading Road all combined to produce a bitter resentment among eastern railway workers. In mid-May, 1877, the Pennsylvania Railroad announced a new 10 per cent cut in wages to become effective on June 1st; other eastern roads announced cuts to become effective on July 1st and simultaneously intensified the discharge and black listing of brotherhood members. Railway workers, thoroughly alarmed, began to organize a secret "trainmen's union" under the leadership of Robert H. Ammon, and to plan a gigantic strike for June 27th. The strike never occurred; for some unexplained reason it was canceled. But the frustration of railway workers ultimately sought release. On July 16th a strike began on the Baltimore and Ohio line at Camden Junction, Maryland, when forty firemen and brakemen stopped work, halting traffic. Police dispersed the strikers. The next day a new outbreak occurred on the same line at Martinsburg, West Virginia, where trainmen seized the depot and refused to allow freight trains to leave until their wage cut was restored. When the strike leaders were arrested, a large crowd released them. State militia proved ineffective, and the governor asked for Federal troops. With their arrival the strike was broken. In the meantime, it had spread eastward to Cumberland, Maryland, and westward into Kentucky and Ohio. Federal troops were brought into Maryland and state militia were called out in Kentucky. By July 22nd the B. & O. was once more in full operation.

But the strike had spread to other lines. At Pittsburgh a strike began among the employees of the Pennsylvania road on July 19th. Trainmen took control of the switches and refused to let freight trains move. The railways called upon the sheriff who read the strikers the Riot Act; the strikers, in possession of the depot, refused to move. The governor mobilized the Allegheny County militia which promptly joined the strikers. Then six hundred militiamen arrived from Philadelphia. They succeeded in dispersing a crowd gathered at the "26th street crossing," killing twenty-six people. But the militia was then assailed so furiously by an ever-growing mob that it was forced to take refuge in the roundhouse. The roundhouse was set

afire. The militia, after fighting the fire all night, retreated out of
the city. A mob took control. For another day the railroad area became the scene of burning, destruction, and looting—$5,000,000 of
railroad property was destroyed. Minor disturbances also occurred
at Altoona, Scranton, Reading, Harrisburg, and Philadelphia in
Pennsylvania. Local forces dispersed strikers everywhere except in
Reading, where three hundred Federal troops were used.

In New York, strikes occurred along the route of the Erie and the
New York Central. The Erie road was most thoroughly involved,
with men refusing to allow trains to move at Hornellsville, Port
Jervis, Corning, and Buffalo. The New York Central alone of the
eastern roads escaped extensive damage. As the employees of the
road went on strike, William Vanderbilt, president of the line, ordered the latest wage cut rescinded and began distributing $100,000
of relief funds. His employees promptly returned to work. Farther
west, strikes occurred on the Lake Shore railroad at Erie and Toledo.
Railway workers quit work at Columbus, Cincinnati, Chicago, and
St. Louis. Vigilantes, militia, and Federal troops countered the activity. By August 2nd railway service had been restored; the strike
had ended. Property damage was upward of ten million; hundreds
had been killed; uncounted numbers had been injured.

The Railway Strike of 1877 thoroughly shocked a large portion
of the public. Not since slaveholders had ceased to be haunted by
dreams of a slave uprising had the propertied elements been so terrified. They became convinced that not only coal miners but railway workers and other laborers were inherently criminal. They were
likewise convinced that immediate steps had to be taken to ensure
law and order in the future. Those steps were taken. The militia
was strengthened by the construction of armories throughout the
nation. Legislatures in many states enacted new conspiracy laws
aimed directly at labor.

The strike involved the largest number of persons of any labor
conflict in the nineteenth century. It was not only a strike of railway
workers. In every community it was aided by other elements. Miners
from the surrounding coal fields supported the strike actively in
Martinsburg and in Pittsburgh; they ran the strike in Scranton; they
turned out in sympathy in St. Clair and Madison counties in Illinois.
Millhands and unemployed workers assisted the strike in Pitts-

burgh; unemployed helped the strike in Cincinnati; 20,000 workmen joined the strikers in Chicago. Negro sewermen in Louisville
and Negro stevedores in Cairo, Illinois, held sympathetic strikes.
Farmers in West Virginia and along the route of the Erie Railroad
in New York joined the movement. Small businessmen aided in
Martinsburg and Pittsburgh. The varied nonlabor elements involved
in this upheavel revealed how bitterly a portion of the American
people hated the railroads with their rate discriminations, stock
manipulation, bribery, and corruption; how willingly they would
join forces with any group in conflict with the arrogant railway owners. But more important as far as labor was concerned was the wide
assortment of workingmen who participated in the strike, revealing
for the first time how widespread was the feeling of solidarity among
labor. The Railway Strike of 1877 was significant primarily because
it gave workingmen a class consciousness on a national scale.

One of the first noticeable results of the Railway Strike was to
turn labor's attention to politics once more. The farmers who organized the Granger-Greenback movement in the Upper Mississippi
Valley had tried to involve labor in an independent political movement through all the first years of the depression. In 1876 they had
gone so far as to invite labor representatives to a joint convention
at Indianapolis. The convention adopted a "Union Program" designed to appeal to labor, and nominated Peter Cooper of New York
as its presidential candidate with Samuel F. Cary of Ohio—ex-labor
leader, ex-general, ex-congressman—as his running mate. The Greenback party did not attract labor votes. Only in Pennsylvania, where
some rising young members of the labor movement, among them
John M. Davis of the *National Labor Tribune* and John P. James,
secretary of the Miners' National Association, put on a campaign, was
there any response. The Cooper-Cary ticket received some 81,000
votes. Four anthracite counties in Pennsylvania gave Cooper the
greatest aggregate of labor votes—2,635.

The Railway Strike produced a remarkable change. The strike
had convinced labor that government was hostile to its aims and
that resort to politics was necessary. Political parties appeared in all
the industrial centers of the nation. The movement reached its height
in New York, Pennsylvania, and Ohio. In New York a convention
of laboring men from all over the state met at Troy. Calling itself

the Labor Reform party, it nominated candidates for secretary of
state and state comptroller and adopted a purely labor platform:
reduction in the hours of labor, abolition of the convict labor system,
prohibition of manufacturing in tenement houses, and establishment
of a bureau of labor statistics. A strong organization was developed
in the areas adjacent to the New York Central and Erie railroads.
Local tickets were placed in the field in most of the state's industrial
centers. An official newspaper, the *Daily Bazoo*, was established in
Elmira.

In Pennsylvania a United Workingmen's Convention met at Harrisburg and named candidates for auditor general and treasurer. Its
platform contained a number of labor demands: abolition of conspiracy laws applying to labor, establishment of courts of arbitration to settle industrial disputes, establishment of labor bureaus,
abolition of the convict labor system, enactment of workingmen's
compensation laws and child-labor laws. A week after the Harrisburg meeting, labor and the Greenbackers merged their forces into
the Greenback and Labor party. In Ohio a convention of workingmen was held at Columbus and organized the "National party." Its
platform, somewhat different from the labor platforms of New York
and Pennsylvania, was an open bid for fusion. Only one real labor
plank was adopted: abolition of truck stores. In addition it called
for the imposition of an income tax and the substitution of Greenbacks for all national bank notes and the remonitization of silver. A
short while later the state's Greenbackers merged with the party.
The fusion adopted a ticket made up of a Greenbacker as candidate
for governor, and laboring men as candidates for the remaining
state offices.

The Labor Reform party in New York and the Greenback-Labor
fusions in Pennsylvania and Ohio enjoyed some success in the fall
elections. In New York the labor ticket polled some 20,000 votes;
one assemblyman was elected from Elmira. In Pennsylvania the
fusion polled 53,000 votes, nearly 10 per cent of the total. In Ohio
the state ticket polled 17,000 votes; Toledo workingmen swept their
whole municipal ticket into office and sent two assemblymen to the
state legislature.

The results of the election made the next development almost
inevitable. Late in the year the National party of Ohio called a con-

vention of "labour and currency reformers" to meet at Toledo in February, 1878. Although few labor leaders attended, and some of those belonged to the previous generation, the convention formed a "Greenback-Labor party." Its platform contained four labor demands which were to form the basis of labor activity for the next decade: reduction of the hours of labor by law, creation of national and state bureaus of labor statistics, prohibition of the convict labor system, and the suppression of the importation of "servile labor." The remainder of the platform was given over to currency reform.

The new party was an immediate success. In the spring it elected mayors in Elmira, Auburn, Utica, and Oswego, New York; and named Terence V. Powderly mayor of Scranton, Pennsylvania, where the opposition attempted to destroy the fusion by calling it the "Molly Maguire Ticket." In the autumn elections success was even greater. In Massachusetts the party joined with the Democrats, nominated Ben Butler as its candidate for governor, and almost won the contest. In New York it received 9 per cent of the votes cast for congressional candidates; in Pennsylvania it secured 12 per cent of the total vote; in Ohio it polled 38,000. Outside the industrial areas its vote was even larger. It secured 30 per cent of the vote in Maine, 15 per cent in Illinois, 22 per cent in Iowa, 17 per cent in St. Louis, 19 per cent in Kansas, nearly 25 per cent in Texas. Its congressional candidates secured more than a million votes; fourteen were elected.

The election of 1878 was the high point of the movement. Shortly after, the Greenback-Labor party began to disintegrate. The alliance had been unstable from the beginning. The agrarian elements were interested primarily in monetary reform. More accurately they wanted inflation. Labor's demands were of little concern to them. In fact they suspected labor's aims, denouncing the "communism of trade unions" as a kind of "labor corporation." Labor, on the other hand, was directly interested in bettering its own conditions and in destroying unfair labor competition. Disintegration was aided by a number of other factors. A few months after the election the Specie Resumption Act went into effect; farmers, recognizing that greenbackism was a dead issue, deserted the movement. A tendency to merge again with the Democratic party developed in labor ranks. That trend had appeared in Massachusetts and New York in the nomination of Butler and several congressional candidates; it in-

creased after 1878—aided by the Democratic party's renewed revelation of concern for the welfare of labor, the first real evidence of
such an attitude since the Civil War. Finally, an industrial revival
which became apparent in the late months of 1878 weakened labor's
grievances and turned its attention once more to economic action.

Efforts were made to keep the Greenback-Labor party alive. The
national convention of 1880 was well attended, but except for delegates from Pennsylvania, eastern labor elements were conspicuous
by their absence. The convention named James B. Weaver as its
presidential candidate, adopted a typical agrarian program and the
labor planks of the Toledo platform. Labor did not respond. Weaver
received a sizable labor vote only in the tier of counties running
across the southern border of Michigan.

The Greenback-Labor movement was only one of the political by-
products spawned by the depression and the Railway Strike. A second, revolving around anticoolie labor sentiment, developed in California. The Chinese first appeared in California in the fifties; as
long as they remained in the mining industry, labor had given them
little thought. After the Civil War, however, the Chinese appeared
in railway construction gangs and among harvest hands. Since they
worked for less, California workingmen revealed immediate and open
hostility; in 1866–1868 they made repression of Chinese immigration
a prime objective, but without result. In 1869 the first transcontinental
railroad reached California; with it came cheaper manufactured
products and eastern workingmen. Thousands of Chinese who worked
on the railroad lost their jobs and became an army of unemployed.
A depression settled upon California. Laboring men, who held coolie
labor responsible, redoubled their agitation for prohibition of Chinese immigration, but the California legislature, powerless to act
upon a subject which came under Federal jurisdiction, would do
nothing. California workingmen turned to the National Labor Union
for aid.

The N.L.U. revealed considerable sympathy for the plight of Cal-
ifornia labor and adopted a resolution calling for rigid enforcement
of the Act of 1862 which prohibited the importation of coolie labor.
But it also approved voluntary emigration of Chinese to the United
States. In the same year the United States and China signed the
Burlingame Treaty specifically authorizing voluntary emigration

between the two nations. In 1870 the National Labor Union changed its attitude, for in that year Chinese strikebreakers were imported into a shoe factory in Massachusetts. The Crispins promptly became the eastern champions of a Chinese exclusion movement and pressured the N.L.U. to demand both the prohibition of coolie importation and the abrogation of the Burlingame Treaty. But employer influence in Congress and the return of prosperity checked the movement.

The Railway Strike revived it. California was prosperous during the early years of the depression of 1873, a condition which resulted in the immigration of 150,000 eastern laborers. When the depression finally descended upon the state in 1877, these additional workingmen made the situation particularly severe. News of the Pittsburgh riots brought discontent to a head. Socialists in San Francisco called a meeting on the "sand lots" in front of City Hall to express sympathy for the railroad strikers. The eight thousand who met there were an orderly crowd. No mention of the Chinese issue was made, but before the meeting ended a group of anticoolie demonstrators arrived and demanded that something be said about the Chinese menace. When leaders of the meeting refused, some of the crowd attacked a passing Chinese; the cry of "on to Chinatown" sent a mob into the Chinese quarter. A two-day riot followed; it was finally quelled through the united efforts of state militia, police, and the "pick-handle brigade."

The riot awoke the latent anti-Chinese sentiment in San Francisco. Among the pick-handle brigade was Denis Kearney who had become well known as an open-air speaker on behalf of the employers and the Chinese. The riot showed him that he was on the wrong side of the fence. When his first effort to shift sides was rebuffed, he set up his own organization, the Workingmen's Trade and Labor Union of San Francisco. His anti-Chinese agitation quickly spread through the state, and in October, 1877, he organized the Workingmen's party of California. Its object was "to unite all poor and workingmen . . . to defend themselves against the dangerous encroachments of capital . . . [and] to rid the country of cheap Chinese labor."

Despite harassment by the courts and the police the Sand Lot party developed rapidly, attracting workingmen, the poor, aspiring politicians, and even socialists. In January, 1878, it held its first state convention. It adopted a platform denouncing the government as the tool of capitalists and demanding legislation which would prohibit the creation of millionaires and monopolists, establish a system of finance "uncontrolled by rings, brokers, and bankers," an eight-hour day, and abolish the convict labor system. Chinese labor was denounced as a "curse" upon the land. That winter the party elected mayors in Oakland and San Francisco. During the following spring the Sandlotters elected fifty-one of the 152 delegates to the state constitutional convention. Their greatest success came in San Francisco; in Los Angeles, where they had united with the Grangers; in the mining areas; and in the drought-stricken counties of Southern California. In the convention they allied themselves with the farmer delegates and secured the adoption of a provision that "no corporation [could thereafter] employ directly or indirectly, in any capacity, any Chinese or Mongolian."

In June, 1879, the Workingmen's party entered its second big contest with the nomination of a wealthy rancher for governor. During the campaign the party formed many fusions—with Democrats, Grangers, and Greenbackers; it elected eleven senators and seventeen assemblymen, becoming the second largest party in the state. In September the party elected its candidate, the Reverend I. S. Kalloch, mayor of San Francisco. But this was the high point. With the return of prosperity the anti-Chinese agitation began to die down. Kearney himself lost enthusiasm; he began to pay frequent visits to the East and in 1880 became a Greenbacker. Meanwhile the party disappeared, fused into the Greenback and Democratic organizations.

It was not long before anti-Chinese agitation revived. Business was slow in California in the early months of 1880; unemployment bulked large. In January a San Francisco painters' union called a meeting which inaugurated a movement to enforce the clause in the constitution which prohibited corporations from employing Chinese. Mobs of men organized into parades to march from factory to factory demanding discharge of all Mongolians. The legislature in session responded with a law implementing the constitution, and a considerable number of Chinese lost their jobs. At this point two events occurred to give the Chinese issue national prominence. A Federal court in the case of *In re Tiburcio Parrott* declared invalid the California statute forbidding corporations to employ Chinese, and Congress ratified a treaty with China in which it was declared that the

United States might "regulate, limit, or suspend" Chinese immigration, but might not "wholly prohibit it." In the next three years a great horde of Chinese descended upon American shores. Alarmed, San Francisco trade unionists now took control of the anti-Chinese movement. The crafts of the city called a state convention to organize anti-Chinese opposition. Delegates of some forty trades attended and formed the League of Deliverance, with Frank Roney as chairman. The league adopted as its weapon a boycott of Chinese-made goods. It was singularly effective. California courts gave it legal sanction, and many factories discharged their Mongolian employees.

Meanwhile labor organizations in the Rocky Mountains, where Chinese labor was semiabundant in the railroad and mining towns, and trade unions in the East took up the agitation. Many manufacturers who suffered from, or feared, Chinese competition joined the movement. The increased pressure brought results. In 1880 both major parties incorporated anticoolie planks in their platforms. In 1882 senators from California and the Rockies secured enactment of a bill to prohibit immigration of Chinese laborers. When President Chester A. Arthur signed the measure providing for a ten-year suspension of Chinese immigration to take effect in August, 1882, California went wild with joy. The menace of coolie labor never again arose to threaten the welfare of American workingmen.

11 ___

The Knights of Labor and Their Rivals: Haymarket

When the depression of 1873 ended, labor was in a weak and disorganized condition. Its old organizations existed mainly on paper. It had a criminal record and a bad reputation. It had no unity of objective. Nevertheless, labor was on the threshold of another period of progress. The major force in this development was an organization with the high-sounding title of the Noble Order of the Knights of Labor.

The order was the offshoot of a Philadelphia garment workers' local which had been black-listed into total ineffectiveness during the recession of 1866–1868. Led by Uriah Stephens, one of the last labor leaders whose intellectual roots were sunk in the politically conscious and reform atmosphere of antebellum days, the members of the local began an investigation into the cause of its decline. After considerable argument they reached two conclusions. The local had failed because its membership was too well known and its members were too readily liable to discharge and the black list; it was necessary, therefore, to adopt secrecy as a means of protection from employer spies and employers' discriminatory tactics. Labor organizations, moreover, would always fail as long as they divided into crafts; they needed to be united into some form of industrial organization. Once the garment cutters reached this conclusion, they acted quickly.

In December, 1869, they dissolved their old organization and created "Local Assembly 1" of the Noble Order of the Knights of Labor. As originally organized, only garment workers were eligible to full membership; men of other callings could join as "sojourners" with the expectation that they would become missionaries to organize workmen of other trades.

The order immediately surrounded itself with ritualism. New members were required to swear that they earned "their bread by the sweat of their brows" and to promise to "defend the life, interest, reputation and family of all . . . members." They also swore never to reveal the name of the order or the names of its members. To ensure secrecy the order was never referred to by name; it was known as the Five Stars or the Five Asterisks. Its meetings were called by mysterious symbols chalked on fences and sidewalks; its members were supplied with grips, passwords, and countersigns.

The order grew slowly. By December 1873, only thirty-one local assemblies were organized—all in the Philadelphia area. At that time "District Assembly 1," a city federation for Philadelphia, was established. In October, 1874, District Assembly 2 was organized in Camden; in August, 1875, District Assembly 3 was set up in Pittsburgh under the leadership of John M. Davis. Total membership at this stage was around five thousand; most members were skilled workers coming from locals which had never been attached to national associations or from the disrupted nationals like the miners, machinists, Crispins, and ship carpenters.

Little attention was given in the early years to the problem of a national organization. In 1875 District Assembly 1 was generally regarded as head of the order, but District Assembly 3 was larger; when it began to claim leadership members began to think of nationalization. Before any strong effort was made to organize nationally the Knights participated in a unifying movement initiated by the Junior Sons of '76, which had been formed at Pittsburgh in 1874. Essentially a political organization which advocated the Greenback program as a solution for labor ills, it called a convention of all labor groups at Tyrone in December, 1875. Sons of '76, Knights, and socialists attended the meeting which adjourned to Pittsburgh. The convention failed in its objective. Greenbackers and socialists disagreed over the importance of monetary reforms; Greenbackers and trade unionists disagreed over the use of political action. The convention's sole accomplishment was the suggestion that labor organize itself "under one head . . . upon a secret basis."

During 1876 and 1877 the rivalry between District Assemblies 1 and 3 for leadership of the Knights grew intense and bitter. Disintegration appeared likely. Then the Railway Strike of 1877 erupted. Although the Knights did not participate officially, the strike produced a sudden rush of labor into the order. By the end of 1877 eleven more district assemblies were created in Massachusetts, New York, West Virginia, Ohio, Indiana, and Illinois. This expansion, together with the problem of what attitude to take toward the Greenback-Labor movement, made a national meeting imperative. District Assemblies 1 and 3, accordingly, laid aside their rivalries to call a convention at Reading on January 1, 1878.

The Reading convention, attended by delegates from eleven districts, transformed the Knights of Labor into a national organization. The convention adopted a constitution and a statement of objectives which formed the basis of the organization until its disappearance in the 1890's. The constitution was a departure from previous attempts to form a national organization of labor. The Knights set up a General Assembly, made up of delegates from the district assemblies and unattached local assemblies, which was given the right to elect officers and to decide all matters of policy. It was given "the power and authority to make, amend, or repeal the fundamental and general laws and regulations of the Order; to finally decide all controversies arising in the Order; to issue all charters . . . [and] to tax the members of the Order for its maintenance." The district assembly was made the "highest tribunal" in its district, the geographical extent of which was not defined. Locals had to consist of at least ten members and were given full right to determine the district assembly to which they owed allegiance. Any person, regardless of race, sex, or skill, over the age of eighteen, "working for wages, or who at any time worked for wages" could become a member. But "no person who either sells, or makes his living by the sale of, intoxicating drink," could be admitted; nor could any lawyer, doctor, or banker.

The cardinal principles of the order were stated in the preamble. "Wealth," it declared, had become so aggressive that "unless checked," it would lead to the "pauperization and hopeless degradation of the toiling masses." If the toilers, therefore, wanted to enjoy the "blessings of life," they had to organize "every department of productive industry." The action of these toilers, however, could not be taken blindly; it had to be guided by knowledge. The ultimate aim of the order would be the establishment of "co-operative institutions productive and distributive." This accomplished, labor and capital could live harmoniously together each enjoying the just fruits of their efforts. Thus, organization, education, and cooperation became the "first principles" of the order.

The platform advocated the substitution of arbitration for strikes whenever employers and employees were willing "to meet on equitable grounds." It demanded establishment of the eight-hour day; abolition of the contract system on national, state, and municipal works; abolition of the importation of servile labor and of the convict labor system; enactment of weekly pay laws and legislation providing for the health and safety of those engaged "in mining, manufacturing, or building pursuits." It called for equal pay for equal work and laws prohibiting child labor under fourteen years of age. It asked for the establishment of postal savings banks and government ownership of railroads, telegraphs, and telephones; and the "abrogation of all laws that do not bear equally upon capital and labor."

Creation of a national organization did not solve all the Knights' problems. During the next six years a number of them produced a constant internal conflict. The issue of secrecy was one of the worst. Older leaders like Uriah Stephens, first Grand Master Workman of the order, regarded secrecy as a sacrosanct principle. They fought bitterly against its abandonment. Ultimately, however, pressure from the membership, the press, and the Roman Catholic Church forced the General Assembly of 1881 to make the name of the order and its activities public. Members, nevertheless, were still forbidden to reveal "to any employer or other person the name . . . of any . . . member of the Order without the permission of the member."

Another persistent source of friction was the question of political action. To a large extent this conflict was between Terence V. Powderly and the leadership on one side and the rank and file on the other. Powderly, a machinist, had joined the Knights in 1874. A man of persuasive personality he soon became the head of District Assembly 5. In 1879, when Uriah Stephens resigned, Powderly became Grand Master Workman of the order. Powderly was deeply interested in political activity. He took part in the Greenback-Labor movement and was elected mayor of Scranton in 1878, 1882, and 1884 on third-party tickets. At other times he favored pressure politics—supporting Democrats or Republicans whom he judged favorable to labor's aims. Since other leaders approved such activity and the platform of the Knights was one which could only be accomplished by legislative action, constant efforts were made to commit the order to a political venture. All such efforts failed: not because the membership was inherently opposed to political action; district and local assemblies often publicly supported Republicans or Democrats for office in the East, or frequently created their own political parties in the West. But the membership was suspicious of the political aims of many of its leaders, who seemed bent on getting labor behind such panaceas as Greenbackism, socialism, or land reform. In addition the economic tide was running strongly against political action. It was a period of prosperity, a period when the attention of labor was more directly centered upon economic action.

A third quarrel within the order arose over the value of strike action and trade unionism. Powderly's ultimate objective for labor was the organization of producers' cooperatives. He was not wage conscious, and constantly emphasized the fact that strikes could not solve issues like apprenticeship, administration of justice, child labor, or the laws of supply and demand. He urged workmen to use their funds for the establishment of producers' cooperatives. But organizers and the rank and file were impatient with such exhortation; they preferred to use strikes and boycotts to achieve higher wages. Between 1878 and 1884 the order conducted a large number of strikes. Many were totally unorganized and involved primarily semiskilled and unskilled labor. Among the most notable were the strikes of the brickmakers and of the tanners and curriers in Chicago in 1882, the strike of railroad freight handlers in New York City in the same year, and the strike of four thousand telegraphers—District Assembly 45—in 1883. In each of these strikes the chief issue was wages. While the public appeared to sympathize with the strikers, only the brickmakers won their demands. There were two principal reasons for failure: the strikes were conducted by unskilled workers who could easily be replaced by strikebreakers; the geographical organization of the Knights, excellent for carrying out general strikes and boycotts, was weak in conducting a strike of tradesmen.

Powderly and other leaders also favored the organization of labor—skilled and unskilled—into industrial unions; they had little sympathy for the trades. The rules of the order prohibited the formation of national trade associations, and the organizing techniques of the Knights gave little consideration to crafts. Organizers were given freedom to act among all laboring elements regardless of trades. The system permitted the organizer, who found it difficult to get in touch with enough members in a single area to form a trade union, to organize members of several trades to form a mixed local. One district organizer could thus do the work of a number of craft organizers, saving duplication of effort and duplication of salaries. The system produced a highly variegated organization. Many locals were developed from workers of one nationality; locals were organized by shops, by departments, and by industries; mixed local assemblies and district assemblies were formed of unskilled and skilled workers in many areas.

In spite of official frowns much organizing was also done on a trade basis. Organizers worked among locals that had been abandoned by nationals, and among trades like those of barbers, shoemakers, horsecar operators, and newspaper printers which felt no outside competition and which had never been nationally organized. Most of these trades were set up as local assemblies. In some areas trades were formed into district assemblies. This happened very early among the printers of New York City, Brooklyn, and Jersey City, and among miners in both the anthracite and bituminous fields. The constant influx of tradesmen into the order ultimately broke down the opposition to their separate organization on a national scale. The change occurred first in 1879 when the windowglass workers were permitted to organize Local Assembly 300 as a national trade association. After 1883 this form of organization became fairly common.

Membership of the Knights in these years increased steadily but fluctuated violently. In January, 1879, the order had about 9,000 members. In 1880 it reached 20,000 members; in 1881, 28,000; in 1882, 19,000; in 1883, 42,000; and by 1884, 52,000. Almost as many members dropped out of the order: between 1879 and 1883 locals initiated 86,000 and suspended 54,000. Although the chief cause for suspension was nonpayment of dues, the main reason for fluctuation was the failure of strikes. After a strike was lost, employers frequently resorted to the courts and to black lists and compelled employees to sign yellow-dog contracts. Numerous locals were forced to disband. This constant fluctuation reduced the effectiveness of economic activity, but it spread the influence of the order over a much larger segment of the laboring population than the membership figures indicated.

The Knights of Labor did not monopolize the labor field in the postdepression years. Other rivals for leadership appeared, each with separate ideologies and techniques, each with its own following. Of these the most radical were the socialists who had appeared in the United States before socialism had been given form, tenets, creed, or methodology. The original leader of the socialist movement in the United States was Herman Kriege who had become a member of the Bund der Gerechten, a secret organization of German workingmen formed and designed in a vague way to overthrow the capitalistic order. Kriege came to America in 1845 and tried to organize a small group of Germans who had been members of the Bund into a socialistic society. But he and the German workingmen soon discovered greater possibilities in the land-reform movement, and the organization died. In 1849 Wilhelm Weitling, who had been leader of the Bund until Marx and Engels had taken control of the organization, arrived in the United States. His objective was the reform of society through the creation of banks of exchange. His plans did not take root; in 1852 his organization contained only three hundred "reliable" members. Meanwhile a third socialistic leader, Joseph Wedemeyer, appeared. Wedemeyer was a true Marxian socialist—as true as was possible before Marxian socialism was clearly defined. Like Marx, he aimed at the direct overthrow of capitalism through trade unions which could be "educated" to work for socialistic objectives. Wedemeyer organized the Proletarian League in New York City in 1852 "for the purpose of reforming the conditions of labor," but the league disappeared in the recession of 1854. Between that date and 1865 little was heard of socialism in America.

It reappeared soon after the Civil War, greatly influenced by the agitation in Germany which was begun by Ferdinand Lassalle in 1863 and by the International Workingmen's Association founded by Karl Marx in London in 1864. Lassalle believed that workingmen could only solve their problems by independent political action; they must organize politically, secure control of the government, and then proceed to establish socialistic cooperatives to replace the capitalistic structure. Marx at this stage emphasized the necessity of organizing trade unions. After that, workingmen could set up producers' cooperatives; when these were functioning the workers could organize politically, seize control of the government, and set up a socialistic state.

The difference in attitude was not at first reflected in the United States. In October, 1865, a small group of Lassalleans formed the German Workingmen's Union in New York City; three years later they reorganized as the Social party with Friedrich A. Sorge as president. Originally the party kept its socialism under cover, announcing typical labor aims. After a miserable showing in the election of 1868, it reorganized as Union 5 of the National Labor Union and Section 1 of the International Workingmen's Association.

For the next several years the Social party tried both to convince the National Labor Union that it ought to cooperate with the International and to create more sections. Its attempt at international labor cooperation, based on a mutual desire to prevent the migration

of workers from one country to another as strikebreakers, produced
no practical results. Its organizing efforts were hardly more successful; by 1871 some seven new sections were formed with a total membership of three hundred. In that year the International attracted the
attention of some native American intellectuals led by William West,
one-time president of the New England Workingmen's Association,
who organized Sections 9 and 12. During the next few years, socialist
influence began to penetrate into Die Arbeiter Union, the German
workingmen's assembly of New York City set up in 1866 and led
by Adolph Douai; it appeared among the furniture workers, in the
German-American Typographia of Chicago, and among the anthracite miners.

But this success was soon menaced by the activities of Section 12.
After the organization of that section, two sisters, Victoria Woodhull
and Tennessee Claflin, strong advocates of woman suffrage and "social freedom," set up a newspaper, *Woodhull and Claflin's Weekly*,
as its organ. While they published considerable material on labor,
they also used a great deal of space to advocate woman suffrage, free
love, sexual freedom, spiritualism, a universal language, and a host
of other reforms. Such preachments horrified Sorge and other International leaders, not only because they deviated from approved International objectives, but because the newspapers of the nation seized
upon the writings of the two sisters and presented them to the nation
as the objectives of the socialist movement. Section 12 was ousted
and a split followed. Twenty-two sections with a primarily foreign
membership organized the North American Federation; thirteen
other sections organized the American Confederation. Each appealed
to the International Congress for recognition. While the congress,
held at The Hague in 1872, gave most of its attention to the struggle
between Marx and the anarchist Mikhail Bakunin, it took time to
settle the American quarrel by recognizing the North American
Federation as its legitimate representative. The American Confederation gradually drifted into oblivion, taking a large share of the American-born socialists with it.

Further disintegration followed. In 1872 the International, fearing
the influence of Bakunin upon European workingmen, transferred
the seat of its organization to New York. Almost immediately Section
1's assumption of leadership produced a revolt on the part of other

New York City sections which ended only when several were expelled. In the early months of the depression of 1873 socialists helped organize unemployment demonstrations to demand relief from the municipal governments of New York City and Chicago. Failure of these movements produced a querulous attitude among the Lassalleans who began to criticize the International's trade-unionist policies and to demand adoption of new techniques. Their agitation ultimately produced two political parties. In the East the ousted New York City sections, a socialist group from Newark, and a small contingent from Philadelphia formed the Social Democratic party of North America. Two later prominent leaders of labor were high in the councils of the organization: Adolph Strasser, cigarmaker, and P. J. McGuire, carpenter. In Chicago the Lassalleans created the Labor party of Illinois. Both parties entered the political campaigns of 1874 but received only scattered votes. After this failure trade unionists began to question the wisdom of political activity. Their criticism so angered the politically minded elements that they withdrew from the Federation almost en masse. The socialist movement was in a shambles.

Attempts to reestablish the unity of the movement were made throughout 1875, but it was not until after the Tyrone-Pittsburgh convention, at the "Union Congress" held in Philadelphia in July, 1876, that the socialists were able to re-form—as the Socialist Labour party. The party decided that its basic structure would be the trade union. Political action in the interest of the working class would be permitted upon a local basis only when a "perceptible influence" could be exercised. Philip Van Patten, an American-born journalist, became the party's first national secretary.

The Union Congress provided the socialist movement only a short-lived harmony. The prevailing trend in the labor world during the depression was toward political action, and the socialists could not resist. The New Haven section entered politics in 1876. The result was so favorable that sections in Cincinnati, Milwaukee, and Chicago entered the municipal campaigns of 1877. In Cincinnati the party secured one-tenth of the votes cast; in Milwaukee six socialists were elected to office; in Chicago Albert R. Parsons, who was the only party candidate for council, secured one-sixth of the vote in his ward. These successes led the political socialists, who had been chafing

under the restrictions placed upon them by the Union Congress, to
begin an agitation for a relaxation of the rules.

In the midst of a bitter intraparty controversy over the issue, the
Railway Strike occurred, catching the socialists unawares. They
quickly rallied, laid aside their quarrels, and made preparations to
give aid to the strikers. Sections of the party in various cities sponsored mass meetings to indicate their support, called for the establishment of the eight-hour day, for abolition of conspiracy laws, and
demanded that the Federal Government purchase the railroads. After
the strike, the socialists succumbed to the political fever sweeping
through labor ranks. At the Newark convention in December, 1877,
the party reversed its former stand, declared that political action was
to be the main function of the party, and shifted headquarters to
Cincinnati, center of the political movement.

The Socialist Labour party entered the election campaigns of 1878
with high hopes, which in some cases were fulfilled. In the spring
Chicago socialists increased their vote from 12 to 14 per cent of the
total and elected two aldermen. In the fall elections New York
socialists, enthusiastically aided by a few trade unions, polled 4,000
votes, and St. Louis socialists elected three members to the state
legislature. In Chicago the party elected three assemblymen and a
state senator in the fall, and three more aldermen in the following
spring. But this was the high tide of the political movement. Trade
unionists remained unreconciled, and during 1879 their discontent
grew bitter. Refusal of the political faction to permit formation of
military clubs, a drop of 60 per cent in the socialist vote in the Chicago
elections in the fall of 1879, and the return of prosperity in 1879 with
its accompanying trend toward economic action contributed to the
dissatisfaction.

Trade-unionist discontent came to a head after the presidential
election of 1880. The party high command decided to cooperate with
the Greenbackers, and named forty-four socialists as delegates to the
Greenback convention held at Chicago in the spring. The socialists
urged the convention to adopt a plank which declared land, light,
air, and water to be the "free gifts" of nature to all mankind and condemned any attempt to monopolize these gifts as detrimental to the
rights of men. Although the Greenbackers refused to adopt this plank
except as a "special resolution" after the platform had been formu-

lated, the socialist delegates endorsed the Greenback candidates, Weaver and Chambers, and called upon the party to support them. The act shattered the socialist movement. German and Scandinavian sections in Chicago, convinced that the action of the Chicago municipal council which had unseated a socialist elected in the spring of 1880 was perfect proof of the futility of political action, demanded a repudiation of the alliance with the Greenbackers. From New York where German refugees were joining the Socialist Labour party in large numbers came similar demands. Lawrence and New Orleans sections refused to support the Greenback candidates. In several cities two socialist tickets appeared.

Immediately after the election the Socialist Labour party divided into several factions. The English-speaking, politically inclined elements in general remained loyal to the old organization, but by 1883 the party was reduced to 1,500 members. Most of the former party members turned to anarcho-syndicalism. The movement had two different bases. In Chicago it arose among the trade-unionist element which urged the creation of military organizations to offer "armed resistance to the . . . capitalist class and capitalist legislatures." In New York and Philadelphia it developed among German refugees who seceded from the party to form social revolutionary clubs. Reform by force was their aim. In 1881 the New York clubs affiliated with the International Working People's Association—the Black International—which had been formed by European anarchists in London. Inevitably the Chicago, New York, and Philadelphia groups moved toward a national organization. At a convention held at Chicago in October, 1881, they became the Revolutionary Socialist party and endorsed the aims of the Black International. The convention rejected political action, endorsed trade unionism, and approved societies which stood "ready to render armed resistance to encroachments upon the rights of the workingmen."

Divergent tendencies appeared almost immediately. In 1882 eastern elements acquired a new leader in Johann Möst, who envisioned a society in which the state would be replaced by an agglomeration of loosely federated producer groups connected by trade agreements. He was a believer in "propaganda by deed"—execution of the capitalists and seizure of their goods. Western elements on the other hand were becoming more and more trade-union conscious. They argued that a strong trade-union movement was a prerequisite to the seizure of the state and the establishment of a "workers commonwealth." A compromise solution was adopted at the Pittsburgh congress, held in October, 1883. The platform, known as the Pittsburgh Manifesto, announced that Revolutionary Socialists regarded trade unions as the foundations of future society. It denounced political action as futile and condemned the state, the church, and the school system as obstacles to the amelioration of the miserable conditions of the working classes. In addition it published aims: establishment of a free society based upon cooperative organization of production; "free exchange of . . . products . . . between the productive organizations without . . . profit"; and regulation of all public affairs by "free contracts between the autonomous . . . associations, resting on a federalistic basis." All these objectives were to be accomplished by force.

The Pittsburgh Manifesto did not entirely unite the Revolutionary Socialists. Differences of attitude concerning the techniques to be employed continued to divide the organization. In New York and the East where Johann Möst dominated, the movement, scorning action through trade unions, remained purely anarchistic. In Chicago trade unionism and anarchism were combined to form something resembling syndicalism. The Chicago wing planned to infiltrate the trades and support them in all their "direct struggles" to obtain such remuneration as would enable workers "to live like human beings should live." But it also planned to educate the trades to work for the overthrow of capitalism and the establishment of cooperative producers' organizations. Of all socialistic groups it was this Chicago syndicalist element which was to have the greatest effect upon the labor world in the eighties.

A second rival of the Knights for leadership of the labor world in the postdepression years was the International Labor Union. The organization, created in 1878, was a product of trade-union socialists like McDonnell, Sorge, and Douai, who had seceded from the party after the Newark convention, and such predepression eight-hour advocates as Ira Steward. The socialists hoped to build a trade-union movement which would turn political at the appropriate moment, secure control of the government, abolish the wage system and set up a cooperative industrial society. The eight-hour group hoped to secure a reform in the wage system through a gradual reduction of hours—

a reform which would inevitably create a cooperative industrial society. At its inception the I.L.U. aimed at organizing all working-men, regardless of calling, into trade unions. Its membership grew slowly until late in 1878 when it helped to organize the victorious strikes of textile workers in Paterson and Fall River. Victory not only increased membership to some eight thousand; it also worked a subtle change in objectives. The I.L.U. now became a movement to organize unskilled workers only. That aim was never accomplished. In 1879 the organization became involved in a number of strikes in the textile industry—the most important occurring at Passaic, New Jersey, and at Clinton and Cohoes, New York. While a few of these ended in victory, the majority of them brought defeat. Membership began to decline; by 1881 the organization was reduced to a single branch at Hoboken.

More important than the socialists or the I.L.U. as rivals of the Knights was the revived "pure and simple" trade-union movement. The revival was paced by Adolph Strasser and Samuel Gompers of the Cigarmakers' Union. Strasser had been a socialist; he had helped organize both the Social Democratic and the Socialist Labour parties, but he ultimately became convinced that socialism was unfeasible in the United States. In 1877 he became president of the Cigarmakers' Union. Gompers, born in England of Dutch-Jewish parents, had come to America at the age of thirteen. Never himself a socialist, he was friendly with a number of them. In 1875 he became head of the cigarmakers' largest affiliate—Local 144 in New York City. Neither Strasser nor Gompers revealed much concern over the condition of the cigarmakers' organization before 1877. Like other trades the union suffered a large loss of membership during the depression; it also suffered from the introduction of machinery and the gradual adoption of the tenement-house system of production.

After the failure of the 1877 strike in New York City, Strasser and Gompers began to act, leading a movement which culminated at the national convention in 1879 when the cigarmakers adopted the British trade-union system as a pattern. The change granted complete authority over local unions to the national association, provided for an increase in membership dues for the purpose of building up a large financial reserve and for "equalization of funds" whereby a strong local was forced to transfer a portion of its treasury to a weak local.

It also provided for a system of sick and death benefits and a plan for lending money to members searching for work. In addition the organization adopted a philosophy of pure "wage consciousness." Its aims were to be practical and immediate.

While the cigarmakers were being reorganized, prosperity returned and the trade-union movement revived. As in previous periods, revival began on a local scale. There were 2,440 locals in existence by 1880. The old city federations—known variously at this period as trades councils, amalgamated trade and labor unions, and trade assemblies—also reappeared and promptly reassumed their old functions: granting financial assistance during strikes, acting as mediation agencies, and leading boycott movements that began on a large scale in 1883. Many of them became pressure groups seeking legislation favorable to labor. The national associations also revived; nearly thirty existed by 1883. In general these associations resembled the nationals of the sixties. Aside from the cigarmakers, only four established benefit features, and none established national control of locals.

Strikes to achieve higher wages constituted the chief activities of the revived trade unions. Most notable was that of 35,000 men led by the Amalgamated Association of Iron and Steel Workers against 116 iron mills in Pennsylvania, West Virginia, Ohio, Indiana, Illinois, and Wisconsin in 1882. Most strikes ended in defeat. Some trades also used the boycott. Perhaps the most significant was that initiated by Typographical Union 6 of New York in late 1883 against the New York *Tribune* because of the discharge of some union men contrary to agreement. The boycott became a factor in the presidential campaign of 1884 when the union publicly opposed the election of the Republican candidate, James G. Blaine, because the Republican party had refused to repudiate the *Tribune* as a party organ. Blaine lost New York by less than 1,150 votes, and thereby lost the election.

Growth in membership of trade unions in the postdepression period was well illustrated in a few trades. The bricklayers increased from 300 to 9,000 between 1880 and 1883; printers from 6,500 to 13,000; cigarmakers from 4,400 to 13,000. By 1883 total trade-union membership was about 200,000: one-half were affiliated with nationals. A characteristic that distinguished this membership from that of the past was the marked predominance of foreign-born elements. The situation in Illinois in 1885 was typical: 21 per cent were American,

10 per cent British, 19 per cent Irish, 33 per cent German, 12 per cent Scandinavian, 5 per cent Poles, Czechs, and Italians.

Not long after the depression lifted, trade unionists once more began to consider the creation of a national organization. The initiative was taken by a group of disaffected Knights from Indiana who joined with the Terre Haute Amalgamated Labor Union in calling a conference in August, 1881. Only a few persons attended—Greenbackers, delegates from trade assemblies, among them the ex-socialist P. J. McGuire, and delegates from three nationals. The conference in turn called another meeting at Pittsburgh for November, 1881. More than a hundred attended from eight nationals, eleven city federations, forty-two craft locals, three district assemblies, and forty-six local assemblies. Of the nationals the Iron and Steel Workers, Cigarmakers, Coopers, Granite Cutters, Printers, Cotton and Wool Spinners, Lake Seamen, and German Printers sent delegates.

After some argument between the nationals and the Knights, the organization adopted the name Federation of Organized Trades and Labor Unions of the United States and Canada. The title was intended to exclude political labor organizations but to include both skilled and unskilled labor. The constitution, however, plainly intended to give control to the skilled element. It provided for the election of a legislative committee of five to act as executive, and an annual convention at which the nationals would receive one vote for each 1,000 members, 2 votes for 4,000 members, three votes for 8,000 members; local trade councils or assemblies were given one vote each, regardless of their size.

The organization declared it would encourage the formation of trade and labor unions on a local and national scale, and seek "to secure legislation favorable to the interests of the industrial classes." The legislative program contained most of the typical demands of labor in the eighties: legal incorporation of trade unions—in order to remove labor organizations from the operation of state conspiracy laws, to protect funds, and to encourge arbitration; adoption of uniform apprenticeship regulations; establishment of a national bureau of labor statistics; enforcement of the Federal eight-hour law; abolition of the convict labor system and of the "truck" system of paying wages; prohibition of the importation of foreign labor under contract; total exclusion of Chinese; perfected mechanics' lien laws;

legislation for the inspection and ventilation of mines, factories and workshops; laws making employers responsible for industrial accidents; compulsory education for children; laws prohibiting the labor of children under fourteen; abolition of conspiracy laws as applied to labor; and a protective tariff. To secure this program it was recommended that "all trades and labor organizations . . . secure proper representation in all law-making bodies by means of the ballot."

The F.O.O.T.A.L.U. was hardly a successful organization. Only nineteen delegates attended the second meeting; the Knights and steelworkers both absented themselves. Although an attempt was made to increase interest by inviting all state federations, district assemblies, locals, and women's trade unions to send delegates, the third convention, held in 1883, was sparsely attended. Even the interest of the nationals which sent delegates was only halfhearted, a fact indicated by the small contributions they made to the treasury. But successful or not the organization of the F.O.O.T.A.L.U. added a right wing to the labor movement of the early eighties. It was not yet a "pure and simple" trade-union organization, but it was a long step in that direction. While it invited the unskilled to join and laid emphasis upon political action to secure legislative aims, it had sloughed off most of the "visionary" principles advanced by the National Labor Union and the Knights, and its platform contained demands for legislation of immediate benefit to labor. In 1884 total membership of the organization was unknown. Judging by the state of the treasury, members could not have numbered more than 25,000. But there were probably another 200,000 trade unionists who were potential members.

When the year 1884 began, labor, as has been indicated, was not a united force. On the left were the socialists; the middle road was held by the Knights; the right was shared by the F.O.O.T.A.L.U. and the independent trade unions. There was disagreement over methods. Socialists were divided between trade unionists, advocates of political action, and advocates of violence; the Knights fostered the "one big union"; the trades were vacillating between economic and legislative action. There was no unity of aim. While most labor organizations advanced similar platforms, the socialists looked to the ultimate overthrow of the capitalistic order; the Knights looked to the destruction of the wage system and the eventual establishment of a "cooperative" economic system which included both owners and laborers; the trades were becoming more and more conscious of the magical quality of high wages to solve all their troubles.

Despite this division, the postwar labor movement came to a climax in the years 1884–1886. New economic conditions, an industrial depression, the Knights, the F.O.O.T.A.L.U., and the anarcho-syndicalists were all involved. The new economic conditions of the early eighties were a culmination of long-term developments. In the fifteen years after the Civil War some 41,000 miles of branch and transcontinental railway lines were laid down. This construction created vast new markets for industry—in small towns, on the farms, and in the West—and ensured the triumph of the factory system. To meet the growing demands manufacturers sank more and more of their capital into machinery.

Neither development boded much good for labor. Expansion of the market brought town mechanics into competition with the factory and forced their wages downward. Expansion of the market also produced new marketing methods. The wholesale jobber, a figure comparable to the merchant-capitalist of earlier days, appeared on the scene to capture the market through traveling agents and advertising. The manufacturer with his capital, credit, and energy tied up in buildings, machinery, and production problems found himself unable to compete. He had the choice of becoming a producer for the jobber or of forming combinations with others in the same industry. In either case labor suffered. If manufacturers became jobber-producers, their gross returns were restricted by contract and their net profits depended upon how much they could deny their labor force. If manufacturers formed industrial pools there was always the danger that such combinations would disintegrate, making for instability and insecurity, periods of high and low employment.

Meanwhile the use of machinery increased the use of the semiskilled and unskilled. By 1886 it was estimated that 65 to 75 per cent of the labor population belonged to these groups. They came from the farm and from Europe. The long depression of 1873, high interest rates on mortgages, high railway rates, poor crops, and low prices forced hundreds of thousands of farmers into the cities. Poor economic conditions in Europe and the recruiting activities of American railroads and industrialists in European villages induced 8,000,000 aliens to migrate to America between 1870 and 1890. The domination of industry by the semiskilled and unskilled workers, weak in bargaining power because they were so easily replaced, also depressed wages.

Fundamentally, therefore, the economic condition of labor in the early eighties was poor, and the depression of 1883 made its condition worse. Although not too much unemployment developed—only about 7½ per cent of the labor force—wages dropped drastically. In 1884 the average cut was 15 per cent; in 1885 the cuts were even deeper. Chief sufferers were the unorganized semiskilled and unskilled workers. Among them a vast and bitter discontent soon appeared, a discontent ripe for eruption.

One early result of the depression was to advance the Knight's cooperative ventures. While leaders of the order, like Powderly, Charles Litchman, and Ralph Beaumont, had always envisioned the establishment of producers' cooperatives as the ultimate method of emancipating labor from the wage system, it was not until 1882, when the Knights decided that their productive enterprises would be centrally controlled, that they took any positive steps toward their goal. At this point the membership still revealed little enthusiasm; but when the full impact of the depression began to be felt, sentiment changed rapidly. Enthusiasm for cooperative ventures developed particularly among the small-town mechanics, shopkeepers, small employers, and farmers. A General Cooperative Board, headed by John Samuel, took upon itself the task of educating members to the dangers and pitfalls involved, of issuing instructions concerning management and credit, and of recommending financial aid. Between 1884 and 1886 at least 135 producers' cooperatives were established. Most of them were conducted on a small scale with an estimated $10,000 investment per unit. Most of the establishments were in the East and Midwest; fifty-one of them were set up in the mining, cooperage, and shoe industries.

More significant than the Knights' cooperative movement was the great wave of strikes that swept through the nation early in 1884. For the most part intended to maintain wage levels, the strikes involved all elements: skilled and unskilled, native and foreign, organized, unorganized, and disorganized. Like the strikes of the seventies they met with bitter opposition: Pinkertons, imported strikebreakers, militia, black lists, and yellow-dog contracts were used to defeat them.

Most famous of the strikes were those conducted by the Fall River spinners, which affected some five thousand men and which was beaten by the importation of Swedish strikebreakers; by New York City plumbers, bricklayers, and stonecutters; by Albany and Troy stove molders, which lasted some five months; by Buffalo bricklayers and longshoremen; by Philadelphia carpet weavers and shoemakers; by the Pittsburgh and Cincinnati molders; by the Cincinnati cigarmakers, which produced a thirteen-month lockout; and by the Hocking Valley coal miners, which involved four thousand men and which was defeated by Pinkertons and state militia.

Toward the end of 1884 labor took up the boycott. There were about thirty boycotts in 1884 and nearly two hundred in 1885. Indeed, the number of products which labor was not supposed to purchase became so large that a correspondent of *John Swinton's Paper* complained that "to be a sincere and systematic boycotter . . . requires the carrying about of a catalogue of the different boycotted forms or articles; and, if you have a family, another catalogue is required for their use." How these boycotts worked was well illustrated by the one conducted against Berg's hat factory in Orange, New Jersey. The boycotting union had matters so thoroughly under control that local brewers refused to furnish beer to saloons which sold drinks to the strikebreakers employed in Berg's factory, and one local hat manufacturer discharged a man because he lived with a brother employed by Berg. A large proportion of the boycotts were successful.

In the last half of 1885 another strike wave developed. Again all types of labor participated. The bricklayers of New York City; street railway workers in New York, Chicago, and St. Louis; quarrymen at Lemont and Joliet, Illinois; and lumbermen in Michigan's Saginaw Valley conducted strikes that received national attention.

The most significant strikes of the year were conducted by the Knights upon the railroads. There were two strikes upon the Union Pacific Railway in 1884 which set the scene. The first began in May when the shopmen in Denver struck to protest a 10 per cent wage cut. Joseph Buchanan, a prominent Knight, stepped in as organizer, and in less than two days every shop on the road from Omaha to Denver joined the strike; Union Pacific officials promptly rescinded the wage cut. Three months later when the company ordered a reduction in the wages of a group of machinists in Kansas and discharged a score of men in Denver, the railway workers tied up the line and the company surrendered again. The major result of these strikes was a large amount of favorable publicity for the Knights among the railway workers which paid dividends the next year. In February and March, 1885, railway workers on three of Jay Gould's lines—the Wabash, Missouri-Kansas and Texas, and the Missouri Pacific— went on strike to protest a 10 per cent wage cut. Buchanan took over the job of organization and success was immediate; the companies rescinded the wage cut. Five months later the Wabash, now in the hands of a receiver, began a campaign to destroy the newly formed organization by discharging men active in local assemblies. The Executive Board of the Knights, after making an attempt to settle the matter by arbitration, issued an order to "all assemblies on the Union Pacific and Gould's Southwestern system" instructing them to "refuse to repair or handle in any manner" the rolling stock of the Wabash railway. The order, which would have affected twenty thousand miles of rails, was never carried out. Jay Gould could not risk a strike at this stage of his fortunes; his pressure upon the receivers and management of the Wabash and the Missouri Pacific resulted in a complete victory for the Knights.

The Gould strikes made the Knights the undisputed leaders of the labor movement. While their membership and influence had been growing steadily through those years, occasioned largely by the assistance the Knights had given the unorganized, the growth had been slow. The Gould strikes completely changed the pace. Labor at last had found an organization capable of wringing concessions from employers. All the bitterness and resentment which had accumulated among workingmen during two years of depression, all the frustration produced by wage cuts, all the fury created by employer use of Pinkertons, black lists, and yellow-dog contracts suddenly burst forth to create a wild rush to join the ranks of the Knights of Labor. Almost overnight the membership of the order doubled and redoubled. In July, 1885, the Knights had 104,000 members; one year later they boasted 703,000 members.

The emergence of the Knights as the nation's leading labor organization was soon mirrored in the newspapers. Strikes conducted by the Knights and the statements of leaders received front-page attention. Feature stories on the purposes and strength of the order were given much space; most commonly circulated was an article which described the Knights as an organization led by five men who "can stay the nimble touch of almost every telegraph operator, can shut up most of the mills and factories, and can disable the railroads." Politicians, both state and Federal, quickly recognized that the Knights had to be propitiated and that failure to do so would cost many of them their legislative seats. Urged on by the lobbyists of the order in state capitals and in Washington, they hastened to take up the problems of convict labor, immigrant labor, and bureaus of labor statistics.

The convict labor issue, a minor one in the antebellum period, had become a major one after the Civil War. Spread of the system through most of the states and the use of machinery in prisons made convicts, producing goods for commercial markets at low wages, a threat to labor welfare. In each of the depressions following the Civil War, labor organizations had demanded abolition of the system. Between 1883 and 1886 Democratic legislatures in Massachusetts, New York, Pennsylvania, and Ohio, and Republican legislatures in New Jersey and Indiana passed anticonvict labor laws. In 1887 the Federal Government put an end to the practice of contracting Federal criminals. Once started the movement spread rapidly. In the late eighties and nineties Massachusetts, New York, and Pennsylvania abolished the use of machinery; Indiana, Minnesota, and Iowa abolished their contract systems; the Omnibus States entered the Union with constitutional limitations or prohibitions upon contract labor by convicts; Connecticut, Colorado, and other states placed severe restrictions upon use of convicts to manufacture goods for sale. By 1900 only the South was still resisting the trend.

The immigrant labor issue developed out of the fact that repeal of the Immigration Act of 1864 had not ended the problem of imported contract labor. Railroads and industrialists continued to hire imported Europeans all through the depression of 1873 and in the eighties. Labor became acutely conscious of the problem when it learned that Swedes had been brought in to break the Fall River spinners' strike, and that thousands of Italians, Hungarians, Slovaks, and Poles had been imported to construct the Nickel Plate and various southern railroads and for use in the coke-making, coal-mining, iron, and glass-blowing industries. In 1884 John A. Foran, former president of the

Coopers, now a Congressman from Cleveland, introduced a bill to prohibit completely the importation of alien labor under contract. A number of the leaders of the Knights of Labor testified for the measure. It became law in February, 1885. The act proved unenforceable and had to be amended in 1887 and several times in the twentieth century, but it was, like the convict labor laws, a tribute to the power of the Knights.

The problem of bureaus of labor statistics, demanded by labor so that it could secure information upon which it could act intelligently, had been raised originally by the trades and the N.L.U. Except in Massachusetts the demand had been ignored until the Knights, who regarded the establishment of the bureaus as the foundation of their educational program, pressed it upon legislators. Congress gave national sanction to the movement with the establishment of a Bureau of Labor in 1884. Maine, New York, New Jersey, Pennsylvania, Ohio, Michigan, and Illinois added bureaus to their administrative machinery during the eighties. By the turn of the century thirty states had set up similar agencies, marking the first steps on the part of the Federal and state governments to grant labor the same recognition as business and agriculture.

The growth of the Knights and the immense prestige that the order acquired in the years 1884–1885 were not accepted sympathetically by all labor. Leaders of the F.O.O.T.A.L.U., who recognized the stagnation of their own organization, looked upon the rise of the order with considerable dismay. Accordingly, the F.O.O.T.A.L.U. convention of October, 1884, determined to make a new bid for leadership by inaugurating a national movement for an eight-hour day. The convention invited the Knights to cooperate. The move brought few results during its first year. The Knights did not respond; they were busy organizing the masses entering the order. Nevertheless, the F.O.O.T.A.L.U. renewed its efforts in October, 1885. It set May 1, 1886, as the deadline for its campaign. On that day a general strike would be called if the eight-hour day had not been granted to all labor.

This time the response was more gratifying. The leadership of the Knights frowned upon the movement; in March, 1886, Powderly issued a secret circular advising the Knights to stay out of the eight-hour movement. But if the leadership of the order was unfavorably inclined, the rank and file threw itself headlong into the campaign. Several circumstances were involved. The mobs of laboring men who entered the order in the year 1885 were primarily unskilled. Neglected and downtrodden for decades, their rush to join the Knights was essentially a reaction against long oppression and degradation. Among this faction two elementary passions developed: an attitude of "give no quarter" and a fierce desire to express the power they felt in their alliance with the Knights of Labor—the great unconquered champion of the underdog. The eight-hour movement was their answer; they seized upon it eagerly as the first issue upon which the battle with employers would be fought.

The Knights' rank and file lost its battle. The forecast of defeat came in a new strike upon Gould's Southwestern Railway system in March, 1886, when railroad officials discharged a Knight in Marshall, Texas. Charging discrimination the Gould employees dropped their tools and paralyzed five thousand miles of railroads in Missouri, Kansas, Nebraska, Arkansas, Texas, and in Indian Territory. Nine thousand men took part; even the engineers, firemen, conductors, and brakemen were forced off the job. Although Powderly and Gould made an effort to arbitrate, the strikers, influenced by the prevailing "give no quarter" sentiment, refused to make any concessions. The strike dragged on for two months, punctuated by hundreds of acts of violence, and finally spent itself early in May.

As the Southwestern strike ended, the long-awaited general strike for the eight-hour day began. It proved a disappointment. While strikes occurred in every industrial center of the nation, they were on a far smaller scale than had been expected. The Knights failed to participate; Powderly's secret circular, ignored for months, stopped cooperation in the campaign at the critical moment. Employers also helped draw much of the energy from the campaign by granting shorter hours to 150,000 workingmen at the last moment. The strike became a trade-union movement; only 190,000 participated. Only 40,000 of those who went on strike secured their hour demands in whole or in part. Of all laboring elements who benefited, only 15,000 retained their gains by the end of the year. The eight-hour movement was essentially a failure.

In the midst of the general strike labor received a setback in Chicago which was to retard its development for decades. It was the anarcho-syndicalists who were largely responsible. That element which had made little impact upon Chicago in the prosperous years immediately after the Pittsburgh convention leaped into prominence during the depression. They set up a newspaper, edited by Albert R. Parsons, in September, 1884, and went to work upon the vast army of unemployed. At the time the Black International had a membership of about one thousand in the city—almost entirely foreign born. Parsons found a way to appeal to American-born workingmen; within a year the size of the International doubled in Chicago.

Meanwhile the anarcho-syndicalists went to work upon the trade unions. In February, 1884, they persuaded the Progressive Cigar-makers' Union, a breakoff from the Strasser-Gompers organization, to create a Central Labor Union which had as its object the "eman-cipation of mankind" through "the open rebellion of the robbed classes," and appealed to the trade unionists of the city, then affili-ated with the Amalgamated Trades and Labor Assembly, to join them in their fight to advance "progressive" principles. For the next eighteen months the Central and the Amalgamated conducted a bitter fight for control of Chicago's trade unions; the Central won the early rounds of the contest: by April, 1886, twenty-two unions—including the eleven largest in the city—had joined it. This success prodded the Amalgamated into action. Since the Central had taken up the eight-hour issue, the Amalgamated formed the Eight-Hour Association made up of its own trades, the Socialist Labour party, and the Knights. Chicago became a beehive of eight-hour activity. On May 1st some 80,000 men went on strike. As the largest turnout in the nation it should have been successful, but its potentialities were destroyed by the events at the McCormick Harvester Works.

There had been labor trouble at the McCormick plant on the out-skirts of Chicago for weeks before the general strike. It had begun with a lockout of lumber shavers. In the weeks following, anarcho-syndicalists took a prominent part in promoting solidarity among the locked-out workingmen. Two days after the general strike began, a large group of lumber shavers held a pep meeting near the McCor-mick plant. August Spies, a syndicalist, was addressing them when the work shift ended, and strikebreakers began to stream out of the gates. A wild mêlée followed. In the midst of it the police arrived, shooting. Four men were killed and many others were injured. Spies, who witnessed the whole incident from the speaker's stand, was horrified. Burning with indignation he rushed home to compose what became known as the "Revenge Circular." It summoned workingmen to "arm" themselves and appear "in full force" at a protest meeting to be held in Haymarket Square the following evening.

About three thousand people braved unusually cold and violent weather to gather in the square on the night of May 4th. It was a peaceful meeting, addressed in turn by Spies, Parsons, and Samuel Fielden—all anarcho-syndicalists. Their remarks were temperate; their demand was for legal redress. After several hours of oratory, the crowd began to disperse; Mayor Carter H. Harrison, who had attended to see that order was maintained, departed between ten and eleven o'clock, certain that no problems would arise. On his way home he stopped at the nearest police station, where a riot squad had been made ready, and instructed the precinct captain, John Bonfield, to discharge his reserves for the night. Instead, Bonfield sent his squad to the meeting. Fielden was speaking when the police arrived, and Captain Ward in charge of the squad ordered the meeting to disperse. Fielden protested and began to argue with Ward. In the midst of the argument a bomb exploded; a police sergeant, M. J. Degan, was killed and about sixty other policemen were knocked down. The police immediately opened fire; the fire was returned and Haymarket Square became a bloody shambles. About ten people were killed and another fifty were injured.

Chicago's citizenry and newspapers, already in the grip of a deep terror produced by the agitation of the eight-hour issue, demanded summary revenge. The police dragged in eight "anarchists"—Spies, Michael Schwab, Fielden, Parsons, Adolph Fischer, George Engel, Louis Lingg, and Oscar Neebe—and charged them with the murder of Sergeant Degan. Their trial, which occurred in June, 1886, was a farce. The jury panel was summoned by a special bailiff instead of being taken from a box containing a hundred names; men who admitted that they were prejudiced against the defendants were admitted to service. No proof was offered that any of the indicted men had thrown or planted the bomb; in fact, only three of the men had been present—Spies, Parsons, and Fielden. No proof was offered that the speakers had incited violence—Mayor Harrison described the speeches as "tame." No proof was offered that violence had been contemplated—Parsons, in fact, had brought his wife and child to the meeting.

But the eight men were convicted because "they had generally by speech and print advised large classes to commit murder and had left the commission, the time, place, and when to the individual will, whim or caprice . . . of each individual man who listened to their advice." Seven of the men received the death sentence; Neebe received fifteen years. Spies, Parsons, Fischer, and Engel were executed in November, 1887; Lingg committed suicide. Schwab and Fielden appealed to the governor for clemency and their sentences were commuted to life imprisonment. Six years later Governor John P. Altgeld reversed the record and granted unconditional pardons to the survivors.

12 ——

The End of an Era

In the public mind the Haymarket affair was a climax to ten years of labor violence. The Molly Maguire Riots and the Railway Strike of 1877 had produced the impression that the nation's labor elements were inherently criminal in character: inclined to riot, arson, pillage, assault, and murder. The Kearney episode in California; the noisy, strike-studded organizing campaign of the Knights; and the Gould-Southwestern strikes had confirmed the impression and had terrified a large portion of the nation. The Haymarket affair, which accented anarcho-syndicalist principles, drove the terror deeper into the nation's mentality and turned it into hysteria. A violent antilabor campaign followed. Fear-gripped state legislatures rushed laws curbing freedom of action of labor organizations onto the statute books. The courts began to convict union members of conspiracy, intimidation, and rioting in wholesale lots. Employers, taking advantage of the situation, instituted widespread antiunion campaigns, with Pinkertons, lockouts, black lists, and yellow-dog contracts as their chief weapons.

Labor's response to this attack was almost instinctive: it turned to independent politics for protection. Its movement, known as the United Front campaign, was paced by a New York City organization which called itself the Central Labor Union. Formed in 1882 by delegates from fourteen trade unions, it helped run the famous freight handlers' strike of 1882 and, upon the motion of P. J. McGuire, created "Labor Day." Between 1883 and 1886 the Central, which enjoyed friendly relations with the Knights, earned a wide reputation for its vigorous support of various boycott campaigns. One of the boycotts attracted nation-wide attention and led directly to the political upheaval of 1886. It was begun in March, 1886, by the Carl Sahm Club, a musicians' local affiliated with the Knights' District Assembly 49, and was aimed at George Thiess, beer- and music-hall proprietor. The boycott lasted for months, until a brewer and a baker who supplied Thiess with beer and bread mediated a settlement; the near bankrupt Thiess paid $1,000 to cover expenses. Shortly after, Thiess brought suit against the five-man committee of the Central Labor Union with whom the settlement had been made, charging intimidation and extortion. The court agreed that the picketing conducted by the Central Labor Union was intimidating and that the $1,000 settlement was extortion under the state's penal code.

The decision, coming at a time when labor was already alarmed over the antilabor campaign that followed the Haymarket riot, produced a political upheaval. The Central Labor Union invited all labor-reform organizations, labor unions, Knights, Greenbackers, antimonopolists, socialists, and land reformers to a conference at Clarendon Hall; some 400 worried delegates from 165 organizations attended. The conference decided that the time had come to take independent political action for labor's protection in the coming mayoralty campaign. Adopting the name Progressive Democracy, it nominated Henry George, father of the single tax, as its candidate. George, whose intellectual followers numbered thousands in the nation's industrial areas, and who was exceedingly popular among Irish labor elements because of his efforts on behalf of Irish relief, was permitted to write his own platform. Labor aims were compressed into one plank which demanded a reform in court procedure so that the practice of "drawing grand jurors from one class should cease, and the requirements of a property qualification for trial jurors should be abolished," demanded also the enforcement of the laws for the safety and the sanitary inspection of buildings, abolition of contract labor on public works, and equal pay for equal work. The rest of the platform was an exposition of the single tax as a cure for all the ills of society.

All labor organizations in New York City and a large number of intellectuals endorsed George's candidacy; even Powderly and Gompers extended their support. The regular parties ignored the new movement at first. Both had strong candidates—Abram S. Hewitt, an iron manufacturer, for the Democrats and Theodore Roosevelt for the Republicans—and they had all the daily papers in the city on their side. But it quickly became clear that the labor upheaval could not be brushed aside. Democrats, Republicans, and their journalistic allies proceeded to heap revilement on George whom they described as an "apostle of anarchy and destruction." Even the Roman Catholic Church became involved. One of its priests, Father McGlynn, who was extremely popular among New York Catholics, supported George's candidacy, and the Church through Thomas S. Preston, vicar-general, was moved to condemnation.

When the official returns were counted, Hewitt had 90,000 votes, George 68,000, and Roosevelt 60,000. Labor hailed the results as a great victory, and the city's editorial writers agreed. The state legislature immediately reacted with a number of new labor laws. It created a board of mediation and arbitration; provided for the labeling of convict-made goods; established a ten-hour day for children under fourteen and for women; and a ten-hour day for labor on street, surface, and elevated railways; amended the penal code to prohibit employers from coercing employees who joined a labor organization; and established a tenement-house code. New York City labor began to anticipate further successes.

But shortly after the election a cleavage developed between single taxers and socialists. The single taxers, supported by Father McGlynn, the intellectuals, the Irish, and the non-German trade unions, were intent upon a movement of all producing classes; the socialists, supported by the German trade unions, were looking toward a movement of laboring men which would eventually work for the socialistic system. Although both sides recognized these dissident aims and tried to prevent an open break, a split was inevitable. In August, 1887, the organization, now established throughout the state and calling itself the United Labor party, ousted the socialists on the ground that they had not conformed to a rule requiring severance of all connections with other political parties. After the break the party nominated a ticket for five state offices, headed by Henry George as the candidate for secretary of state. The socialists, meanwhile, organized the Progressive Labor party and wrote a platform demanding a reduction of hours; abolition of child and convict labor; sanitary inspection of buildings, factories, and mines; and abolition of conspiracy laws.

Election returns disappointed both parties. The United Labor party secured 72,000 votes in the state, 37,000 from New York City. The Progressive Labor party received only 5,000 votes in the state. A number of factors contributed to the decline: the return of prosperity and the spate of laws passed by the legislature the previous winter which allayed a certain amount of discontent; the excommunication of Father McGlynn which caused many Irishmen to drift back to Tammany; and the failure of the Knights to give the movement any aid.

The political movement of labor in New York City in 1886–1887 was not an isolated event; the antilabor campaign following the Haymarket riots produced a similar upheaval in scores of other industrial centers. The same elements participated: Knights, trade unionists, socialists, single taxers. In the areas west of the Wabash River the movement was frequently joined by agrarian organizations as well. The platforms were remarkably similar. The greatest attention was given to the same labor demands which had been incorporated into the program of the New York movement.

In 1886 this movement outside New York brought happy results. Labor tickets won municipal elections in Lynn, Rutland, Naugatuck, and South Norwalk in New England. A labor man won an assembly seat in Newark. A labor movement carried the municipal elections in Richmond, Virginia, and Key West, Florida. In Chicago the Central Labor Union, the Amalgamated, the Knights, socialists, and single taxers created the United Labor party in the summer of 1886 and elected a state senator and six assemblymen. In Milwaukee a farmer-labor coalition elected a congressman, a state senator, and six assemblymen. In Leadville, Colorado, the Knights elected a state senator and three legislators. Coalitions developed in several areas. In Massachusetts, Connecticut, upstate New York, and Paterson, New Jersey, labor men won assembly races on the Democratic ticket. In Cleveland Martin A. Foran was reelected to Congress on the same ticket. In St. Louis two Knights won election to the legislature as Republicans. The total effect of the upheaval in 1886 was one of victory.

The spring elections of 1887 seemed to bear out the promise of the previous year. In Chicago the United Labor party named Robert Nelson, head of the Knights' District Assembly 24, as its candidate for mayor and polled better than 25,000 out of 77,000 votes cast against a Democratic-Republican coalition. Labor tickets carried local elections in nineteen midwestern communities. But the spring election of 1887 marked the climax of the movement. The same forces that destroyed the movement in New York City appeared in other industrial centers. Joseph Buchanan described the situation well when he declared: "Men representing a dozen different shades of opinion . . . come together ostensibly to pool their issues and amalgamate the elements variously represented. When they . . . come to write the 'union' platform . . . each claimed that he had the cure-all. . . . The upshot of the business has been a few truces, and the stronger faction has written the platform, while the rest have gone home sore-headed." Everywhere the movement split into two wings—conservative and socialist. In most places the conservative wing captured control of the organization, leading to a socialist ouster or secession. In two cities, Philadelphia and Denver, the situation was reversed, but with no better results.

Labor was not yet through with political action. From the start of its political upheaval a movement to form a national farmer-labor party had appeared. In the summer of 1886 the Chicago *Express* issued a call to "Knights of Labor, the Farmers' Alliance . . . Grangers, Greenbackers, [and] Anti-Monopolists" which resulted in a convention at Cincinnati in February, 1887. The meeting, dominated by farmers, was attended by labor leaders from the Midwest. It adopted the name Union Labor party, and wrote a platform copied from the program of the Knights of Labor. Most midwestern labor parties and the socialists merged with the new organization, but Henry George's organization refused to join because the new party would not endorse the single-tax program, and labor parties in Philadelphia, Baltimore, Cincinnati, Milwaukee, and San Francisco gave the movement a cold reception. During most of 1887, therefore, the Union Labor party enjoyed a precarious existence. In the meantime the single taxers, led by Gaybert Barnes and Father McGlynn, developed plans for their own national organization.

In May, 1888, Union Labor and United Labor conventions met at Cincinnati. The simultaneous meetings were called with the obvious intention of merging the two movements. All efforts failed: the stumbling block was the single tax. The two conventions drew up almost identical platforms; the chief difference was a proposal for an income tax in the Union Labor program and a proposal for a single tax in the United Labor program. The Union Labor party nominated Alan J. Streeter, president of the Northern Farmers' Alliance, as its candidate for the Presidency; the United Labor party named Robert H. Cowdrey.

In the campaign of 1888 labor was badly split, reflecting the conditions which had become evident the previous year. Many of the prominent labor leaders worked for the major parties. In most industrial centers, local parties, assemblies, and trade unions, many of which had once affiliated with the Union Labor party, became side shows of the Democratic and Republican organizations. Even the socialists, once so enthusiastically vigorous in their desire to advance a united front, gave no aid. Very early in the campaign the Union Labor efforts focused on the agrarian Mississippi Valley. Only one industrial center, Milwaukee, gave the party real support. The United Labor party never campaigned seriously outside New York. Cowdrey's votes came almost entirely from that state. The last important independent political movement of labor in the nineteenth century had disintegrated.

The political upheaval of labor which followed the Haymarket riot marked the near end of an era in labor history. There were still a few years left, but these were characterized by the slow decline and disappearance of the Knights of Labor. The order emerged from the Haymarket affair seemingly uninjured. It had not taken a major role in the eight-hour strike; it had apparently cleared itself of any complicity in the Haymarket bombing by refusing to aid the defendants on trial. For a short while after Haymarket the membership of the Knights continued to grow. Nevertheless, the Knights soon found themselves under attack because the public decided that the Knights —the noisy, tempestuous, strike-happy Knights—were at the bottom of the whole labor upheaval.

The first of the Knights' ventures to feel the full effect of the post-Haymarket reaction were their cooperative enterprises. In part the very nature of such enterprises worked against them. The successful ventures became joint stock corporations; the wage-earning shareholders became owners and managers hiring labor like any other industrial unit. In part the cooperatives were destroyed by inefficient managers, squabbles among shareholders, lack of capital, and injudicious borrowing of money at high rates of interest. Just as important was the attitude of competitors. Railroads delayed the building of tracks, refused to furnish cars, or refused to haul them. Manufacturers of machinery and producers of raw materials, pressed by private business, refused to sell their products to the cooperative workshops and paralyzed operations. By 1888 none of the order's cooperatives were in existence.

But cooperative enterprises were a small part of the Knights' activities; it was against their power as a labor union that the most bitter war was waged. Leaders of the campaign against them were the employers from whom the order had secured concessions. Shortly after Haymarket, employers once more began to organize into associations which openly and deliberately moved to destroy the order by systematic violation of trade agreements, refusal to arbitrate industrial disputes, and resort to lockouts, black listing, and yellow-dog contracts. Such activity led to some fearsome conflicts. Nearly 100,000 Knights were involved in strikes and lockouts in the latter months of the year 1886. Most important were the lockouts of 15,000 laundry workers at Troy; of 20,000 knitters at Cohoes and Amsterdam, New York; and of 20,000 packing-house workers in Chicago. All were lost—to the great damage of the prestige of the Knights. In 1887 the Knights lost a strike of railway coal handlers—who were joined by longshoremen, boatmen, shovelers, grain handlers, and freight handlers—on the New York waterfront.

The Knights also became involved in an inevitable war with the trade unions. The Knights, essentially more realistic than the trade unionists in their attitude toward the nation's industrial structure, recognized that the factory system had come to stay, and that the majority of workmen, semiskilled and unskilled, were at the mercy of the machine. They worked for the union of all labor elements in order to use the power of the strategically placed skilled workers on behalf of the unskilled. The trades, on the other hand, were more self-centered. For them there was always the hope that they might halt the growing spread of machinery which was destroying their importance, and the fear that unskilled labor, allied to the machine, was a natural enemy. Recognizing their strategic position in industry they sought to take advantage of it by acting without the encumbrance of the unskilled.

During the early eighties these differing attitudes had produced no conflict. Since the skilled element which the Knights attracted were primarily those neglected or deserted by the trades, they did not actively transgress upon the fields which the trades had mapped out for themselves. The F.O.O.T.A.L.U. revealed some covert jealousy, but it was too weak to fight the Knights. Trouble did not arise until 1885 when trade unions began to complain of the Knights' raiding activities. One of these "raids" finally led to open warfare. It began among New York cigarmakers, divided into Local 144 and Progressive Union No. 1. In January, 1886, the New York Cigar Manufacturers Association announced a reduction in wages. Urged by District Assembly 49 and the Central Labor Union, the Progressives refused to accept the change; Local 144 joined them. The manufacturers promptly ordered a lockout which involved ten thousand men. Ultimately the Progressives came to an agreement with the manufacturers. In exchange for the use of the Knights' white label, and permission to use bunching machines, wages were restored. As an aftermath of this settlement the Knights incorporated the Progressive Union into the Order. Local 144 was furious; the Cigarmakers' International promptly began a boycott of all cigars which did not bear their own blue label.

Out of this conflict developed a larger one. Samuel Gompers, head of Local 144, who had long revealed opposition to the Knights, was selected by the cigarmakers to arouse other trades to the threat presented by the Knights and to work for a closer federation of the trades. Gompers's agitation resulted in the foregathering of a large trade-union conference at Philadelphia about two weeks after the Haymarket affair. The strongest trade organizations sent delegates; among those present were W. H. Foster, secretary of the F.O.O.T. A.L.U.; Strasser and Gompers; McGuire of the carpenters; P. J. Fitzpatrick of the iron moulders; Jonah Dyer of the granite cutters; William Weihe of the iron workers; Chris Evans of the miners; and Daniel Boyer of the printers.

The conference quickly revealed its object. While recognizing the "solidarity of all labor interests," it pointed out that the introduction of machinery was reducing the number of the skilled. Accordingly the conference proposed that the Knights and the trade unions should come to an agreement on the following terms: (1) that the Knights should not initiate any person in, or form any assembly in, any trade already organized on a national basis; (2) that the Knights admit no person who worked for less than wages fixed by the trade unions in his craft, or who had scabbed against his craft; (3) that the charter of any assembly of Knights in any trade where a national existed be revoked and the members be requested to join the trade; (4) that any agent of the Knights who tampered with a trade union be dismissed; (5) that no assembly of Knights interfere in any trade union strike or lockout; and (6) that the Knights establish no label in competition with a trade-union label.

No one could have expected the Knights to accept such terms. The General Assembly of the order promptly indicated its belief that "the time [was] approaching, when all who earn their bread by the sweat of their brow shall be enrolled under one general head, as we are controlled by one common law." It recognized that the trade unions contained within their ranks "a very large proportion of laborers of a high grade of skill and intelligence" who could rightfully demand "that excess of compensation paid to skilled above the unskilled labor." But the unskilled laborer had to receive attention, "or in the hour of difficulty the employer will not hesitate to use him to depress the compensation of the skilled." Accordingly the Knights suggested: interchange of working cards, mutual warfare against scabs, adoption of uniform standards of hours and wages in each trade, and joint conferences to bring about cooperation and common action against employers. The counterproposals were categorically rejected by every national trade association to which they were presented.

For several months open war was forestalled by continued negotiations between leaders. But in October, 1886, the Knights met at Richmond and brought the issue to a head by ordering all members who were affiliated with the Cigarmakers' International to withdraw from it or forfeit their membership in the Knights. The resolution may have been the impulse needed to create a new trade-union federation. In December the F.O.O.T.A.L.U. and a general trade-union conference both gathered at Columbus. After the F.O.O.T.A.L.U.'s legislative committee congratulated itself on its leadership of the eight-hour movement, the organization dissolved. The trade-union conference then declared itself to be the first convention of the American Federation of Labor. As such it represented twelve nationals, six trade assemblies, seven locals, and about 140,000 members.

The A.F.L. made one more attempt to negotiate with the Knights and then declared open war. The Knights countered by reorganizing to give craftsmen a preferred position. Basis of the reorganization was the old practice which permitted the formation of trades into local assemblies and district assemblies on a nation-wide scale. While the leaders of the order had frowned upon this custom before Haymarket, their attitude now changed. The rules were amended to permit crafts to form national trade assemblies; all local assemblies made up of a single trade were ordered to withdraw from their district assemblies and to join the national assemblies of their trade as soon as organized. In 1887 twenty-two national assemblies, with a membership of 50,000, sent delegates to the annual convention.

Reorganization did not halt the struggle. The component parts of the Knights and the federation scabbed against each other, invaded each other's territory, encouraged revolt, and eagerly accepted disaffected locals into their own organizations. The tide of battle ran against the Knights. The employers' opposition to the Knights hampered their fighting abilities. The order's uniform lack of strike success after 1886 worked against them. The effort of district assemblies to keep their local assemblies and tradesmen from joining national assemblies alienated many of the skilled. National Assembly 198 composed of patternmakers, foundrymen, blacksmiths, machinists, boilermakers, and their helpers withdrew from the Knights "because the odium which the Order has gained is damaging to us," and formed the National Association of Machinists.

In the meantime the unskilled were forgotten. They had joined the Knights with their hopes at high pitch; to them the events of 1887–1890 were a great psychological shock. Knowledge that Powderly had refused to support either the eight-hour movement of 1884–1886 or the Haymarket anarchists on trial, loss of every industrial conflict in 1886–1887, and total neglect of their welfare in the war with the trades brought deep discouragement and demoralization. The unskilled began to desert the order in hordes.

By July, 1887, the Knights' membership had declined from a high of 700,000 to 510,000. At this point it was not a uniform decrease in all areas. Most of it came in the big industrial centers. The ten district assemblies of Portland, Lynn, Boston, Providence, Hartford, New York, Newark, Philadelphia, Baltimore, and Chicago, which had a membership of more than 290,000 in mid-1886, lost 178,000 of that number by mid-1887. Membership also fell off in the smaller cities and towns of the Midwest, the South, and the Rocky Mountain and Pacific Coast areas. But this loss was partially offset in the same years by the creation of new assemblies in the same areas. Membership in the smaller industrial centers thus remained fairly stationary. Thereafter the decline was more precipitous. Membership dropped to 260,000 by mid-1888, to 220,000 by mid-1889, and to 100,000 by mid-1890 when the bulk of the order was found among the mechanics, shopkeepers, small employers, and farmers in the nation's small cities and towns. But the Knights were not yet dead; they had one more role to play.

Their last important activity was taken in conjunction with those agrarian agglomerations known as the "alliances." There were two alliances. One was formed in the South in 1887. It was essentially a revolt against the South's merchant-storekeeper who kept the southern farmer in economic subservience through crop liens and high interest rates. Its object was to relieve this burden by cooperative purchases and marketing. The other alliance was formed in the upper Mississippi Valley in 1880. It was originally a revolt against the domination of the northern agricultural areas by the railroads; after 1887 low prices for crops, oppressive mortgages, and droughts were added to the grievances of its members. Like the Southern Alliance it stimulated cooperative buying and selling ventures.

In 1889 these agrarian movements secured national attention when the Southern Alliance met at St. Louis and decided to enter into the political campaigns of the southern states and to establish a lobby at Washington in order to further a program which included currency inflation, the later famous subtreasury plan, and other agrarian reforms. At this point the Knights of Labor informally allied with the movement. Three leaders of the order—Powderly, Beaumont, and A. W. Wright—attended the St. Louis meeting. Either because they recognized that the order needed strengthening, or because they recognized that the declining membership of the order was being concentrated in the cities and towns closely allied to agrarian interests and that the logical step was to draw those interests into closer unity, they drew up an agreement with the alliance leaders. They endorsed the demands of the alliance, agreed to merge their lobbying activities with those of the alliance in Washington and to support for office "only such men as could be depended upon to enact alliance principles into law."

Meantime the semiautonomous branches of the Northern Alliance had also determined upon an active political role. The result was a widespread political upheaval in the agrarian areas of the nation. The Southern Alliance, operating through the Democratic party, elected governors in three states and sent some thirty-odd alliance members to Congress. The Northern Alliance, organized into third parties along state lines, elected two United States senators, eight congressmen, and secured the balance of power in the legislatures of four upper Mississippi Valley states. In this campaign the local and district assemblies of the Knights in the South and West took a prominent part; they deserved some of the credit for the success of the movement.

The next step was inevitable. Sentiment for a merger of agrarian and labor organizations developed. At the last moment, however, both the Southern Alliance and the Knights lost enthusiasm. The Northern Alliance, nevertheless, met with other organizations at Cincinnati in May, 1891, and created the Populist party; it met again at Omaha in July, 1892, to name James B. Weaver of Iowa and James G. Field of Virginia as its presidential ticket. It also adopted a now famous platform in which labor interests were recognized in several planks. The platform demanded government ownership of the means of transportation and communication and a graduated income tax; condemned the continued importation of pauper, criminal, and contract labor and demanded further restriction of "undesirable" immigration which crowded American wage earners from their jobs; announced a sympathy for workingmen's efforts to shorten hours of labor; condemned the use of Pinkertons as a menace to civil liberties; and announced support of a Knights' boycott against a group of Rochester clothing manufacturers.

Although the Knights' leadership had helped call this political movement into existence, their attitude toward it now became strangely equivocal. The General Assembly refused to give official sanction to the new party. In the East what remained of the order gave the party but little attention; the rank and file retained affiliation with the Republican and Democratic parties. In the South and West, however, the assemblies gave the new party their cordial and vigorous support, contributing to the heavy vote that the Populists polled in the western farm areas.

Flirtation with the Populists was followed by a further decline of the order. By 1893 membership had dropped to less than 75,000. The order still existed in the East—District Assembly 49 continued to function in New York; the United Mine Workers were secretly affiliated; locals of the United Brewery Workers maintained their status within the organization—but most of the members were located in agrarian areas. In 1893 the Socialist Labour party considered the order enough of a labor organization to try to secure control of it. But in 1893 Powderly was removed as Grand Master Workman; the socialists and farm delegates combined to replace him with James R. Sovereign, an Iowa farm editor. Thereafter, the order quickly lost all status as a labor organization. By 1896 it regarded itself no longer as an organization intended to adjust relations between employer and employee, but rather as an organization intended to adjust "natural resources and productive facilities to the common interests of the whole people."

The decline of the Noble Order of the Knights of Labor from its position of labor leadership in 1886 to a state of futility in the midnineties did not mean that the organization had been a failure. Its accomplishments during its short period of domination—the hope for a better economic world it developed among the semiskilled and unskilled workers, the sense of unity and power it produced among the rank and file of labor, the legislation it sponsored—were in themselves enough to give the order a position of major significance in the history of American labor.

But the influence of the order extended beyond its brief moment of triumph. The unity it fostered among workingmen has remained a labor dream to the present day, and the concept of industrial unionism it produced remained a major goal of large numbers of laboring men and ultimately brought about reorganization of labor unionism in the New Deal period. More immediate to its own time, the order sparked a movement that led to the enactment of a great volume of labor legislation by the states between Haymarket and the twentieth century.

The Knights were not directly responsible for the passage of the laws. The United Front parties of 1886–1887, the socialists, the American Federation of Labor, the Populists, a public fearful of its own welfare in the conflict between capital and labor, a public whose humanitarian instincts were aroused by the miserable condition of some labor elements, were more directly responsible. But the Knights provided the basic platform—written at Reading in 1878—for the whole movement; the Knights provided the spirit of labor unity which created the United Front, the program which the United Front parties advanced, and much of the rank and file of United Front voters; the Knights provided the Populists with their labor planks and contributed to the success of the party.

Labor legislation enacted between 1886 and 1900 centered primarily upon six major points: arbitration of industrial disputes; child labor; women's labor; factory, sweatshop, and mine safety; responsibility for industrial accidents; and the eight-hour day.

The most widespread type of labor legislation enacted by the states was the laws providing for voluntary arbitration of industrial disputes. Although the National Labor Union and the Knights of Labor had suggested such laws, it was not until after Haymarket, when the United Front parties took up the issue and the public began to recognize that strikes and lockouts might be injurious to the community, that the movement showed results. The United Front campaign led to the enactment of voluntary arbitration laws in New York and Massachusetts. These provided for the establishment of permanent state boards of arbitration which could be called into any threatened or actual dispute by either party; acceptance of such services by both parties would make the decision of the board final. By 1900 twenty-two states in the industrial North and the Rockies had similar boards.

Legislation on behalf of children in industry was more complex, involving minimum age, night work, maximum hours, and employment in hazardous occupations. Although interest in the minimum age of children working in industry dated back to antebellum days, only seven states had enacted laws before 1880. The agitation of the Knights, supported to a degree by the socialists, the F.O.O.T.A.L.U. and the A.F.L., and a humanitarian instinct that became active in the nineties increased the number of states with such laws to twenty-six by 1900. The problem of maximum hours for children, a part of the ten-hour and eight-hour movements between 1845 and 1872, had a similar history. The Knights renewed the agitation; by 1900 all northern states except Illinois had enacted legislation setting a ten-hour day and a sixty-hour week as the limit for children working in industry. Agitation to check night work and employment of children in hazardous occupations began with the Knights. By 1900 eight northern states banned night work and most states prohibited employment of children in dangerous industries.

Legislation on behalf of women was less extensive. Massachusetts enacted a law limiting the hours of women in factories in 1874. The Knights, working through district assemblies, took up the issue in the mid-eighties; the United Front parties, the A.F.L. and various middle-class women's organizations added their strength to the movement with the result that twelve more states, mostly in the North, joined the list by 1900. Four states prohibited night work for women in the same period.

The agitation of the Knights of Labor created the original movement for factory, sweatshop, and mine inspection laws. Reenforced by the United Front parties, by the socialists, and by the A.F.L. in the next decade, the agitation led to enactment of a large amount of legislation. Almost all industrial states passed factory inspection laws between 1894 and 1900, establishing rules concerning fire escapes,

ventilation, adequate guards on dangerous machinery, cubic air content, cleaning of machinery in motion, and handrails on stairs. Nine
northern states enacted sweatshop laws between 1892 and 1900, defining sweatshops as places of manufacture normally used for living
and sleeping purposes. Most states provided that only members of
the family were to work in such shops; some required that sweatshop
goods be labeled "tenement made." Twelve coal- and metal-mining
states enacted mine-inspection laws providing for regular examination of scales, escape shafts, and hoisting machinery, boilers, cages,
ventilation, doors, lamps, and props.

The Knights and the A.F.L. together developed the issue of responsibility for industrial accidents. The rules on the subject, established by state courts in the 1840's, required that the employer must
provide a safe place to work, must furnish employees with safe tools
and appliances, must establish proper rules of conduct, and must
warn employees of special dangers. If a worker wanted to recover
damages for injury, he had to prove that the employer had been
negligent in these duties and that such negligence was the cause of
the injury; he had also to prove that he himself was not negligent
and that the accident had not been caused by another worker or
"fellow servant." In addition he had to prove that he had not assumed
the risk of the conditions under which he worked by contract. Recovery of damages under such conditions had been nearly impossible.
Between 1886 and 1900 a number of states began to modify portions
of the rules: ten made employers responsible for accidents caused by
defective machinery; eleven abolished the fellow-servant rule; seventeen forbade manufacturers or railroads to rid themselves of responsibility through contracts.

The most controversial legislation enacted by the states during the
period from 1886 to 1900 concerned maximum hours for men. Although seventeen states had enacted laws limiting the working day
by 1886, the laws were ineffective because they permitted contracts
for longer hours and the courts assumed that such contracts existed
where longer hours were customary. The agitation of the Knights,
strongly aided by the United Front parties, the socialists, and the
A.F.L., brought some changes. Ten states established maximum
hours for public contract workers between 1892 and 1900. Labor
activity and the appallingly large number of railroad accidents which

threatened the lives and limbs of passengers—accidents due largely to fatigue from overwork—brought further hour laws. Between 1892 and 1900 seven northern states enacted legislation limiting railway labor to fifteen hours of continuous duty in any twenty-four, and twelve states limited hours of street railway employees.

Little of the legislation enacted by the states during the period was effective. Employers were seldom willing to use arbitration machinery. Minimum-age laws for children generally applied only to those under twelve and to those working in factories or mercantile houses. Maximum-hour laws for children (between twelve and eighteen) were rarely enforced. Few states defined dangerous enterprises in which children could not work. Maximum-hour laws for women generally provided penalties only for "willful" violations which were difficult to prove; all such laws, moreover, were called into question by the decision of the Illinois Supreme Court which declared its own statute a deprivation of freedom of contract. Factory, sweatshop, and mine-inspection laws rarely provided for adequate enforcement. New rules concerning responsibility for industrial accidents made it no easier to recover damages for injuries received on the job. Maximum-hour laws for men in specific callings were declared unconstitutional in five states—making enforcement in all states haphazard. But for all the ineffectiveness of such legislation, it was a monument to the Knights, forming a base upon which the more effective legislation of the Progressive era was built.

PART THREE

The Modern Era

13 ___

The Triumph of the Machine

The Modern Era in the history of American labor, which began about 1890, is a period of ever-growing domination by the machine. When the era began, the machine already had a commanding position in the major industries of the nation. Its sources of power were all in use: coal, natural gas, petroleum, and hydroelectricity. Its engines of power, the steam engine, the steam turbine, the dynamo, and the internal combustion engine were tried and tested. Transportation and communication facilities were to a large extent mechanically operated. By 1890 there were more than 160,000 miles of railroad operating over good roadbeds on heavy steel rails. Street and elevated railways, operated electrically, handled most urban traffic. Waterway traffic was almost completely mechanized. While highway travel was still largely horse drawn or man powered, the production of wagons, carts, carriages, and bicycles was thoroughly mechanized. Most of the nation's messages were still sent by post; but the telegraph was in extensive use and the telephone was in a lusty infant stage.

Among the basic industries iron and steel were essentially machine produced. Bridgebuilding, shipbuilding, the manufacture of iron pipe and steel wire had become mechanized. Lathes, planes, drilling machines, grinding machines, trip hammers, and hydroelectric presses had taken over the foundries. Copper refining and the production of virgin aluminum, lead, zinc, silver, and cement had become largely machine processed. Among the consumer-goods industries meat packing, by virtue of refrigeration, had become a factory enterprise. The cereal, brewing, distilling, and sugar industries were carried on in factories. Cigarettes, and to a lesser extent cigars and smoking tobacco, were produced by machinery. Cotton, woolen, and silk textiles and the shoe industry were almost totally mechanized; machines had invaded the clothing industry. The manufacture of bathroom fixtures, furniture, stoves, and hardware was done by machines. Office equipment, arms, papermaking, and printing had become factory enterprises.

Indeed, American transportation and communication facilities and industry had become so overwhelmingly mechanized by 1890 that it was difficult to foresee any further mechanization. Yet, in the next forty years the advances made by the machine were phenomenal. Three factors paced the development: new uses for known fuels, extension of existing industries, and construction of new industries.

In 1900 coal supplied 90 per cent of the nation's power and heat; by 1928 coal supplied only 61½ per cent of the nation's energy, a reduction which led to a considerable mechanization of the coal industry in the form of mechanical loaders and strip mining by steam shovels. Coal's decreasing importance occurred because of advances made by natural gas, petroleum, and hydroelectricity. Between 1901 and 1930 production of natural gas increased 308 per cent, of petroleum more than 880 per cent, of electricity more than 1,900 per cent. These increases created vast new industries; at the same time they encouraged further mechanization of transportation, communication, and manufacturing.

Transportation was changed both in kind and degree between 1890 and 1930. The least important developments occurred upon the railways. The rolling stock was made over—heavier locomotives and rails, more luxurious cars, and more safety devices were installed, keeping old manufacturing industries in operation—and toward the end of the period railways began to use petroleum and electricity as fuels. Street and elevated railway systems continued to expand along with the cities they served until 1924. Waterway transportation declined until the First World War when the Federal Government began to canalize the Ohio and Missouri rivers, and industry, particularly steel, built its own fleets to haul bulk materials. Construction of river boats and barges once more became a highly important business. Meanwhile, business on the Great Lakes expanded;

ships increased in size, and mechanical loading and unloading equipment was developed to a new point of efficiency.

The greatest development in transportation was the automobile. Gasoline-driven cars appeared for sale in 1896. Ten years later Henry Ford entered the field with his concept of mass production. By 1915 nearly a million cars and trucks were being manufactured annually. The greatest expansion came between 1920 and 1929 when annual production increased from 2,225,000 vehicles to more than 5,600,000 vehicles and the number of registered cars increased from 9,000,000 to 26,500,000. The automobile had a highly beneficial effect upon the steel, rubber, glass, copper, leather, textile, and petroleum industries. It served to boom a suburban home-building industry, and it led to a new era of road, bridge, and tunnel building. The automobile also revolutionized personal transportation and much commercial transportation. The horse, the hansom, and the wagon gradually disappeared to be replaced by personally owned cars, and by taxicabs, busses, and trucks. City deliveries, farm-to-city transport, and short-line hauls became almost completely mechanized. By 1929 the nation's investment in motor vehicles and highways was greater than its investment in railroads.

Important mechanical developments occurred in the field of communications. The amount of mail increased nearly sevenfold between 1890 and 1930, and use of the telegram by businessmen brought a great expansion in the telegraphic industry. In the telephone business the dial phone, the automatic telephone exchange, and relay stations for sending messages long distances extended telephone service into every hamlet in the nation. By 1929 transfer of the human voice by mechanical means had become an everyday matter both in the business world and in the social world. The most spectacular development came in radio. Invented in 1896, it mushroomed into a great industry after 1919. Transfer of information, entertainment, and advertising over air waves more than anything else revealed the triumph of the machine in the twentieth century.

Mechanization of the nation's basic industries also advanced rapidly. Blast furnaces became almost completely mechanical, increasing steel production 1,300 per cent between 1890 and 1929. Machine tools which had been introduced in the nineteenth century were enlarged and made more efficient. The value of machinery and transportation equipment increased twenty-five times between 1899 and 1929. The nonferrous metals—copper, lead, zinc, and aluminum—increased in use, and production of alloys grew steadily more mechanical. The cement, crushed-stone, sand, sulphur, lime, gypsum, salt, and phosphate industries were virtually taken over by machinery. After the First World War a large chemical industry developed; the building of chemical equipment became one of the nation's largest enterprises.

There were vast changes in consumer industries. In the meatpacking industry machinery helped meat packers to utilize many previously wasted portions of slaughtered animals. Bread baking became mechanized. The "tin can" revolutionized the fruit, vegetable, and fish industries; the touch of the human hand had become unknown in most canneries by 1929. The cigarette industry, growing ever more mechanized, increased production from three billion to nineteen billion in the first three decades of the century. In the textile industry new machinery vastly increased the output of cotton and silk mills. In 1910 a new, highly mechanical textile industry—rayon—appeared. By 1929 the United States was the world's largest producer of the chemical fiber. Between 1900 and 1929 the making of men's clothing—except for shirts and rough clothing which were sweatshop produced—had become a factory enterprise. The millinery business was taken over by the machine. Women's clothing also began to succumb to the machine. The rubber-goods business was completely transformed. In 1900 it had been a part of the clothing business; by 1930 it was a highly mechanical adjunct of the automobile business. Glassmaking became a mechanized industry during the period. A whole new electrical appliance industry which included such things as irons, vacuum cleaners, washing machines, and refrigerators developed into one of the nation's giants between 1914 and 1929. The phonographic industry made its appearance and grew to huge proportions, and the movie-camera industry was developed into one of the nation's largest.

The growth of mechanized factory enterprise was only one feature of early twentieth century industrial developments. The factory system also spread over a wider geographical area. The East, which had produced 58 per cent of the nation's manufactured goods in 1890, produced only slightly more than 40 per cent by 1929. The old

Northwest increased its production to 30 per cent in the same period, and the rest of the nation—about evenly divided between the South and the trans-Mississippi West—produced the rest.

The trend toward concentration begun in earlier decades continued. In spite of the enactment of the Sherman Act and other laws between 1890 and 1921, in spite of the trust-busting activities of Theodore Roosevelt, William Howard Taft, and Woodrow Wilson, the tendency toward combinations was never curbed. Between 1890 and 1900 new combinations were formed or reorganized in almost every industry. By 1900 there were 185 industrial combinations in the nation; they constituted less than ½ of 1 per cent of the establishments but owned 15 per cent of the capital. Four years later the number of such combinations had doubled, and their control reached 40 per cent of the nation's manufacturing capital.

After 1904 some of these combinations were dissolved by government action, but they generally managed to reform under some arrangement—as "voluntary mergers," as "gentlemen's agreements," and as trade associations—which accomplished the same ends. After the First World War, the Federal Government obligingly lifted the restrictions upon expansion, and a new era of consolidation began. Banking houses decreased from 30,000 to 23,000 between 1921 and 1931. Half of the total bank resources of the nation were controlled by 1 per cent of the banks by 1930. Holding companies which had appeared in the public-utility field even before the First World War enjoyed a heyday of expansion in the twenties. The Bell telephone system secured control of three-fourths of the nation's telephones and seven-eighths of the revenue. In 1929 it was estimated that out of the nation's 4,362 electric power corporations, nearly three-fourths were controlled by forty-one holding companies; thirty-five of these companies were in turn controlled by six financial groups.

New consolidations also developed in the manufacturing and mining industries. The phenomenon was apparent in old as well as in new industries. In steel the number of establishments was reduced from 719 in 1890 to 591 in 1929; four companies produced 64 per cent of the iron and steel output. In the newer automobile industry the number of establishments was reduced from 315 in 1919 to 244 in 1929; three corporations accounted for nearly 90 per cent of the product. The same sort of combinations appeared in the infant radio industry. The Radio Corporation of America, owned by General Electric and Westinghouse, secured control of 95 per cent of the radio apparatus sold in interstate commerce; and a subsidiary, the National Broadcasting Company, monopolized twenty-eight of the forty cleared radio channels by 1930. Between 1919 and 1930 nearly six thousand independent manufacturing and mining companies disappeared as a result of mergers.

In 1904 the public had been concerned because three hundred companies had a total capitalization of $7,000,000,000. Yet by 1930 there were thirteen corporations in the United States with a capitalization ranging from one to four billion dollars each; the thirteen together were nearly twice as large as the old three hundred. In 1910 the two hundred largest corporations in the country did 33 per cent of the business; by 1930 the two hundred largest were just about equal in size to their 300,000 smaller competitors; they controlled half the corporate wealth, a third of the business, and one-fifth of the total wealth of the United States.

Technological and structural changes in American industry after 1890 brought other changes; they created or helped to create new social habits; in many cases they brought about an increase in productivity; and, what was most important for labor, they changed traditional employment patterns.

Between 1900 and 1940 the physical output of American industry tripled, and the number of those gainfully employed increased from 29,000,000 to 53,000,000—an increase of about 83 per cent. But not all industries followed the national pattern. While American consumption of agricultural products increased, the number of people working in agriculture declined from 40 per cent to 18 per cent of those gainfully employed. The number of those employed in manufacturing grew from 6,200,000 to 9,200,000 between 1900 and 1940— an increase of about 50 per cent. But this increase in number represented only a small increase in percentage of all employed. The 1900 figure represented about 22 per cent of those gainfully employed; the 1940 figure represented 24 per cent. The increase in manufacturing employment, moreover, was less than the increase in total employment.

In the mineral industries various trends appeared. In the industry as a whole output increased 300 per cent and full-time wage earners

. increased about 5 per cent—from 594,000 to 622,000. In anthracite, however, the number of full-time wage earners declined from 95,000 to 57,000 between 1902 and 1937; in bituminous full-time employment decreased by 7 per cent; in metal mining employment dropped from 120,000 to 90,000. On the other hand the number of employees in the oil and gas industries leaped from 32,000 to 160,000.

Combined passenger and freight traffic of all commercial transportation agencies increased 500 per cent between 1889 and 1939 and doubled again between 1939 and 1946. Employment in the industry increased 150 per cent—from 1,000,000 to 2,500,000—but the increase was not the same in all branches of transportation. The number of railway workers increased from 750,000 in 1903 to 2,000,000 in 1920—when they made up 80 per cent of the transportation labor force—and then dropped to 1,400,000 by 1946. At the same time waterway workers increased from 97,000 to 151,000; pipeline workers increased 80 per cent between 1921 and 1946; and the airways hired 80,000 workers between 1926 and 1946. The greatest change occurred on the highways. Although definitive information is lacking, it is estimated that the intercity trucking business, which carried 58,000,000,000 ton miles of traffic in 1940, employed at least 1,000,000 workers that year—more than the railroads had employed in 1903.

The most startling change in the employment pattern occurred in the service industries—wholesale and retail trade, insurance and real estate, banking and finance, domestic service, the professions, hotels, laundries, barber and beauty shops, entertainment. Taken as a whole the number employed in the service industries increased from 6,900,-000 in 1900, 24 per cent of those gainfully employed, to 27,300,000 by 1950, 47 per cent of those gainfully employed. In some services there was an absolute decline in employment: hotels; in some there was a relative decline: domestic service, law, and medicine; but some experienced large increases: barber and beauty shops, 300 per cent; retail trade, nearly 400 per cent; banking, insurance, and real estate, nearly 400 per cent. In 1900 the number of those engaged in trade was less than half those engaged in manufacturing; by 1950 the number of "traders" was greater than the number of manufacturing employees. In 1900 the numbers of those engaged in service industries other than trade was about one-third of the number engaged in agriculture, mining, and transportation; in 1950 the number employed in service industries other than trade was almost double the number of those employed in agriculture, mining, and transportation.

14 ——

The A.F.L.'s First Decade—
Homestead and Pullman

The dominant organization of the first fifty-odd years of the Modern Era of labor history was the American Federation of Labor. As it was conceived and organized in December, 1886, the A.F.L., with Samuel Gompers at the helm, was the climax of skilled labor's long efforts to form a union of all crafts. It borrowed its structure from the F.O.O.T.A.L.U. At the top was an Executive Council, charged with the following tasks: (1) To aid the organization of trade assemblies, to set up state federations for the purpose of influencing legislation, and to assist in the establishment of national trade associations based upon "strict recognition of the autonomy of each trade"; (2) To secure national legislation and to influence public opinion "by peaceful and legal means"; (3) To pass judgment on boycotts begun by affiliated organizations; (4) To investigate strikes and lockouts and issue appeals for voluntary financial contributions for labor organizations whose cause it approved. The council was elected by an annual convention dominated by the nationals which received one vote for every one hundred members represented. Revenue was to be secured from charter fees and from a per capita tax of one-half cent per month for each member in good standing.

The A.F.L. was not an inevitable success. Its first ten years included struggles with the Knights, with "recalcitrant" trades, with socialism, with strike failures, and with a depression. The struggle with the Knights ended in victory, but the federation threw so much of its strength into the effort to destroy its rival that it made only negative gains. While membership in the Knights dwindled, membership in the federation did not advance appreciably. A number of factors were involved. Many nationals refused to join because they were fearful of turning over any power to a superior body; a large number of locals refused to join because they resented the fact that they were given no voice in the new organization; many tradesmen refused to join because they believed in industrial unionism and labor unity. In addition, the federation was still unproved.

A.F.L. leaders were conscious of the organization's weakness, recognizing the need for an attention-attracting effort. Late in 1888 the annual convention determined to renew the eight-hour drive which would culminate on May 1, 1890, in a general strike. The campaign misfired; the 1889 Convention decided to begin a new eight-hour drive with the carpenters, strong in number and possessed of a large strike fund. The carpenters' campaign, inaugurated in May, 1890, was largely successful. According to Gompers the trade secured the eight-hour day in 137 cities, and the movement helped local campaigns for shorter hours among other building tradesmen in a number of industrial centers.

Elimination of the Knights and the eight-hour campaign of the carpenters gave the federation somewhat greater prestige in the early nineties; it was becoming clear that the organization was emerging from its infant stage, and some complacency became evident in the statements of its leaders. But that complacency was rudely shattered in a series of disastrous strikes which shook the labor world in 1892. Chief of these was the Homestead Strike involving the Carnegie Company and the Amalgamated Association of Iron, Steel, and Tin Workers.

Andrew Carnegie had purchased the Homestead mills in 1889, placing Henry Clay Frick in charge. At the time he had renewed the long-standing trade agreement between the Company and the well entrenched Amalgamated for a period of three years. In February, 1892, Frick and Amalgamated leaders began negotiations for a new agreement. Since the steel business was booming, the Amalgamated asked for an increase in tonnage rates; Frick countered with a request for decreases. After more than three months of negotiations, Frick announced that either an agreement would be reached in twenty-nine days or the company would cease dealing with the union. Promptly with the expiration of the ultimatum the Homestead workers were locked out. Both sides made ready. Frick erected barbed-wire fences around the plant and hired three hundred Pinkertons to serve as company guards. The Pinkertons were assembled at a point on the Ohio River below Pittsburgh on the night of July 5; they were armed, placed aboard a barge, and towed up the Monongahela to Homestead. Despite efforts at concealment, steelworkers met them in the mill yards. In the battle that followed, a dozen men were killed on each side, scores were wounded, and the Pinkertons were driven off.

Meanwhile the "strike" had spread to other mills. Workers at the Carnegie plants in Pittsburgh and Duquesne and men in various other steel mills in Pittsburgh dropped their tools in sympathy. On July 23rd, as the lines of conflict were growing tighter, Alexander Berkman, a half-crazed New York anarchist, who had read about the oppressed workmen of Homestead, attempted to assassinate Frick. Though he failed, the act fastened the attention of the nation on Homestead. Almost instantly it became apparent that the public was on the side of the strikers, primarily because Carnegie had asked for an increase in the tariff on steel in 1890 and then had sought to reduce the wages of his workmen. So widespread was the attitude that the Republican party, in the midst of a campaign to reelect President Benjamin Harrison, intervened. Vice presidential candidate Whitelaw Reid appealed to Carnegie to end the strike, and the party sent an emissary to negotiate with Frick. But the effort was vain. Carnegie and Frick were determined to crush the Amalgamated, as Frick declared, "If it takes all summer. . . . Yes, even my life itself." The strike dragged into fall, through the presidential campaign—in which the Republicans were defeated—to November 20th when the Amalgamated, its treasury empty, officially announced its end. The men went back to their jobs as nonunion workers. The Amalgamated was shattered at Homestead, and steel unionism was virtually eliminated in the mills of the Pittsburgh area.

Three other industrial battles were fought and lost in 1892. One, in the silver mines at Coeur d'Alene, Idaho, in July, was defeated by Federal troops. A second, conducted by switchmen employed by the railroads in Buffalo, in August, was broken by militia. The third, involving coal miners in the area around Tracy City, Tennessee—a series of strikes which sought to force convict labor from the mines—was also defeated by militia.

The four defeats were a shock to all labor. They revealed only too clearly that the corporations of the late nineteenth century were much more powerful fighting units than was generally realized, capable of defeating the strongest labor organization, and that capital had secured a firm grip on state and local governments and would use the state's power to protect its own interests. Many laboring men began to argue that reorganization of the whole labor movement was necessary if labor expected to maintain or advance its standard of living. Two roads were open: conversion of the A.F.L. into a political movement or the development of industrial unionism.

Those who believed that political action was the solution made themselves felt at the 1892 A.F.L. convention. Led by socialist trade unionists, they pointed out that the "recent defeats" of labor were signal evidences of the "impotency" of trade unions "to cope with the great power of concentrated wealth," and demanded that the federation take the lead in an independent political movement. Gompers' hostility helped head off the movement. Nevertheless, the convention endorsed two planks in the Populist platform—the initiative and referendum, and government ownership of the nation's telegraph and telephone systems. The political movement grew stronger in 1893, aided by the depression that began in May and threw a pall of defeatism over the trade unions. When the socialists introduced a "political programme" calling for the establishment of a legal eight-hour day; abolition of the contract system upon public works; abolition of the sweatshop system; governmental inspection of mines and workshops; adoption of the initiative and referendum; compulsory education; municipal ownership of public utilities; nationalization of telegraphs, telephones, railroads, and mines; and "the collective ownership by the people of all means of production and distribution," the A.F.L. convention accepted it and recommended it to the consideration of affiliates.

During 1894 a large number of labor organizations acted upon the program. Most nationals, state federations, and city assemblies endorsed it without reservations. Only one union—the bakers'—rejected the program in its entirety. During the year hundreds of locals plunged into politics, often forming active alliances with the Populists. Some three hundred trade unionists ran for elective office. When the A.F.L. convention met, it was obvious that the membership had enthusiastically endorsed political action. Yet the convention failed to adopt the political program. Gompers and other federation leaders, fearful that approval would make the organization an adjunct of the socialist movement, set themselves against it and proceeded, through some tricky parliamentary procedure, to defeat it. Gompers ruled that the program had to be considered piecemeal. The preamble recommending political action was defeated, all the planks were approved separately with nullifying amendments, and the plank endorsing collective ownership was altered beyond recognition. When the amended program was presented to the conventions, its original friends, disgusted with the changes, helped to defeat it by a vote of 1,173 to 735.

But political thinking was not submerged. In 1895 the old political program, its potentialities now weakened, was adopted as a "legislative platform," and Gompers began to encourage "nonpartisan" political action. In the following year free silver became the most loudly publicized political issue in the nation. The Democrats, repudiating their titular leader, adopted a free-silver plank and nominated William Jennings Bryan as their candidate for the Presidency. Although the federation and the Executive Council maintained an official attitude of neutrality upon the candidates for the Presidency, a large number of trade-union leaders announced themselves in favor of the election of Bryan; even Gompers, inclined to be a Republican and hostile to free silver, gave support to the Bryan campaign. Although no careful study of the election has been made, it seems clear that a large portion of rank-and-file labor voted for Bryan. Had he won, the A.F.L. might have entered politics by the back door. His defeat, however, ended any immediate danger; after the election, pressure to convert the A.F.L. subsided.

Meanwhile the second post-Homestead movement—industrial unionism—had developed around the railway workers. The first permanent national railway association had been organized by the locomotive engineers. Although the brotherhood had begun with orthodox aims and tactics, the influence of Charles Wilson who became head in 1864 and the disastrous Michigan Southern strike soon brought a change. Thereafter the organization aimed to "advance the moral, social, and intellectual condition of the locomotive engineers and to thereby elevate their standard of character as a profession." Any attempt by members to place the body in a position of "antagonism" to employers was to be checked immediately. While there were deviations from this attitude in the next twenty years, the engineers in general did not act as an orthodox labor organization. Meanwhile they began to develop their insurance and benefit system. Railway engineering was considered a highly hazardous trade in the nineteenth century, and private companies charged the trade prohibitive rates for insurance. To circumvent the problem the organization set up a widows', orphans', and disabled members' fund, and a death-benefit system.

The Brotherhood of Railway Conductors and the Brotherhood of Locomotive Firemen, organized in the sixties, had gone through the same transformation. The tradition that skilled railway labor which made up the train crews was organized primarily for insuring itself against the risks of their trade was so well established by the eighties that the Brotherhood of Railway Trainmen, the Switchmen, and the Yardmasters, who organized during the decade, didn't even pretend to be labor unions; they organized as mutual aid societies.

During the depression of 1873, however, men who worked in the yards, depots, roundhouses, and railway machine shops began to develop a more orthodox attitude. The Railway Strike of 1877 served to increase the feeling that railway workers needed to become more aggressive. After the depression railway labor with this attitude joined the Knights.

The two railway elements, with their varying traditions, managed to exist harmoniously side by side until after Haymarket when the brotherhoods became involved in a struggle with the Knights. The fight reached a climax in 1887–1888 when brotherhood scabs defeated a strike of the Knights against the Reading Road, and the Knights' scabs in turn defeated an engineer-fireman strike against the Burlington. The two conflicts started some significant trends. Among train crews it produced a movement for greater unity. A few months after the Burlington strike, the brotherhoods and the switchmen formed the United Order of Railway Employees to bring about greater cooperation among railway workers. A quarrel between trainmen and switchmen led to the dissolution of the Order in 1891. E. E. Clark, head of the conductors, promptly began a new movement of brotherhoods, switchmen, and telegraphers. The Cedar Rapids Plan, as the program was called, provided for a federation of railway service men by railway systems; cooperation to the point of a general strike was envisioned. The plan never became effective. The Burlington strike had caused so much damage and had so thoroughly alarmed railway managers that they adopted a highly conciliatory attitude toward the strategically placed brotherhoods, granting full recognition, wages so high as to make the operating employees the élite of the labor world, and job security through seniority rules. The brotherhoods, well satisfied, went their independent ways. In the meantime unionism among the yard, depot, shop, and maintenance workers deteriorated. Even the tradition of solidarity and industrial unionism, handed down from the Knights, became dormant.

The industrial conflicts of 1892 changed the whole picture. They reopened the issue of trade versus industrial unions and gave the industrial unionists a leader in Eugene V. Debs, secretary-treasurer of the Brotherhood of Locomotive Firemen. In 1892 he was regarded as one of the most conservative of railway labor leaders. But the weakness of trade unionism in conflict with big business convinced him that a drastic change was needed. Railway workers had to organize into one union if advances were to be made. In the fall of 1892 he began a campaign for a new railway organization. His campaign reached fruition in the creation of the American Railway Union at Chicago in June, 1893. The A.R.U. was patterned directly on the Knights, with control vested in a central organization. Its objective, like that of the Knights, was a union of all railway employees. Its dues were low. Its aim was the amelioration of the economic condition of all railway workers. It pledged itself to stay out of the insurance field.

The success of the American Railway Union was almost instantaneous. The depression which began with the failure of the National Cordage Company in May, 1893, formed the background. Within a year after the depression began, no dividends were being paid on 60 per cent of the nation's railway stocks. Banks, feeling the strain, began to call in their loans; businesses unable to make repayments collapsed—over 15,000 business failures were recorded. Commercial enterprises cut orders, and factories cut production or closed their doors; wages were reduced; men were discharged by the thousand. In the midst of these conditions the unorganized railway workers on the Great Northern walked off their jobs in protest against a wage cut and appealed to the American Railway Union for help. Reluctantly, because he doubted the possibility of leading a successful conflict at the time, Debs went to Minneapolis to organize the strike. The Great Northern surrendered. The American Railway Union was made; railway workers of every type flocked to the organization. The movement was less apparent among engineers and conductors, but the rush of firemen, brakemen, car men, yard, depot and shop workers into the new organization was almost too rapid to handle. At its second convention the A.R.U. could boast 150,000 members.

Among the railway men who joined the American Railway Union in the spring of 1894 were the employees of the Pullman Palace Car Company. They were different from other railway workers in that they lived in a model town and paid their rent, utility bills, and taxes to the company. In September, 1893, the company cut wages 22 per cent without making any reduction in rents and other services. Eight months later when the employees asked for an adjustment, they were bluntly refused and some members of the committee who had tried to negotiate with the company were discharged. Pullman workers promptly walked off the job and appealed to the A.R.U. for help. Debs first tried to persuade the Pullman Company to arbitrate. When George Pullman refused, the A.R.U. began a sympathetic boycott of Pullman stock on June 26th. In a few hours some 60,000 men ceased work along the western railway lines; Pullman traffic from Chicago westward was paralyzed. Then the boycott spread slowly to the South and East. The public, fearing disorder, held its breath. Then the picture changed.

While the strike and boycott were not aimed at the railroads, the railroads became involved when the General Managers Association, a half-secret combination of twenty-four railroads centering on Chicago, decided to help the Pullman Company. Their aim was expressed by their chairman on the eve of the boycott: "We can handle the railway brotherhoods, but we cannot handle the A.R.U. . . . We cannot handle Debs. We have got to wipe him out." The General Managers Association turned to Attorney-General Richard Olney for help.

Their appeal met with instant response. Olney, a railway lawyer and a member of the board of several railroads, asked President Grover Cleveland to send Federal troops to Chicago to prevent interference with the mails and with interstate commerce. But Cleveland refused unless it was necessary to support "judicial tribunes."

Olney promptly began working on a plan to make it necessary to use troops. The first step was to find judicial authority for repressive action. He did not find it difficult. As he himself expressed his views: A railway was not a mere private enterprise; it was a "public highway." Any obstruction in that highway could be dealt with by Federal authorities as a restraint of commerce. Employees who in concert quit work on highways were in reality obstructing it; they could be dealt with as a "conspiracy in restraint of trade." To carry out his plan, he appointed a railroad lawyer, Edwin Walker, as special counsel to the Federal District attorney in Chicago, and instructed him to resort to "all legal remedies" to break up the strike, suggesting that it was not necessary to wait until some criminal or illegal act was committed because it was possible to file bills in equity enjoining persons from interference with the mails in violation of the Sherman Anti-Trust Act. He likewise suggested that the number of deputy marshals in Chicago be increased.

Walker, District Attorney Milchrist, together with Federal Judges Peter Grosscup and C. D. Wood, responded with an injunction ordering all persons "to refrain from interfering with or stopping any of the business of any of the railroads in Chicago engaged as common carriers" on the ground that such action was interference with the mails and an unlawful restraint of commerce. At the same time the number of marshals was increased from fifty to one thousand. In the afternoon of July 2nd United States Marshal Arnold, at the head of 125 deputies, read the order to a crowd gathered on the Rock Island tracks at Blue Island, halfway between Chicago and Joliet. He was hooted; he and his deputies were jostled and roughhoused. Arnold, in conjunction with Walker, Milchrist, and Grosscup, thereupon sent Olney a highly misleading dispatch:

When the injunction was granted yesterday a mob of from two to three thousand held possession of a point in the city . . . where they had already ditched a mail train, and prevented the passing of any trains whether mail or otherwise . . . [After reading of injunction to them] the mob threw a number of baggage cars across the track, since when mail trains have been unable to move. I am unable to disperse mob, clear the tracks, or arrest the men who are engaged in the acts named, and believe that no force less than the regular troops can procure the passage of the mail trains or enforce the orders of the court. It is my judgment that the troops should be here at the earliest moment.

When Arnold's message reached Washington, President Cleveland ordered the commandant at Fort Sheridan to move his force into Chicago. The army poured into the city on July 4th. Simultaneously Marshal Arnold added 2,600 deputies to his staff, all armed and paid for by the railroads, and described by Chicago police as "thugs, thieves, and ex-convicts." The atmosphere of the strike changed instantly. Large excited mobs gathered about the railway yards and tracks. On July 5th the burning of freight cars began at the Rock Island yards. For several nights thereafter freight cars, ties, signal towers, and merchandise in the yards throughout the city were destroyed by fire. By July 6th Chicago was gripped in a wave of hysteria. Law and order had ceased to have meaning.

At this point Governor Altgeld stepped into the situation. Altgeld, who had been following the strike very closely, was amazed and angered by Cleveland's dispatch of Federal troops into Illinois without invitation. On July 5th he sent Cleveland a strongly worded message protesting the use of troops as "unnecessary," "unjustifiable," and unconstitutional. The next day, in response to requests from local authorities, he dispatched five thousand state militia into Chicago to suppress the riotous disorders that had developed after the arrival of Federal troops. Their appearance led to the first bloodshed of the strike. A mob, infuriated by the growing numbers of troops, attacked one Illinois regiment, which fired point blank into it, killing twenty to thirty people and wounding scores of others. Between July 7th and July 9th the same incident was repeated each day. Cleveland and Altgeld, accordingly, both poured more troops into the city until fourteen thousand state and Federal soldiers patrolled the streets and railroad right of ways.

In the meantime Debs, who had been indicted for conspiracy in restraint of commerce and for obstructing the mail, recognized that the boycott was being defeated and appealed to the Chicago trade unions to strike in support of the railway workers. Although sympathetic, the trades held back until Samuel Gompers arrived in Chicago, worried by the rumor of an impending general strike. Gompers went to see Debs, who informed him that there was no hope for victory and asked him to secure an agreement from the General Managers Association to rehire the strikers without discrimination. Gompers refused, and the Pullman Strike collapsed.

Public reaction to the strike was bitterly divided. Many recalled labor's involvement in violence during the previous decade, and their impression that workingmen were criminal in character. Olney's use of such strong expressions as "We have been brought to the ragged edge of anarchy," together with the use of the injunction and of troops, and the arrest of some seven hundred union leaders convinced them that the nation was being threatened with revolution. They could hardly find words sufficient to express their approval of the action taken by Cleveland and Olney.

On the other hand farmers of the Grange and Alliance country were happy to have the railway workers strike a blow against their old enemies. There were many, moreover, who were passionately critical of the use of Federal troops to quell domestic violence against the wishes of a state governor and of "government by injunction." Criticism, in fact, became so persistent that Cleveland appointed a commission to investigate the strike. The commission's report served to give good foundations to the criticism. It denounced the unfeeling paternalism of the Pullman Company, castigated the General Managers Association as a shrewd device to evade law, and exculpated the American Railway Union from the charge of provoking violence.

The report came too late to help labor; before it was issued the courts had already given approval to the chief by-product of the strike—the injunction. The injunction was nothing new; courts had been issuing them in England and America for centuries. Nor was the use of injunctions in labor disputes new. A large number of injunctions were granted by state courts during the Southwestern Strike of 1886; Federal courts issued injunctions during the Burlington Strike of 1888. But the injunctions issued before 1890 were of doubtful legality. In most cases they were issued to prevent strikers from committing acts already prohibited by criminal laws. Since the injunction was a remedy in equity, and it was a well established principle of jurisprudence that equity would not interfere with crime, use of the injunction to prohibit criminal acts was probably illegal.

Between 1890 and 1894 state and Federal courts began to issue injunctions in greater number, particularly during the railway strikes in the early part of the decade. These injunctions had a different basis. They were justified either as orders designed to prevent violations of the Interstate Commerce Act or the Sherman Act, or as orders designed to protect private property. In the former instance the injunction was on doubtful legal ground. The exact meaning of the acts was not defined at this early period; there was grave doubt that they were meant to be applied to labor.

Injunctions used to protect property were on much firmer legal ground, but there were difficulties involved. The problem was to establish the fact that irreparable injury to property had occurred. When the strikers were guilty of trespass, arson, sabotage, the matter was simple. But most injunctions were issued to prevent strikes, picketing, and boycotting. Strikes were designed to destroy relations established between employers and employees; boycotts were designed to undermine the profitable relations which the employer had developed with his customers. What was being threatened was not property but future expectancies or good will. By 1895 the courts were beginning to recognize the principle that these expectancies were property rights with a market value. But mere recognition of "probable expectancies" or good will as property did not justify the use of the injunction in labor disputes; it was a well-established principle of law that no recovery could be secured for losses resulting from the exercise by others of that which they had a lawful right to do. It was necessary, therefore, to establish the principle that strikes, picketing, and boycotting were unlawful; in the nineties the courts began to use the old common-law doctrine of conspiracy to this end. The old doctrine was that conspiracy was a criminal offense because it threatened the public. The new doctrine being developed from the old was that conspiracy was a civil offense because it endangered the property involved in probable expectancies.

When the Pullman strike occurred, the United States Supreme Court had not given a decision on any of these precedents. During the strike Federal courts issued a rash of injunctions which gave rise to a number of cases. The most important was the injunction issued against Debs and other A.R.U. leaders in Chicago. Debs was twice arrested, once for conspiracy and once for contempt of court. The conspiracy case was never brought to a conclusion. The contempt trial became one of the best known in American history.

Justice Brewer read the decision for the United States Supreme Court in what became known as the *In re Debs* case. He was careful to point out that the Supreme Court was not examining the right of the lower court to issue the injunction under the Sherman Act. There were instead two questions involved in the case: Did the Federal Government have authority to prevent forcible obstruction of interstate commerce and transportation of mail? If it had such authority, did one of the Federal courts of equity have the right to issue an injunction "in aid of the performance of such duty?" Under the constitution, Justice Brewer explained, power over interstate commerce and the transportation of the mails was vested in the national government; since Congress had exercised that power, it followed that the national government could prevent any unlawful and forcible interference with either. If necessary, it could also "appeal to the civil courts . . . and invoke the powers of these courts to remove or restrain . . . obstruction[s]." The right of the courts to interfere in such matters by injunction had long been recognized; it did not matter if obstructions were "accompanied by or consisted of acts in themselves violations of the criminal law." The Chicago court had full jurisdiction to issue the injunction and to judge whether it was obeyed or not.

In re Debs was significant to labor because it gave the highest legal sanction to the growing concept that conspiracy in restraint of trade was not only a criminal but a civil offense, thus widening the possible judicial use of the old doctrine of conspiracy as it applied to labor. It meant that thereafter labor activities could be forestalled by civil action. *In re Debs* also gave sanction to the concept that the injunction could be used to protect property in the form of probable expectancies, which meant that the injunction could be used in almost any industrial conflict where an employer's future relations with employees or customers were involved. *In re Debs* put the finishing touches upon a new and devastating antilabor weapon. In 1897 the Supreme Court in another case, known as *In re Lennon,* declared that all persons who had actual notice of the issuance of an injunction, whether specifically directed to them or not, were bound to obey its terms. The Lennon case thus gave legal sanction to the "blanket injunction."

15 ——

The A.F.L.: Advance and Regression

The full significance of the Pullman Strike was not immediately recognized by workingmen. While organized labor in general was alarmed by the alliance of business and government that had been revealed in the strike, and while the American Railway Union was visibly weakened, the A.F.L. emerged unscathed, looking forward to a brighter future. The confidence was not misplaced, for the organization was on the eve of one of its most remarkable periods of growth. The depression of 1893 began to lift in the summer of 1896. Factories resumed full production and the demand for labor increased. With returning employment trade union membership began to recover, and the A.F.L. reaped the reward.

The growth was not all happenstance. At the turn of the century both the nationals and the federation made conscious efforts to strengthen their structures. Nationals adopted the British system of the cigarmakers, gradually increasing control over locals and funds, destroying some aspects of local autonomy, and building the principle of trade solidarity. The movement met with resistance; local unions, jealous of their prerogatives, often split off from the national to go their independent ways or to form other organizations, sometimes of an industrial nature. By 1909, however, the nationals—or internationals as some were called—had become the leading units of the labor world: it was to them rather than to the locals and city federations that craftsmen looked for guidance.

The A.F.L., meanwhile, adopted a policy of opportunism toward its affiliates. In 1901 it issued the "Scranton Declaration," a statement which made "craft autonomy" the cornerstone of its organization. In some cases the federation followed its policy. The printing trade was an example. A printer had once been a craftsman able to do all the jobs in a print shop. Introduction of machinery and new printing techniques had broken the trade into a number of "operations": compositors, pressmen, feeders, stereotypers, bookbinders, electrotypers, and photoengravers. Although all of these craftsmen had been members of the Typographical Union, between 1889 and 1903 all but the compositors broke away to form their own nationals. The matter was arranged *entre famille* with the blessings of the federation. The same separation of crafts was accomplished in the shipping business where in spite of efforts to form an industrial union the men engaged were divided by trade into the International Longshoremen's Association and the International Seamen's Union.

But the principle of craft autonomy sometimes surrendered to the principle of might. An excellent example was found in the woodworking trade, in which the A.F.L. had three affiliates: the United Brotherhood of Carpenters and Joiners, the Amalgamated Society of Carpenters, and the Amalgamated Wood-Workers International. There was no clear distinction between the Brotherhood Carpenters and the Amalgamated Carpenters; both did the same kind of work. When, therefore, the federation revoked the charter of the weaker Amalgamated Carpenters in 1911—after nine years of jurisdictional warfare—it was upholding the principle of craft autonomy. There was a distinct difference between the carpenters and the wood-workers who worked in planing mills and built sashes, frames, doors, and furniture. Between 1901 and 1911, during which time the carpenters became the most powerful international in the nation, the two crafts waged a bitter war. A threat by the carpenters to secede from the federation finally solved the issue: the A.F.L. forced the weaker wood-workers to submerge their separate trade.

At times powerful industrial unionism also outweighed the principle of craft autonomy. The very convention which issued the Scranton Declaration violated its own proclamation by granting the United Mine Workers, an industrial union, the right to retain the craftsmen —hoisting engineers, firemen, blacksmiths, carpenters—who worked around the coal mines and who by all rules of craft autonomy belonged to other unions. Similarly in 1908, after eight years of unceasing effort to break them down into separate crafts, the A.F.L. conceded the right of the United Brewery Workers to enroll coopers, teamsters, stationary engineers, and stationary firemen in their industrial union.

This policy, with all its inconsistency, was essentially beneficial. It served to promote strong nationals and internationals which in turn were able to produce "trade" solidarity, and it helped to promote an increase in membership. On the other hand it also bred some dissatisfaction among those labor elements which were on the losing end of decisions. That dissatisfaction was to prove worrisome to the federation in later years.

Equally important for A.F.L. growth after 1896 were several spectacular victories in the coal fields. The period was one of utter chaos in the bituminous industry. Operators were engaged in a fierce competition for markets which reduced the price of coal 28 per cent between 1891 and 1897. Wages and working standards had dropped in the same proportion, a decline made easier by the appearance in the coal fields of Slav and Italian migrants willing to take lower wages. It was a situation in which no one in the industry appeared to profit.

In 1897 the United Mine Workers, with a mere ten thousand members, decided to remedy their situation with a bid for higher wages throughout the whole Central Competitive Field: western Pennsylvania, Ohio, Indiana, and Illinois. The wages they asked were adjusted to place the whole field upon terms of competitive equality. The request met with a generally favorable response from operators, but there were some recalcitrants. When these refused to come to terms, Michael Blatchford, president of the U.M.W., ordered a strike. The response was staggering: almost 100,000 miners walked off their jobs in the first four days. The Central Competitive Field was completely paralyzed, and mining operations were suspended even in Kentucky and Tennessee.

The operators surrendered. In the following year miners and operators met in conference to form the "Interstate Agreement" which established an eight-hour day for miners, a uniform wage scale for all day laborers, and a scale of wages for miners in each district which would equalize costs of production among all operators and thereby

establish equality of competition. It was a great victory for the
U.M.W.—evidenced by a 1,000 per cent increase in membership
during the year.

In 1898 Johnny Mitchell, a shy young man of twenty-eight, became
president of the miners' union. It was a propitious moment. Prosperity
had returned; the Spanish-American War was making industry hum;
the U.M.W. boasted 100,000 members. On the other hand the U.M.W.
was weak in anthracite. Unionism had disappeared from the five
hundred square miles of Pennsylvania known as the hard-coal fields
after the Molly Maguire trials. In the next quarter of a century the
English-speaking workers drifted away, to be replaced by some
twenty different nationality groups. They were an element willing to
work for lower wages and under far worse conditions than natives.
Suspicious of each other they appeared to be almost impossible to
organize.

Mitchell began a quiet organizing campaign in the area in 1898
and so quickly captured the imaginations of the "dagoes" and "hunk-
ies" that he was able to call a strike in two years. More than 100,000
joined in the walkout. Then Mitchell laid his case before the public:
The average annual wage of anthracite workers was $250. They were
paid by the ton, which Pennsylvania defined as 2,400 pounds but
which mine operators had increased to as much as 4,000 pounds by
the simple expedient of forcing miners to load cars eighteen inches
above the edge. Miners were forced to pay high prices for powder, to
trade at company stores, and to pay a monthly doctor's fee without
having the right to select their own physician. The miners demanded
an increase of 20 per cent in wages, payment on the basis of a 2,400-
pound ton, the right to employ checkweighmen, semimonthly cash
payment of wages, abolition of the doctor's fee, and reduction in the
price of powder.

The response of the public was so heartening that the Republican
party high command became alarmed. In an election year a coal
strike made mockery of their statement that Republicanism meant
prosperity and contentment for all Americans. Mark Hanna rushed
to confer with J. P. Morgan, whose banking house had immense
financial interests in anthracite, and with the presidents of the railroads which owned the anthracite fields. Shortly afterward, the Reading Road announced a 10 per cent increase in wages; other roads

followed. Fearful of a "back to work" movement, Mitchell accepted the offer.

Anthracite operators did not like the agreement which Republicans and Morgan had forced upon them. Nor, on second thought, did the miners. Wages had been increased but not enough to meet rising living costs, and all other grievances still remained. Accordingly, in 1902 the U.M.W. made new demands: for recognition, an increase in wages, and an eight-hour day. Mitchell appealed to the National Civic Federation for aid. Brain child of Ralph Easley, the Civic Federation had been created in 1900 to prevent industrial conflicts by bringing together the "reasonable" leaders of industry and labor so that they could settle their disputes around a conference table. Gompers and Mitchell both became members; Mark Hanna supported the organization; Morgan and August Belmont supplied it with money. Appeal to this body to intervene in the impending coal dispute was an effort to settle differences amicably.

The National Civic Federation failed, and on May 12, 1902, the U.M.W. called a strike. Almost all miners quit work within ten days. The strike was not so peaceful as the previous one. During the first two weeks the operators commissioned some 1,600 coal and iron police; in June they began to advertise for strikebreakers. Sporadic violence began in July and continued through August, but the total amount of violence was comparatively small. Mitchell's public statements—mild, conciliatory, and indicating willingness to arbitrate—counteracted any unfavorable impression and, in fact, won much public sympathy for the strikers. The attitude of the operators reenforced the sentiment. One incident was outstanding. In mid-July a Wilkes Barre photographer wrote a letter to George F. Baer, president of the Reading Road and leader of the anthracite operators, urging him as his religious duty to end the strike. Baer's reply has become a classic in labor history:

I see that you are a religious man; but you are evidently biased in favor of the working man to control a business in which he has no other interest than to secure fair wages for the work he does. I beg of you not to be discouraged. The rights and interests of the laboring men will be protected and cared for—not by the labor agitators, but by the Christian men to whom God in his infinite wisdom has given control of the property interests of this country.

Meanwhile the public, worried over a coal shortage, began to appeal to the White House for intervention. Theodore Roosevelt hesitated until September, when the price of coal reached $30 a ton; and he began to receive ominous reports of the probable effects of the strike upon the approaching election. Through Hanna he again approached Morgan, but this time the banker was unable to shake Baer, who refused to make any settlement except one that only starving men would accept. On October 3rd Roosevelt called a conference of the disputing parties, and appealed to both sides to consider the "terrible nature of . . . a winter fuel famine." Mitchell announced that the strikers were willing to submit the case to arbitration at any time. But Baer assumed an intransigent attitude, accusing the miners of sabotage, and rebuking the President for "negotiating with the fomenters . . . of anarchy."

While the conference was a failure, it made a tremendous impression upon Roosevelt, who was both angered by the "insolent and abusive language" used against him, and worried because the obstinancy of the coal operators had doubled "the burden on us" who stood between the people and "socialistic action." After ten days of deliberation, he informed Morgan that he would seize the mines unless the coal operators would accept a plan of arbitration. The operators capitulated, but with the proviso that no representative of labor would sit upon the arbitration commission. Ultimately a solution was found; a seven-man commission was set up without a labor man, but Edgar E. Clark of the Order of Railway Conductors was seated as an "Eminent Sociologlist." The commission handed down its award in March, 1903: wages were increased 10 per cent; provision was made for the employment of checkweighmen; and discrimination against union men was prohibited. The commission also recommended the creation of a board of conciliation to adjudicate all disputes arising between employers and miners. Although the award fell short of labor goals, it was rightfully considered a victory. Taken as a whole the coal conflicts were of great significance to the A.F.L. They were the first outstanding victories won by an affiliate, more important than the carpenters' eight-hour victory of 1890–1891. They created a powerful union, about 200,000 strong, in one of the few basic industries in which the federation ever secured a firm foothold. More than any other single event they were responsible for a six-fold increase in A.F.L. membership, which by 1904 reached 1,675,000.

This figure, however, became a temporary high point in the federation's history; during the next six or seven years the organization experienced a serious decline. Employers, alarmed over the aggressiveness and success of A.F.L. affiliates, were primarily responsible. Their movement began in a desultory fashion in the late nineties with the appearance of employer associations, which publicly acknowledged their intention to "investigate" and "regulate" labor relations. Their aim was the "open shop."

One of the first employer associations developed in the Chicago building industry. Locals involved in the industry had formed a Building Trades Council in 1888, and by using the sympathetic strike had secured a tight grip upon the city's construction work. In 1899 Chicago builders formed a Building Contractors Council and challenged trade-union domination with a demand for modification of contractual agreements which would once more place hiring in the hands of employers, permit use of nonunion materials, and abolish rules limiting output. In the year-long strike that followed, the builders managed to maintain complete unity; the strike ended with the disintegration of the Building Trades Council and with contractors in complete control of Chicago construction work. Similar organizations developed on a national scale in the metal trades. In 1901 the International Association of Machinists, with 60,000 members, struck for a nine-hour day in the industrial centers of the North. Employers formed a Metal Trades Association, defeated the machinists, and then adopted a policy barring "outside interference" with business operations. Simultaneously employers in the job foundry industry, long dominated by the International Moulders Union, organized the National Founders' Association, and demanded abrogation of long-established rules governing minimum wages, hiring and firing, apprenticeship, and use of machinery. Four years of intermittent conflict followed, ending with the industry once more under employer control.

The lesson of these conflicts was not lost. In 1901 employers from thirty-eight companies in Dayton, Ohio, where the A.F.L. had made considerable advances and had won a number of small strikes, formed a city-wide, industry-wide Dayton Employers Association. In the following year the association opened a united campaign against union labor. Two companies closed their plants "for repairs," informing employees who wished to return that they would have to make written application for reemployment and declare their willingness to work alongside nonunion men. The lockout, four weeks long, was successful. In the short space of one year labor-union membership dropped an estimated 85 per cent, and Dayton became an open-shop city. Meanwhile, Chicago employers, led by Frederick W. Job, also established an association and began a vigorous antiunion campaign. Its operation became typical of the whole later movement. It organized employers by trades and pledged them to fight as a unit for the open shop; it recruited nonunion workers, hired spies, organized strikebreaking agencies, and provided both financial aid and leadership in strikes. Simultaneously another movement began in Sedalia, Missouri, where J. West Godwin and other industrialists formed the Sedalia Citizens' Alliance, composed not only of industrial employers but also of a large majority of the city's business and professional men. The Sedalia alliance added vigilante action and credit restrictions to the weapons forged in Dayton and Chicago, and soon reduced local unions to impotence.

Two years after the open-shop movement began in Dayton, employers' associations and citizens' alliances were organized in almost every industrial center of the nation. Some were created by missionaries from the three pioneering cities—Job and Godwin were the two most important proselyters. Some were indigenous. In either case their objectives were the same. They proposed to obliterate the whole concept of an organized labor movement from the pattern of American life. The commonly accepted picture of labor as a victim of industrial oppression was to be reversed. Instead the employer was to be portrayed as the victim of the tyrannical and corrupt union business agent who, backed by his credulous followers, was interfering with the inalienable right of the employer to run his own business.

In 1903 the National Association of Manufacturers assumed leadership of the movement with a resolution opposing further recognition of unions and with the creation of the Citizens' Industrial Association, with David M. Parry as chairman, to coordinate an open-shop drive. During the next two years the C.I.A. made great advances. Its educational campaign attacked the closed shop as "un-

American"—contrary to the spirit of American institutions and to the spirit of free enterprise—and laid the blame for all industrial disturbances on the doorstep of labor. Thousands were converted. Even ministers and educators concluded that labor unions oppressed the workingman. Charles W. Eliot, president of Harvard University, went so far as to glorify the strikebreaker as an example of the finest type of American citizen whose liberty had to be protected at all costs.

The results of the campaign became evident in a long series of major strike losses suffered by A.F.L. affiliates after 1903. One of the first to suffer was the New York building tradesmen who had not only merged into the United Board of Building Trades and had secured effective control of labor conditions, but had also secured affiliation of labor employed by building-material dealers. In 1903 the power of the United Board appeared supreme. Nevertheless, material and lumber dealers organized an association and declared a lockout, bringing New York's construction industry to a standstill. Contractors promptly formed a Building Trade Association. The two employer groups then united in a campaign to rid themselves of union domination. First they demanded that building tradesmen agree to work with any kind of material that contractors used. The demand split the United Board. About half the unions agreed and formed their own organization. Then employers demanded that the unions agree to establishment of a General Arbitration Board, made up of representatives of all unions and employer associations, with power to adjudicate all differences; they also insisted that the sympathetic strike had to be outlawed. The proposal, accepted by the skilled trades, was rejected by the semiskilled and unskilled. When contractors threatened to create dual organizations among the "recalcitrant trades," most of them capitulated; the employers once more assumed control of the New York building industry.

The A.F.L. suffered another serious defeat in the meat-packing industry, which the Amalgamated Meat Cutters had started to organize in the nineties. In 1904 the union, with a membership of 56,000, demanded that the Beef Trust—Armour, Swift, Morris, National Packing, Swartzchild, and Cudahy—grant a uniform wage scale to all workers, skilled or unskilled, throughout their plants from coast to coast. When the packers made a counteroffer of a minimum wage for the skilled with nothing for the unskilled, the meat cutters, recognizing that such an offer would be followed by a reclassification of skilled workers into unskilled categories, rejected the terms. In July 50,000 packing-house workers and 12,000 auxiliary tradesmen in nine cities went on strike. Both sides settled down for a long contest. The packers recruited strikebreakers, and the union threw up picket lines; violence flared in several cities. In September New York City locals accepted the packers' terms, and the strike front began to disintegrate. The Executive Committee of the union, recognizing that its treasury was empty and that further struggle was futile, declared the strike at an end. The Beef Trust established an open shop.

A.F.L. teamsters also tasted defeat. The trade performed a wide variety of tasks ranging from cellar excavations to milk deliveries. The common denominator among its members was the fact that they drove a team of horses. The most important center of the International Brotherhood of Teamsters, organized in 1899, was Chicago. The union in that city grew very rapidly after 1900 chiefly because of two men, Albert Young who organized the Coal Team Drivers and John C. Driscoll who organized the Coal Team Owners Association. The two men, acting in their own trade, secured an employer-teamster agreement which in two years doubled wages but passed the increases on to the consumers. The agreement was then extended without trouble to other similar branches of teaming. It was even forced upon employers for whom teaming was only incidental to business and who could not easily pass on the increased costs to consumers, like breweries, department stores, and commission houses. By 1902 Young and Driscoll, because of their ability to cripple any firm by a boycott, had become arbiters of Chicago's industrial life.

While teamsters found nothing wrong with the situation, other elements in the Chicago labor world became alarmed. In 1904 the Chicago Federation of Labor began an investigation of Young-Driscoll activities which ended with both men resigning their positions. But the structure they erected remained. In April, 1905, the Chicago Federation requested the Teamsters to intervene in a strike of garment workers against Montgomery Ward. Eager to clear themselves of the suspicions raised by the Young-Driscoll investigations, the teamsters promptly paralyzed Montgomery Ward's business. Almost instantly the conflict spread. The Chicago Employers Association stepped in to organize an Employers' Teaming Company, and to persuade teaming employers, who had once worked hand in glove with the teamsters, to discharge all drivers who refused to haul for Montgomery Ward.

A wave of violence engulfed the city; drivers for the Employers' Teaming Company were mobbed, their wagons were attacked and merchandise was destroyed. Federal Judge Christian Kohlsatt issued an injunction against interference with deliveries; the violence increased. Charles B. Dodd, president of the Chicago Federation, and Cornelius Shea, head of the teamsters, and other labor leaders were arrested for ignoring the injunction. Shea was charged with corruption and was indicted for conspiracy; about nine hundred others were arrested and charged with rioting. The combined attack finally told. The strike ended in mid-July, with the trade on an open-shop basis.

The A.F.L.'s most important defeat in the early twentieth century developed out of a long conflict in the steel industry. The struggle was preceded by a gigantic consolidation movement begun by Carnegie-Phipps' purchase of controlling interests in coal fields, coke ovens, natural gas fields, limestone quarries, and iron mines between 1882 and 1896—purchases which made the company self-sufficient in the production of raw steel. Simultaneously various entrepreneurs began a consolidation of raw-steel-producing plants so that by 1900 three combines—Carnegie-Illinois, Federal, and National—controlled the whole crude and semifinished steel supply. In the meantime producers of finished steel joined the movement, and huge combinations appeared in the tin plate, tubing, wire, sheet, and structural steel industries. In 1900 integration of the whole industry from mine to finished product was accomplished by the formation of the United States Steel Corporation.

Labor was directly affected. In 1900 the only union in the steel industry was the Amalgamated Association of Iron, Steel, and Tin Workers. Formed in 1876 by the highly skilled, the Amalgamated immediately recognized that the new corporation, only partially unionized, could destroy unionism completely by playing nonunion mills against union mills. In 1901 an Amalgamated committee approached the Steel Hoop, Sheet Steel, and Tin Plate divisions of the company with a demand for unionization of all mills. Executive officers of each company indicated a willingness to meet the union wage demands in those mills which were already unionized and to extend the scale to some nonunion plants, but they insisted on keeping some mills on a full nonunion basis. The Amalgamated promptly issued strike calls, and 46,000 men quit work.

United States Steel's board of directors was perturbed. While it had no use for unionism, it could not afford a clash with labor. Most of the stocks and bonds of the corporation had not yet been sold to the public. An industrial conflict might destroy much of the value of these securities, and might even destroy the new corporation. The board, therefore, decided to grant union wage demands in all but a few mills of the strike-bound subsidiaries. The Amalgamated merely renewed its demands and called a strike against all mills of the corporation; 16,000 answered the call. The strike never had a chance. The Amalgamated had not won the sympathy of the unskilled workingmen, most of whom stayed on the job or returned to work after a few days' "vacation." The corporation imported strikebreakers and the mills reopened. The Amalgamated capitulated. Its wage demands were granted, but it surrendered its right to use the sympathetic strike, agreed not to attempt to extend unionism, agreed to work alongside nonunion men, and gave the corporation the right to discharge men for union activities.

The defeat set the stage for the next action—total destruction of unionism. The corporation moved slowly: in 1902 it initiated a profit-sharing plan, aimed particularly at the lowest-paid unskilled workers; in 1906 it began a safety program to reduce industrial accidents and began to provide vocational, social, and medical facilities for employees; in 1910 it inaugurated a voluntary accident-insurance policy, an old-age pension system, and a home-building program. Meanwhile, the Amalgamated continued to decline. In 1904 it lost a strike in the mills of the American Hoop Steel Company over wages. By 1908 the only unionized mills of the corporation were in the American Sheet and Tin Plate division. In June, 1909, that branch of United States Steel announced that it would henceforth operate as an open shop.

The announcement stirred the Amalgamated to final action. The response to its strike call was enthusiastic—even the unorganized workers, convinced that the welfare program of the company had been promoted by fear of the union, answered. All but one of the company's mills closed. The strike lasted some fourteen months, but not on a full scale. The company imported strikebreakers. In many towns it secured injunctions against picketing. In others, local officials systematically harried all strike activities. In one month all the non-union mills resumed operation, and the strike deadlocked. In November the A.F.L. denounced United States Steel as a "soulless corporation," and granted financial aid to the strikers to continue the fight. But to no avail; in March, 1910, the company announced a new, higher wage scale. The strike front collapsed, and in August, 1910, the Amalgamated officially recognized that United States Steel had become an open-shop corporation.

Meanwhile, unionism in Great Lakes shipping—one of steel's subsidiaries—had also been destroyed. Unionization of Great Lakes seamen dated back to 1903 when the Lake Seamen's Union secured its first contract from the Lake Carriers Association, a contract which limited the working day and provided for overtime payment. Five years later the Lake Carriers, led by Cleveland owners closely connected with steel, began an open-shop campaign. All men caught "agitating" were discharged; all men hired were compelled to sign affidavits renouncing allegiance to their unions. In addition all employees were given "continuous record discharge books" in which kind and quality of service performed were to be recorded each year. Only men with such record books were to be given employment. The Lake seamen, recognizing the plan as an elaborate black-listing system, protested. When Lake Carriers paid no attention, the seamen, marine firemen, cooks, and stewards in the union went on strike. It was hardly effective. The carriers were readily able to hire docile strikebreakers from among the myriad of southern and eastern Europeans who lived around the Great Lakes and who found the relatively wretched conditions aboard ship a considerable improvement over their normal living conditions. By the spring of 1910 the open shop was a reality upon the Great Lakes.

Another subsidiary of steel which became the scene of an open-shop campaign in the early years of the twentieth century was the structural iron industry. Union organizing in that industry had begun with the formation of the International Association of Bridge and Structural Steel and Iron-Workers in 1896. The structural iron-workers were not as highly skilled as members of other crafts; ironwork, moreover, was casual, migratory, and dangerous—it attracted men with considerable strength, courage, and recklessness but with little stability. Accordingly the Iron-Workers Union had remained weak until 1902 when it won a strike against the American Bridge Company, dominant concern in the field. A year later the ironworkers established a union shop in the whole industry.

The twin victories prompted employers to form the National Erectors Association and to hire Walter Drew, of the Battle Creek Citizens' Alliance, to lead its drive. Under Drew's guiding hand the Erectors Association refused to deal with unions, gave subcontracts only to open-shop contractors, hired spies and stool pigeons to invade the unions and *agents provocateurs* to stir up trouble, and used an extensive black list. By 1907 the Iron-Workers Union was reeling. In desperation it resorted to terror and dynamite. Between 1908 and 1911 there were forty-three explosions on jobs of the Erectors Association and twenty-seven on jobs of nonunion independent contractors. No lives were lost and very little property was damaged. But in October, 1910, the Los Angeles *Times* building, owned by Harrison Gray Otis, a leading open-shop advocate, was blown up by a blast of dynamite. Twenty-one persons were killed by the explosion and fire; property damage was huge.

A wave of hysteria swept the nation. The Erectors Association and the Los Angeles Merchants' and Manufacturers' Association hired a one-time "T-man," William J. Burns, to find the killers. A nation-wide manhunt followed. In April, 1911, Ortie McManigal and J. B. McNamara were secretly arrested in Detroit for the crime. A few days later J. J. McNamara, secretary-treasurer of the Iron-Workers Union, was secretly arrested in Indianapolis and, without much regard being given to extradition proceedings, was taken to Los Angeles. Burns then made the arrests public, announcing that McManigal had confessed and that his confession had named J. J. McNamara as director of the dynamiting campaign and J. B. McNamara as the *Times* dynamiter.

The arrest of the three men was a profound shock to labor. Convinced that the McNamaras were innocent, primarily because of the manner in which they had been spirited from the Midwest to Los Angeles, the A.F.L. organized a defense committee and employed Clarence Darrow as attorney. Meanwhile, in Los Angeles the

McNamara brothers were indicted for murder and for a whole series of other dynamiting crimes. Their trial began in October, 1911. Darrow soon realized that his clients, particularly J. B. McNamara who had actually committed the *Times* job, had little chance, and arranged a settlement. Both men pleaded guilty: "J.B." received a life sentence; "J.J.," a less severe sentence; all other prosecutions were dropped. The McNamaras' trial did not end the case. Ortie McManigal's confession had implicated other members of the Iron-Workers Union. In 1912 forty officials of the union were indicted in the Federal courts on charge of conspiracy to transport dynamite and explosives. Thirty-eight were found guilty, including Frank Ryan, the union president. The union was wrecked.

The long series of open-shop conflicts had a very harmful effect upon the American Federation of Labor's public relations. They reenforced the open shop advocates' contention that the closed shop was an un-American institution by emphasizing the point that labor unions which secured a closed shop used their power in a manner contrary to public interest. Building trades unions, for example, had checked introduction of apprentices, had retarded use of labor-saving machinery, and had limited output; they had, in short, increased the cost of construction. Teamsters' unions had acted in the same highhanded fashion: they had increased their own incomes at the expense of the consumer.

The building-trade and teamster strikes had also turned the spotlight upon the "insidious" operations of the union business agents. In the Chicago building-trades strike, contractors had charged that Martin Madden, head of the Building Trades Council, was a grafter. The charges had been unsubstantiated, but in the next ten years a number of Chicago business agents, including Madden, were convicted of extortion. The activities of Albert Young and John C. Driscoll and the indictment of Cornelius Shea of the teamsters on charges of corruption in 1905 were part of the pattern. The most important revelations had come in New York City where Sam Parks, business agent of the local Structural Iron-Workers Union, had been charged with extortion and brought to trial. His case had revealed in detail the versatile tactics which enabled a business agent both to dominate industry and to feather his own nest. One method was to call a strike on any pretext and then to accept a bribe to cancel the strike; another method was to threaten a strike and to accept money to prevent it; a third method was to call a strike against a competitor of a favorite contractor for which the agent was paid. The long conflict between the Erectors and the Iron-Workers had revealed that unions, when crossed, were more than willing to resort to violence, willing to destroy life and property to gain their ends. Finally, several events had revealed the shamelessness of the trade-union rank and file. Even after Sam Parks was convicted of extortion, his own union had reelected him as business agent. Even after Frank Ryan was convicted of conspiracy to transport explosives, the Iron-Workers had reelected him president.

Such revelations convinced a large part of the public, particularly the small-town and rural public, that trade unions were essentially selfish, that all business agents were crooked and that their activities were condoned by the labor rank and file, that labor was completely irresponsible and immoral and, therefore, to be condemned. The reaction reversed the pro-labor trend which had begun during the Homestead Strike and which had increased and intensified during the Pullman and anthracite strikes. After 1902, in short, public opinion once more turned against labor.

The open-shop conflicts also revealed internal divisions in the labor world. Some strikes made clear that the policy of organizing only the skilled left A.F.L. affiliates at the mercy of the unskilled. In the steel industry the unskilled workers, neglected by the Amalgamated, gave little support to successive steel strikes and helped, thereby, to undermine the strikers. In the shipping industry the unorganized foreigners along the Great Lakes, held in contempt by unionists, helped defeat the seamen's strike. Some conflicts drove a wedge between cooperating labor elements. Notable was the New York building-trade strike from which the unskilled emerged highly suspicious of the skilled unions which had revealed a willingness to throw them over to make separate agreements with contractors.

The conflict that created the greatest discontent was the Steel Strike of 1901. Early in the strike the Amalgamated asked Gompers to throw the full force of the A.F.L. behind the fight to maintain unionism in steel. He refused. After the strike was lost, the Amalgamated charged Gompers with "lukewarmness" and Mitchell of the U.M.W. with failure to keep a promise to support steelworkers.

Although Gompers and Mitchell were exonerated by a committee of the federation, the indictment made an impression. It served to focus attention upon Gompers' and Mitchell's association with industrialists in the National Civic Federation. The more aggressive labor leaders began to reveal a suspicion of the alliance; socialists became convinced that Gompers had sold out; even some middle-class reformers sympathetic to labor began to doubt. Such attitudes became the basis for Mitchell's removal as U.M.W. head in 1908 and for attacks upon Gompers by radical labor elements until his death in the midtwenties. They served to retard the A.F.L.'s development for more than a generation.

The decline of the A.F.L. could not be attributed solely to the open-shop campaign; the organization was also attacked by employers in the Federal courts. Use of the Sherman Act and the injunction during the Pullman Strike had alarmed the A.F.L. at first; but as time passed and the judicial proceedings were applied only to "outlaw" unions, the organization began to assume that it, as a respectable junior partner of industry, was immune. This complacency was rudely jolted after 1902 when the A.F.L. and its affiliates became involved in more than a score of cases designed to weaken or crush unionism.

The Danbury Hatters case, first of the series, developed out of the efforts of the United Hatters of America to organize the nation's hatshops. Their campaign, which made extensive use of the boycott, was highly successful wherever it was tried. In 1902 the hatters began a campaign in the shop of D. H. Loewe and Company of Danbury, Connecticut. Unlike most hat manufacturers, Loewe fought back; accordingly the hatters at Loewe's went on strike and declared a nation-wide boycott against Loewe products. In August, 1903, Loewe and Company sued the 250 individual union hatters who were on strike for $240,000 under Section 7 of the Sherman Act which allowed triple damages to persons injured by conduct contrary to the act. The suit was significant because the demand for damages and the suit against individuals was without legal precedent and because the legality of the use of the Sherman Act against labor had never been settled.

It was many years before the Danbury Hatters case ended. In the original proceedings the district court ruled that the individual members of the Hatters Union were liable for damages since they had violated the Sherman Act. The hatters appealed, contesting the applicability of the act. In 1908 the Supreme Court handed down its decision. The Sherman Act, it declared, was designed to prevent conspiracies in restraint of interstate commerce. While the hatters had not interfered physically with the transportation of hats between states, there were other forms of interference: the hatters' boycott was that kind. A boycott, then, was a conspiracy in restraint of trade and those guilty of conspiracy were liable to pay damages.

While the Danbury Hatters case was still in litigation, several officers of the A.F.L. were confronted by another legal problem which arose out of a conflict between James Van Cleve, president of the Buck's Stove and Range Company of St. Louis, and the metal polishers' union. In 1906 Van Cleve ordered the metal polishers in his St. Louis factory, who had been working nine hours for several years, to return to a ten-hour day. The metal polishers went on strike, threw up a picket line, declared a boycott of Van Cleve's product, and appealed to the A.F.L. to place the company upon its "We Don't Patronize" list, published regularly in *The Federationist*.

The A.F.L. moved cautiously, but in May, 1907, after all negotiations had failed, it placed the company's product upon its "We Don't Patronize" list and sent out circulars asking all affiliates and members to call upon businessmen, urging their cooperation and asking them to write to the company to make an honorable adjustment of its relations with labor. It was the A.F.L.'s first large-scale attempt to use aggressive boycott measures. Van Cleve asked for an injunction. It was granted by Justice A. M. Gould of the Supreme Court of the District of Columbia in December, 1907. The order restrained the A.F.L. and its officers from "interfering in any manner" with the sale of Van Cleve's products; from "declaring or threatening any boycott" against Van Cleve's company "or in any manner assisting such boycott; or printing or distributing through the mails any paper" which contained any reference to the name of Van Cleve's company, its business, or product in connection with the term "unfair" or "We Don't Patronize."

The injunction was a shock to A.F.L. officials; they had judged themselves immune from hostile governmental action. Their subsequent actions were moderate. The proceedings of the Norfolk convention of 1907 in which the company was referred to as under boycott were extensively circulated. Gompers criticized the injunction in a speech at Indianapolis, and Mitchell presided over a convention at which the boycott was mentioned. Nevertheless, one year after the injunction was issued Judge Wright of the Supreme Court of the District of Columbia declared Gompers, Frank Morrison, A.F.L. secretary-treasurer, and Mitchell in contempt. Gompers was given a one-year sentence, Morrison six months, and Mitchell nine months. All three appealed in March, 1909; the Court of Appeals of the District of Columbia announced that the lower court had erred in issuing the injunction by making it too sweeping. But in November, after the injunction was amended, Gompers, Morrison, and Mitchell were again adjudged guilty of contempt. The new sentences were also appealed. In the midst of the hearings Van Cleve died, and at the company's request the United States Supreme Court dismissed the case.

Of the two cases, that of the Danbury Hatters was the more important because it made individuals responsible for actions of the union to which they belonged and because it called into question the very legality of a trade union. While the case had involved a boycott intended to bring about union recognition, the Supreme Court had decided that the boycott was intended to prevent Loewe from engaging in interstate commerce and was, therefore, an unlawful conspiracy. To labor the doctrine was most alarming: it invited the courts to decide that any act to raise wages, shorten hours, or improve labor conditions might be construed as an unlawful conspiracy because it incidentally interfered with commerce.

Between 1908 and 1914 labor's worst fears were realized. In the New Orleans Dock case a district court declared that all strikes which tied up interstate commerce were unlawful under the Sherman Act. In the Hitchman Coal and Coke Company case, another district court declared that the U.M.W. was in and of itself an unlawful combination under the Sherman Act. The decision was reversed by a Federal circuit court, but for two years the U.M.W. was unlawful.

The Buck's Stove Case, while not so significant, was also alarming. It marked a revival of the use of the injunction; it made impractical the use of the boycott, one of labor's most potent weapons; it threatened the most respectable of labor leaders with jail sentences;

it seemed to reveal that in any dispute between capital and labor the
government was on the side of capital.

The over-all effect of the open-shop campaign and of employers'
resort to law could be read in the A.F.L.'s membership rolls after
1904. In that year A.F.L. membership stood at 1,675,000; it dropped
to 1,490,000 in 1905, to 1,450,000 in 1906. Membership increased
slightly in 1907–1908, but it was still well below the 1904 figure in
1910. At the beginning of 1911 it appeared that the growth of the
federation had been checked.

16 ——

The Labor Radicals

Troubles with employers and the Federal courts were not the
only problems which the American Federation of Labor faced during
the decades after the Pullman Strike. It was also confronted by
several rivals for the allegiance of labor—rivals with different ap-
proaches and solutions to the problems of labor, rivals which collectively presented a challenge to the A.F.L.'s leadership of the
labor world.

Most significant were the socialists, whose organization, the Socialist Labor party, shattered in the early eighties, emerged from
obscurity during the United Front campaigns. The politically conscious elements—largely English-speaking and led by V. L. Rosenberg—dominated the organization at the time, but their ascendancy
was short-lived. The small vote cast for socialist candidates in the
election of 1888 created an intense dissatisfaction with political programs, and the A.F.L.'s eight-hour movement revived hopes of trade-
union success. In 1889 the trade unionists revolted, ousted Rosenberg,
and adopted a platform pledging the party to cooperate in the formation of trade unions and promising support for the A.F.L.'s eight-hour
movement.

The trade unionists' hope that they could establish friendly relations with the federation was soon destroyed. The A.F.L.'s refusal to charter a socialist-sponsored trade assembly in New York in 1890, causing the withdrawal of the party from trade assemblies in sixteen cities, and the efforts of A.F.L. socialists, under the leadership of Thomas Morgan, to convert the organization to politics with the "political programme" of 1893 made cooperation impossible. Relations between the organizations, in fact, became hostile.

Meanwhile leadership of the Socialist Labor party changed. The man who rose to the helm was Daniel De Leon, who became editor of the party's newspaper *The People* in 1891. His accession to power was revealed in a sudden change of direction. In 1892 the party nominated the first socialist presidential ticket in American history: Simon Wing and Charles Matchett; the ticket polled better than 21,000 votes. More important was the change created by De Leon's obsessive desire to head a trade-union movement. In 1892 he began to write about "new," "militant," "energetic" trade unionism, willing to enter politics and to struggle not for mere "groveling improvements or hunger-aggravating crumbs," but for a "co-operative commonwealth." He set out to capture the dying Knights of Labor as the most suitable vehicle for achieving his aims.

His first step was to induce the United Hebrew Trades, found primarily among needleworkers, to affiliate with District Assembly 49. As a reward he and several other socialists were elected as delegates to the General Assembly. There he joined the agrarian contingent to unseat Powderly as Grand Master and to replace him with Sovereign. Success seemed certain, but differences shortly developed between Sovereign and De Leon over policy, and De Leon lost his seat as a delegate. The failure to take over the Knights led De Leon to independent action. Late in 1895 he issued a call to "all Knights of Labor assemblies and all progressive organizations to join . . . in establishing a national body on the . . . lines plainly marked out in the class struggle." District Assembly 49, the New York, Brooklyn, and Newark Central Labor federations, and the United Hebrew Trades responded. In December, 1895, they organized the Socialist Trade and Labor Alliance, which promptly declared war on both the A.F.L. and the Knights. Many socialists were pleased with the developments that followed. Party membership increased, and the

1896 presidential ticket won a larger vote than it had four years earlier. The Socialist Trade and Labor Alliance also showed progress. Starting with about one hundred unions in the New York area, its campaigns kept the East Side of New York in a turmoil and in addition attracted garment workers, textile workers, cigarmakers, coal miners, and glass-bottle makers from New England, New Jersey, and Pennsylvania.

De Leon's tactics, however, ultimately caused trouble. A group of Jewish radicals in New York announced their opposition to the policy of dualism, seceded from the party and set up their own newspaper, the *Vorwärts*, in 1897. De Leon, master of invective, promptly unloosed a flood of scurrilous language upon their heads. Shortly afterward the New York assemblies which supported the *Vorwärts* secession were expelled from the party. These were followed by sections in Haverhill, Cleveland, and St. Louis. A large contingent of the party, recognizing that such expulsions would ultimately reduce organized socialism to an impotent economic sect, began to grow restive. Late in 1898 the *Volkzeitung*, a newspaper dominated by German trade unionists, issued a bold criticism of De Leon's policy of dualism. When De Leon demanded a retraction, the *Volkzeitung* replied by an attack upon the Socialist Labor party in general. The De Leon-dominated National Executive Committee of the party promptly censured the newspaper and announced that the issue of severing relations completely with that publication would be brought up at the next meeting of the General Committee. But the *Volkzeitung* faction called its own meeting, named its own Committee—Morris Hillquit among them—descended upon the party offices where the printing plant of *The People* was housed, and demanded possession. In spite of a pitched battle De Leon managed to maintain control.

His victory was not a real one. In 1900 the Socialist Labor party adopted his policies as its platform. Its aim, thereafter, was the ultimate overthrow of the wage system. To make sure that this aim would not be compromised, all members of the party were forbidden to accept office in a "pure and simple" trade union. The party nominated Joseph F. Malloney and Valentine Remmel as its presidential ticket. At this point advance stopped. The party had received better than 82,000 votes in the elections of 1898; it polled less than 38,000 votes in the election of 1900. The Socialist Labor party never changed after that. Although its name and that of its leader was to be seen and heard for two decades, its membership remained static; its offshoot, the Socialist Trade and Labor Alliance, made no further gains; and its influence gradually disappeared.

While the Socialist Labor party was tearing itself into conflicting factions, a new socialist movement appeared on the scene. The development had a number of forces behind it: first was the old Rosenberg faction; a second was Eugene V. Debs; a third was the appearance in the nineties of what has been termed "Yankeefied" socialism.

The Rosenberg socialists had seceded from the Socialist Labor party in 1889 when the trade unionists had assumed control. Small in number and their philosophy repudiated, they had quickly sunk into oblivion. Revival began in 1893 with the appearance of Victor Berger, a Marxian who believed in political action and who joined the faction's small wing in Milwaukee. Berger set out to persuade the political socialists to surrender their Marxian theorizing about the class struggle and the ultimate establishment of a proletarian state and to replace this with practical immediate demands that were possible of achievement. His vigorous activity soon created a considerable following in Milwaukee and in the Chicago area. In 1894 the faction cooperated with the Populist party, but in 1896 it withdrew its support because it was unable to understand how Bryan or Free Silver would do anything for the "exploited toilers." In the late nineties the element was seeking a new course of action.

Meanwhile Eugene V. Debs had become a convert to socialism. After the Pullman Strike, Debs had spent six months in jail where he read countless socialistic writings and was visited by Berger. When he was released, he was not yet a socialist. After the election of 1896, in which he and his American Railway Union supported Bryan for the Presidency, Debs announced his conversion. His socialism was still a bit strange; its objective at this point included colonization of a western state, assumption of political control, and establishment of a cooperative commonwealth within its limits. Debs broached his ideas to various leaders of the American Railway Union. Their response was enthusiastic—primarily because of the influence of the new brand of socialism which was being preached in the Midwest.

"Yankeefied" socialism had its origin in Edward Bellamy's *Looking*

Backward, published in 1888, which presented a picture of a social-istic utopia in the United States some two hundreds years later. Per-haps because the book revealed little, if any, Marxian influence, it profoundly affected many intellectuals. They began to organize "Na-tional Clubs" to educate the public in the direction of making Bel-lamy's vision a reality. While these clubs did not penetrate deeply into society, they made thousands of Americans who had always regarded socialism as a "foreign importation" conscious of a socialistic dream world. More important than the clubs was J. A. Wayland who in 1893 began publishing the *Appeal to Reason* with the intention of establishing a "government of, by and for the people as outlined in Bellamy's *Looking Backward*." His campaign was directed at the midwestern agrarians who had created the Populist party. It was written in a language they understood, taking the form of vigorous attacks upon trusts, the rich, and the money power; and an equally vigorous advocacy of antimonopoly laws and the government owner-ship of transportation and communication facilities. The *Appeal to Reason* reached several hundred thousand midwesterners. Debs's suggestion that something be done to implement socialistic ideology fell on this fertile group.

In June, 1897, the American Railway Union dissolved itself. Then it joined a host of other individuals representing trade unions, social-ist clubs, religious organizations, or merely their own humanitarian instincts to form the Social Democracy of America. Their funda-mental objective was the creation of a cooperative commonwealth in some western territory from which they would spread socialistic principles to the rest of the nation. The organization lasted one year. At the second convention Meyer London's *Vorwärts* socialists of New York and Berger's Milwaukee followers demanded a removal of the colonization plank from the platform; defeated, they promptly se-ceded. Debs, who had become convinced that colonization was chimerical, went with them. The next day the seceders, announcing their belief that trade unionism and independent political action were "the chief emancipating factors of the working class," estab-lished the Social Democratic party with a platform calling for public ownership of all monopolies, all means of transportation and com-munication, and all mines; reduction of the hours of labor; adoption of the initiative and referendum, and proportional representation.

The party quickly expanded. While it secured only 12,000 votes for various candidates in 1898, it elected a mayor in Haverhill and named two members of the Massachusetts legislature. In the next two years some groups ousted by De Leon from the Socialist Labor party drifted into its ranks. By 1900 the new party could claim nearly five thousand members.

At this point a disrupting force appeared in the form of the anti-De Leon faction of the Socialist Labor party. Led by Morris Hillquit, that faction had assembled at Rochester in January, 1900, to recommend that all members of the party "join the organization of the trades to which they belong[ed]," and to reaffirm its faith in the trade-union movement as an "inevitable manifestation of the struggle between capital and labor." The assembly also nominated two of its leading figures, Job Harriman of California and Max Hayes of Ohio, as its presidential ticket for the coming election and appointed a committee to seek a merger with the Social Democratic party. The suggestion threw the Social Democrats into an uproar. Debs, Berger, and other leaders were opposed: the Hillquit faction was essentially trade unionist and might be infected with the virus of De Leonism. But the party rank and file were highly enthusiastic. Taking control of the annual convention, they not only nominated Debs for the Presidency and Job Harriman of the Hillquit faction as his running mate, but also appointed a committee to discuss merger.

Months of negotiation and delay followed. Several referendums were held, but the leaders of the Social Democratic party remained adamant. No agreement was reached. Nevertheless, both factions supported the Debs-Harriman ticket. This support, more than any other factor, tipped the scales. It convinced many of the previously hostile leaders that they had a great deal more in common than they had originally recognized. The high vote given the ticket—97,000—produced a further spirit of cooperation. Accordingly, in June, 1901, a unity convention met at Indianapolis and established the Socialist party of America.

The party's platform, written after a long and acrimonious debate, was a mixture of many socialistic principles. The party decided that its main effort to establish a cooperative commonwealth would be through independent political action, but it also approved the formation of trade unions both as a means of indoctrinating labor with socialistic principles and as a means of lessening the exploitation of labor. The party decided furthermore that its ultimate aim was the establishment of a socialistic society, but that it was also expedient to work for immediate goals: regulation of trusts, mines, transportation, and communication facilities; shorter hours for labor; abolition of child labor; a graduated income tax; and adoption of the initiative and referendum.

Between 1901 and 1905 the Socialist party made large advances. Its membership increased from less than 10,000 to more than 20,000. On the political front it waged vigorous campaigns, winning thousands of voters, particularly in the area covered by Wayland's newspaper. In the election of 1904 the party nominated Debs and Ben Hanford as its presidential ticket and polled 420,000 votes. The trade-union element of the party renewed its boring-from-within tactics inside the A.F.L., seeking to convert the organization into an independent political party which would work for the ultimate overthrow of capitalism. Max Hayes introduced such a resolution in 1902; it was defeated by a vote of 4,897 to 4,171, an indication of how strong socialism became in these years.

The American Federation of Labor's second rival for the allegiance of labor was the Western Federation of Miners which appeared in 1893 among the metal miners of the Rocky Mountain area. One of its roots lay deep in the structures which the Knights had created among coal and metal miners of the trans-Mississippi area. Another lay in the conditions that existed in the mining areas. The mining communities of the nineties were still part of the frontier. The people who lived in them were still highly individualistic, still resentful of control of any kind—yet quick to unite against any menace to their welfare. The W.F.M. was thus in part an almost instinctive frontier reaction against danger.

The immediate reason for the appearance of the Western Federation of Miners was the events that occurred in the gold-, silver-, and lead-mining regions around Coeur d'Alene, Idaho. Early in 1892, after introducing the machine drill which could do the work of five hand drillers and which automatically reduced 80 per cent of the skilled underground workers to the position of shovelmen, mine operators, acting in concert, closed every mine in the Coeur d'Alene area and announced that they would reopen only on condition that the miners would accept a dollar a day wage reduction. When the miners refused, trouble began. The operators imported strikebreakers who were promptly induced to leave—at the point of rifles. The operators secured a Federal court order enjoining interference with the strikebreakers and persuaded the governor to issue a proclamation to the same effect. The miners ignored both. The operators then hired a large number of armed guards. In July, 1892, a guard killed a striker; the miners, several hundred strong and armed with rifles, attacked and forced the guards to leave the area. The governor promptly dispatched the whole state militia to the scene and appealed to the Federal Government for aid. The War Department sent General Carlin who quickly restored order. He forced the miners to surrender their arms, brought back the strikebreakers and put them to work. Then he erected a bull pen, arrested several hundred known union men, and incarcerated them in it. Meanwhile, he removed all local officials sympathetic to the strikers, replacing them with persons willing to carry out his commands, and ordered the mining companies to discharge all active union men. As a final gesture eighty-five men were taken from the bull pen and charged with contempt of court; thirty more were charged with conspiracy. Sixteen of the two groups were found guilty.

The events of Coeur d'Alene produced a strong reaction throughout the whole mining country from Montana to Arizona. In May, 1893, some forty delegates from northern mining camps, led by Ed Boyce, Charles Moyer, and "Big Bill" Haywood, met in convention at Butte, Montana, and established the Western Federation of Miners —designed to organize all miners, mill men, smelter men, and engineers in the metal-mining industry; and to secure for the metal miner "an earning compatible with the dangers of the employment"; payment in lawful money instead of company scrip; laws establishing safety regulations in the mines; and laws prohibiting the employment of company guards. Boyce became first president; Haywood, secretary.

From the moment of its formation the Western Federation of Miners became involved in a long series of strikes. Its first major test came in the Cripple Creek region of Colorado in January, 1894. This was followed by major struggles—interspersed with many smaller conflicts—at Leadville, Colorado, in 1896, at Coeur d'Alene in 1899,

and at Telluride, Colorado, in 1901. The conflicts followed a remarkably similar pattern. Regardless of instigation the miners in almost
every strike were quickly confronted with a determined and ruthless
employer front which created Citizens' Alliances to harry strikers
with credit boycotts and beatings, which hired strikebreakers and
armed guards, and forced local authorities to recruit deputies to
"protect private property." Almost every conflict became, at some
time during its history, a miniature war with guards and deputy
sheriffs—organized at times even into machine-gun and cavalry divisions—facing equally well organized strikers. The terrorization of the
local population by armed guards and deputies and the dynamiting of company property, by parties unknown, were common features
of every struggle. When company and local resources failed, employers persuaded state authorities to dispatch the militia to restore
"law and order." With the militia came the removal of local officials
sympathetic to the strikers, the erection of bullpens, the incarceration
of strikers and their friends, elaborate black-list systems, and deportations. In spite of the forces arrayed against them, the W.F.M. locals
won more conflicts than they lost, and even in defeat they continued
to grow until by 1902 the organization could boast two hundred
locals and fifty thousand members.

In the meantime the Western Federation of Miners had also
plunged into politics in Idaho, Utah, and Colorado. Its activities
varied. While it most frequently allied itself with the Populists, it
also worked with the Democrats and occasionally named its own
"Miners' Ticket." The W.F.M.'s chief political aim was an eight-hour
law for all mine, mill, and smelter workers: a movement which the
small U.M.W. contingent in the Rockies and labor in general also
supported. The W.F.M. campaign was an easy success in Idaho and
Utah. Although corporate interests in the latter state fought the law
on the ground that it violated the Fourteenth Amendment, the United
States Supreme Court in the case of *Holden* v. *Hardy* approved the
legislation as a valid exercise of the state's police power to protect
the health of men employed in the mining industry.

In Colorado the results were different. The W.F.M. secured an
eight-hour statute in 1899, but it was promptly declared unconstitutional by the state supreme court. Undeterred, the W.F.M., supported
by the whole Colorado labor movement, began a campaign to amend

the state constitution. The desired amendment was overwhelmingly approved in a popular referendum in 1902. But W.F.M. success now ended; a powerful lobby of mine operators, smelter owners, and ranchers defeated all attempts at enactment of a new law.

The failure of the political eight-hour campaign in Colorado proved to be a turning point in the history of the W.F.M. In its frustration the organization launched a drive to secure the eight-hour day by economic action and plunged, thereby, into the dramatic and destructive second Cripple Creek Strike. The conflict began early in 1903 when the W.F.M. asked mill managers in Colorado City for an eight-hour day and an increase in minimum wages. When the manager of the Standard mill, largest in the area, rejected the demands on behalf of the owners, a walkout followed in all mills. The strike developed along customary lines. Mill hands established a picket line, and the managers began hiring strikebreakers. The sheriff appointed a large body of deputies, paid for by the operators, to protect mine property; and the governor, without investigating, ordered the Denver militia into the area. In March the W.F.M. and three of the mills came to an agreement whereby the mill managers granted an eight-hour day, pledged themselves not to discriminate against union men, to reinstate strikers, and to recognize the union. The troops were withdrawn.

But the Standard manager proved recalcitrant. After five months of unsuccessful effort to bring him to terms, the W.F.M. ordered the men employed in mines which shipped ore to the Standard mill to drop their tools. The sympathetic strike produced trouble. The mine operators began to grumble about being punished because of a dispute for which they were not responsible. When they announced that they would reopen their mines, the carpenters erecting a fence around one mine were immediately assaulted. The governor promptly flooded the area with one thousand militiamen. Led by Brigadier-General Chase, the military force began wrecking the local union: active leaders were arrested without charge and incarcerated in a bull pen; several government officers and the entire staff of the Victor *Record* suffered the same fate. In the midst of this action an explosion in which two men were killed occurred at the Vindicator mine. The governor immediately announced that the Cripple Creek area was in a state of insurrection and rebellion, declared martial law, and

suspended the writ of habeas corpus. The military commander issued
a vagrancy order threatening idle men with deportation. Arrest of
miners multiplied; officers of the W.F.M. from outside were refused
admission. Slowly all commotion died down and in February, 1904,
troops were withdrawn.

The Cripple Creek strike, nevertheless, continued. The final series
of episodes began in June when a train loaded with strikebreakers
was blown up at Independence. Mine operators and the Citizens'
Alliance promptly forced the sheriff to resign his office and appointed
one of their own men in his place. In a meeting at Victor the new
sheriff harangued the mob with a denunciation of the W.F.M. as a
gang of cutthroats and called upon the people to take the law into
their own hands. A wild mêlée followed in which five men were killed,
and the union hall was destroyed. The governor restored martial law
in the person of General Bell. The new military commander acted
without any regard for civil liberties; his troops were allowed to
destroy a miners' camp at Dunville; the Citizens' Alliance, clad in
white caps, was allowed to run wild: overthrowing governments, destroying property, terrifying citizens, beating and robbing miners, and
deporting any out of sympathy with their activity. A committee of the
Alliance was set up as a Military Commission to "try" miners for
deportation; more than 225 were shipped to Kansas and New Mexico.
The Portland mill, permitted to operate by the W.F.M. because it
was fair to labor, was closed; storekeepers were ordered to cease
selling goods to union men and their families; relief supplies sent into
the territory were seized by the military. By July, 1904, quiet was
restored to Cripple Creek, but the W.F.M. local was destroyed.

The defeat in Colorado was a crushing blow to the W.F.M. The
officers of the union, most of them fleeing warrants charging them
with responsibility for every crime committed in Colorado in the
previous year, recognized immediately that the whole organization
might dissolve unless some drastic action was taken. Their decision
was not long in the making; almost immediately they concluded that
survival depended upon some amalgamation to give their organization greater strength.

The W.F.M. had attempted to find allies before; the miners had in
fact affiliated with the A.F.L. in 1896. But when the federation had
failed to grant financial aid during the Leadville strike, they had

promptly seceded. In 1898 W.F.M. leaders had tried again. At a convention held at Salt Lake City and attended primarily by former Knights, they formed the Western Labor Union. Although its constituency consisted of 14,000 miners and only 400 individuals from other trades, the organization alarmed Gompers. A delegation from the A.F.L. visited the Western Labor Union convention of 1901 to plead for a reunited labor movement, but the only result had been to convert the Western Labor Union into the American Labor Union. Neither the W.L.U. nor the A.L.U. was a successful organization. Their chief affiliates consisted of a small group of Colorado railway workers, some Colorado coal miners' locals, and western hotel and restaurant workers.

When the W.F.M. began a search for new allies in 1904 the A.F.L. promptly suggested reaffiliation. The W.F.M. recognized, however, that there was too great a gulf between the organizations: it was geographically remote from A.F.L. centers; the conditions it faced, bordering upon class warfare, were not understood by eastern labor; and its philosophy of political action, industrial unionism, and direct economic action was foreign to A.F.L. ideology. In addition the leaders of the W.F.M. had begun to show socialistic inclinations, an attitude that emphasized the width of the gap between the two organizations.

W.F.M. leaders were looking in another direction. Late in 1904 they invited about thirty persons, sympathetic to the idea that the "working classes if correctly organized on both political and industrial lines were capable of successfully operating the industries of the country," to a conference. Twenty-three attended. Among them were three from the W.F.M.; five from the A.L.U. and its affiliates; William E. Troutmann, editor of the United Brewery Workers newspaper; Charles O. Sherman of the United Metal Workers Union which had seceded from the A.F.L.; De Leon and several other members of the Socialist Trade and Labor Alliance; Debs of the Socialist party; and individuals, like "Mother" Jones, who represented only themselves.

The conference promulgated a statement of principles to be used as the basis of a new labor organization. The "manifesto," as it was named, denounced the A.F.L. for attempting to divide labor by creating an aristocracy of skill, criticized it as an organization which had failed to recognize the mechanization of industry and the resulting degradation of labor, and condemned it as an organization out of step with current developments, totally incapable of resolving the "irrepressible conflict between the capitalist class and the working class." The solution was to organize labor into "one great industrial union embracing all industries—providing for craft autonomy locally, industrial autonomy nationally, and working class autonomy generally." The conference invited all labor groups sympathetic to this statement of principles to meet in convention in June, 1905.

About two hundred of the most heterogeneous delegates attended; in addition to those at the first conference they represented dissatisfied A.F.L. locals among miners, longshoremen, printers, hotel and restaurant workers, switchmen, street railway employees, barbers, metal polishers, carpenters, and tailors. Full of wild enthusiasm they adopted the name Industrial Workers of the World, announced their determination to organize labor into industrial unions which would take direct and vigorous action to ameliorate labor conditions, and to create an independent third party which would work for the overthrow of capitalism and the establishment of a "co-operative commonwealth." The convention placed executive power in the hands of a president, Charles O. Sherman; a secretary-treasurer, William E. Troutmann; and a five-man board which included Moyer of the W.F.M. It provided for organization of the rank and file into thirteen departments covering all industries in the United States. The W.F.M. became the mining department; the Amalgamated Society of Engineers and the Metal Workers was formed into the engineering department; and the railway men into the transportation department.

When the first I.W.W. convention adjourned, its leaders confidently expected to see a great horde of wage earners join the new organization. The stampede never materialized. The trend was all in the other direction. In the next three years the I.W.W. lost practically its whole original membership. First to break was the Socialist party of America. Its unwillingness to cooperate had a number of motives. The Hillquit-Hayes faction opposed cooperation because it considered the A.F.L. a better field for socialistic activities. The Debs-Berger element was alienated by the I.W.W. platform which rejected alliance with other parties and seemed to make futile any hope of attaching the new organization to the Socialist party. Both groups, moreover, were alarmed by De Leon's apparent satisfaction with developments. After 1905 no official delegates of the Socialist party attended any convention of the I.W.W. In later years some party sections announced their approval of I.W.W. objectives, and the party itself often supported I.W.W. campaigns and strikes with its funds. But officially and in fact the Socialist party and the "Wobblies" traveled separate roads.

During the next ten years the Socialist party reached its greatest strength. Internally the organization achieved a previously unattainable unity. Between 1905 and 1917 the party was made up of a strange conglomeration: Yankeefied socialists who had no Marxian background, intellectual Marxians who believed in political action, Marxians who were more interested in trade unionism than in politics—laboring men, college professors, social workers, ministers, small businessmen, and farmers. All these elements formed into two wings: a left led by Haywood, Frank Bohn, and Leon Greenbaum; and a right led by Berger, Hillquit, Hayes, and London. Between these two wings there developed a ceaseless argument over party principles. In general the left wanted to emphasize the class struggle, to advocate sabotage and mass action, to preach revolution and the inevitability of a violent final struggle to overthrow capitalism. The right insisted that the class struggle was not important in the United States, that the party must at all times emphasize legal and peaceful action, that socialism could be instituted through the ballot box, and that socialists must think first of today, only secondly of the millennium.

The two wings quarreled over many specific issues. The left wanted a highly centralized party structure; the right insisted upon decentralization and flexibility. The left demanded that membership be limited to proletarian laborers; the right argued that all elements— proletarians, intellectuals, farmers, and the poor—must be welcomed. Although both wings agreed that political activity was desirable, the left objected strenuously to any alliance with a "labor" party; while the right wing was willing to support a "bona fide" labor party if one was created. The left wanted no restriction placed upon immigration; the right insisted that the party was obligated to protect the standards of the American worker, and, therefore, advocated restriction. The left called the farmers "property owners" and insisted that no concessions be made to them; the right sought to hold the farmers in line by assuring them that the party had no desire to nationalize their landholdings within the foreseeable future.

The longest and most bitter quarrel occurred over industrial and trade unionism. A large right-wing faction argued that the policy of boring from within the A.F.L. was the most certain way of advancing socialistic doctrines. Many rightists and most leftists, however, favored industrial unionism as the more realistic approach to the problem of organizing labor; but this group quarreled over the proper attitude to take toward the I.W.W. The left advocated support of the Wobblies, but the right denounced the I.W.W. as dualistic and syndicalistic and its members as saboteurs and anarchists, and insisted upon keeping the two organizations as far apart as possible.

The internal quarreling did not shatter party harmony. The right wing boasted a large majority, and its domination paid dividends. Inside the A.F.L. socialist strength increased until 1912 when Max Hayes received about one-third of the votes cast in the contest with Gompers for the presidency of the organization. Socialist pressure, moreover, undoubtedly influenced the A.F.L. to undertake its "amalgamation" policy and to adopt a more forceful nonpartisan political philosophy after 1906. Socialist party membership also increased. In 1905 the party had 10,000 members; by 1910 the number had jumped to 58,000; by 1912 to 118,000. In 1915, 70 per cent of the party was native born. Socialist election totals also advanced. Although 1908 election totals showed only a slight increase over the previous national election, in 1912 when the party nominated Debs and Emil Seidel, mayor of Milwaukee, its vote reached 897,000—5.9 per cent of the total. Much of the increase came from the western farm areas; the party was making a strong appeal to its normal enemies, the agrarians. By 1912 the party had more than one thousand of its members in public office, including one Congressman, fifty-six mayors, and three hundred aldermen. But election returns did not tell the whole story; between 1905 and 1917 the Socialist party also became the advance guard of the progressive movement. Its honest and unwavering stand won it so much support from so many discrete sources that ultimately both major parties were forced to reckon with socialist influence upon elections. The socialists, in short, could claim some of the credit for the progressive legislation enacted during the era.

Shortly after the Socialist party detached itself from the I.W.W., the Western Federation of Miners also seceded. The W.F.M. with-drawal was caused, fundamentally, by the Haywood case which began in December, 1905, when Frank Steunenburg, former gov-ernor of Idaho, was killed by an explosion of dynamite. A few days later police in Denver arrested Harry Orchard and turned him over to James McParlan, then head of the Pinkerton agency in Denver. Orchard confessed to a long series of crimes of violence in the Coeur d'Alene and Cripple Creek areas and to the murder of Steunenburg, but he swore that Moyer and Haywood of the W.F.M. had paid him to murder Steunenburg, and that George Pettibone, a Denver businessman, had suggested the method. A month later the Canyon County, Idaho, district attorney swore out warrants for the arrest of Moyer, Haywood, and Pettibone. After the governor of Colorado secretly signed extradition papers, Moyer, Haywood, and Pettibone were arrested, conveyed under guard to the railway station, and taken by special train provided by the railway to Idaho. In March, 1906, they were formally indicted for murder.

The proceedings immediately aroused labor throughout the na-tion. Denouncing the act of officials as a "kidnaping," they raised a large defense fund and retained Clarence Darrow and W. F. Rich-ardson, one of the leading attorneys in the West, to defend the three men. Meanwhile, another witness, Steve Adams, who was turned over to McParlan, made a confession corroborating Orchard's story. But before the trial he repudiated his confession and charged that Governor Frank R. Gooding of Idaho had threatened to have him hanged if he did not support Orchard's story. Adams was promptly indicted for the murder of two claim jumpers and brought to trial. The Moyer-Haywood-Pettibone defense charged that the trial had only one purpose: to force Adams to corroborate Orchard's confes-sion. If such was the aim, it was not successful; the jury disagreed.

The main trial began in May, 1907, with Bill Haywood under in-dictment. The chief witness was Orchard, who confessed to a long criminal career which included bigamy, theft, arson, and murder. In addition he testified that as a member of the W.F.M. he had been employed by an "inner circle" as a professional assassin and dyna-miter. As the tool of this inner circle, he had committed twenty-six murders and had dynamited both the Vindicator mine and a rail-road depot in Cripple Creek. The obvious object of his testimony was to show that the W.F.M. leadership had inspired Steunenburg's murder. But the defense tore Orchard's confession to ribbons. It charged that McParlan had "fixed" the confession; it produced witnesses to contradict a vast amount of Orchard's testimony. Its objective was to show that Orchard had been motivated solely by personal malice in murdering the former governor. The jury returned a verdict of "not guilty."

The Haywood case, which began shortly before the second I.W.W. convention, scared the W.F.M. A substantial portion of the public had already concluded that the metal miners were in truth advocates of violence and murder; their affiliation with the I.W.W., a "revolutionary" organization, did nothing to mitigate the belief. W.F.M. leaders, realizing the potential effects of a hostile public opinion, became cautious. At the 1906 convention of the I.W.W. this attitude caused a split in the organization. The leadership of the W.F.M. demanded that the I.W.W. repudiate revolutionary principles and launch a drive to create a more efficient industrial labor organization. Two factions developed: the conservatives led by I.W.W. president Sherman who supported the W.F.M. demands; and the radicals led by I.W.W. secretary Troutmann, De Leon, and Vincent St. John. In the showdown that followed, the radicals secured control and Sherman and most of the W.F.M. delegates promptly bolted.

The action precipitated a new struggle. The Sherman faction secured legal control of I.W.W. properties, and the Troutmann faction set up its own I.W.W. Both organizations, judging that survival depended upon the attitude of W.F.M. rank and file, began proselyting among the metal miners. At this point the W.F.M. became involved in another disastrous conflict in Goldfield, Nevada, whence a large number of miners had moved from Cripple Creek. During the panic of 1907, when Goldfield mineowners tried to force miners to accept wage payments in scrip, the W.F.M. locals went on strike. They were joined by I.W.W. elements among cooks, waiters, and bartenders who resented efforts of local businessmen to force them into the more tractable A.F.L. unions. The governor asked for Federal troops and broke the strike. Loss of the contest was the culminating defeat for the W.F.M. It reduced the leadership to despair and forced the rank and file to conclude that it must eschew its radical past. At the 1907 convention the organization decided by an over-whelming vote to support the more conservative Sherman I.W.W. A minority, headed by Vincent St. John, refused to accept the deci-sion; it joined the Troutmann I.W.W.

W.F.M. support for the Sherman I.W.W. did not last long. Con-ditions were changing in the mining country. No longer a raw fron-tier, it was becoming throughly respectable and middle class. The leadership of the miners was also changing. Old and weary of fight-ing, it was becoming more and more sympathetic to A.F.L. ideology. In May, 1911, the W.F.M. withdrew from the Sherman I.W.W. and "returned" to the fold. As a federation affiliate it made one half-successful effort at revival in the Michigan Copper country in 1913, and it became involved in a suicidal internecine quarrel with the Butte Miners' Union in 1913–1914. A few years later, its one-time strength dissipated, it became the International Union of Mine, Mill and Smelter Workers.

The W.F.M. decision to join Sherman reduced the Troutmann I.W.W. to a seemingly impotent little group of former W.F.M. mem-bers and De Leon's followers. But the organization quickly shrugged off the effects of the schism and began proselyting among elements previously untouched by the labor movement: the migratory agri-cultural workers of the Great Plains, the lumber workers of the Pacific Northwest, and the dockworkers along the Pacific Coast. The cam-paign was led by Troutmann, St. John, John H. Walsh, and the "over-all brigade." Dressed in blue denim overalls, black shirts, red necker-chiefs, and sporting I.W.W. buttons, the brigade toured the country between Chicago and the Pacific by freight car. Their campaign, undertaken in the midst of the 1907 panic, was no overwhelming tri-umph; but when the Troutmann I.W.W. met for its fourth conven-tion in 1908 it was once more vibrant with life.

The new members produced a final split. A stubborn-willed crowd, believing in organization for economic ends and willing to use any weapon to achieve those ends, they scorned theory and politics—and thereby ran squarely into De Leon. With characteristic scurrility the head of the Socialist Trade and Labor Alliance began to criticize the new members for their crudities, their rawness, and their inabil-ity to perceive the more "civilized" methods needed for gaining their ends. It was an ill-advised attack. The overall brigade took control

of the 1908 convention and summarily ousted De Leon on the charge
that he represented a union in a different industry from his own. De
Leon promptly organized an I.W.W. with headquarters at Detroit,
but he secured no new followers. The organization soon became another propagandist appendage of the Socialist Labor party.

With De Leon's expulsion the Troutmann I.W.W. became the
"real" or "Chicago" I.W.W., legitimate descendant of the original organization set up in 1905 and mouthpiece of the nation's laboring
"rabble." It made its first major impression upon the nation through
its involvement in the "free speech" fight begun in Spokane, Washington, employment center for the casual labor elements of the Pacific
Northwest. The fight developed late in 1908 when the I.W.W.
launched an extensive speaking campaign with the slogan "Don't
Buy Jobs" in the streets around the Spokane employment agencies
which had become skilled in the art of swindling men who applied
for jobs. The agencies promptly countered by pressuring the city
council to pass an ordinance forbidding street speaking. The I.W.W.
obeyed the regulation for nearly a year, until Spokane religious
groups, which habitually used the streets, secured a new regulation
exempting them from the street-speaking ordinance. Angered by the
discrimination on behalf of "the Christers," the Spokane I.W.W. renewed its campaign. In one day 150 men were arrested and crowded
into jails that could hardly accommodate them. Reinforcements
promptly arrived from the surrounding territory. At the end of
twenty days four hundred men had been jailed. The effort brought
results: the W.F.M. declared a boycott of all goods coming from
Spokane, and taxpayers began to protest against the cost of feeding,
housing, and policing the prisoners. When Vincent St. John publicly
appealed to all Wobblies to come to Spokane to renew the struggle,
city officials capitulated. The I.W.W. was granted freedom of assembly, freedom of the press, and the right to distribute its literature.
The free-speech fight in Spokane was followed during the next two
years by others in Kansas City, Missouri, in Aberdeen, Washington,
in Fresno, California, and in San Diego. Each developed along much
the same lines as the Spokane struggle with one major exception. In
San Diego beatings, clubbings, and forceable deportation of Wobblies
by masked vigilantes replaced incarceration. The results, nevertheless, were always the same: the I.W.W. won every fight.

Meanwhile, the Wobblies became involved in a campaign on behalf of the textile workers of the East. Textile labor, which worked in the nation's most completely mechanized industry, was divided into two groups—a small minority of skilled and a huge majority of unskilled. The skilled were organized as the United Textile Workers, affiliated with the A.F.L. Their condition was fair, and they gave no attention to the many nationalities which made up the unskilled, partially because they regarded the unskilled as socially inferior and partially because they considered the foreigners as unorganizable. The condition of the unskilled made a travesty of the widely vaunted American standard of living.

In January, 1912, a state law providing a fifty-four-hour week for women and children went into effect in the Massachusetts mills. Although the average wage for the unskilled was only $8.76 for a fifty-six-hour week, mill operators promptly reduced wages. Workers in the weaving department of the American Woolen Company in Lawrence revolted and in three days 25,000 men, women, and children were on strike. The I.W.W. sent one of its most able organizers, Joseph Ettor, to the scene. Ettor immediately organized a strike committee and drew up demands: a 15 per cent increase in wages and double pay for overtime. He formed a relief committee to secure funds from sympathizers and ordered demonstrations to be made against the only two mills in Lawrence still operating. Although four companies of local militia ordered to duty as soon as the strike began broke up Ettor's carefully arranged demonstration, the mills were shut down. More militia descended upon Lawrence; under the protection of their bayonets some of the mills began to reopen. Then Ettor organized a parade. During its passage, and at a considerable distance away from it, a woman striker was killed. Lawrence authorities immediately arrested Ettor as an accessory to the murder of the woman striker. The act, intended to break the strike, failed. Big Bill Haywood arrived to take charge and the strike front held firm. In March millowners who had stood out adamantly against all negotiations broke down. The victory was followed by wage boosts in all New England woolen mills.

Before the tumult of the Lawrence strike had died down, the I.W.W. became involved in another conflict in the silk industry of Paterson, New Jersey, where in 1912 the mills began to replace the two-loom with the four-loom system, increasing the wear and tear on the weavers without any increase in wages. The I.W.W. promptly began organizing. In February, 1913, it called a strike against the city's largest establishment, the Henry Doherty Company, demanding reestablishment of the two-loom system, the eight-hour day, and a minimum wage of $12 a week. Local authorities, announcing that they were determined to "nip the strike in the bud," ordered I.W.W. leaders out of town and forbade picketing. Despite the action, the strike spread; when Bill Haywood arrived to take charge Paterson industry was paralyzed. The police, determined to break the strike, forbade his making any speeches. When Haywood tried to circumvent the order by holding a meeting in the adjacent town of Haledon, he was arrested by Paterson police on a charge of disorderly conduct as he was about to cross the city line. The strike, nevertheless, continued until starvation finally forced the strikers to return to work.

Defeat in Paterson hardly checked the Wobblies, for they were already engaged in their most significant campaign, outlined by the overall brigade, among the migratory workers of the grain fields of the Great Plains. The work was slow until 1915 when the rudimentary locals already established among the harvest hands created the Agricultural Workers Organization which adopted a platform calling for a ten-hour day, a $3.00 wage, fifty cents an hour for overtime, satisfactory board, and clean sleeping places. It was an ambitious campaign. Harvest hands came from cities and farms; they began working in southern Oklahoma and moved northward to Canada as the wheat became ripe. Each job was a short one; much time was spent in the "jungles" where the hands rested, and in traveling from job to job by freight trains. In the jungles and on trains their earnings were menaced by hold-up men and small-time gamblers. The 1915 campaign was a success. In the following year pay demands were increased and secured; armed committees cleaned out the jungles and, before the season ended, the A.W.O. established a virtual closed shop by securing physical control of the means of transportation with the connivance of railway police, who permitted only holders of I.W.W. cards to ride the freight trains. By October, 1916, the A.W.O. had enrolled 18,000 members and had become the mainstay of the I.W.W.

From the Great Plains the Wobblies turned to the lumber industry of the Pacific Northwest, where the Knights had created a 2,000-member district assembly in the eighties, and the A.F.L. had established both shingle weavers' and timber-workers' unions. When the I.W.W. had first entered the area in 1907, it had little success; its victories in the harvest fields and the Everett strike spurred it to greater efforts. The Everett conflict began in 1915 when wages of shingle workers were reduced with the promise of restoration when the price of shingles increased. But the promise was not kept; in 1916 the shingle weavers called a strike which the small I.W.W. local joined. The city's businessmen promptly formed a vigilante committee and began to seize, arrest, beat, and deport every Wobbly they could find. The I.W.W. countered, in characteristic fashion, with a call for a mass descent upon Everett. The Seattle local chartered two small vessels which, loaded with nearly three hundred men, steamed down Puget Sound. But when the passengers attempted to disembark at Everett, some two hundred armed vigilantes who were waiting on the dock opened fire. Thirty-six Wobblies and twenty-one vigilantes were killed or injured. On their return to Seattle the passengers were arrested, and seventy-four were charged with murder. But the first men tried under the charge were acquitted, and the rest were freed.

In the following spring the I.W.W. set up the Lumber Workers Union in Spokane and began a new organizing drive. It was quickly successful; by the summer of 1917 I.W.W. strikes, aimed at increasing wages and improving the unbearable living conditions in the lumber camps, had tied up the whole lumber area from Montana to the Pacific coast. Lumber companies accused the strikers of sabotage and pro-German sympathies, but the charges had little effect. Nor were the suppressive tactics of state authorities any more effective. Not till the I.W.W.'s treasury was empty did the Wobblies return to work, and they returned only in order to "strike on the job," which meant doing eight hours' work in ten—a slowdown. Although men who engaged in such tactics were fired, the result was a labor turnover which multiplied costs and reduced production, and which finally brought the intervention of the War Department. The army brought peace to the lumber country, with machinery for settling grievances and an eight-hour day.

The results were different in the copper-mining industry, which the I.W.W. entered with the Metal Mine Workers Union in 1916. After a year of organizing and a number of small victories, the union decided on a major drive with strikes for higher wages and for semimonthly pay days in cash instead of company scrip in two copper centers at Jerome and Bisbee, Arizona. The strikes never had a chance to develop. In both towns the strike was met by ruthless vigilante action. In Jerome the local committee seized and deported seventy Wobblies, and the strike promptly collapsed. In Bisbee a huge posse made a systematic roundup of all I.W.W. strikers and sympathizers, twelve hundred in all, loaded them on a train of cattle cars, and dumped them in the middle of the desert. Thirty-six hours later Federal authorities rescued the men, took them to Columbus, New Mexico, and lodged them in a detention camp. Although a few ultimately returned to Bisbee, they returned to a town where the I.W.W. had been completely wiped out.

The I.W.W.'s "free speech" fights, its activities at Lawrence and Paterson, its violence-studded campaigns among agricultural, lumber, and mine workers in the West have given it a reputation as a bitter, irresponsible organization of malcontents bent upon overthrowing traditional American institutions. Its campaigns—which organized about fifty thousand casual, migratory, and unskilled workers—have been judged failures. But the reputation which the Wobblies earned is not entirely deserved, and the judgment pronounced upon them is inaccurate.

The objectives of the I.W.W. campaigns between 1908 and the First World War revealed little that was revolutionary. Its demands were commonplace: increased wages, shorter hours, semimonthly paydays, and better working conditions. Nor did these campaigns reveal much that was radical. The Wobblies were inclined to use flaming language in their pronouncements, strike calls, and speeches. They were more inclined to strike than to negotiate to achieve their ends. While their strikes were often raucous and sometimes violent, much of the violence was initiated by local authorities and vigilante groups, and I.W.W. members were often the victims of the violence. Their one innovation was the strike-on-the-job, or slowdown.

Wobbly activities did have unfortunate results. I.W.W. campaigns in Lawrence and Paterson incurred the bitter hostility of employers accustomed to a docile labor force. Its campaigns in the West aroused the primitive, "I'll run my own business" spirit of western employers. Once aroused, these employers resorted to the old, lawless methods of the frontier. They attacked the I.W.W. with any and every physical and legal weapon, and they attacked the organization with words. Their verbal attack was the more significant because it convinced many Americans with economic interests to protect that the Wobblies were bent upon destruction of those interests. That conviction became the basis of a fierce attack upon the organization during and after the First World War.

On the other hand, the I.W.W. made important contributions. Its campaigns revealed, contrary to A.F.L. philosophy, that the migratory, casual, unskilled laborers, with their diverse languages, customs, prejudices, religions, and animosities, were organizable. More significant was the impact of the Wobbly campaigns upon the "progressives." Wobbly strikes revealed how thoroughly industry controlled local governments, and how willing it was to use its control with a brutal ferocity that gave no regard to civil rights. This made a lasting impression upon men who believed implicitly in the democratic process as the surest technique for solving all the nation's problems; it made them friends of labor because the laboring men were being denied their democratic rights. The strikes also revealed that a very large segment of the laboring population was living under deplorable economic circumstances in the midst of splendor. This appealed to the progressives' humanitarian instincts; it lent much force to their determination to alleviate industrial conditions. The Wobblies, in short, gave a tremendous spiritual impetus to the progressive movement.

17 —

The Federation's Revival

The years between 1904 and 1911 were very unhappy ones for the American Federation of Labor. They were years when the very existence of the A.F.L. was seriously challenged by an open-shop campaign that swept it from a vast number of the nation's towns and small cities, when internal disgruntlement became strong, and when many of its activities were hampered by the Federal courts. They were also years when the A.F.L. was challenged in the labor world itself—by the socialists whose constant reiteration of the idea that labor could better itself by political action won many supporters, and by the W.F.M. and I.W.W. forces which appealed to many laboring men with their doctrine of industrial unionism and direct action.

The American Federation of Labor was keenly aware of its problems. It had recognized the threat presented by the doctrine of industrial unionism at the Scranton convention when it had permitted the U.M.W. to enroll the craftsmen who worked around the mines. With the formation of the I.W.W. it also surrendered to the United Brewery Workers. But it had regarded these concessions as exceptions to, and not as contraventions of, its principle of craft autonomy. When the demand for recognition of industrial unionism continued to grow, the A.F.L. began to realize the need for a more practical solution. It found the answer in the trades council, which had long been used locally in the building trades. As late as 1905 the A.F.L. denounced as dual unionism any attempt to federate local building-trade councils into a national organization. In 1907 its attitude on the subject suddenly changed. It created a Building Trades Department of all building trade unions inside the federation for the express purpose of adjusting jurisdictional disputes and of aiding each other through the sympathetic strike. Other similar organizations followed: a Metal Trades Department was set up in 1908 to offset the secession of the United Metal Workers; a Railway Employees Department made up of the railway shop crafts was established in the same year; a Mining Department was evolved out of the U.M.W. and the Smelters Union in 1912. Despite all attempts to justify these actions in craft-union terms, they were obviously efforts to compromise with "industrialism." Their purpose was to unite a number of trades into a fighting unit upon an industry-wide front, almost exactly the object of an industrial union.

"Departmentalization" satisfied many, but not all, industrial unionists. In 1912–1913 the industrial-union movement was given a boost by the spectacular activities of the I.W.W. in the East and by the election of officials who favored industrial unionism to the leadership of the machinists, miners, and tailors. The Executive Council, recognizing the trend, bent a little more, with the announcement that the Scranton Declaration did not prevent the extension of union membership to the unskilled, nor did it prevent an amalgamation of labor unions. The announcement, and the opiate-like effects of the prosperity that preceded the opening of the First World War, temporarily ended the agitation.

The A.F.L.'s recognition of the threat contained in the Socialist party's campaign to secure labor objectives through political means was somewhat more belated. Socialist pressure worried A.F.L. leaders; Gompers' scathing attack upon the socialists in every annual convention was symbolic. What bothered A.F.L. leaders was not the demand for political action, but the demand for united action. Although leaders of the federation were often actively engaged in politics, their party allegiance was divided. Although state federations and city centrals also entered politics—often in order to secure support of public officials for the hiring of union labor on public contract jobs—these bodies had a varied allegiance: they were Republican in Republican states, Democratic in Democratic states. United political action seemed impossible.

The situation began to change after 1905. The socialists' political agitation, the National Association of Manufacturers' open participation in the congressional and senatorial campaigns of 1904 which resulted in defeat for men friendly to labor, and the attack upon the Danbury Hatters all contributed. In 1906 representatives of 118 internationals met in Washington and formulated a document known as "Labor's Bill of Grievances," which called for enactment of an eight-hour law for all labor, elimination of what remained of convict labor competition, total exclusion of the Chinese, a limitation upon immigration, exemption of labor from the application of the anti-trust laws, and elimination of the injunction in labor disputes.

When Congress ignored the demands, the A.F.L. Executive Council decided to enter directly into the congressional campaign of 1906. This was not an entirely new activity. The council had always urged affiliates to support their friends and punish their enemies, but the urgings had been casual. Now the council organized more thoroughly: it named a Labor Representation Committee to conduct a nation-wide campaign; it suggested that all city centrals and locals scrutinize the labor records of nominees for office and publicly announce the names of the men whom labor would support and whom labor would work to defeat. In addition it suggested that where no satisfactory Democratic or Republican candidates could be found, an independent labor candidate be nominated. The Labor Representation Committee itself entered actively into the campaign, invading the home districts of antilabor congressmen with speakers, propaganda, and money. When the campaign ended, the A.F.L. could look back with some pride: its efforts had greatly reduced the pluralities of its enemies and had brought the election of six A.F.L. cardholders.

The Buck's Stove injunction of 1907 and the Supreme Court decision in the Danbury Hatters case of 1908 intensified the A.F.L.'s interest in politics. The Executive Council appeared before the resolutions committees of both the Republican and Democratic parties in 1908 and asked for the adoption of several labor planks: the right of labor to organize, prohibition of the use of injunctions in labor disputes, trial by jury in contempt cases, extension of the eight-hour day to all public workers, endorsement of an employers' liability law, woman suffrage, and the creation of a department of labor and a bureau of mines. The Republican answer to the request was a statement upholding the authority and integrity of the courts; the Democrats incorporated the planks into their platform. During the campaign the A.F.L. officially maintained its nonpartisan attitude; in congressional contests it supported Democrats, Republicans, and even Socialists. In the presidential contest the organization maintained a constant attack upon Taft's labor record, thus unofficially supporting Bryan.

Although the A.F.L. was disappointed by the results, no one suggested that its political activities be abandoned. In the next four years the conviction of Gompers, Morrison, and Mitchell upon contempt charges; Taft's veto of the Speight-Wilson bill designed to ameliorate the condition of seagoing labor; further use of injunctions against labor unions; and the Hitchman case, which actually questioned the legality of trade unions, kept the organization politically conscious. The climax of its activity came in 1912. The Socialist party produced a highly attractive labor platform: government relief for unemployment, an eight-hour day, a forty-four-hour week, more effective factory and mine inspection laws, prohibition of the transportation of child-made and convict-made goods in interstate commerce, minimum-wage laws, and accident, unemployment, and death insurance. The A.F.L. Executive Council approached the major parties again. The Republicans, not so hostile as before, adopted several planks. The "Bull Moosers" and the Democrats were even more cooperative; both endorsed the whole A.F.L. platform and added some labor planks of their own. This success made it difficult for the A.F.L. to make a choice of presidential candidates, but it managed. Its leaders and newspapers dismissed Debs with the gratuitous charge that his "Red Special" was paid for by the enemies of labor, repeated their attack upon Taft, questioned Roosevelt's sincerity, and wholeheartedly praised Wilson. The A.F.L. was genuinely pleased with the results of the election, which it interpreted as a double triumph —a victory over socialism and a victory for its principles.

The A.F.L.'s main answer to the problems it confronted after 1904 was not found in its compromise with industrial unionism nor in its active efforts to reward friends and punish enemies. Rather it consisted of efforts by affiliates to maintain and increase trade-union membership, efforts which began to show positive results after 1910 and brought A.F.L. rolls to a new high of 2,000,000 by 1914. Although the increase was spread through all trades, 70 per cent of it came in four fields: railways, building, clothing, and coal mining. The increase in railway union membership was largely the result of strong organizing campaigns carried out by both the railway

brotherhoods and the railway shop crafts. The rise in membership
among the building trades was the result of a steady campaign conducted by affiliates to offset the exposés of building-trade agents.

The increase in the clothing industry had a different basis. The
needle trades of the early twentieth century were organized as they
had been in the early merchant–capitalist system: work upon gar-
ments was done in teams; payment was made by the piece and each
member of the team shared in the total. Piece rates were very low,
and hours of labor were inhumanly long. Labor organizations in the
trade were haphazard arrangements. Most of the tradesmen were
Jews. Although they had a natural affinity for one another, they
were unable to maintain a united front for any length of time. Some
became employers and operators of fearsome sweatshops; others
shifted to other industries. Nevertheless, three unions existed in the
needle trades in 1905: the Journeymen Tailors, the United Garment
Workers, and the International Ladies' Garment Workers Union.
None were large or strong; they were confined chiefly to New York
City where they were torn by ideological conflicts between non-
socialists, socialists, and anarchists. They had all become victims
of the "open shop" drive.

In September, 1909, a change began with the strike of the I.L.G.
W.U. against the Triangle Shirt Waist Company. The strike, caused
by the company's continuous discharge of union labor, was furiously
resisted by company guards who assaulted and beat pickets, mostly
girls, and by the police. The brutality boomeranged when 20,000
workers in the industry walked off their jobs. The strike was finally
ended by arbitration in mid-February, 1910, with the strikers winning wage increases and a closed shop in almost all shirtwaist establishments. The victory gave unionism in the needle trades a strong
boost. In the summer of 1910 the I.L.G.W.U. went on a carefully
planned strike for abolition of the "inside" system which created
sweatshop conditions, establishment of a forty-eight-hour week, and
union recognition in the cloakmakers' industry. A long deadlock
followed. Gradually, however, the I.L.G.W.U. was able to persuade
small shops, which feared they would be sacrificed by the larger concerns, to grant the demands; cloak manufacturers surrendered and
signed the "Protocol of Peace."

The Protocol became a milestone in the history of the needle trades.

It abolished the "inside" system, homework, and charges for electricity and materials. It established a perferential union shop, a six-day, fifty-four-hour week, limited the total working day to the hours between 8:00 A.M. and 8:30 P.M., limited overtime to two and a half hours a day, and provided that piece rates be fixed by the employer and a committee of employees. It also set up an industrial government which included a Board of Arbitration to settle all major grievances and a Board of Sanitary Control to act as factory inspectors. The whole settlement was rightfully regarded as a tremendous victory for the I.L.G.W.U., which now became one of the most important A.F.L. affiliates with a membership approaching 60,000.

Developments in the men's clothing industry, which was scattered over a wider geographical area, followed another course. In Chicago the industry was divided into three types: a factory system typified by Hart, Schaffner and Marx; a home system; and a subcontracting system. Keen competition among these various types kept the wages of the unorganized mass of nationalities in the industry inordinately low. In September, 1910, however, a revolt occurred when one Hart, Schaffner and Marx shop reduced the piece rate; in a few weeks 41,000 were on strike. At this point A. T. Rickert, president of the U.G.W., arrived to take charge. Rickert revealed a highly skeptical attitude toward the immigrants' ability to maintain a united front and promptly concluded an agreement which provided for submission of all grievances to a board of arbitration and for reemployment of all strikers without discrimination. Profoundly shocked, the strikers rejected the terms and set up a new committee to carry on the struggle. But gradually the condition of the strikers, who were without sufficient funds, grew desperate, and in January, 1911, they accepted terms substantially the same as those approved by Rickert. Although the results were disappointing, the strike had far-reaching effects. It set up the original machinery for adjusting industrial disputes in the men's clothing industry: the original Board of Arbitration established a fifty-four-hour week and granted a 10 per cent increase in wages. In addition the strike made thousands of Chicago clothing workers union conscious, thus adding to A.F.L. membership rolls.

Meanwhile, the small U.G.W. locals in New York City had begun to agitate for a general improvement in the men's clothing industry.

When employers struck back by a wholesale discharge of union members, U.G.W. locals called a strike in December, 1911, to secure a 20 per cent wage increase, a forty-eight-hour week, and the abolition of subcontracting and tenement house work. One hundred and ten thousand workers responded. Almost immediately violence flared: employers secured injunctions against picketing, strikers ignored the writs, and clashes with the police became frequent. Late in February, 1912, Rickert stepped into the situation. Without consulting local leaders he concluded an agreement providing for an immediate general wage increase of $1.00 a week, abolition of subcontracting, and the appointment of an arbitration board to settle all other grievances. The strikers, aghast, denounced the settlement as "treachery." But Rickert's behind-the-scenes action proved costly. Mayor William Gaynor, taking the attitude that the strikers were recalcitrant, ordered the suppression of all picketing and provided strikebreakers with police protection. Enthusiasm died rapidly and in March, 1912, local leaders accepted Rickert's agreement. Although the strikers were disappointed, membership of the U.G.W. increased by some 66,000.

The growth of A.F.L. membership in the coal fields after 1910 developed primarily out of conflicts in West Virginia and Colorado. The West Virginia fields were among the richest in the nation; the seams were unusually thick, the topography made mining operations relatively easy, and the fields were located close to the nation's industrial centers. The U.M.W. began a unionizing campaign in West Virginia in 1902. The odds against success seemed unsurmountable; the miners themselves were poverty-stricken and illiterate, and local officials were brutally hostile. The campaign ended abruptly in a strike of 16,000 which was ruthlessly crushed by the state militia.

Not until 1912, when there were 70,000 miners in West Virginia, did the U.M.W. start another campaign. Activity was touched off in April in the Cabin Creek district of the Kanawha Valley by a local strike for higher wages and union recognition. Operators immediately hired guards from the Baldwin-Felts agency and began evicting strikers from company houses. Bloody warfare followed, reminiscent of earlier struggles in the Rockies, until the governor declared martial law and the strike ended. Peace was short-lived. A few days after the strike ended, U.M.W. organizers, led by the redoubtable "Mother" Jones, arrived in the Cabin Creek district; the companies promptly fired all union men and another strike began. In September the governor again imposed martial law. Under its protection the companies renewed eviction activity, hired strikebreakers, and reopened the mines. But when the militia was withdrawn, the strikers promptly resumed picketing and halted operations. The strike continued peacefully until February when mine guards, operating from a specially chartered Chesapeake and Ohio train, machine-gunned a tent village at Holly Grove. The miners retaliated by a counterattack upon the guard encampment at Mucklow. The governor again imposed martial law; 125 union leaders and strikers were arrested for murder. The strike appeared to be lost. Nevertheless, the tide was shifting. The nation was thoroughly shocked by the attack upon Holly Grove and demanded an end to the atrocities. In March, West Virginia inaugurated a new governor, Henry D. Hatfield, who ordered the release of miners imprisoned by military courts and suggested terms to end the strike: the right to organize, no discrimination against union men, and a nine-hour day. Both operators and miners accepted.

The end of the West Virginia strike proved to be only a pause in the struggle between coal miners and operators. Late in 1913 a new conflict broke out in the coal fields of Colorado. Unionizing activity had begun in that state in 1900 and had culminated in a year-long strike against the Rockefeller-owned Colorado Fuel and Iron Company in the Trinidad district in 1903–1904. It had been crushed by deportations and military law. In 1913 the U.M.W. sent a host of organizers into southern Colorado. Increase in union membership became apparent almost immediately. But when the U.M.W. asked for a conference with mine operators, it was refused. The U.M.W. issued a strike call, demanding an increase in wages and union recognition. Almost immediately the conflict became violent. The operators hired several hundred Baldwin-Felts agency guards who cruised the area in armored automobiles. They attacked the tent colony which evicted miners set up at Forbes and a strikers' mass meeting at Walsenburg. The governor sent General Chase of Cripple Creek fame to impose martial law. Chase promptly began breaking up picket lines, arresting strikers, and deporting strike leaders.

The climax came in April, 1914, when a detachment of militia attacked the strikers' tent village at Ludlow. The fight, in which two strikers and a boy were killed, ended with the troops capturing the camp and setting it afire. The main tragedy was discovered the next day: two women and eleven children, seeking escape from the militia, had been smothered to death in a cave. The "Ludlow Massacre" turned the striking miners into furious avengers. They attacked and destroyed a half-dozen mine properties, attacked mine-guard encampments and the militia. For a week southern Colorado was a battlefield. The governor called for Federal troops. With their arrival peace was restored. The strike continued all through the summer and fall, but all attempts at settlement, including two suggestions by President Woodrow Wilson, failed. Finally in December, 1914, the U.M.W. rescinded the strike call.

Although the failure to unionize West Virginia and the defeat in Colorado were disappointing, the campaigns were beneficial to the U.M.W. and the A.F.L. Attacks by company guards and state militia upon tent colonies at Holly Grove, Forbes, and Ludlow had horrified the nation. The public suddenly forgot the "un-American" closed shop, grafting business agents, and the McNamara case and gave its sympathy unstintingly to unionism. A larger portion of the public now became convinced that much of the blame for industrial strife could be laid upon the doorsteps of employers, and that a reform in industrial conditions was needed. In addition the strikes indicated that the U.M.W. had begun to revive after the open-shop campaign. Unsuccessful as they were, the strikes added some 150,000 miners to the federation's membership rolls.

The increase was not at first apparent, for in 1914 A.F.L. membership leveled off. There were several reasons: a minor recession which prevented some members from paying dues; the federation's preoccupation with politics and legislation; and the fact that the federation had reached its limits in many industries and areas where unionism had secured a foothold. In addition an internal conflict caused a secession. The conflict was a by-product of the 1911–1913 strikes in the men's clothing industry during which the national officers of the United Garment Workers had revealed a strong skepticism of the immigrant workers' attachment to unionism and an overabundant eagerness to come to terms with employers. In 1913 local leaders and the rank and file who resented the attitude and looked upon the settlements as acts of treachery began a movement to oust the national officers. The movement was quickly checked at the U.G.W.'s convention where the Credentials Committee ruled that most of the rebellious delegates were ineligible to hold seats because their locals had not paid all dues into the treasury. The act precipitated a break. The ineligible delegates, forced from the floor of the convention, proceeded under the leadership of Sidney Hillman to create their own U.G.W. After a year-long battle for recognition from the courts and the A.F.L., the Hillman faction formally ended the contest by announcing its secession and, with the Journeymen Tailors Union, formed an independent union—the Amalgamated Clothing Workers. The secession cost the A.F.L. approximately 50,000 members.

In 1915 the trend changed again, and membership once more began to increase. The A.F.L.'s claim of credit for the growing body of labor laws passed in states and in Congress, concerted activities among old members in small cities, and the increase in business activity created by the war in Europe were all responsible. On the eve of the First World War the A.F.L. could boast 2,370,000 members.

There were other satisfactions. In the previous twenty years there had been a marked reduction in the hours of organized labor. In 1897 few skilled laborers had worked as little as forty-eight hours a week. Their hours had run from forty-eight to seventy-two; the general average ran between fifty and fifty-four hours. By 1917, however, some skilled labor worked as little as forty hours a week; building tradesmen normally worked forty-four hours, and comparatively few skilled tradesmen outside the factories and the less advanced industrial states worked more than forty-eight hours. This was in contrast to factory labor and the unorganized unskilled which still averaged fifty-four to sixty hours a week. There had also been increases in wage rates. Between 1897 and 1917 the cost of living increased some 40 per cent. To a large degree A.F.L. members had kept pace with that increase: building tradesmen had increased their hourly wages as much as 140 per cent; other A.F.L. members had not fared so well, but their average earnings had risen 60 per cent in the same period. This was, again, in contrast to the unskilled whose earnings had risen a mere 25 to 30 per cent. Thus, on the eve of the war the federation was inclined to regard itself as an economic success.

18 ____

Progressive Labor Legislation

There was more for labor, however, in the early years of the twentieth century than economic gains for the A.F.L. skilled. The period was also one of general reform when the self-centered agrarian movements of the nineteenth century, which came to a climax in the Populist revolt and the election of 1896 and with which labor had been loosely allied, became the Progressive movement. Leadership of the new movement was assumed by medical men, college professors, teachers, journalists, ministers, and welfare workers. Highly articulate and unselfish, they aimed at bettering conditions for the entire population—at democratizing and making more efficient the political system by taking control of government from the vested interests and giving it once more to the public, and at democratizing the use of the nation's resources and wealth by forcing the owners of the nation's economic structure to share their good fortune with the less fortunate majority. The movement enlisted farmers, small businessmen, women, and workingmen; it cut across party lines, obliterated sectional differences, and shattered traditional urban-rural cleavages.

For many reasons the Progressives gave much attention to labor and its demands. Their left wing, the Socialist party, was essentially a workmen's organization which demanded that the nation give attention to labor problems. The very nature of the Progressives' movement involved labor. Aiming, as they did, at the "interests" which had secured control of the nation's government and resources and were using that control in a manner contrary to the public good, it was only logical for Progressives to assume that the "interests" also acted contrary to the welfare of their employees. Examination of employer-employee relationships became inevitable. Popular reaction to industry practices was involved. The use of the injunction in the Pullman and subsequent strikes and the application of the Sherman Act to labor in industrial disputes alarmed a large share of the public, which recognized in these actions both a misapplication of the law and the existence of an alliance between big business and government which threatened to destroy democratic processes. Use of Federal troops, militia, the state constabulary, sheriffs' posses, and city police; use of brutality, deportations, bull pens, *agents provocateurs*, spies, Pinkertons, and black lists; disregard of civil liberties of strikers in the northwestern lumbering districts, in the metal mines of the Rockies, in the coal mining areas of West Virginia, in the steel towns of Pennsylvania, in the textile towns of Lawrence and Paterson, in the needle-trade districts of Chicago and New York outraged the public's sense of fair play and created a demand for redress.

Labor itself contributed. The existence of a multitude of labor organizations made the public labor conscious. Quarrels between labor leaders added to the public interest and knowledge of labor's aims. Every strike became an exposé of sordid conditions—of unbearably long hours, intolerably low wages, unhealthful and unsafe working conditions, lack of sanitary facilities, brutal and avaricious foremen, exploitation through company stores, broken men, miserable women, wretched children, slums, tenements, filth and squalor—which aroused the nation's humanitarian impulse. The A.F.L.'s resort to politics was a final reason. The activation of its policy of rewarding friends and punishing enemies forced politicians to take a greater interest in labor's welfare.

The result of the Progressive movement was the enactment of a vast body of legislation by state governments designed either to protect the public from the consequences of industrial strife, to ameliorate the lot of the most helpless and to protect the health of future generations, or to correct palpable injustices. To a large degree this legislation attempted to solve much the same problems as those called to public attention by the Knights, the United Front parties, the Socialist Labor party, and the A.F.L. in the nineteenth century.

Only one earlier problem—that of providing machinery for voluntary arbitration of industrial disputes—received less attention. So many industrial states had erected boards of arbitration by 1900 that the problem slipped into the background, overwhelmed by more pressing issues. Most attention in the field was given to the new experiment in Colorado which provided for semicompulsory arbitration by prohibiting strikes and lockouts until an investigation could be made. The example, roundly condemned by labor because it was placed at a disadvantage in timing its strikes, did not spread.

The issue of child labor was a different matter. Although many states had enacted legislation prohibiting the labor of "children," had provided maximum hours for teen-agers, or had banned night work, and most states had prohibited employment of children in dangerous industries, the legislation was faulty. Minimum-age requirements were low, maximum-hour laws still permitted a sixty-hour week, and except for mining, hazardous occupations were seldom defined. Enforcement of all laws, moreover, was lax. The Progressives, strongly aided by A.F.L. lobbies, made a concerted effort to correct the situation. Almost all states which had no minimum-age requirements enacted such laws by 1917, even in the South where the movement encountered the violent opposition of textile interests. Almost all states raised minimum-age requirements to fourteen and extended the coverage of their laws so as to include not only manufacturing and mercantile establishments, but also business and telegraph offices, restaurants, hotels, apartment houses, messenger and delivery services, the street trades, and canneries. Nineteen states established the eight-hour day in factories and stores for children under sixteen. Thirty-seven states passed laws which forbade children under sixteen employed in manufacturing establishments and stores to work between 7:00 P.M. and 6:00 A.M.; twenty-three states defined hazardous occupations; and four drew up comprehensive lists of specific occupations forbidden to children.

The Progressives also gave considerable attention to legislation concerning hours of women in industry. When the twentieth century began, all previous state laws on the subject were under a legal cloud because of a decision by the Illinois Supreme Court which declared a statute limiting women's working hours unconstitutional on the ground that it deprived women of freedom of contract. In 1907 this decision was reenforced by the New York Court of Errors which declared the state's law prohibiting night work for women unconstitutional on the same ground.

A year later, however, the whole legal situation was reversed when the United States Supreme Court in the case of *Muller* v. *Oregon* sustained the right of a state to enact a ten-hour law for women in order to protect health. The decision produced a legislative avalanche. Between 1909 and 1917 forty-one states wrote new or improved maximum-hour laws for women. Most of these extended the scope of the laws to cover both factories and mercantile establishments and limited the working day to nine hours or the work week to fifty-four. In addition, five states prohibited night work for women.

Laws establishing minimum wages for women were also added to state codes. Leadership for the movement came almost entirely from middle-class women, shocked by the unbelievably low wages paid to women in the textile and needle trades. Labor gave the movement only desultory support; in fact, the California State Federation fought against the legislation because it feared that minimum wages would become maximum wages. Nevertheless, between 1912 and 1917 twelve states passed laws providing for the establishment of minimum rates for women. Although the rapidity of the movement seemed to indicate the dawn of a new era, the results were disappointing. Some states set inflexible rates which soon fell below the cost-of-living indexes; some set no wage rates; some did not enforce their wage rates; and others found enforcement hindered by injunctions. Just as the war began, however, the movement was given additional impetus when the United States Supreme Court—by a tie vote—upheld the constitutionality of the Oregon minimum-wage laws in the case of *Stetler* v. *O'Hara*.

An issue of great importance in the nineteenth century—that of safety and health in factories, tenements, and mines—might have been forgotten in the early twentieth century if it had not been for the Triangle Shirt Waist Factory fire in New York City in 1911. The tragedy, which cost more than one hundred young girls their lives, renewed the older movement. Under the pressure of the Progressives, led in this case by state federations of labor, northern and western states refurbished their old laws, defining safety regulations in factories more specifically and providing more severe punishment for violations. Some states also enacted more exacting tenement- and mine-safety laws.

The labor problem which the Progressives made the strongest effort to solve was that of responsibility for industrial accidents. Between 1901 and 1908 they approached the problem essentially as it had been approached in the nineteenth century—by securing a modification of the old common-law rules. Their efforts increased markedly the number of states with laws prohibiting employers from ridding themselves of responsibility for industrial accidents by contract, the number which made employers liable for accidents caused by defective machinery, and the number which abolished the fellow-servant rule.

But the Progressives' most significant contribution to a solution of the problem involved the suggestion that insurance systems be established to cover industrial accidents. The suggestion was based on the idea that workmen should be compensated for accidents regardless of cause and that compensation for accidents was to be regarded as a part of production costs. Maryland passed a voluntary insurance law in 1902; Montana followed with a compulsory law in 1909. Both were crudely and loosely drawn, and they were quickly declared unconstitutional by state courts. Between 1909 and 1913 thirty-two states appointed committees to investigate the problem. With almost phenomenal unanimity every committee made the same recommendations: they called for complete abrogation of the old doctrines and the adoption of a workingmen's compensation system. A deluge followed. Prodded by A.F.L. lobbies, thirty states, including all those of the North, passed compensation legislation by 1917. The laws were not entirely effective. Most states enacted laws which encouraged employers to join an insurance system but which, at the same time, permitted them to evade responsibility. This wariness was due to the action of the New York Court of Errors which in the Ives case of 1911 declared the compulsory New York law unconstitutional because it knew of "no principle on which one can be compelled to indemnify another for loss unless it is based upon contractual obligation or fault." New York amended its constitution, and new legislation was passed. It was challenged again, and brought to the United States Supreme Court as the case of the *New York Central Railroad Co.*

v. *White*. The court ruled that since the act was intended to replace the old common-law doctrine with another system, and that the principle of liability without fault was not an innovation in law, the New York statute was valid. Thus, when the war began, the legality of workmen's compensation was well established.

The most controversial labor legislation in which the Progressives became involved concerned, as in the nineteenth century, that of maximum hours for men. At the turn of the century all laws on the subject were of doubtful legality. Although the United States Supreme Court in the case of *Holden* v. *Hardy* had declared that a Utah act, which applied to miners, did not violate the Federal Constitution, five states had declared comparable hour legislation—applied generally or to specific occupations—contrary to their own constitutions.

In 1905 the situation was partially clarified when a Kansas statute providing maximum hours for men employed upon public works was brought before the United States Supreme Court in the case of *Atkins* v. *Kansas* and was declared legal on the ground that the state as one party to a contract could set the terms of the contract. The decision was followed by a rewriting of many old laws, and enactment of some new legislation. By 1917 twenty-seven states had laws governing labor of persons working upon public works, direct or contractual. Meanwhile the Progressives continued their pressure for legislation in other occupations with some success. Between 1901 and 1907 fourteen states limited hours of railway workers; in the same period ten states enacted hour legislation for telephone and telegraph operators engaged in directing the movement of trains. Twelve states adopted hour legislation for miners—though none of the great coal-mining states, where the laws were needed most, became involved in the movement. North Carolina enacted an eleven-hour law for all manufacturing establishments; South Carolina and Georgia passed eleven-hour legislation for workers in textile plants; four states regulated the hours of bakers; New York, those of brickmakers; and Montana, those of stationary engineers.

The whole movement was suddenly given a setback by a United States Supreme Court decision enunciated in 1905 in the case of *Lochner* v. *New York* in which the court declared that legislation regulating hours of bakers was unconstitutional because there was no special hazard to health in that occupation. The movement was not entirely halted; it might have developed into a strong effort if the A.F.L. had begun an active campaign on the issue. But the powerful internationals who were able to secure shorter hours through economic pressure opposed legislation on the subject. The movement, accordingly, continued only on the Pacific Coast where most labor unions were relatively weak and unable to secure shorter hours through strike action; it was partially successful in Oregon where a ten-hour day for all manufacturing establishments was provided in 1913. Even the Pacific Coast campaign ended in 1915 when the federation condemned legislative action on the issue on the grounds that the benefits were illusory and that the law was of dubious legality. Two years later the United States Supreme Court handed down a decision on the Oregon law, the *Bunting* v. *Oregon* case, and declared it legal, primarily because it followed a customary and reasonable average.

The same forces which persuaded the states to enact legislation on behalf of labor between 1900 and 1917 also influenced the Federal Government. The pressure of the Progressives brought about an enactment of laws for the District of Columbia and for Federal employees that followed much the same patterns as those already established by the states. The congressional child-labor laws passed during the period for the District of Columbia established fourteen years as the minimum age at which children could enter employment, provided an eight-hour day for youths between fourteen and sixteen, prohibited all night work, and regulated the street trades. On the eve of the war Congress provided for an eight-hour day for women employed by private enterprise in the District. Two Federal laws, in 1908 and 1916, were enacted to establish a workingmen's compensation system for Federal employees. In 1892 Congress provided legislation which closed some loopholes in the old eight-hour law for mechanics and laborers and which extended the law to all Federal employees in the District of Columbia and to labor employed on Federal contract jobs; in 1914 it established an eight-hour day for all Federal employees.

More important, however, were the Progressive and labor campaigns that resulted in legislation on behalf of children, seamen, and railway workers throughout the whole nation. In 1914 the National

Child Labor Committee became very pessimistic about the future of child labor. While much legislation had been passed by the states, even the most enlightened did not meet the committee's standards. There were still two million children under sixteen gainfully employed; more than one-fourth were outside agriculture. The committee turned to Congress for help in establishing national standards. By 1916 every political party and a large number of organizations, including the A.F.L., had lined up behind the movement. Despite powerful opposition from the cotton-mill interests of the South and the National Association of Manufacturers, both of which argued that the matter should be left to the states, the Owen-Keatings bill was enacted in 1916. The act prohibited the transportation in interstate commerce of manufactured goods which were the product of a factory in which children under the age of fourteen were employed, or where children between the ages of fourteen and sixteen years were permitted to work more than eight hours in any day, or more than six days in one week, or between 7:00 P.M. and 6:00 A.M. When the war began, it appeared that the problem of child labor in industry had been solved.

The campaign on behalf of seagoing labor began in the late nineteenth century. At the time the American sailor's condition was at its worst. He lived under the full control of the captain at sea; he was unable to quit his job at will for fear of being punished as a deserter; and he was unable to join in concert to improve his condition on pain of being punished as a mutineer. In addition, he had become the prey of the "crimp," a combination shipping master and boarding-house keeper. The crimp had obtained control of the sailor's employment by taking the sailor into his boardinghouse between jobs and keeping him there until he ran up a huge board bill. When the bill was large enough, the crimp provided the sailor with a voyage, making him sign over several months' pay, which the shipping company paid as soon as the ship cleared, keeping the sailor in a perpetual state of peonage.

In 1894 Andrew Furuseth came to Washington as lobbyist for the Sailor's Union of the Pacific Coast. Within four years he persuaded Congress to pass the White Act which limited the penalty for desertion in any port of the United States, Canada, Mexico, Newfoundland, and the West Indies to a forfeiture of wages earned, reduced the penalty for desertion in foreign ports to one month's imprisonment, prohibited corporal punishment, and provided for a survey of the seaworthiness of a ship upon application of a majority of the crew.

In the early years of the twentieth century Furuseth's efforts further to ameliorate the condition of seamen met with constant failure, partially because the seamen were devoting much of their energies to combating an effort to merge them into an industrial union of all seagoing and longshore labor groups and partially because they were fighting for their very existence on the Great Lakes. The latter struggle earned them the sympathy of the Progressives who made "seamen's liberties" a leading issue of the campaign of 1912. When Congress met, Robert M. La Follette, Senator from Wisconsin, introduced far-reaching reform legislation. Opposed only by shipowners, the La Follette Seamen's Act became law in March, 1915. Applying to all American vessels and foreign vessels in American ports, it abolished imprisonment for desertion in a safe harbor and limited the penalty for desertion to a forfeiture of personal effects left on board; gave seamen the right to demand half of the wages earned and still unpaid in any port where cargo was loaded or discharged; prescribed living conditions and food allowances; provided a nine-hour day in port; protected the seamen's wages from allotment to original creditors, a blow at the crimps; made owners liable for infliction of corporal punishment aboard their ships; and established safety regulations.

Of all campaigns the one which most thoroughly involved the Federal Government concerned the railway workers. As has been indicated, the dual traditions of nonmilitancy and aggressiveness which had characterized railway unions before 1886 had begun to change after the Burlington strike. Among brotherhoods and shop crafts there had appeared a tendency toward unity and direct action. The Pullman strike intensified the trend. In the late nineties the brotherhoods began to form "system federations": combinations of all train-crew lodges on one railroad, designed to act as a unit in negotiations with railway managers. This type of cooperative activity was soon proved inadequate; it permitted railway managers to counter demands for higher wages and shorter hours with the argument that the railway would not be able to compete with other roads. In the twentieth century the brotherhoods changed their tactics. Profiting by the example of the A.F.L., they strengthened their internal organization and conducted drives for new members—activities in which the railway shop crafts also engaged. Simultaneously the brotherhoods broadened their cooperative activity. In 1902 conductors and trainmen on the roads west of Chicago formed the Western Association. When the association was able to secure an increase in wages and a reduction in hours, conductors and trainmen on eastern and southern railways created the same kinds of organizations. In 1908–1909 engineers and firemen copied their example—organizing three associations—with similar success.

Meanwhile, the Federal Government's interest in railway workers had been growing. Federal interest originally centered on the problem of protecting public welfare against the consequences of railway strikes. After the Burlington strike Congress provided for voluntary arbitration of disputes on interstate carriers. The Pullman strike led to additional legislation, the Erdman Act of 1898. The law named the Chairman of the Interstate Commerce Commission and the Commissioner of Labor as a permanent board of mediation whose services could be requested by either party to a dispute involving railways. If unable to reach a settlement, the mediators were required to propose arbitration by a special three-man board. If accepted, the board's award was to be compulsory on both parties.

Federal interest in railway workers did not remain confined to arbitration. In the Erdman Act, Congress outlawed the use of yellow-dog contracts by railroads, which the Supreme Court later declared unconstitutional in the case of *Adair* v. *United States* on the ground that it was an unwarranted interference with freedom of contract. In 1907 Congress enacted a law applying to all employees engaged in the movement of trains between states, which provided ten hours' rest after sixteen consecutive hours of work for all operating employees and a nine-hour day for train dispatchers. The act was upheld by the Supreme Court in the case of the *Baltimore and Ohio Railroad Co.* v. *Interstate Commerce Commission.* In 1908 Congress enacted an Employers' Liability Law, providing for workingmen's compensation on railroads. The act was declared unconstitutional on the ground that its wording was too vague. When Congress rewrote the act, it was upheld.

Of all this legislation, the Erdman Act affected railway workers most thoroughly. Applied in only minor conflicts at first, it was used on a large scale in 1907 by the Western Association of Conductors and Trainmen, which won substantial gains. Between 1907 and 1910 other associations won awards in the same way. But in 1912 the situation changed when an Erdman arbitration board failed to grant wage increases to eastern engineers. Warren S. Stone, head of the brotherhood, announced that he would never again consent to arbitration of railway problems by men both ignorant of railroad conditions and imbued with an antilabor attitude. The firemen, who had simultaneously experienced the same disappointment, made a similar pronouncement.

This open hostility to the Erdman Act so impressed Congress that it passed the Newlands Act setting up new machinery for settling railway disputes. The act established a United States Board of Mediation and Conciliation, with a permanent commissioner and two other officials, empowered to act on its own initiative in offering mediation. If this failed, the board could increase its membership and become a board of arbitration empowered to act if requested by both parties. In the meantime, the engineers and firemen had put aside their long-standing feud over the status of firemen who had become engineers, and had drawn into close alliance. In August, 1913, they made common wage demands on the western roads. The new board was called in to arbitrate. Its award produced a bitter reaction among all rail workers and proved to be the factor which induced all four brotherhoods to take concerted action.

Late in 1915 the executives of the four brotherhoods met in conference and drew up demands to be presented to the railroads: in all road service one hundred miles or less, eight hours or less, would constitute a day's work—except in passenger service; overtime would be paid whenever eight hours of duty had been served, or whenever the time on duty exceeded the miles run divided by 12.5 miles per hour; overtime would be compensated on the minute basis and would be paid at time and a half; reduction in hours or mileage was not to bring any reduction in pay. In March, 1916, these demands, backed by 300,000 rail workers, were presented to the management of 459 railroads. When negotiations accomplished nothing, the brotherhoods called for a strike vote. Although railway managers attempted to influence the vote with open letters, warnings, pleas for loyalty, and veiled threats of loss of pension rights, 92 per cent of the men cast their votes for extreme action. Brotherhood leaders called a strike for September 4th. President Wilson, who had been unsuccessful in persuading either railway labor or management to arbitrate, appealed for a postponement. When brotherhood chiefs denied their power to suspend the order, the President, in desperation, turned to Congress with the request that it enact an eight-hour law for railway employees.

Congress showed only slight hesitation in putting Wilson's suggestion into law. On September 3rd the Adamson Act established an eight-hour day for railway workers and provided that there should be no wage cuts for the shorter working day. The railroads immediately challenged the act on the ground that it was a regulation of wages. The brotherhoods awaited the decision quietly for several months but finally lost patience. In March, 1917, they demanded immediate institution of the eight-hour day; simultaneously they announced a strike for March 17th. President Wilson managed to postpone the strike twenty-four hours, and on March 18th the railroads agreed to grant the eight-hour day regardless of the court decision. On the next day the court upheld the constitutionality of the act in the case of *Wilson* v. *New*. Congressional power to enact both hour and wage legislation for railway employees was recognized.

The Federal Government's most significant legislation during the period concerned not special labor groups but labor as a whole. An indication of this interest in all labor was given as early as 1903 when a Department of Commerce and Labor was set up in the cabinet. Ten years later the two divisions were separated; a Department of Labor was established with William B. Wilson, former Knight and a member of the U.M.W., as secretary. The new department had three bureaus: labor statistics, children, and a conciliation service. Labor was thus recognized as one of the major concerns of government.

More important was the fruition of the A.F.L.'s campaign for relief from the application of the Sherman Act and the use of the injunction. The campaign, strongly supported by Progressives and carried directly to Congress by Samuel Gompers himself, ended in the passage of the Clayton Act of 1914. That act, designed to define more specifically the antitrust laws, contained two sections of importance to labor. Section 6 read:

The labor of a human being is not a commodity or article of commerce. Nothing contained in the anti-trust laws shall be construed to forbid the existence and operation of labor . . . organizations, instituted for the purpose of mutual help . . . or to forbid or restrain individual members of such organizations from lawfully carrying out the legitimate objects thereof; nor shall any organizations, or the members thereof, be held or construed to be illegal combinations in restraint of trade, under the anti-trust laws.

Section 20 read in part:

That no restraining order or injunction shall be granted by any court of the United States . . . in any case between . . . employers and employees . . . involving, or growing out of a dispute concerning terms or conditions of employment, unless necessary to prevent irreparable injury to property, or to a property right, of the party making application, for which injury there is no adequate remedy at law. . . .

Gompers hailed the act as a "Magna Carta upon which the working people will rear their constitution of industrial freedom." In 1914 such words did not seem extravagant. The act recognized the legality of labor organizations; it likewise appeared to free labor from the antitrust laws and the application of "judicial ukases."

Thus, on the eve of the First World War, labor, and particularly the American Federation of Labor, could look back upon a period that was successful not only economically but politically. Heavy blows had been struck at child labor; the hours and even the wages of women had been partially regulated; provision had been made in many states for inspection of factories, sweatshops, and mines; the whole concept of responsibility for industrial accidents had been changed and provision had been made for workingmen's compensation; hours of labor for men in some industries had been partially limited; and all labor had been given relief from the application of the antitrust laws and the injunction. As the war began, labor appeared to be on the threshold of a new era.

19 ——

Trade-Union Success •

The entrance of the United States into the war against the Central Powers provided organized labor with a fortuitous opportunity for advancement. Not that the opportunity was entirely clear at first. On the eve of the war the A.F.L., offering a wholehearted cooperation in support of the "democracies," pointed out that its support would be weakened if labor's interests were neglected. The Federal Government heard the warning. From the opening of the war, it adopted the policy that production could not be halted and that disgruntled trade unionists had to be satisfied. The War Department was among the first to face labor problems. In the spring of 1917 men engaged on the construction of cantonments began to complain about housing conditions and wages in the overcrowded cantonment construction areas. Secretary of War Newton D. Baker promptly established the Cantonment Adjustment Commission, representing the Army, the A.F.L., and the public, with instructions to determine basic union standards on wages, hours, and working conditions in the locality of each cantonment, and to use these standards to make any adjustments that were required to prevent a halt in construction. The department also set up similar commissions for the adjustment of labor disputes in the clothing industry, in the harness and saddlery industry and, with the cooperation of the Labor Department, in the meat-packing industry.

The Navy Department and the United States Shipping Board also faced labor problems early in the war. Their solutions were similar to those of the Army. When the men in the shipbuilding industry, living in overcrowded areas in which living costs had skyrocketed, began demanding higher wages and the adoption of a policy of no discrimination against union men, the Secretary of the Navy, Josephus Daniels, appointed a Shipbuilding Wage Adjustment Commission which settled the grievances with a 31 per cent increase in pay. The Navy also created an Arsenal and Navy Yard Wage Commission to keep its employees satisfied. The Shipping Board's biggest labor problem during the war was raised by the seamen, whose trade became so highly significant when the war opened that the government attempted to prevent trouble in advance. In May, 1917, the board met with representatives of the Atlantic Coast Steamship Owners and the International Seamen's Union and drew up an agreement setting a new wage scale, with a bonus of 50 per cent for seamen employed on vessels passing through the war zone and $100 compensation for loss of personal effects due to war accidents; the seamen in turn relaxed their apprenticeship regulations. The "May Agreement" was quickly accepted by Pacific Coast shipowners; two strike threats and government pressure also forced the Lake Carriers into line.

The governmental agency that left the heaviest imprint upon the nation's labor relations was the War Labor Board, created by a conference of labor leaders and manufacturers early in 1918. The board —consisting of five representatives from the A.F.L., five from industry, and Frank P. Walsh and former President Taft as cochairmen—was given jurisdiction over all fields of production needed for the successful prosecution of the war except those coming under an already established adjustment commission. It was to be guided by certain principles: no strikes or lockouts, recognition of the right of collective bargaining, recognition of the right of unions to organize but not their right to alter the status of nonunion shops, the eight-hour day, the fixing of wages in accordance with local standards, and equal pay for women. The War Labor Board operated until August, 1919, during which time it heard 1,250 cases and made awards affecting 1,100 industrial units and more than 700,000 workmen. Its attitude was generally liberal; left to itself it would probably have taken some strong steps to aid unionism. Since the terms upon which it was founded prevented any such action, it did what it considered the next best thing: it promoted the formation of shop representation committees in 125 industrial establishments where no union existed, with the expectation that such organizations would ultimately become full-fledged unions.

The benevolent attitude that the Federal Government displayed toward labor during the war undoubtedly worked in favor of the trade unionists. The government fostered a spirit which encouraged increases in wages, decreases in hours, and better working conditions. War conditions in turn gave substance to the spirit. The war created an abnormal demand for labor; at the same time it made labor scarce by reducing migration to practically nothing and by removing 4,000,000 men from the ranks of actual or potential labor and placing them in the armed forces. The need for labor led industry, which was itself making huge profits, to raise wages. The result could be read in the statistics. Wages in general increased from 100 in 1914 to 104 in 1918; for men engaged in manufacturing, transportation, and coal mining the real wages increased from 100 in 1914 to 120 in 1918. Demand for labor also led to a shorter basic working day. Not that industrial labor worked less, but in many industries, steel being the main exception, the eight-hour day and the forty-four-hour week became standard; overtime was compensated at a higher rate of pay. All this advance, widely publicized by the A.F.L., led in turn to an increase in union membership. On January 1, 1917, the organization had 2,370,000 members; by January 1, 1919, its membership had increased to 3,260,000.

When the First World War ended, the A.F.L. was in a jubilant mood. It looked back upon two years of "unshakable" advances which made the future look so bright that it confidently prepared an extensive "reconstruction program" which called for recognition of the right to organize, shorter hours, abolition of child labor, equal pay for women, government ownership of public and semipublic utilities, improved workmen's compensation laws, a drastic limitation upon immigration, a progressive tax on inheritances and incomes, and improved housing. The railway brotherhoods, in a similar mood, advocated government purchase of the railroads and their operation by a board representing government, management, and employees.

To a certain extent the A.F.L. achieved a portion of its program in the months immediately after the war but not in the way it expected, for the postwar years were hardly a period of peaceful advance. The eighteen months following the war constituted a period of "prosperity," in which industrial production remained high and the cost of living, at 150 in 1918, reached 205 in 1920. These conditions produced strong pressure for direct action from the rank and file.

Not all A.F.L. affiliates became involved in strikes. Many internationals adopted the attitude that time and prosperity were on their side, and they proved right: the high profits of the postwar months induced many employers to grant wage increases on mere demand.

Other A.F.L. elements, while generally successful, had to fight for their gains. Four days after the Armistice the Amalgamated Clothing Workers, anticipating a demand for civilian clothes, precipitated a strike which ended with the establishment of a forty-four-hour week in the men's clothing industry throughout the nation. Almost simultaneously the United Textile Workers, swelled by wartime accretions, struck for an eight-hour day and increases in wages. When U.T.W. leaders accepted a compromise, locals in the larger New England textile towns rebelled. Led by A. J. Muste, a socialist clergyman, about 100,000 workers seceded from the U.T.W., created an independent union and won their demands. Dock workers and longshoremen won shorter hours and higher wages in strikes that paralyzed the New York port area for weeks in 1918 and 1919. New England telephone operators forced Postmaster General Albert S. Burleson, director of the nation's telephone and telegraph lines during the war period and a bitter opponent of unionism, to grant wage increases.

Railway workers also became involved. In January, 1919, and in February, 1920, the brotherhoods and shopcrafts asked Walter D. Hines, Director-General of Railroads, for wage increases to meet rising living costs. Hines refused on both occasions, the second time because the government's control of the roads was due to end. Shortly afterward Congress enacted the Esch-Cummins Act, which provided for the settlement of disputes on interstate carriers by collective bargaining and for the appointment of a Railway Labor Board to act as arbiters of disputes if collective bargaining failed. Acting under the law the unions once more asked the railways for wage increases. Turned down, they appealed to the Railway Labor Board. At this point an explosion occurred among Chicago switchmen when a foreman in the yards of the Milwaukee Road was replaced by a road conductor from the Brotherhood of Railroad Trainmen. The action, a minor affair which ordinarily would have been handled without trouble, precipitated a strike in the Chicago yards. The Switchmen's Union and the brotherhoods, fearing that the walkout would prejudice their plea for wage increases, ordered the strikers to return to work. When the order was ignored, the unions began recruiting strikebreakers. Switchmen in Chicago countered by forming a "Yardmen's Association" and appealed to the Railway Labor Board for help. Although the board refused the association a hearing, causing the strike to collapse, the incident had its effect; it probably helped persuade the Railway Labor Board to grant railway employees a large wage increase in July, 1920.

Labor also made gains on the legislative front. State concern with the problem of arbitration of industrial disputes—which the Federal Government had brought to a new peak of efficiency during the war—revived in 1919. In the next three years a large number of states which had previously provided for temporary boards of arbitration set up permanent commissions. One state, Kansas, provided for compulsory arbitration. The law guaranteed labor a theoretical right to organize and to bargain collectively, but it also outlawed strikes in industries especially concerned with the public interest and provided that all labor disputes had to be submitted to the arbitration of the Industrial Relations Court. The A.F.L. fought the law as a deprivation of its rights, and a number of industrialists challenged its constitutionality. In 1922 the United States Supreme Court, in the case of *Wolff Packing Co.* v. *Court of Industrial Relations*, seriously emasculated the Kansas statute by declaring that Kansas' effort to set wages in the meat-packing industry was unconstitutional and that since such regulation was necessary to enforcement of the law compulsory arbitration in the meat-packing industry was unconstitutional.

A large number of states refurbished their child-labor and women's labor laws. Between 1917 and 1922 eleven states enacted legislation prohibiting labor of children under sixteen in specific industries. Six states wrote new laws which either provided for a forty-eight-hour week or prohibited night work for women; the United States Supreme Court approved the latter type of statute in the case of *Radice* v. *New York*. Four states and the District of Columbia enacted minimum-wage laws for women.

A remarkable number of states gave new attention to workmen's compensation legislation. Eight enacted new accident compensation laws between 1917 and 1919. The most important advances were made in the states which had enacted laws before the war. A number amended their old elective statutes to make accident compensation systems compulsory. About half of them changed their methods of administering the laws. The tendency had been to allow employers and employees to determine enforcement of the law by agreement and to let the courts settle any differences. It was soon learned that such methods were slow and costly, and that injured workmen often lost a portion of their compensation to attorneys. Administration was accordingly turned over to special commissions, a development which made compensation quicker and more certain. Several states also widened the scope of their legislation. Laws passed before 1917 limited to employees in hazardous occupations were amended to cover occupations in general—an action which brought about 65 per cent of all workers under compensation laws.

The most significant pieces of "labor" legislation enacted during the postwar period involved restrictions upon immigration. Between 1891 and 1920 more than 18,000,000 aliens entered the United States. The influx, not unusual in relation to the total population, alarmed two groups: the superpatriots and the trade unions. The former were particularly alarmed because most immigrants were of Latin and Slavic stock. Concluding that this new immigration was largely responsible for the crime, disease, and pauperism of which the nation was becoming conscious, they assumed the lead of a movement for restriction in the late nineteenth century and secured the passage of laws which prevented the admission of various "undesirables." Such restrictions had little effect on the tide. Accordingly, in the twentieth century, the superpatriots began to urge literacy as a test for admission. For several decades after the passage of the anticontract labor law, trade unions had not revealed any particular concern over immigration. In the early years of the twentieth century, however, the A.F.L. began to show interest, primarily because it recognized that immigrants, whom it regarded as unorganizable, were becoming more and more of a competitive threat to the skilled. The A.F.L. joined the movement for a literacy test, and a bill barring illiterates from entering the country was enacted over the President's veto in 1917.

The act marked the beginning of a restricted immigration policy. After the war a large number of Americans, alarmed by the growth of revolutionary ideologies in Europe, joined a movement for additional restrictions in order to prevent the entry of persons who might overthrow American institutions. Trade unionists again added their strength to the crusade, for a different reason. Immigration had all but halted during the war period—only about one million Mexicans, who had been used in agriculture, had been permitted to enter the country under contract—and the wages and hours of labor had been vastly improved. The conclusion was inescapable. Scarcity of labor would improve labor conditions in the future. Since the war had created a tremendous backlog of Europeans who wanted to enter the United States, that scarcity would be hard to achieve. The only answer was severe restriction. The result was the passage of the Immigration Act of 1921 which restricted immigration in any one year to 3 per cent of the number of a given national origin already in this country in 1910. The act, which was made a permanent part of the national policy by the even more restrictive act of 1924, was unquestionably a labor victory. While its full effect was not immediately evident, even at the time of its passage it was expected to benefit labor by reducing the nation's available labor supply and by checking competition.

The war and the postwar months thus constituted a period of considerable advance for trade-union labor. Economically the advance was recorded in statistics: by mid-1920 hours had been reduced to the point where many skilled laborers worked no more than forty-four hours a week, most skilled laborers worked no more than forty-eight hours a week, and the nation's work week averaged fifty hours; real wages of persons engaged in manufacturing and transportation were 35 per cent higher than before the war. Politically the advance was recorded in legislation: a lessening of child-labor competition, gains in hour legislation for women, improvements in workingmen's compensation, and a restrictive immigration policy. The success of trade-union labor was reflected in the growing membership rolls. By January 1, 1920, the A.F.L. boasted 4,078,000 members; another 1,032,000 members in other unions, most of them in the railway brotherhoods, brought the total to 5,110,000. Organized labor in 1920 appeared stronger than ever. It was due for a rude awakening.

20 ——

The Attack on the Radicals

The "cold shower" which the trade unions received after 1920 had its origins in wartime developments. With the entry of the United States into the First World War a wave of antiforeign hysteria swept through the nation. Directed at first against minority nationality groups suspected of sympathizing with Germany and the Central Powers, it soon transformed itself into a campaign to eradicate all elements which in any way seemed to be obstructing the war effort. It was a campaign based on fear that had its roots deep in the nineteenth century. Because of the Molly Maguire riots, the Railway strike of 1877, Haymarket, the Pullman strike, and the activities of the W.F.M. the insecure and the misinformed had developed a vague terror of labor. In the twentieth century this irrational fear had been further nurtured by the activities of socialists and Wobblies. Before the war the fear had manifested itself in the brutal attacks of employers and citizenry upon western Wobblies, culminating in the episodes at Everett, Washington, and Bisbee, Arizona. During the war, with the nation and its institutions in danger, it manifested itself in more concerted fashion.

The legal basis for the campaign was provided by the Federal Government, which passed the Espionage Act in June, 1917, and the Sedition Act in May, 1918, and by the states which vied with one another in a wild haste to pass criminal-syndicalism laws throughout 1917 and 1918. The Espionage Act provided punishment for anyone who interfered with the draft or who attempted to encourage disloyalty. The Sedition Act was intended to punish anyone who might obstruct the sale of bonds, incite insubordination, discourage recruiting, "wilfully utter, print, write, or publish any disloyal, profane, scurrilous, or abusive language about the form of government of the United States, or the Constitution . . . or the flag . . . or the uniform of the Army or Navy . . . or bring the form of government . . . or the Constitution into contempt . . . or advocate any curtailment of production in this country of anything necessary or essential to the prosecution of the war." The criminal-syndicalism laws provided for the punishment of persons who in any way advocated the overthrow or subversion of American institutions.

First to feel the effect of the wartime hysteria were the socialists. In a sense they invited the attack, for within a week after the war began a socialist convention declared the party opposed to the war and pledged itself to unyielding opposition to conscription and money-raising campaigns. Prosecution of the socialists began in May, 1917, when raids were made on the party's Indianapolis offices. The big drive, however, was launched in September, 1917, when Department of Justice agents raided the party's headquarters throughout the nation, seized literature and records, and arrested leaders. A mass trial of socialists accused of obstructing the war effort occurred in Chicago in February, 1918. The trial resulted in the conviction of several highly prominent figures in the party—among them Adolph Germer, the secretary; Louis Engdahl, editor of the official paper; Irwin St. John Tucker; and Victor Berger. Debs was convicted separately. Other trials of lesser figures followed with similar results.

The party, nevertheless, managed to maintain a sturdy existence. While Debs made no attempt to escape his fate, the men tried in Chicago never served a day of their sentences; their convictions were set aside on a technicality. A great many other convicted socialists served only a part of their terms, and some, like Hillquit and London, managed to escape scot-free. A factor which helped was the socialists' partial retreat from their original antiwar stand after the Russian revolutions and Wilson's announcement of his peace aims. Thus, in 1918, seven socialist aldermen in New York City announced themselves as favorable to the third Liberty loan, the party executive committee called for the extinction of "kaiserism," and the socialist needle trade unions became open advocates of war. Party membership during most of the war remained practically stationary at 80,000, increasing to 108,000 early in 1919. Socialist voting strength also continued high; during the 1917 elections the party polled better than 20 per cent of the vote in some fifteen cities and elected public officials in a dozen of them. The party's vote was equally large in the spring of 1918.

While the Socialist party emerged from the war with its influence still strong, the I.W.W. was almost destroyed. Like the socialists the Wobblies did not help themselves. They issued several pamphlets denouncing the war as a capitalistic plot; many Wobblies, moreover, were obvious draft dodgers. In the summer of 1917 President Wilson appointed Judge J. Harry Covington of the Supreme Court of the District of Columbia to investigate the organization. His report led to a Federal campaign of extermination. In September, 1917, Department of Justice operatives, making simultaneous raids on I.W.W. headquarters and homes in more than a dozen cities, arrested Bill Haywood, the members of the I.W.W. Executive Board, the secretaries of all industrial unions, the editors of I.W.W. newspapers, and all men who had at any time played an important role in the organization's affairs. The initial raid was soon followed by others, carried out both by Federal and by state authorities. Mobs supplemented the action with raids on Wobbly headquarters in California, in the oil fields of Kansas and Oklahoma, and in the lumber areas of Idaho and Washington. In all, some two thousand were arrested.

In the spring of 1918 the government brought 105 Wobbly leaders to trial in Chicago. They were charged with conspiracy to hinder and delay the execution of the Espionage Act, to injure citizens selling munitions to the government, to encourage draft dodging and desertion, and to cause insubordination and disloyalty in the military and naval forces. In effect the whole I.W.W. was placed in the dock. After four months of argument, all but thirteen of the defendants were found guilty. Throughout 1918, trials of I.W.W. members continued in all areas of the nation in both Federal and state courts. At least one-quarter of those originally arrested received penitentiary sentences. Nor did the campaign stop after the first blow was delivered. The Federal Government arrested and indicted any new figures that arose to lead the I.W.W. The effect was disastrous. The government's original campaign removed the ablest and most experienced leaders from the helm of the organization; its continued campaign destroyed the second- and third-rate leaders. By the end of the war the organization was beginning to disintegrate.

In the first months after the war, the hysteria that had formed the basis for the campaign against the socialists and the Wobblies began to recede, a reaction quite normal after high public excitement. It was, however, only a temporary recession: by mid-1919 a new wave of hysteria, known as the Red Scare, swept across the nation. The phenomenon had several causes. From Europe came news of "Bolshevik" victories in Russia, of radical revolutions in Finland, Hungary, and Bavaria, and of the organization of a Third International designed to spread communism throughout the world. News of this kind was in itself enough to strike terror into the hearts of those Americans who feared that they might be the targets of a similar movement.

To make matters worse a Bolshevik movement appeared in the United States, the result of a split in the Socialist party over the future of Marxism. From the fall of 1917 to early 1919 American socialists watched the Russian upheavals and the socialist-communist seizures of power in Finland, Hungary, and Germany with great interest. European events raised the hope of socialism's ultimate triumph throughout the world. As the war ended, however, this hope turned to trepidation, for it became clear that the European movements had no unity. There were two groups of Marxists: the socialists who had supported the war and were in a majority in most European countries, and the communists who had opposed the war and dominated Russia. The socialists, eager to re-create their prewar international organization, scheduled a conference at Berne for February, 1919; the communists scheduled a conference in Moscow for March, 1919. Although American socialists were invited to both, the party sent delegates only to Berne. The American left wing was outraged, but it took no action until after the Moscow conference, which established the Third International, proclaimed an undying hatred for all socialist groups which had failed to oppose the war, and set up a program calling for the overthrow of all capitalistic governments and the immediate establishment of a dictatorship of the proletariat. Adopting this program as its own, the left wing set out to impose it upon the Socialist party.

A change in party character made their goal achievable. In prewar days 85 per cent of the party rank and file had been American, German, Scandinavian, or British born. In 1910, however, the party, in an effort to reach the large Slavic and Latin immigrations of the previous decades, had created autonomous "language federations" which would devote themselves exclusively to the task of spreading the socialist gospel among people of their own nationality. By 1919 fifty-three per cent of the members, most of them immigrants from Russian or former Russian territory, belonged to these federations. Left-wing success among this element was phenomenal; in a few weeks it won control of the strong Brooklyn, Bronx, and Queens sections of New York City and of the seven largest language federations.

Then the right wing, which regarded the revolutionary movement as impracticable and dangerous, took action. Still in control of the party's executive machinery, it suspended the divergent sections and federations and began a reorganization drive. The left promptly met in conference to determine future action, but found itself unable to agree. While a majority, determined to secure control of the party, set up a council to plan strategy, the minority, led by the Russian Federation, bolted.

Shortly thereafter a national convention of the party, attended by the right wing in full force and a large left wing, gathered in Chicago. With the right wing in command the convention reaffirmed the old platform, which emphasized immediate demands, and rejected an alliance with the Third International. Most of the left wing walked out of the convention, reducing the Socialist party to a rank and file membership of some 30,000. The party was not destroyed. In May, 1920, it held its regular convention and named Debs, still serving a prison term, and Seymour Stedman as its presidential candidates. The party's campaign on behalf of its ticket was mild and conservative; it attracted almost a million voters.

The party left wing also reorganized. The original bolters, who claimed to represent some 58,000 former socialists, met at the Smolny Institute in Chicago simultaneously with the regular Socialist convention. While they were in the process of organizing, the second group of seceders asked permission to join them. Spurning the request, the Smolny gathering proceeded to organize the Communist party, with C. E. Ruthenberg as executive secretary. Its aim, it declared, was to establish industrial unions which through mass strikes would "educate" the workers to the importance of industrial struggles in the overthrow of capitalism. Meanwhile, the rebuffed group, representing some 30,000 former socialists, created the Communist

Labor party, with Alfred Wagenknecht as executive secretary. It advocated the use of revolutionary trade unionism and political action to secure the dictatorship of the proletariat. The two parties, in short, were different only in the emphasis they placed on means to secure their goals.

In addition to the appearance of the two communist organizations, which convinced many Americans that the very foundations of the nation were in danger, several strikes, all given "scare handling" by the press, struck further terror into the public mind. The first of the strikes occurred in Seattle in February, 1919, when the Shipbuilding Adjustment Board established a uniform wage scale for shipyard workers on both the Atlantic and Pacific coasts, thereby destroying a traditional wage differential favorable to the Pacific Coast workers. When metal trade workers failed in their efforts to restore the differential, they appealed to the Seattle Central Labor Council for help. Sixty thousand men dropped their tools, bringing every industry in the city to a standstill. Although the strike, mildly and cautiously conducted, lasted only four days, it had a wide effect. On the last day, Ole Hanson, Mayor of Seattle, denounced the strikers as Bolsheviks and revolutionaries. The denunciation, quickly circulated throughout the nation, convinced many who noticed the ease with which labor had paralyzed a city that they were witnessing the beginning of a violent revolution.

Equally alarming was the strike of Boston police which began in early September, 1919, after the police commissioner suspended nineteen members of the police force who had led a movement to affiliate Boston police with the A.F.L. The move caught Boston by surprise; large-scale rowdyism broke out in many parts of the city. Hastily recruited volunteers proved powerless to check the increasing lawlessness. Not until the third day of the strike when the mayor called out the Boston militia companies was order restored. The episode, short as it was, left its mark. As a direct threat, by negligence, to the established order, it not only alarmed the public but created a hysterical attitude which magnified the strike into a movement to destroy the major pillars of the nation's society—a threat to home, family, and the sanctity of womanhood.

This reaction greatly colored the public's attitude toward the next industrial conflict in steel. At the outbreak of the war the steel industry was the most powerful open-shop organization in the nation. Nevertheless, in the summer of 1918, A.F.L. leaders in Chicago, led by William Z. Foster, ex-Wobbly and ex-syndicalist with industrial-union tendencies, proposed an organizing drive and persuaded officers of the internationals with jurisdiction over various crafts and trades in the steel industry to form a National Committee for the Organizing of the Iron and Steel Industry. Foster became its secretary.

The campaign, which began in September, 1918, was a difficult one. The people who lived in the steel towns of Pennsylvania, Ohio, Indiana, and Illinois were immigrants of a dozen different nationalities, suspicious of each other and with little knowledge of English. They were divided into a mutually mistrustful skilled minority and an unskilled majority; the skilled in turn were broken into twenty-four crafts, each jealous of its prerogatives. In addition the companies owned many of the steel towns; they controlled the political machines and the press; and their ability to suppress undesirable persons or conduct and to destroy civil liberties was almost unlimited. Despite these handicaps the National Committee made progress. Steel company response indicated the growth of the movement. United States Steel granted its skilled labor an eight-hour day in the Chicago-Indiana area in October; Bethlehem granted the same concession to all its skilled laborers several months later. But the vast majority of steelworkers received nothing. About one-third of them were still working twelve hours a day, seven days a week, for miserable wages; another 50 per cent were still working a ten-hour day.

In May, 1919, the National Committee, which had signed up nearly 100,000 men, presented demands: recognition of the right of collective bargaining, reinstatement of all men discharged for union activities, the eight-hour day, one day's rest in seven, abolition of the twenty-four-hour shift, a living wage, double pay for overtime, adoption of the checkoff and seniority, and abolition of company unions. Steel companies answered the demands by stepping up their discharges. A strike began on September 22nd with 375,000 workers out. The steel companies fought back with all their resources. Expert publicity men were hired to produce the impression that steel workers were highly paid, that the majority of them were opposed to the strike, and that the mills were operating at nearly full capacity. A strong effort was made to discredit the whole movement by attacking Foster as a Bolshevik hireling. In the field the steel companies used other devices. Although the civil liberties of the strikers were fairly well respected in West Virginia and Ohio, civil rights were completely suppressed in Pennsylvania: no meetings were permitted, organizers were beaten and run out of town, mounted state troopers rode their horses through the towns, clubbing strikers. Two months after the strike began the steel companies, with the aid of Negro strikebreakers, restored production to 75 per cent of normal. By January, 1920, the slender resources of the strike committee were exhausted, and the strike was canceled.

The effect of the strike on the public was profound. Securing its knowledge of the strike from newspapers which were decidedly anti-labor, which made no effort to report the strikers' case, and which sought to discredit the whole conflict as a movement led by a revolutionary and composed of immigrants instilled with foreign "isms," the public concluded that the strike was a Bolshevik plot, aimed at destroying the economic stability of the nation's society by paralyzing its chief industry.

The nation's catharsis for the Red Scare was a campaign of extermination, conducted on many fronts over a period of several years. The socialists suffered least. In New York City a mob of ex-soldiers and civilians wrecked the office of the New York *Call;* several states jailed socialists for violating criminal-syndicalism laws; and Federal authorities deported a few. In 1919 the New York Assembly declared five members of the party, including Morris Hillquit, ineligible to hold their seats. When the five were reelected in September, 1920, three were expelled. Congress took action against Victor Berger, expelling him twice, but allowing him to keep his seat after his third election in 1922.

The communists received more drastic treatment. During the summer and fall of 1919 many states took action against members of the Communist and Communist Labor parties under their criminal-syndicalism laws. Communist leaders in New York, Illinois, and California, among them Ruthenberg and Benjamin Gitlow, were sent to jail. The Federal Government became involved through the act authorizing the Secretary of Labor to arrest and deport any alien who advocated revolution or belonged to any organization which advocated the overthrow of government by force. Secretary of Labor William B. Wilson used the law in December, 1919, when 249 aliens, most of them communists, were placed aboard the "Red Ark" and sent to Russia.

Meanwhile Attorney-General A. Mitchell Palmer was preparing an even heavier blow. During the fall and early winter Department of Justice agents infiltrated communist ranks to secure the names of leaders and members. Then, on January 2, 1920, they made simultaneous raids upon communist meeting places throughout the nation and upon homes of known or suspected radicals, arresting everyone found on the premises. Persons who attempted to visit the suspects in jail were arrested on suspicion of being communists. The total thus seized has never been officially stated; estimates ran from four to ten thousand. Although the raids brought considerable protest from liberal elements and from the Department of Labor, which alone had jurisdiction over aliens destined for deportation, trials of the suspects began immediately—often without counsel or the usual judicial safeguards. The obvious intention was to deport as many of the seized men as possible. Secretary of Labor Wilson partially checked the effort when he ruled that the Communist Labor party was not illegal and that membership in that party was not cause for deportation. This brought the release of about 75 per cent of the suspects. Of the remainder about 550 were eventually deported and another group was turned over to state authorities for punishment under criminal-syndicalism laws.

The raids temporarily shattered the communist movement and drove it underground. For a while it groped in darkness, seeking means to unite. A host of organizations were established—the United Communist party, a Proletarian party, an Industrial Communist party, and a Rummager's League—all claiming to be the "true" organization. Several "legal" offshoots of the underground also appeared, among them the American Labor Alliance and the Trade Union Educational League, which was designed to "educate" the trade unions to the need of revolutionary activity. Early in 1921 various communists began to urge that the movement come out of hiding. Since the Red Scare had not abated, the leaders scheduled an underground conference to argue the matter in the woods outside

Bridgman, Michigan. In the midst of its deliberations the conference was raided by government agents; a large number of delegates were arrested. Among them was William Z. Foster, now an avowed communist and head of the Trade Union Educational League. The Bridgman raid was the last important blow struck at the communist movement. In December, 1921, the communists formed the "Workers' Party of America," which quickly united all but a few dissidents and emerged from the underground. For communists the Red Scare had ended.

For the Wobblies, however, it continued for several years. The I.W.W. came out of the war without effective leadership and bitterly divided into "centralists" and "autonomists." Ultimately the centralists won control and provided, as they had planned, for universal dues and initiation fees. The act, however, cost them the support of Philadelphia longshoremen and New York City bakers, both of which had been among the steadiest financial supporters of the general organization. In addition the Wobbly rank and file became suspicious of its own leaders and forced the adoption of a rule limiting executive officers to a maximum term of one year. Thus the organization weakened its financial position and destroyed the effectiveness of its already poor leadership. It was hardly ready to fight the new campaign directed against it after the war.

The anti-Wobbly drive developed out of events in Centralia, Washington, in the heart of the lumber area where the I.W.W. reopened its meeting hall, which had been wrecked during the war. On Armistice Day, 1919, a parade of American Legionnaires, urged on by a Citizen's Protective League created by lumbermen to combat "radicalism," rushed the hall. The forewarned Wobblies opened fire, killed three Legionnaires and wounded two others. Ultimately twelve Wobblies were captured and thrown into jail; one of the twelve was later removed and lynched. The Centralia episode released a fearful blood lust. Hysteria-ridden mobs attacked and demolished I.W.W. meeting halls throughout the state; police cooperated by making wholesale arrests until the number of Wobblies jailed in Washington reached at least one thousand.

Meanwhile, the anti-Wobbly hysteria spread through the nation. In Weirton, West Virginia, 150 Wobblies involved in the Steel Strike were forced by the police to kneel in the street to kiss the flag. In

Kansas, Oklahoma, Idaho, Oregon, and California more than a thousand Wobblies were arrested and brought to trial during 1920, charged with vagrancy, criminal syndicalism, and sedition. A letdown occurred in 1921, but during the two following years the effort to destroy the organization was renewed. California showed the way. Wherever a Wobbly-led strike occurred, authorities immediately began prosecution for criminal syndicalism. Most notable were the cases involving 1,700 construction workers on the Hetch Hetchy aqueduct in 1922, and 3,000 longshoremen at San Pedro in 1923. California reduced its campaign to simplest terms: it used professional witnesses to secure convictions; when juries began to rebel the authorities continued the campaign with an injunction which forbade I.W.W. organizers to solicit new members—Wobblies bold enough to disobey were jailed for contempt of court without a jury trial. Against such tactics the I.W.W. was powerless. By 1924 the organization had been reduced to a hollow shell; all that remained was its jailed leaders and a handful of die-hard followers. In 1924 this remnant reduced itself to a state of futility when it split into two parts over the question of whether jailed leaders should accept pardons. For all practical purposes the I.W.W. was dead, victim of the most systematic campaign of extermination in American history.

21 ___

A Decade of Decline

The drives against "radicals" and "reds" during the First World War and after were not aimed at orthodox labor unions. The public at large supported these campaigns because it feared that socialists, communists, and Wobblies were either enemies of the nation during wartime or enemies of cherished American institutions in peacetime —fit to be destroyed, therefore, as a measure of self-defense. But eventually a subtle change occurred. In the midst of the campaign against the reds, leaders of industry began to point out that they were part of the labor world; they insinuated that all labor was tinged with radicalism, that labor if not "red" was at least "pink." Labor, in short, was becoming un-American; it would have to be hobbled and forced to return to time-hallowed American principles.

The campaign to accomplish this end began during the Great Steel Strike when President Wilson called an industrial conference to discuss methods whereby the wartime harmony in industrial relations could be maintained. The labor contingent demanded that the conference recognize labor's right to organize, to bargain collectively, and to be represented by individuals of its own choosing in any negotiations with industry. Employers, on the other hand, insisted that any such recognition "must not be understood as limiting the right of any wage earner to refrain from joining any organization or deal[ing] directly with his employer if he chooses." Shortly after the meeting, a concerted campaign to reestablish the open shop spread through the nation. It had no obvious focal point. The press, speech-making employers, bankers, and farm leaders simultaneously began to talk about an "American Plan" designed to restore certain traditional American rights: among them the inalienable privilege of every American to enter any trade or business he chose and to accept employment under conditions satisfactory to himself without interference from a union business agent. The campaign was an almost instant success. During 1920 the whole nation was covered with a network of organizations which under one name or another became advocates of the open shop. The results became evident in 1921 when employer groups set out to recover their old ascendancy over labor.

The year 1921 was a propitious time for launching an antilabor campaign. The nation was rapidly sinking into a postwar depression which had begun in the spring of 1920. Causes of the event were complicated: a reduction on loans to European countries which reduced European orders for American goods, a reduction in government spending, a drop in the volume of goods bought by American consumers no longer able to pay inflated prices, a decline in building activities caused by investors' recognition that building costs had reached a level which practically precluded a reasonable return on investments. The result was a drop in industrial production from a level of 119 in 1919 to 102 in 1921, and a sharp drop in employment —between 1919 and 1921 the number of wage earners engaged in manufacturing was reduced almost 25 per cent.

It was the kind of period which organized labor had faced before, and its response was similar. It sought to check the deterioration of its condition by keeping wages high and hours short. The effort gave rise to another strike wave, full of bitterness and violence. Labor won some of the strikes. The printing trades managed to maintain their forty-four-hour week. The Amalgamated Clothing Workers of New York City won a six-month struggle, involving some 65,000 workers, to maintain control of jobs but were forced to recognize the need for a 15 per cent wage cut. The I.L.G.W.U. prevented reestablishment of piecework and the forty-eight-hour week. The United Textile Workers and the Amalgamated Textile Workers combined to win a two-month strike for restoration of wage cuts against cotton manufacturers of Massachusetts and Rhode Island.

These victories were in sharp contrast to events in other industries. In 1921 the International Seamen's Union went on strike against a proposal to cut wages and abolish the three-watch system, completely paralyzing shipping from Maine to Texas. The United States Shipping Board combined with the American Shipowners Association to defeat the effort. Black listing and discrimination once more became rampant in the industry. In 1922 meat packers lost their wartime wage gains in a strike involving 45,000 butchers and cutters in thirteen cities.

The building trades became involved in several antiunion movements. Although these movements originated with a public angry over high building costs, they were also designed to reestablish the open shop. The most spectacular public attack occurred in New York where the Lockwood Committee, created by the state legislature in response to public demand for investigation of strikes and high costs in the building industry, exposed a sordid picture of graft and corruption involving a union business agent, a lawyer who "ran" some building associations, and certain material dealers. In spite of Gompers' efforts to explain the situation, the public revealed a strong resentment that boded no good for the unions. In Chicago, where the building trades' practices were investigated by the Dailey Committee of the Illinois legislature, a similar exposure began an open-shop movement. In May, 1921, builders offered members of the Building Trades Council a new wage scale 20 per cent lower than the old. A walkout followed. Immediately, however, a Citizens' Committee raised $3,000,000 and began to import strikebreakers; it hired detectives to keep contractors under surveillance and provided for the boycott of contractors who hired labor at higher wages. The Citizens' Committee broke the strike. An equally successful drive against the building trades also occurred in San Francisco.

The most important strike of the period involved the railway shop crafts. In the fall of 1920 railroad managers asked the Railway Labor Board to authorize a cut in wages to match the drop in railway traffic and to abolish the shop craft rules established during the war. The board imposed a 12 per cent cut and released the roads from paying overtime wages for work performed on Sundays and holidays. Two years later in August, 1922, when the board approved a second 12 per cent cut, the shop crafts went on strike. The walkout was denounced by the chairman of the Railway Labor Board and by the press as an illegal act, and the board threatened loss of seniority rights; but the strikers, refusing to retreat, demanded that the issue be negotiated. Railway managers, confident of victory, refused and the strike stalemated.

With the public growing steadily more restive over the threatened paralysis of the roads, Attorney-General Harry M. Daugherty obtained a temporary order from the Federal Court in Chicago forbidding the unions from doing anything in support of the strike. The injunction, as issued by Judge James H. Wilkerson, was based on the charge that the unions had conspired to violate both the antitrust laws by interfering with interstate commerce and the Esch-Cummins Act by going on strike against a decision of the Railway Labor Board. Although the unions pointed out that the Clayton Act specifically exempted labor from the operations of the antitrust laws when it was engaged in a direct dispute with employers and that the Esch-Cummins Act did not prohibit strikes, the injunction remained in effect. The strike continued, but it soon began to weaken. Early in October, Daniel Willard, president of the Baltimore and Ohio line, suggested separate agreements for each road. The unions accepted. By mid-October eleven large systems and many smaller lines, employing some 225,000 shopmen, made settlements. But the Pennsylvania and others, employing some 175,000 shopmen, refused to arbitrate. On those roads the open shop was once more established.

Meanwhile, organized labor began to receive setbacks on the legal front. Between 1921 and 1924 neither the states nor the Federal Government enacted any significant laws dealing with children, women, working conditions, workmen's compensation, or hours. In addition the Federal courts proceeded to emasculate many of the legislative gains labor had made during the progressive era and in the immediate postwar period. The Supreme Court's decision on the Owen-Keatings Act which was challenged in the case of *Hammer* v. *Dagenhart* in 1918 foreshadowed the trend. In spite of the fact it had approved the use of the commerce power to regulate impure foods, lotteries, and the white slave traffic, the court found the act unconstitutional. Congress sought to offset the damage with an act which provided for a 10 per cent tax in excess of all other taxes on the net profits from the products of a mining or manufacturing establishment in which children under fourteen were allowed to work, or in which children between fourteen and sixteen were permitted to work more than eight hours or at night. In 1922 the Supreme Court in the case of *Bailey* v. *Drexel Furniture Co.* declared the act unconstitutional, although it had previously upheld a regulatory tax on narcotics and on colored oleomargarine. In 1923 the court declared unconstitutional the law providing for the establishment of minimum wages for women in the District of Columbia in the case of *Adkins* v. *Children's Hospital,* a decision which cast doubt on the legality of all minimum-wage laws. The court also nullified attempts to place longshoremen under state compensation laws. In 1917 the court had ruled that longshoremen were not entitled to accident compensation under state laws on the ground that they were under the jurisdiction of the Federal Government. In 1920 Congress attempted to remedy the situation by providing that all persons under the maritime and admiralty jurisdiction injured on the job would have the "rights and remedies" provided by the laws of the states in which the incident occurred. But the Supreme Court in the case of the *Knickerbocker Ice Co.* v. *Stewart* declared this law unconstitutional on the ground that Congress did not have the right to transfer its powers and jurisdiction to the states.

The changed attitude of the Federal courts toward welfare legislation was also revealed in decisions which revolved around the use of the injunction in labor disputes and the application of the antitrust laws.

Labor had assumed that the Clayton Act had given it immunity from the use of the injunction. It learned that the anti-injunction provision, permitting the issuance of injunctions when necessary "to prevent irreparable injury to property or to a property right," was no protection at all. Since almost any action that labor took during an industrial conflict could be construed as an action injurious to property or a property right, the courts continued to issue injunctions as freely as ever. Labor unions, in fact, were swamped with injunctions after 1920; one in the Red Jacket Coal Company case went so far as to forbid all attempts to organize coal miners. The attitude of the Supreme Court on this issue was clearly revealed in the case of *Truax v. Corrigan*, tried in 1921. The case involved an Arizona statute which was modeled after the Clayton Act. Lower courts in Arizona issued an injunction; the Supreme Court of Arizona declared the injunction illegal. But the United States Supreme Court announced that the Arizona Supreme Court had erred in denying the injunction because such action constituted a denial of the right to resort to equity in a specific case and amounted to a denial of the equal protection of the law.

Labor also learned that the provision granting immunity from the antitrust laws was nearly useless. The pattern was set in the Duplex case. The Duplex Printing Press Company, located in Battle Creek, Michigan, was a manufacturer of printing machinery. In 1913 it broke relations with the Machinists Union and restored a ten-hour day. When the union called a strike and instructed its members and those of other locals to refuse to install and service Duplex presses, the company asked for an injunction on the ground that the union was an illegal combination designed to monopolize the machinists' trade. Lower Federal courts denied the request, but the Supreme Court, in a judgment handed down in 1921, reversed the decision. It pointed out that the Clayton Act applied only to employers and employees directly involved in an industrial conflict and not to other persons; the involvement of these other persons was, therefore, an unlawful secondary boycott. Even more important, the Court also pointed out that Section 6 of the Clayton Act applied to labor organizations which were "lawfully carrying out legitimate objects." There was nothing in the section which permitted labor organizations to engage in any activity that would "enable a normally lawful organization to become a cloak for an illegal combination in restraint of trade," nor did the section exempt a labor organization or its members "from accountability where it or they depart from . . . normal and legitimate objects and engage in an actual combination or conspiracy in restraint of trade." What was "lawful" and "legitimate" was to be defined by the courts.

In subsequent decisions the court made some definitions. In the Tri-City Trades case, tried in 1921, the court decided that all picketing was unlawful and that the courts could limit the activity to "peaceful picketing" which would permit one man—a former employee on strike—to be stationed at the entrance to the plant. In the Coronado case of 1922 the court went further, pointing out that labor unions on strike could be held liable where the strike affected interstate commerce for destruction of property or a property right—a decision that threatened all future labor activity.

The open-shop campaign, by-product of the war on radicals and reds, and the antilabor attitude assumed by the Supreme Court in its interpretation of the Clayton Act were severe shocks for orthodox labor. How severe was revealed in membership statistics. While unionism remained in the old, well organized trades, it disappeared in the trades and industries organized during the war. Between 1920 and 1924 membership in all labor organizations declined from 5,110,-000 to 3,600,000, and the A.F.L.'s membership dropped from 4,078,-000 to 2,866,000. But the combined economic and legal attack did not paralyze labor's will to struggle. In spite of setbacks a substantial portion of trade-union leadership and the rank and file of the early twenties were still imbued with the belief that they could create a Utopia. The problem was to find the means to halt decline. They did not seek far. Almost immediately they turned to the two solutions offered by previous generations: political action and industrial unionism.

The political development, known as the Progressive movement, had several forerunners. Among the first was the Non-Partisan League, founded in North Dakota in 1915. On the eve of the war the league appeared in Minnesota where, in 1918, it joined the Minnesota State Federation of Labor in voting for designated candidates in the Republican primary. While the coalition failed to name its choice for governor, the electorate sent fifty-one of its endorsees to the legislature. In 1922 the coalition became the Farmer-Labor party of Minnesota and elected Magnus Johnson governor and Henrik Shipstead senator.

In the meantime, local labor groups, eager to speed the postwar millennium, began a movement reminiscent of the United Front campaign of the eighties. The movement began with the creation of labor parties in Connecticut industrial towns; in 1919 trade unionists in New York City organized the American Labor party, and the Chicago Federation, led by John Fitzpatrick, organized the Labor party of Cook County. Although A.F.L. leaders like Gompers and Dan Tobin opposed the trend, it continued to grow. The Pennsylvania and Indiana State federations and District 12 of the U.M.W. endorsed the development; state labor parties appeared in New York, Pennsylvania, Michigan, Illinois, and Utah. In November, 1919, a conference of over one thousand delegates met at Chicago and created the National Labor party, inviting all laboring men, farmers, and socialists to join. The response was disappointing. Gompers proceeded to remove presidents of city centrals who were prominent in the movement and threatened locals which showed strong tendencies toward political action with loss of charters. The socialists criticized the movement as dualistic and urged its backers to throw their efforts into the Socialist party. Despite this discouragement, the National Labor party met again at Chicago in mid-1920 to formulate plans for the coming presidential campaign.

Another body, the Committee of 48, met at the same time. The Forty-eighters were professional and businessmen who wished to keep alive the spirit of Theodore Roosevelt's progressive party. Strong defenders of civil liberties and the democratic process, they also sympathized with labor's objectives. As was expected the two movements merged into the Farmer-Labor party. But that was as far as the agreement went. The Laborites, with greater numbers and greater experience in rough-and-tumble debate, wrote a platform which called for increasing participation of labor in the affairs of industry, and most of the Forty-eighters, unable to accept so radical an objective, walked out. The convention then nominated Parley P. Christensen, a Forty-eighter and Utah lawyer with a long record as a labor sympathizer, as its presidential candidate and Max Hayes as his running mate. The party made little additional headway. Farmers failed to join the movement; even the Farmer-Labor party of Minnesota held aloof. The A.F.L. continued its policy of proscribing trade-union leaders who showed any inclination to support the movement, and socialists, who had their own candidate, revealed open hostility. Christensen received less than a quarter-million votes.

Unsuccessful as it was, the movement laid the psychological foundations of the larger Progressive movement. In 1921 William H. Johnston, president of the railway machinists, alarmed over the growing antilabor trend, called a meeting of several railway chiefs to discuss means of protecting the interests and welfare of labor. The meeting in turn called a Conference for Progressive Political Action, for February, 1922, to take action on behalf of all the nation's discontented. Response was excellent. Delegates attended from some fifty brotherhoods and internationals, from the Socialist party, from the Farmer-Labor party of Minnesota, from the Non-Partisan League, from the Farmers' Union, and from various socio-political and religious organizations; many were members of the National Labor party. The C.P.P.A. was immediately confronted with the question of what action to take. The Socialists and the Farmer-Labor party of Minnesota urged immediate formation of an independent political party. But the majority decided on other tactics: they provided for the organization of local conferences which would be free to take any political action deemed appropriate in the next election. Wherever Socialists or Farmer-Labor candidates had a chance for victory the conferences were to throw their support to them; elsewhere the boring-from-within tactics of the Non-Partisan League were to be used.

The C.P.P.A. held a second, stock-taking meeting in December, 1922. Since a large number of progressives had been elected to both Federal and state offices in the previous election, the conference was more than pleased with itself. But success created a crisis. The Farmer-Labor party of Minnesota again demanded that the movement turn to independent action. When its demands—supported by the Missouri and Wisconsin federations, by the needle trades, and by the socialists—was defeated, it walked out of the meeting. The act might have been shattering, but at this stage the conference majority, dominated by railway leaders, was looking forward with considerable confidence to the next campaign. Their candidate for the presidency was William Gibbs McAdoo, wartime Secretary of the Treasury and Director-General of the railways. Since McAdoo appeared to have an inside track for the Democratic nomination, C.P.P.A. leaders expected to win a large-scale victory as allies of the Democratic party.

They were doomed to disappointment. The Republicans nominated Calvin Coolidge to succeed himself, and the Democrats named John W. Davis, a Morgan partner. While both parties announced their support for a Federal child-labor amendment and an eight-hour day and denounced the Railway Labor Board and compulsory arbitration of industrial disputes, C.P.P.A. leaders suspected that neither was sincere. Accordingly they called another conference. Some six hundred delegates swarmed into Cleveland to attend the fourth C.P.P.A. meeting, which adopted the name Progressive party and nominated Robert M. La Follette, a long-time progressive and friend of labor, as its candidate for the Presidency with Senator Burton K. Wheeler of Montana as his running mate. It also adopted a platform written by La Follette himself. The platform, not as strong as many elements would have liked, was a mixture of labor and farmer demands. The aim of the movement, it declared, was to break the power of private monopoly over the government, the courts, and industry. It demanded public ownership of the nation's water power, recovery of oil reserves involved in the Teapot Dome scandal, heavy inheritance taxes, reduction of taxes upon individuals and legitimate business; it called for a reduction of tariffs, reduction of railway rates, and legislation for relief of the farmer. On behalf of labor it denounced the power of the courts to nullify acts of Congress, demanded abolition of the injunction in labor disputes, repeal of the Esch-Cummins Act, and prompt adoption of a child-labor amendment.

The campaign opened in a mighty burst of enthusiasm and optimism. Many there were who expected victory; even cautious supporters of the movement expected to poll ten million votes. The Socialist party abrogated its rule requiring support for a member of its own party to endorse La Follette's candidacy. The A.F.L. in turn abandoned its long-time nonpartisan policy and officially endorsed La Follette's candidacy. But the campaign proved to be no joyous crusade. In many states the party had trouble in getting its candidates on the ballot. The task was ultimately accomplished in all states but Louisiana under one name or another, but it used up much of the movement's energy. The problem of making nominations for lesser offices also proved troublesome. The party adopted the policy of supporting congressional and state candidates with progressive principles who were nominated by other parties, a policy which created much discontent because it spawned a movement with a head but no body. The communists proved embarrassing. Although their proffered support was repudiated by La Follette, their willingness to help the movement gave opponents an opportunity to attack La Follette as a dangerous radical. The campaign was handicapped by inadequate financial support and by the lack of precinct and ward machinery. Labor, moreover, was disappointed because La Follette concentrated his campaign upon agrarian voters, and discouraged because many leaders did not support the movement—among them John L. Lewis, William Hutcheson of the carpenters, and Terrence V. O'Connor of the longshoremen who supported Coolidge, and George L. Berry of the pressmen who supported Davis.

The La Follette-Wheeler ticket polled nearly 17 per cent of the vote—4,822,000 out of a total of 28,935,000. It was the largest vote given to a third party since the Republicans had appeared on the national scene in 1856. La Follette carried Wisconsin and ran second in ten other western states. He polled better than 17 per cent of the vote in Illinois and Ohio, better than 14 per cent of the vote in Pennsylvania and New York; he carried the city of Cleveland. The movement also helped elect six senators and twenty congressmen. Labor, nevertheless, was disappointed. Perhaps the labor leaders in the movement had expected too much, and their disappointment impelled them to readopt the A.F.L.'s old nonpartisan policy. Perhaps they never intended to operate politically for more than one election and used the "poor vote" merely as an excuse to return to old policies. Whatever the reason, the C.P.P.A. dissolved early in 1925, and what had appeared to be a promising political movement died in its infancy.

The movement was not without results. In 1926 the Congress

elected in the La Follette campaign abolished the Railway Labor
Board. In its place it enacted a Railway Labor Act which erected
a permanent Board of Mediation composed of five members. The
new board was charged with the task of attempting to mediate any
railroad dispute not settled by direct negotiation or by adjustment
boards. If mediation failed the board was to urge the parties to submit to arbitration which would provide a mandatory award. If one
or both parties refused to arbitrate and an interruption in interstate
commerce threatened, the President was empowered to name an
emergency board to investigate and report recommendations for a
settlement; during investigation and for thirty days afterward no
change could be made in labor conditions. The act, intended to eliminate the compulsory tendencies of the Esch-Cummins provisions
and to safeguard the public against any hasty action, satisfied railway
labor.

The movement to check decline by converting the A.F.L. into an
industrial union was also known as "progressivism." It was a movement based on logical considerations. Many laboring men recognized
that skills were becoming less important in American industry, that
machinery had eliminated some skills entirely and had divided and
subdivided others to the point where almost no time was needed to
learn them. In addition they recognized that organization of industry
by skills made it difficult to secure a united front in any industry;
craft jealousies prevented the creation of fighting combinations and
gave industrial managers a chance to use "divide and conquer" tactics. Finally, there was the fact that more than 80 per cent of the
workers in industry were not members of the skilled group. A labor
movement that rested upon 20 per cent of the workingmen could
never be strong.

Progressivism became an issue inside the federation immediately
after the Great Steel Strike. Its chief exponents were the needle trade
workers, members of unions with strong socialist admixtures, and
the A.F.L.'s younger element. The movement revealed itself most
clearly for the first time in 1921 when John L. Lewis, president of the
United Mine Workers, challenged Gompers' reelection. Lewis, no
progressive himself, received one-third of the votes cast. This manifestation of strength alarmed A.F.L. leaders. Realizing that the very

foundation of the federation was in serious danger, they set out to stop the movement—by tarring it with the brush of communism.

As has been indicated the communists had created several public "fronts" during their period underground; among them was the Trade Union Educational League, designed to work within the trade unions to convert members to communism. The T.U.E.L. proved moderately successful; it converted thousands and secured a strong grip upon the needle trades of New York City. Its converts and sympathizers within the federation became strong exponents of progressivism. It was this situation that A.F.L. leaders used. In 1922 the official organs of a number of internationals opened a concerted attack upon progressivism as "communist inspired." Simultaneously the Executive Council of the federation began a war upon the communists inside the organization, revoking charters of small locals which were dominated by the T.U.E.L. and forcing the expulsion of hundreds of communists from positions of importance within the federation. In 1925, after the C.P.P.A. was dissolved, the A.F.L. issued an official denunciation of the Soviet régime, a declaration which it continued to repeat for many years. In the following years it began a purge of the strong needle trades. Using unsuccessful strikes as an excuse, it dissolved the communist-dominated New York Furriers' Joint Board and the I.L.G.W.U.'s Joint Committee and communist-led locals of both trades in New York and Chicago and began reorganization. The task, which took two years to accomplish, cost the federation thousands of members who joined the communist-created Needle Trades Workers Industrial Union, but it rid the leadership of a troublesome element. To complete the campaign the Executive Council ordered all affiliates to withdraw their support from the Brookwood Labor School because it suspected that the institution was teaching progressive doctrines.

The anti-communist campaign wrecked the industrial union movement within the A.F.L. Because they disliked the communists as much as trade unionists did, the progressives supported the communist purge. They did not help themselves thereby; they not only lost the support of the communists inside the A.F.L., but at the same time found that their own program had become synonymous with communism. Placed on the defensive, the progressives were unable to develop their attacks upon trade unionism and unable to develop a strong drive for conversion. Accordingly, they lapsed into silence.

The defeat of progressivism contributed to the continued decline of organized labor after 1924. Inside the A.F.L. it created an old guard, led after Gompers' death by William Green and Matthew Woll, which steadfastly refused to recognize that the organization needed strengthening. It was content to rest upon past performances, to confine membership to the élite among workingmen, and to remain the junior partner of management in the nation's economic system. In addition, the campaign against progressivism took up so much of the federation's energy that little remained for organizing purposes— an astonishing failure, considering that labor had made its greatest organizational advances in eras of prosperity.

The inertia of A.F.L. leadership was illustrated by the fact that throughout the late twenties the federation made only one major effort to enlarge its area of operation—in the southern textile industry. In the summer of 1927 a walkout among unorganized workers in Henderson, North Carolina, aimed at preventing the introduction of the "stretch-out," indicated that unionizing efforts might have some success. Accordingly, an A.F.L. convention approved an organizing drive. The campaign inspired one strike for higher wages in the rayon factory of Elizabethtown, Tennessee, which ended in the reformation of a company union, and another strike at Marion, South Carolina, which ended in complete defeat. In 1930 the A.F.L. decided on a more concerted drive and appealed to the whole labor movement for aid. The new campaign resulted in one incident. Employees in the Riverside and Dan River Cotton Mills of Danville, Virginia, revolted against a 10 per cent wage cut. When the strike was crushed by police and militia, the A.F.L. gave up its campaign.

Failure of A.F.L. leadership was not the only cause of organized labor's continued decline after 1924. A contributing factor was the agricultural situation. While retail food prices remained fairly constant at a level 60 per cent above the 1913 figure between 1921 and 1928, hourly money wages of labor rose to roughly 100 per cent above 1913 after 1926. Laboring men who secured benefits from this situation were not inclined to join unions in order to keep wages from lagging behind cost of living.

Population movements had an effect. There was a steady movement during this period from agricultural areas to the cities, and a particularly strong movement of Negroes and poorer whites from the South to the North. Both increased available labor supply in industrial regions, provided competition to established labor, and made established labor somewhat more docile. The shifting of industry had similar effects. During the period oil wells in Ohio, Indiana, Illinois, West Virginia, Louisiana, Kansas, and Wyoming; lumber camps in the Northeast, around the Great Lakes, and in the South; copper mines in northern Michigan; lead and zinc mines in the Mississippi Valley were abandoned. Textile and shoe factories in New England were moved to the South and Midwest; clothing and printing establishments moved from large to small cities. All these shifts left behind a labor supply which in some cases had been unionized but which under the stress of making a living gave up its unionism to get jobs.

Rapid introduction of machinery also contributed. It reduced the need for labor, even skilled labor. Use of new products often destroyed old industries; better quality machinery reduced the workers needed to maintain machinery and equipment. A great many of these workers, "the technologically unemployed," were members of unions. It might have been expected that they would have induced union action to protect their jobs, but this element, large nationally, was broken into small groups, too small to force those who retained their jobs to help them. They served only to contribute to the decline of labor by adding to the available labor supply.

More important than any of these factors in the decline of unionism after 1924 was the adoption by large portions of industry of "welfare capitalism." In the later twenties the term involved many things: company unions, profit sharing and benefit schemes, scientific management, and union-management cooperation.

Although company unions—organizations of workers created or inspired by the employer in order to provide a docile labor supply—originated in the prewar period, the institution was given its strongest boost by the War Labor Board, which promoted employee representation plans where no regular unions were recognized or existed with the hope that the shop committees thus created would become a wedge which would ultimately result in opening the way to organization of real unions. After the war industrial managers quickly recognized that these plans could be used to bring management and labor into closer relationship. The "unions" had no share in this development. They merely elected committees to make suggestions. The real improvements were made by management itself. Ideas were borrowed from many places: from Frederick W. Taylor's early experiments with time and motion studies, from psychologists, from United States Steel's profit-sharing and pension policies, and from the Colorado Fuel and Iron Company's social and recreational facilities.

When all the ideas were assembled and put into effect, industry produced a highly adequate substitute for union-management contractual relations. It erected special industrial relations departments designed to put men into jobs where they would be best satisfied and to take charge of the problem of hiring and firing, factors which seemed to make discharges less arbitrary. Through more careful long-range planning, greater regularity in production and consequently greater regularity in employment were assured. By introduction of the most efficient machinery, which generally entailed a cutting down of the working force, industry assured good wages and an eight-hour day to the remaining employees. It gave workmen a stake in the company by introducing profit-sharing and stock-distribution plans. It gave the workingman security against the hazards of industrial life by setting up plans which took care of life insurance, disability, and old-age pensions. It also offered hygienic and pleasant shop conditions. Finally, it provided club houses, swimming pools, playgrounds, and hospitals.

Not all labor revealed itself satisfied with company unionism and managerial benevolence. In 1926 a portion of the Interborough Transit employees in New York City revolted and tied up the New York subway system for a month. More significant was the uprising in Colorado coal mines, all of which used welfare capitalism. In 1928 remnants of the I.W.W., some small U.M.W. locals, and Colorado labor leaders in other fields decided that a demonstration by six thousand miners against the execution of Sacco and Vanzetti revealed opportunities for unionization. A strike to secure wage increases, the eight-hour day, and the right to organize in all Colorado mines followed. Poorly organized, it soon collapsed, but it left a heritage—the Colorado Industrial Plan, which was to provide labor leaders with many ideas for contractual relations in future years. The new plan, introduced by Josephine Roche, who took control of the Rocky Mountain Fuel Company at the height of the strike, involved making a labor leader vice president of the company, provided for recognition of the U.M.W., and the establishment of a medical and sanitary department supervised jointly by union and company to take care of the health and safety of employees and their dependents. In return the union pledged itself to cooperate in securing maximum efficiency.

Although the Interborough and Colorado conflicts revealed that welfare capitalism was not always accepted, for the most part it was successful. The appeal of organized labor had always been based on the fact that it was the only force capable of fighting exploitive and calloused employers. When the exploiting employer was replaced by a benevolent gentleman eager to take care of his labor force, unionism was greatly weakened.

Organized labor's answer to this situation was an attempt to prove that it was industry's most able helpmeet. William H. Johnston and Otto S. Beyer, an engineer, worked out the first plan of cooperation. Accepted by Baltimore and Ohio management, it provided that the railroad, which usually had its new stock built and its major repairs done in outside shops, should utilize its own irregularly operating shops to build and repair all B. & O. equipment. Labor in turn would set up machinery to provide the most efficient and economical service in those shops. The plan worked well, bringing increased employment and wages, better working conditions, a reduction in grievances, and lower costs. The Amalgamated Clothing Workers also joined the movement. In 1925 that union persuaded Hart, Schaffner and Marx to allow it to take over shop discipline in order to install more economical methods. The union proceeded to abolish hallowed shop customs and to introduce hundreds of small economies and dozens of short cuts which greatly reduced costs. So successful was the experiment that nonunion establishments began to welcome the union.

The union-management cooperation movement soon spread through a considerable portion of industry. Even the A.F.L. gave the movement its blessings in 1925 when it promulgated the theory that prosperity depended upon high wages and low cost of production—which cost could be kept low by the use of modern equipment and modern managerial techniques. The implication was obvious: labor must do its part in making industry more efficient. But such a philosophy was only an unconscious admission that labor was in decline. Union-management cooperation in the interest of efficiency did nothing to bolster the labor movement. Trade unions paid a price for being allowed to cooperate. Railroads which adopted the cooperative plan divided their working forces into two groups—permanent and temporary employees. The permanent employees were guaranteed full-time employment; the rest worked only during the rush periods. In industry the experience of the Chicago needle trades was typical: in 1925 the trades employed 23,000 workers during the height of the season; three years later as a result of union efficiency methods the number had dropped to 14,000 and total production had increased. Thus, welfare capitalism had dire effects. While it gave relatively permanent employment, good wages, short hours, and fine working conditions to a portion of labor, it also reduced another portion of labor to the status of casual and part-time workers.

Evidence of the declining strength of unionism could be seen in many quarters after 1924, but nowhere was it better revealed than in the coal fields. The United Mine Workers emerged from the war under terms of a contract known as the "Washington agreement," which was intended to last until April, 1920. Long before the contract expired, however, the bituminous miners, faced by a rapidly rising cost of living, began to grow restive. Accordingly, in November, 1919, John L. Lewis, newly elected president, began negotiations for a new contract. When the operators refused to make any changes before the Washington agreement expired, the miners began a strike which almost completely paralyzed the coal industry. Attorney-General Palmer promptly secured an injunction which ordered U.M.W. officers to cease all activities tending to encourage and maintain the strike. Although John L. Lewis responded with the cryptic phrase, "We cannot fight the government," no miners returned to work until President Wilson persuaded them to accept a temporary 14 per cent increase in wages and to submit all other issues to a newly appointed Bituminous Coal Commission. The commission's award, handed down early in 1920, provided for an increase of 20 per cent in wages for monthly- and day-men and a 30 per cent increase in tonnage rates for machine men, pick miners, and loaders.

The award was the last real victory the bituminous miners won for many years. Between 1920 and 1924 they met with many defeats and only a few partial victories. It was a period when the mine operators discovered that they could produce all the coal they could sell on a part-time production basis, a period when the open-shop movement invaded the coal fields. The two factors gave the operators the whip hand, and they used their advantage mercilessly. The U.M.W. started on a long road toward disintegration.

Several calamitous events aided the process. The award made by the Bituminous Coal Commission created one. Dissatisfaction over the commission's wage scale finally produced a total suspension of mining operations in the Indiana and Illinois fields in the summer of 1920, a strike which ended only when President Wilson appealed to Lewis to send the miners back to work. Lewis' compliance caused a breach. Frank Farrington of District 12 (Illinois), angered over the "surrender," demanded that the U.M.W.'s unified negotiations with operators be ended in favor of district negotiations. Unable to suggest an alternative, Lewis consented and thereby opened the way to divisions in the U.M.W.'s previously united front.

The Mingo County War in the West Virginia fields was another calamity. The conflict developed over a U.M.W. attempt to organize the mines opened by United States Steel and other corporations in Mingo County. When Union organizers entered the territory, Mingo County operators began to discharge union men. In May, 1920, a strike, which also encompassed Logan County, broke out. Quieted by Federal troops, it flared again in May, 1921, in both counties. Sporadic fighting between company guards and strikers followed for months. Then, in August, the strike became a miniature civil war when Logan County was invaded by unionized miners from the Paint and Cabin Creek fields. Federal troops were again rushed in. A year later the strike ended with the union defeated. A bitter antiunion campaign, which broke the backbone of the U.M.W. in West Virginia, followed hard upon defeat.

The "Herrin massacre" also contributed to decline. Early in 1922 Lewis began negotiations for a new contract with operators in the Central Competitive Field. When operators balked—they recognized that district negotiations would be more to their advantage—a strike began. Miners from the Connellsville area—where there had been no union successes for thirty years—from the Pittsburgh area, Ohio, Indiana, Illinois, the South, and the Southwest walked off their jobs. For two months, except in the Connellsville region where operators tried every form of suppression, the strike was peaceful. Then a southern Illinois company reopened operations with members of a Chicago Steamshovel Men's Union. Hostilities began immediately: strikers who attempted to confer with men who were taking their jobs were met with machine-gun fire and responded by attacking the company's stockade. When the stockade was captured, the nineteen strikebreakers who had surrendered were killed. The Herrin massacre turned the public against the miners, and Lewis was forced to make concessions. He secured new contracts for only the miners of Ohio, Indiana, and Illinois. He lost western Pennsylvania, Maryland, Virginia, West Virginia, Alabama, Texas, Utah, and Colorado. Equally bad was the desertion of the miners of the Connellsville fields. John Brophy, head of District 2, sought to secure protection for these nonunion men by keeping his district miners out, but Lewis peremptorily ordered them back to work.

In 1924 the U.M.W., recognizing its tenuous position and the growing number of nonunion mines, pulled itself together and made a firm stand in its negotiations with the operators. Its efforts brought a three-year agreement, signed at Jacksonville, for the whole Central Field and other areas.

Almost immediately, however, operators began to evade it. Before the year was out the unionized mines in West Virginia returned to 1917 scales; the Rockefeller-controlled Consolidation Coal Company and the Mellon-controlled Pittsburgh Coal Company and one hundred other Pennsylvania operators repudiated the agreement and established the open shop; Ohio operators shifted their operations to nonunion mines. Simultaneously, mineowners introduced more machinery with the result that 200,000 miners were squeezed out of jobs; those who found employment worked only 171 days a year.

The situation produced a revolt against Lewis' leadership. The miners' chieftain had made a number of enemies in the mine fields: Alexander Howatt, president of District 14 (Kansas), whom Lewis had removed when he refused to accept the award of the Bituminous Coal Commission in 1920; Frank Keeny, a leader of the badly riddled West Virginia unions; Frank Brophy, who had been working on the idea that miners would become prosperous only when they owned the mines themselves and whose hatred for Lewis became proverbial after the desertion of the miners in the Connellsville field; and the communists who appeared in small number in the anthracite fields and whom Lewis fought with bitter invective and expulsions.

During 1925 Howatt, Keeny, and Brophy—who called themselves the "progressives"—and the communists began organizing their revolt under the slogan "Save the Union." Their campaign, carried throughout the organized and disorganized mine fields, was a loud denunciation of Lewis' policy, which, they contended, had resulted in a transfer of operations from union to nonunion mines and in the loss of the southern fields. They proposed that the U.M.W. adopt a policy which would force northern operators to include their southern mines in any contracts. The revolt, carried to the 1926 convention, failed.

The next year Lewis' negotiations for a new contract with Central Field operators broke down. The U.M.W., forced to authorize negotiations by districts, provided that no contract with scales below those of the Jacksonville agreement should be signed. Eventually, District 12 surrendered; after a six-month strike it signed a contract 18 per cent below the old agreement. Indiana, Missouri, and Kansas miners followed. That was all the U.M.W. was able to salvage. In western Pennsylvania and Ohio miners on strike were so ruthlessly harassed by the coal and iron police that Lewis was forced to cancel the strike and order the men to return to work.

The act rearoused Lewis' old enemies. A "Save the Union" committee, headed by Frank Brophy, organized a national conference of anti-Lewis forces, which demanded that the U.M.W. endorse a program calling for readoption of the Jacksonville agreement on a national scale, a six-hour day, five-day week, nationalization of the mines, and democratic election of union officers. Lewis acted quickly. Denouncing the "Save the Union" element as reds and dual unionists, he expelled its leaders from the union; expulsions of rank and filers throughout the bituminous and anthracite areas followed. But Lewis' action in turn led to an open division. The communists, led by Patrick Toohey, organized the National Miners' Union, which soon boasted 40,000 members.

More divisions were in the offing. During 1929 a rumor that District 12's leaders were guilty of a long series of petty corruptions began to spread through the organization. Lewis, who had long battled

against the district's tendency toward autonomy, seized the opportunity to establish his own ascendancy by dismissing a large number
of district officials on charge of corruption and replacing them with
his own men. When District 12 officials barred their headquarters
to Lewis officials, Lewis revoked the district charter. At this point
the Brophy, Howatt, and Keeny forces joined with District 12 in a
move to reorganize the U.M.W. The progressives, meeting at Spring-
field, elected Howatt president of a reorganized union. A bitter feud
followed. The progressives, strong in Illinois and in Kansas, invaded
Pennsylvania and Ohio. The Lewis element in turn invaded southern
Illinois. The feud, carried into the courts and reaching the proportions of armed warfare in the field, gradually stalemated. A compromise was arranged: Lewis was recognized as U.M.W. president
and the old District 12 leaders were restored, but progressives like
Brophy, Howatt, and Keeny were re-proscribed. Though Lewis had
won the quarrel, it was hardly a victory. In the Belleville region
U.M.W. rebels created an independent "Progressive Miners Union."
In West Virginia, Keeny also erected an independent union. The once
powerful U.M.W. had been split four ways; by 1930 the organization, which had once enrolled 450,000 of miners, had been reduced
to 150,000 members.

The decline in the economic position of labor after 1924 was
matched by a similar decline in the political field. The fate of child-
labor legislation was typical. In 1925 Congress proposed a child-
labor amendment giving the Federal Government power to regulate
and prohibit the labor of persons under eighteen. The amendment
made no progress. The National Association of Manufacturers, the
southern textile interests, and the American Farm Bureau Federation
immediately launched an extensive, well conducted campaign against
the measure. They denounced it as "socialism," attacked it as a measure to destroy state rights, and raised the fear that the privacy and
sanctity of hearth and home would be invaded. Only six states ratified the amendment by 1932. Nor did the failure of the amendment
encourage state legislation. Instead a tendency toward relaxation
of laws became apparent. By 1930 enforcement of age and hour requirements had practically ceased in the South and was beginning
to weaken in the North.

Legislation on behalf of women suffered the same fate. Only

North Carolina enacted hour legislation. No state made any effort to enact effective minimum wage legislation after the Adkins decision; those states in which such laws remained gradually ceased to enforce them. Developments in the field of workmen's compensation after 1924 almost stopped. In a measure this was to be expected, since forty-two states had previously enacted laws. While Missouri and North Carolina provided new legislation, and the Federal Government enacted laws for the District of Columbia and for longshoremen, no state shifted from elective to compulsory systems or established public systems; the failure left the field to an uncontrolled and expensive private enterprise. Hour legislation for men made a little progress. Illinois enacted an eight-hour law for its public employees, and seven states limited the hours of bus drivers.

Labor also received some new legal setbacks as the Federal courts continued their vigorous application of the antitrust laws. The Coronado case was reargued and brought to the Supreme Court a second time. The court decided that the new evidence revealed that the strike, purely local, constituted illegal interference with interstate commerce and was punishable under the antitrust laws. In 1927 the Supreme Court extended the meaning of a secondary boycott in the Bedford case, which arose out of a rule adopted by the Journeymen Stone Cutters' Association providing that no member should work on stone cut by nonunion men. When fourteen employees of the Bedford Cut Stone Company went on strike to enforce the rule, the union was hailed into court. Although no effort had been made to influence any but union members, the court ruled that the act was a secondary boycott and therefore an illegal interference with interstate commerce.

The effect of the late twenties upon labor was well illustrated in union rolls. Over-all union membership declined from 3,600,000 in 1924 to 3,400,000 by 1930. A.F.L. membership also dropped about 100,000 to 2,770,000 by 1930. But this figure did not reveal the situation clearly. The federation maintained its high membership because of gains in the building trades, where employment remained high, and in the printing trades, where expansion in advertising and publishing redounded to the advantage of the printers. The development of trucking and bus industries and of commercial amusements also added members. At the same time 60 per cent of the A.F.L.'s old unions either experienced no gains or suffered reductions. The older membership, in short, was declining more rapidly than the statistics revealed. But worse was yet to come.

22 ⸺

The Impact of the Great Depression

Late in 1929 the "Great Depression" began. It came as a surprise to the nation, for the national economy appeared to be in excellent condition: production was high, dividends were huge, value of sales was at a peak, the credit market was "sound," and the stock market was reaching astronomical heights. Federal officials and business leaders were announcing that a "new economic era" in which poverty was eliminated had been achieved. Nor did the stock-market crash of October, 1929, change the feeling of optimism. Prominent bankers and industrialists assured the nation that the crash was only an "investors' panic," and President Herbert Hoover announced that business was still on "a sound and prosperous basis."

Within the nation's economic fabric, however, there were a number of weaknesses. Farm income had been low for nearly a decade, and the annual real income of labor, including both employed and unemployed, had been sinking for years. The situation was reflected in the declining volume of sales of durable goods, in growing inventories, in a slowing down of house building. The stock-market crash, moreover, did have an influence upon the nation's economy. Thousands of individuals who lost heavily in the crash promptly curtailed purchases. Thousands who had not been caught saw the value of their securities decline and reduced their spending. An atmosphere of gloom settled upon the nation. Luxury and then semi-luxury items of industry—automobiles, household and electrical appliances—experienced a drop in trade. This in turn affected steel, rubber, glass, coal, oil, copper, and textiles. Plans for industrial expansion were dropped; wheels of production were slowed. The nation started to slide down the long incline into its severest depression.

Although few recognized how deep the nation's economy was destined to sink, the Federal Reserve Board quickly informed President Hoover that the situation was serious. He acted promptly. Adopting the philosophy that high wages would enable the nation to weather the storms ahead, he began a series of conferences with business and labor leaders. From these conferences a policy developed: industry pledged itself to continue and even increase its construction and expansion programs and at the same time maintain high wage rates; labor in turn pledged itself to avoid strikes and demands for wage increases. The President promised an increase in government expenditures for public works.

Although less than 10 per cent of the nation's big corporations cut wages during 1930, the depression grew worse. Small and weak companies began to cut wages and to dismiss employees as early as the spring of 1930; larger and stronger corporations began to stagger employment at the same time. By November, 1930, estimates of unemployment ran between 2,900,000 and 6,900,000. In the following year the situation grew worse. Ever increasing numbers of smaller companies cut wages and their labor forces; more large companies rationed work. While big corporations still hoped that business would recover, it became apparent by the fall of 1931 that these hopes were vain: in the previous two years the net income of the nation's 550 largest industrial corporations had declined 68 per cent. In September, 1931, United States Steel surrendered with the announcement that wages would be reduced 10 per cent; despite A.F.L. protests the announcement started an avalanche of wage reductions. Business, accordingly, slid deeper into the depression. A second wholesale round of cuts was imposed in the spring of 1932 a third round began in the fall of 1932. Meanwhile, big industry and the railways abandoned their work-rationing programs and began to make permanent layoffs. By November, 1932, the number of unemployed was estimated to run between eleven and seventeen million, with the median figure at around 13,500,000—a total which amounted roughly to one-third of the nation's wage earners.

When labor recovered from the initial shock of the depression, its first impulse was to turn to the government for aid. Not with any unanimity: while many demanded huge increases in the public works program, others raised a demand for direct relief to the unemployed. In the first year of the depression relief had been handled as a local problem through private and public agencies. By October, 1930, however, it became clear that the problem was growing too complex for the uncoordinated and miserably financed local organizations. Although President Hoover responded with announcements that appropriations for public works would be increased, he stubbornly opposed any movement to bring the Federal Government into the relief business. Instead he appointed a committee, under the direction of Arthur Woods, to coordinate relief work. Woods secured the establishment of nearly three thousand local organizations which did yeoman service in collecting extra funds and in coordinating relief activities of state, municipal, and private agencies; but neither additional appropriations for public works, state funds, nor increased philanthropies proved enough to offset the growing unemployment rolls, destitution, and even starvation.

In 1931 labor pressure for relief continued to grow. Though A.F.L. leaders announced, "Labor wants jobs, not a dole," rank-and-file trade unionists and unorganized labor called ever more loudly for Federal handouts. President Hoover relaxed his adamant stand: he asked for further expansion of public works and announced that he would allow the Reconstruction Finance Corporation to lend $300,-000,000 to the states for relief. But he refused to approve bills for the erection of public works which would not be self-liquidating and he vetoed a measure permitting the R.F.C. to lend money to states without regard to their financial ability to repay. Hoover's measures proved entirely inadequate, and the nation's labor force sank deeper and deeper into economic misery. By the summer of 1932 its average weekly earnings had declined from $25.03 to $16.73, and its total income had dropped 48 per cent. The situation was reflected in membership figures. By 1933 organized labor's rolls had fallen to less than 2,500,000, and the A.F.L. membership had dropped to 2,125,000.

To many workingmen the increasing misery, destitution, and starvation evident not only in their own lives but all around them indicated that the American labor movement and the American economic system had finally collapsed. Although some turned once more to socialism and began to make proposals for nationalization of the railroads and the coal mines, the more vociferous portion of this element turned to communism. The communists had never ceased their activities in the twenties. Rejected by the C.P.P.A., ousted from control of needle trade locals, forced out of the U.M.W., their influence destroyed in the A.F.L., they had continued their infiltration of the labor movement through the Needle Trades Workers' Industrial Union, and the National Miners' Union. In 1927–1928 they became involved in bitter industrial conflicts in Passaic, New Jersey, and Gastonia, North Carolina. The Passaic conflict, led by a communist, Albert Weisbord, and a "United Front Committee," was caused by a demand for union recognition, a 20 per cent increase in wages, and a forty-four-hour week. Lasting more than a year, shunned by the A.F.L., and punctuated by violence and a disregard of civil liberties, it ended in partial victory. The Gastonia strike—organized by communists around a demand for a minimum wage of $20 and a forty-four-hour week—attracted national attention when militia permitted a masked mob to destroy strike headquarters and police to invade the strikers' tent colony. A raid resulted in the death of four people. In spite of repressions the strikers made some gains. Both conflicts earned the communists much publicity among labor as organizers.

During the depression the communists gained friends by their constant agitation for unemployment relief. In the large cities they organized soup kitchens and bread lines and led deputations to municipal authorities to demand increased relief funds. Their voices rose loudest in the chorus of those who demanded Federal relief funds for the starving and down-trodden workers. At the same time the communists spread their own propaganda. The depression, they insisted, had been caused by the capitalist class, which had been reaping the fruits of industrial earnings ever since capitalism had first been erected and had left only the crusts to the poor workingman. The capitalists had created the depression in order to make the working classes more subservient and docile. But under the Soviets, they maintained, the economic system was operated in the interest of the proletariat: the masses alone received the rewards of their labors; there was no unemployment, no starvation; everybody worked and everybody was taken care of. The solution was simple: working classes needed only to unite to seize control of the state in order to operate the economic system in their own interest.

The propaganda was most effective where misery was deepest: in the big cities of the North where unemployment figures reached as high as half the working population and where relief sources had run dry; in the needle trades; in the textile and mining industries which had been depressed throughout the twenties; among the foreign-speaking population employed as unskilled labor in the mass-production industries and against whom discrimination was used even in the distribution of relief; among Negroes in the northern cities who had long learned that they were the last to be hired and the first to be fired; among youth which had found it increasingly difficult to secure jobs. By 1932 communism had filtered through a large part of the labor world as the only hope in the midst of despair.

Communism was not the only technique which attracted working-men as the depression deepened. In some quarters there was a return to the idea that the depression could be conquered by old-fashioned union methods. The coal miners of Harlan County, Kentucky, suggested the movement. The mines in Harlan County, primarily of the captive type, had never been unionized; conditions had been miserable in the twenties and grew impossibly bad during the depression. The miners endured until early in 1931 when two successive wage cuts led 18,000 of them to revolt. The strike turned into a sniping war between guards and strikers and culminated in a pitched battle at Evarts. Local authorities then arrested forty-four miners for murder and inaugurated a ruthless campaign of suppression. Harlan County became the focus of the nation's attention. Remnants of the I.W.W., communists, literary men, social workers, and college students poured into the area to aid the indicted miners. The invasion served only to increase local prejudices; seven of the miners were convicted.

Support for a revival of militant trade unionism also came from Illinois where, in February, 1932, District 12 miners went on strike to prevent further wage reductions. Three months later the district president and operators agreed on a new wage scale and a partial six-hour day, but the miners rejected the agreement. With the help of John L. Lewis another agreement, containing some small concessions, was arranged. After the usual referendum, Lewis and district officials announced that the agreement had been approved. A majority of the rank and file promptly rebelled. At a gigantic meeting in the center of the district the membership decided to continue the strike. An automobile caravan made up of thousands of miners descended upon the mines and shut them down. In September the revolting miners, together with delegates from Indiana, formed a new union, the Progressive Miners of America. The new organization, representing some 30,000 miners, proceeded to make its own contracts.

To some laboring men, however, neither communism nor revived trade unionism provided an answer to labor's problems. They turned for solution to the movements which had appeared after Homestead and during the early twenties. Early in 1929 a group of socialists and trade-union progressives, headed by A. J. Muste, organized a Conference for Progressive Labor Action. Using a magazine, the *Labor Age,* as its chief medium, the organization renewed the old campaign to convert the A.F.L. to industrial unionism and more direct action. Its chief demands were for the organization of the semiskilled and unskilled labor elements, establishment of a five-day week through legislation, and enactment of a social-insurance program. Although the conference disintegrated when socialists and progressives quarreled over future programs, it helped revive the idea of industrial unionism and sparked a movement toward solution of labor problems through legislative action. By 1932 the C.P.L.A.'s political program had become the common property of a large share of labor.

This trend toward political action was encouraged by a more thorough public recognition of labor's problems. Unemployment, bread lines, soup kitchens, destitution, the Harlan County war, and other events which reached the front pages of the nation's press created an atmosphere that revived interest in labor's welfare. Encouraging also was the apparent change in attitude on the part of Federal officials. In 1930 the Supreme Court handed down a startling decision in the case of *Texas and New Orleans Railway Company* v. *Brotherhood of Railway and Steamship Clerks.* The action began when the union secured an injunction against the company's efforts to promote a company union, which the clerks charged was a violation of the Railway Labor Act, granting each side the right to be represented for the purpose of collective bargaining by representatives of their own choosing. The Supreme Court approved the grant, thereby giving implicit sanction to unionism. In the same year the United States Senate also revealed an attitude of friendliness when it refused to confirm the appointment of Circuit Judge John J. Parker to the Supreme Court in part because of his decision approving yellow-dog contracts in the Red Jacket case.

More important was the attitude that the Congress, elected in 1930, revealed toward labor welfare. Dozens of bills for huge public works programs, for direct Federal relief, for maximum-hour laws, for unemployment insurance and old-age pensions were introduced. None of them were passed, but Congress did enact one bill of vital significance to labor: the Norris-La Guardia Act. The measure, intended to solve the problems of injunctions and yellow-dog contracts, indicated congressional recognition of the fact that under prevailing economic conditions an individual worker was unable to "exercise actual liberty of contract" or to "protect his freedom of labor." It announced further that it was necessary that the laboring man be granted "full freedom of association, self-organization, and designation of representatives of his own choosing to negotiate the terms and conditions of his employment, and that he . . . be free from the interference, restraint, or coercion of employers . . . in his activities for the purpose of collective bargaining or other mutual aid or protection."

The courts were denied the right to issue injunctions in any labor dispute contrary to this policy. More specifically they were denied the right to issue injunctions which would uphold yellow-dog contracts, prevent work stoppages, joining of unions, payment of benefits or insurance monies to men on strike, lawful aid to persons on trial, union publicity, and peaceable assemblies; they were denied the right to issue an injunction on the ground that any person engaged in a labor dispute was engaged in an unlawful combination or conspiracy. The courts, moreover, were denied the right to issue any injunctions until after hearing testimony in open court and had found that unlawful acts had been threatened and would be committed unless restrained, that substantial and irreparable damage to property would occur for which no adequate remedy at law existed, and that public officers charged with the duty of protecting property were unable or unwilling to furnish protection. In cases arising under the act in which a person was charged with contempt of court, the accused had to be given a speedy and public trial by an impartial jury, except where contempt was committed in the presence of the court.

The Norris-La Guardia Act put an end to labor's four-decade struggle to obtain recognition of its right to organized existence and its efforts to free itself of the restrictions placed upon it by court order. The act marked the beginning of a new period in labor history, one in which the government became the friend of the laboring man.

23 ——

Labor's New Deal

In the summer of 1932 the significance of the revival of labor activity, of the new trend toward political action, and of new legislation was not apparent to labor. The nation's economy was in a state of disintegration. Hundreds of banks heavily laden with frozen assets had declared themselves insolvent during the previous two years. Insurance companies, with their heavy investments in industry, commerce, and real estate, were shaky. Industry, bellwether of the nation's prosperity, was approaching collapse. Between 1929 and 1933 the number of units of manufacturing enterprise had dropped from 133,000 to 72,300; production had declined nearly 48 per cent; and industrial income had declined from $29,000,000,000 to $2,900,000,000.

The condition of labor was only a reflection of this situation. Of the workingmen normally employed in the nondurable-goods industries 26 per cent were out of work; of those employed in the durable-goods industries 51 per cent were out of work. The number unemployed in the larger cities was staggering. It was estimated that half the nation's unemployed were found in the seven industrial states of Massachusetts, New York, New Jersey, Pennsylvania, Ohio, Illinois, and California. In addition large numbers of those not counted upon the unemployment rolls were working only part time at lower wages. Between 1929 and 1933 labor income had declined from $51,000,000,000 to $26,000,000,000—a drop of 48 per cent.

The nation's industrial areas had become scenes of desolation. Thousands of laborers lost their homes because they could not meet mortgage payments or pay rent. These built shacks made of scrap metal and egg crates on city dumps, creating villages which were named "Hoovervilles." In the coal fields miners eked out a precarious existence upon Red Cross flour, scraggly gardens, and wild blackberries. In the cities bread lines and soup lines stretched endlessly. Destitution was common: many a family literally lived on bread and coffee; some on what they could scavenge from garbage cans; others on dandelion greens. Youth hung around street corners or took to bumming; in 1932 there were more than two million "on the road," living by theft and beggary.

Amidst this cheerless situation faint glimmerings of hope appeared with the nomination of Franklin D. Roosevelt as the Democratic candidate for the Presidency. To most laboring men Roosevelt was an unknown quantity. Some who had supported Alfred E. Smith were inclined to take an unfriendly attitude; others looked skeptically upon his Hudson Valley-Harvard background. But a number of factors made workingmen into hopeful, if not enthusiastic, supporters. His dramatic air flight to Chicago to accept the party nomination captured the imagination: it revealed a man willing to employ new techniques. His campaign tour of the nation revealed a man full of vitality; his campaign speeches appeared to make a confidante of the man in the street. While examination of his record as Governor of New York revealed no spectacular acts, it did indicate concern for the unemployed and willingness to use public resources to relieve suffering. During the campaign, moreover, Roosevelt listened sympathetically to labor leaders who related to him the sorry plight of various labor elements, and he promised privately and publicly to do what he could to relieve distress and improve labor conditions.

322   A HISTORY OF AMERICAN LABOR

The strongest factor which made labor support Roosevelt's candidacy was its growing and bitter hatred for Herbert Hoover. It was weary of hearing the President described as a "great humanitarian" and tired of his oft-repeated belief that rugged individualism would see the nation out of its depression. It was angered by his concern for industry, railways, banks, and insurance companies; his willingness to use hundreds of millions of dollars to relieve big business of its distresses; and his refusal to use Federal money to relieve unemployment. It was even more tired of hearing his declaration that public relief would sap the moral fiber of its recipients. In the summer of 1932 Herbert Hoover stood before the nation as a symbol of governmental inhumanity. The reaction of labor was well summarized by a young mine leader: "I don't know about this Roosevelt. . . . But his heart seems to be in the right place as far as labor is concerned. I am going to vote for him. Anything to get rid of Hoover."

When Franklin D. Roosevelt took office with his promise of a "New Deal," he was already surrounded by advisers with various plans to bring the nation relief from its distress, to reverse the depression, and to make reforms which would prevent future economic catastrophes. Among them were men who had become sincerely concerned with labor's plight and labor's problems, and who revealed a willingness to use the powers of the Federal Government to solve those problems. Given the sympathetic support of the President, they threw themselves headlong into the job.

The New Dealers' first task was to relieve immediate distress. No question concerning use of government money to ameliorate the effects of unemployment was raised. Pushed by Harry Hopkins, Congress, in May, 1933, set up a Federal Emergency Relief Administration and gave it $500,000,000 which it would allocate among the states as gifts. Specific distribution of the funds was left in the hands of state and local authorities who could provide either for work relief or for an outright dole. Since the dole was far more economical, it was used almost exclusively. In February, 1934, Congress appropriated another $950,000,000 for the same purpose. By the end of the year four million families, one-sixth of the population, were receiving benefits. The relief granted in this way did not satisfy New Dealers. FERA Administrator Harry Hopkins, in particular, found it objectionable on the ground that the public did not like charity. He argued that work relief was preferable because its recipient retained his self-respect; it was an argument firmly supported by the A.F.L., which was again announcing that labor wanted jobs and not a dole. The New Deal's first work relief agency was the Civilian Conservation Corps. Personally proposed by the President, it was designed to create work for about 250,000 men between the ages of eighteen and twenty-five, who were to receive wages of a dollar a day, most of which was to be sent to dependent relatives. Their job was to clear forests, plant trees, improve roads, and erect dams to prevent floods. Although the CCC was severely criticized at first as an effort to increase the strength of the army, it soon justified itself. It helped partially to cut down the available labor supply; it made vast improvements in the nation's parks and forests. In 1935 provision was made for doubling the enrollment.

The CCC had only limited application. It was not an answer to the demand for work relief. The New Dealers' original solution to that problem was enacted in June, 1933, in Title II of the National Industrial Recovery Act which provided for the institution of a gigantic public works program designed to create business for heavy industries in particular and all industry in general and thereby to stimulate recovery and to provide employment for large numbers of men. Congress appropriated $3,300,000,000 for the purpose. To carry out this program the President created a Public Works Administration with Harold L. Ickes, the Secretary of the Interior, in charge. The PWA was a huge disappointment. Administrator Ickes' determination to get full value for government money and to examine all details of construction before he granted approval, together with the task of getting states and local governments to contribute part of the costs of many projects, created long delays. In the fall of 1933 the PWA was still in the blueprint stage. It had not answered the demand for a work-relief program.

Accordingly, in October, 1933, the President created the Civilian Works Administration as a branch of the FERA to provide work relief on projects of civic value for able-bodied men over the winter. By January, 1934, more than four million men were at work on CWA projects. Wages ran from $1.00 to $1.20 an hour for skilled labor and forty to fifty cents an hour for unskilled; average weekly earnings were less than $15. Despite a widespread impression, only a very small portion of these men raked leaves and shoveled snow. One-third of the money expended by the CWA was used to repair roads and streets; most of the rest was used to improve school buildings, and to construct stadiums, swimming pools, parks, and airports. The program ended in spring—at a cost of more than $900,000,000. What the CWA accomplished was doubtful. While relief recipients liked it, and the community secured something for its money, it was expensive. The program was not renewed during the winter of 1934–1935.

Meanwhile, the New Dealers had also begun work on a "permanent" solution of the unemployment problem. They recognized that their relief programs—nothing more than palliatives for an emergency—were based on principles that belonged to the nineteenth century when the almost universal attitude had been that "any man who really wants a job can get it" and when the unemployed had been handled primarily as charity problems. New Dealers repudiated this philosophy. Instead they adopted the attitude, suggested in the nineties by the A.F.L., that unemployment was caused by economic forces beyond the control of labor; and the conclusion, expressed in the early twenties by various state industrial commissions, that a partial solution for the problem might be found in the establishment of public employment offices to enable labor to move more readily from one job to another.

Employment agencies had existed in the United States since the colonial period when various trades on strike had created "houses of call" to enable skilled workers to find jobs. In the nineteenth century all such agencies had been privately owned and operated and had earned bad reputations for misrepresentation, fraudulent advertising, fee splitting, and other evils. In the eighties the Knights of Labor had begun to demand regulation. Between 1883 and 1930 some forty-four states passed legislation providing for licensing and fee fixing. Since the laws were crudely drawn, few had been effective; in the 1920's enforcement was made more difficult by various decisions of the United States Supreme Court: most important was the case of *Ribnik* v. *McBride* which declared a fee-fixing law of New Jersey, and by implication the laws of thirty other states, unconstitutional.

In the period after 1890 a movement for the creation of public employment offices began when Ohio created agencies in its five principal cities. Between 1890 and 1917 about sixty-five such offices were established in various portions of the nation. Since they were regarded primarily as relief agencies and appropriations made for their support were usually inadequate, they did not have the expected salutary effects. During the First World War the Federal Government became involved. American entrance into the war created a chaotic labor market: employers stole men from one another; labor scouts appeared in cities to recruit laboring men by the hundreds; and the turnover in jobs increased to tremendous proportions. In 1918 the Department of Labor responded by establishing a United States Employment Service. Although the agency did yeoman service in recruiting agricultural labor and common labor for war work, it never entirely succeeded. Too many of the men named to administer the task were inexperienced; many were connected with private employment offices and used their position on behalf of private agencies; and industry used its own competitive methods.

After the war use of public employment offices as a means of mitigating the problem of unemployment rapidly deteriorated. Employers feared that the USES would reduce their control of the labor market, and they objected to the USES policy of refusing to send men to work at any strike-bound plant. Accordingly, the National Association of Manufacturers, other employer associations, and open-shop groups began to denounce the USES because it "discriminated against non-union men." The attacks had their effect. After 1919 congressional appropriations in support of the USES were drastically reduced; by 1928 the USES had offices in only eleven states. State employment offices also declined. After 1919, nine of the twenty-four states which had offices appropriated no money to support them; most of the others had such small resources that they operated almost exclusively by mail.

While the value of public employment offices declined in the twenties, the service was not forgotten. With the advent of the depression, demands for a more effective structure became so loud that Congress passed a measure, introduced by Senator Robert Wagner, providing for the establishment of a Federal agency designed to supervise and subsidize state employment offices. President Hoover vetoed the bill on the ground that it would destroy the "well established" USES. After the veto, the Department of Labor announced that it was reorganizing and expanding its services. Appropriations were increased, and four hundred special agents were appointed.

It was to this agency that New Dealers turned for aid in solving the unemployment problem, seeking first to enlist the agency's facilities in selecting men for the Civilian Conservation Corp. They quickly discovered that the "reorganized USES" had been nothing more than a political agency working for the reelection of President Hoover; it was unable to accomplish even rudimentary tasks. Accordingly Congress enacted the Wagner-Peyser bill which provided for the refurbishing of the United States Employment Service as a bureau in the Department of Labor and for the establishment of a Federal-state system of employment service. The USES, which was to be headed by a trained director, was empowered to set up a national system of employment offices wherever no public offices existed and to assist in coordinating and maintaining employment services in the states where public offices did exist. Coordination and maintenance of state offices was to be accomplished by an agreement whereby the states accepted the Federal regulations and standards regarding salaries, selection and training of personnel, record systems, premises used for offices, and the policy of informing potential employees of the existence of strikes and lockouts in any plant where workers were in demand; in return the USES financed 75 per cent of the cost of maintaining state offices. In its first year of operation the USES set up Federal offices in twenty-nine states; nineteen other states accepted the terms of the act and became affiliates. By 1941 the USES had become a permanent feature of the economy.

Important as it was, the refurbished USES was not the New Dealers' main answer to the problem of unemployment. They recognized that restoration of normal employment and a permanent improvement in the condition of labor depended, primarily, upon industrial recovery. In the early days of the New Deal, proposals to achieve this end were numerous. Businessmen suggested that industry could recover most readily if it were freed from the restrictions of the antitrust laws. John L. Lewis, who had been advocating imposition of government controls over production, prices, and wages in the coal industry, suggested that business recovery could be quickly accomplished if his plan were extended to all industry. On the other hand A.F.L. leaders pointed out that industry had become so highly mechanized that it could operate without reemploying all labor; they advocated the passage of legislation establishing a thirty-hour week as a means of spreading work. The President, however, announced that he was skeptical of the value of a maximum-hour law unless it was accomplished with legislation designed to maintain wages. Although New York had enacted a mandatory minimum-wage law, gradual in its application in 1933, and six other states had followed, Roosevelt's suggestion immediately provoked a storm of opposition. Among the critics was the A.F.L., which advanced the old argument that minimum wages would in reality become maximum wages. Meanwhile, other elements voiced additional proposals concerning industrial recovery and the condition of labor. They pointed out that even though the Federal Government had recognized the right of labor to organize and bargain collectively and had outlawed the yellow-dog contract in the Norris-La Guardia Act, employers were successfully evading the law by forcing workers to join company unions. Industrial recovery would mean nothing unless this situation were corrected.

The net result was seen in Title I of the National Industrial Recovery Act passed in June, 1933. The act was intended to aid business recovery by permitting industry to write codes of fair competition; such codes, however, had to contain safeguards for labor. These safeguards were specifically mentioned in Section 7(a), which required that every code must provide "that employees shall have the right to organize and bargain collectively through representatives of their own choosing, and shall be free from the interference, restraint, or coercion of employers . . . in the designation of such representatives . . . or in other concerted activities for the purpose of collective bargaining or other mutual aid or protection; that no employee and no one seeking employment shall be required as a condition of employment to join any company union or to refrain from joining . . . a labor organization of his own choosing." An additional clause provided that employers must comply with labor conditions of the codes. What kind of labor conditions the New Dealers had in mind was revealed in the President's Re-employment Agreement, a blanket code published in July, 1933, which all employers were asked to sign until their own industry code had been established. The blanket code bound signers to employ no one under the age of sixteen, to pay clerical and service workers a minimum of $12 to $15 for a forty-hour week, and to pay factory workers a minimum of forty cents an hour for a thirty-five-hour week.

Labor was loud in its acclamation of the N.I.R.A. and the National Recovery Administration set up under Hugh Johnson to administer it. William Green joyfully announced that Section 7(a) gave "millions of workers throughout the nation" their first opportunity to stand up and receive "their charter of industrial freedom." The enthusiasm seemed warranted at first. Industry, anticipating a quick revival in business and an increase in material and labor costs, promptly began to step up its output. By October 1, 1933, production had increased 50 per cent and 2,500,000 workers had been re-employed.

Equally important was the sudden revival of labor unionism. Labor interpreted Section 7(a) as an invitation to form independent unions under governmental protection. The response was in many ways reminiscent of the sudden rise of the Knights of Labor fifty years earlier. Long-dormant unions quickened into life, forming new locals and invading territory in which they had previously regarded themselves as trespassers. While the impulse sometimes came from A.F.L. headquarters, more often rank and file laborers began activity themselves, forming their own locals and then applying for charters. One-third of the federation unions increased their rolls; one-fourth doubled their membership. The greatest increase came in the industrial unions. The U.M.W., which had a mere 60,000 members in 1932, added 300,000 workers in a few months. The tiny United Textile Workers trebled in size—reaching 80,000 by 1934. The International Ladies' Garment Workers secured 100,000 new members, and recaptured New York and the "runaway" shops which had moved to other portions of the nation in the twenties. The Amalgamated Clothing Workers added 125,000 to its rolls. Oil workers built up their almost nonexistent union into an organization of more than 40,000.

The most significant development came in the mass-production industries. In one year more than 1,700 Federal and local unions were organized in the automobile, steel, lumber and sawmill, rubber, and aluminum industries. By mid-1934 estimates of membership in these industries ran as high as 350,000. For the first time since the heyday of the Knights, unionism was appearing on a large scale among the semiskilled and unskilled. So spectacular was the expansion of unionism in the months that followed the adoption of the NRA that William Green could announce in October, 1933, that the A.F.L.'s goal was ten million members.

But the revived unionism rested on shaky foundations. That industry was in no mood to grant concessions first became apparent when the New Deal announced its blanket code. While most manufacturers hastened to accept it, they pointed out that labor conditions in their industry or section were peculiar, and they received exemptions from code provisions regulating hours and wages. Industry's attitude was further revealed in the code-making process. It was anticipated that the codes were to be made as a bargain between industrial trade associations and labor unions. Instead, the codes were made by industry and the N.R.A.'s Labor Advisory Council—a well meaning but not entirely effective body, handicapped by its ignorance of trade practices and labor conditions and by the fact that it was thoroughly overworked. The result was that some codes did not contain the principle of unionization and collective bargaining. Eighty-four per cent of the codes, covering 57 per cent of industrial employees, adopted a forty-hour week; 64 per cent of the codes, covering 61 per cent of the employees, either established a forty-eight-hour week, or permitted it under certain conditions. Many codes did not mention minimum-wage scales.

Industry's general unwillingness to accept the principles of Section 7(a) was further revealed after the codes went into operation. What industry feared most was establishment of independent unions which could force "collective bludgeoning." Almost immediately, therefore, a large part of industry set out to nullify the intention of the codes. Some corporations flatly prohibited organization of any union; others turned to employee representation plans: between 1933 and 1935 almost four hundred company unions were created. Membership in such organizations increased much more rapidly than in regular unions. By 1935, 43 per cent of industry had no union organization, 20 per cent had company unions, 7 per cent had both company and independent unions; only 30 per cent had independent unions. Collective bargaining under such conditions was hardly an established fact. Nor did N.R.A. authorities help the situation. They actually allowed proportional representation to company unions in collective bargaining and permitted industry to overlook an independent union which enrolled a majority of workers to "bargain" with a minority company union.

Labor leaders protested loud and long both against company tactics and against the "interpretations" of the N.R.A. by governmental authorities. As early as the summer of 1933 they began to denounce the N.R.A. as the "National Run Around" and to question the New Deal's labor objectives. Complaints grew so numerous that in August, 1933, President Roosevelt established a seven-man National Labor Board, with Senator Robert F. Wagner as impartial chairman and with equal representation granted to industry and labor, to supervise labor relations. The National Labor Board was confronted with a difficult task. Although it set up rules providing that a majority of workers in any plant were to be allowed to bargain for the whole plant, that secret elections be held to determine bargaining units, and that bona fide efforts be made to secure agreements, the board had no power to enforce its decisions.

Labor soon recognized the N.L.B.'s inefficiency. Its reaction was inevitable: a wave of strikes spread through the nation until, in 1934, almost one-seventh of the total labor force of the nation became involved in industrial conflicts. Some of the strikes threatened to assume national proportions. In the automobile industry, workers at the Fisher Body Company, enrolled in A.F.L. locals, began a revolt with a call for a strike to secure recognition, a wage increase, and a thirty-hour week in March, 1934. New Dealers, from the President down, worked frantically to prevent the call from becoming effective and eventually persuaded management and labor leaders to accept the creation of an Automobile Labor Board with power to hold an election in the industry and to award proportional representation to all unions, including company unions, on any collective bargaining committee. While the act averted the strike, automobile workers who were not consulted in the settlement charged that they had been "sold out." A longshoremen's conflict arose in San Francisco in July, 1934, when demands for recognition, control of hiring halls, and higher wages were rejected. The strike soon spread to other trades until more than 125,000 were involved and San Francisco was nearly paralyzed. Vigilantes appeared and a wave of antiunion hysteria seized the city. Mediators rushed to the scene and secured a compromise with union leaders. The men returned to work, but in a mood that bespoke suspicion both of their own leaders and of the government.

Most violent and far-flung of the conflicts occurred in the textile industry. That industry had suffered from overproduction even in the twenties, and the code it had prepared had been intended solely to reduce output. Although it contained the usual labor provisions, they were hardly observed. Alabama mill hands finally kicked over the traces in July, 1934, with a strike calling for recognition, abolition of the stretch-out, and a thirty-hour week with no reduction in pay. By September 1st between 400,000 and 500,000 textile workers in twenty states were on strike—the largest strike in history to that time. It was a violent conflict. In the South where striking workers organized "flying squads" to persuade mill hands to drop their tools, some 11,000 militia were called out. Clashes between strikers and militia became common. When government mediators were unable to find a basis of settlement, President Roosevelt intervened with the appointment of a Textile Labor Relations Board to study conditions in the industry. Union leaders called the strike off, leaving textile workers openly disgruntled.

Temporarily, however, labor discontent was quieted by a new event. In July, 1934, the National Labor Board was abolished, and Congress authorized the creation of a three-man National Labor Relations Board to replace it. The new board, made up of "experts," was no more successful. Although its principles were somewhat more severe—it ruled that company unions were not proper bargaining agents—it, likewise, had no power to enforce its decisions. In some ways its task was more difficult since by the summer of 1934 industry, beginning to see its way out of the depression, was becoming more and more truculent. It flatly and openly defied N.L.R.B. decisions and began a strong campaign to roll back the union tide through careful discrimination in the hiring and firing of its labor. Contributing to this attitude was a decision handed down late in 1934 by a Federal district court, which in the Weirton Steel case declared Section 7(a) unconstitutional. The effect upon labor was discouraging. In the fall, winter, and spring of 1934–1935 much of unionism's gains began to melt away. Some six hundred Federal unions were disbanded; the number of automobile workers unionized declined to less than 10,000; several hundred thousand workers who had joined the textile union during the strike dropped their membership.

By the spring of 1935 criticism of the N.R.A. became almost universal. Big business, as it commenced to recover, began to regret its partnership with the government and showed anger over even feeble attempts to enforce the labor provisions of the codes. Little business saw itself squeezed between monopoly and labor. Workingmen, seeing themselves betrayed, added their voices to the chorus of denunciation. On May 27, 1935, the United States Supreme Court in the Schechter case declared the N.R.A. unconstitutional on the grounds that Congress had extended its authority over interstate commerce to intrastate business and that Congress had delegated legislative authority without specifying sufficiently how it should be exercised.

What effect the N.R.A. had upon labor is difficult to determine. It failed to bring about the establishment of collective bargaining or minimum-labor standards; it failed to abolish child labor. Nevertheless, there were some results. Employment increased during the first six months after the N.I.R.A. was enacted by some 2,500,000. Not all this increase could be attributed to the act, but it was significant that employment in code industries increased 11 per cent while in other industries it increased only 4 per cent and in agriculture almost nothing at all. Hours of labor decreased: in spite of the fact that few codes met the government's suggested standards, average hours of labor worked in all industries decreased from 43.3 to 37.8 per week by October, 1933. Wages also increased: although the N.R.A. made no real effort to provide a decent living wage and permitted sectional and sexual differentials, minimum wages in industry rose from 43.8 cents to 52.15 cents an hour by October, 1933, and reached 57.2 cents an hour by May, 1935. Annual earnings—in manufacturing, construction, and mining—which had stood at $874 in 1933, reached $1,068 by 1935.

Invalidation of the N.R.A. marked the end of the early New Deal. For New Dealers concerned with the plight of labor it had not been a happy period. Far too little had been accomplished. Although the bite of economic distress had been softened, relief remained a major problem. Although the employment service had been strengthened and the ranks of the unemployed had been cut by a minor industrial recovery, unemployment still bulked large. Labor, moreover, had not secured its rights. Many New Dealers expected workingmen to turn against the administration in the congressional elections of 1934. But their fears proved groundless. As the congressional elections approached, a movement to keep the New Deal in office appeared among both organized and unorganized workingmen. In spite of disgruntlement labor sensed the good will inherent in the New Deal experiments; in spite of disappointments it was filled with a hopefulness that it had not felt for nearly a decade. Since the same spirit appeared among other elements, the result was the election of a Congress with a stronger New Deal majority.

Heartened by the popular mandate, New Dealers reapproached their task with a determination to solve the problems of labor once for all. Again they turned to the problem of relief. Wiser and bolder, now, they pressed for solution through a work program which they expected not only to relieve distress but also to maintain labor's dignity, to preserve its skills, and to stimulate business recovery by increasing purchasing power. In April, 1935, Congress inaugurated the new program in the Emergency Relief Act which authorized the establishment of an agency which would provide relief work for the able-bodied unemployed on useful projects. Agency officials would help in planning and administering projects, would prescribe rules for selection of workers, and would regulate conditions of labor. Nearly $5,000,000,000 was appropriated to carry out the act. Businessmen and the A.F.L. were critical: business lamented the cost; the A.F.L. feared the development of a low wage rate on governmental projects which would be reflected in private enterprise. Despite opposition, the new program was put into effect when the President created a Works Progress Administration in May, 1935, with Harry Hopkins in charge.

In six months Hopkins had nearly three million workers on W.P.A. rolls. The original work-relief projects were not always useful; many of them, as opponents pointed out, were merely "boondoggling projects." In time, however, useful projects were created for all kinds of workers. They ranged from the construction of highways to the extermination of rats; from the building of stadiums to the stuffing of birds; from the improvement of airplane landing fields to the making of books for the blind; from the building of over a million privies to the playing of the world's greatest symphonies. Skilled, semiskilled, unskilled, and even white-collar workers found jobs.

In the first six years of its existence the W.P.A. spent more than $11,000,000,000, three-fourths of it on construction and conservation projects and the remainder on community service programs. In the same six years the W.P.A. employed some 8,000,000 different workers. Average monthly employment was 2,112,000. Wages paid during the period varied. They were based originally both upon classification of workers as to jobs and upon assumed sectional differences: in 1935 rates in the South varied from $19 a month for unskilled to $75 a month for professional workers; the rates in the North varied from $40 to $94. By 1939 when the sectional differences were removed, the wages varied from $31 to $95. Monthly earnings for all types of workers averaged $41.50 in 1935 and $59 in 1939.

Meanwhile the Public Works Administration also made some contribution to the problem of relieving unemployment. In its earliest days most P.W.A. projects involved slum clearance and the erection of new housing; only gradually did other heavy construction projects develop. The recession of 1937 resulted in a huge increase in activity; by 1939 the P.W.A. had spent or allocated some $6,000,-000,000 for construction in all but three counties in the nation. Money was used primarily for improvement of waterways and harbors, for construction of Federal aid highways, and for building of post offices, courthouses, warehouses, and other structures needed by the Federal Government. Considerable sums were spent upon the building of naval and coast guard vessels, for the improvement of Army camps, aviation fields, and national parks. Large amounts were also used for construction of municipal waterworks, sewage and electric-light plants, public buildings, hospitals, and schoolhouses. The P.W.A.'s employment rolls generally ran between 200,000 and 300,000 a month.

The total effect of the New Deal's work relief and public work policy is difficult to assess. Although it never entirely relieved economic distress—wages were often too low to provide even barest living essentials—the New Deal did ameliorate misery. For millions, and particularly for the families of unskilled labor which made up from 60 to 70 per cent of W.P.A. rolls, it meant the difference between starvation and sustenance. Nor did it solve the problem of unemployment. There were at least ten million unemployed in 1935, and there were still eight million unemployed in 1940. These figures, however, do not reveal the whole story. A considerable portion of those unemployed in 1940 were young people who had never been employed. Since 1933 this group had been joining the ranks of employables at the rate of 700,000 a year, a total of nearly 5,000,000. The New Deal had, in short, taken care of a large proportion of the 1933 unemployed element, but it had failed to take care of the year-by-year accretion. The figures, moreover, counted those working on emergency work projects as "unemployed." If that element were counted as employed, the 1940 figures would be reduced by nearly three million. Such calculations indicate that the New Deal's program was more of a success than its detractors concede.

The W.P.A. constituted only one phase of the New Dealers' renewed efforts to solve labor's problems. As in the previous two years they continued to seek a permanent answer to the question of industrial unemployment. The solution they now adopted was based on the conclusion that unemployment was inevitable but predictable and insurable. While suggestions for the creation of an unemployment insurance system had been made by socialists in the 1870's, the first real effort to provide compensation for industrial unemployment began in the early twenties in Wisconsin when John R. Commons, professor of economics at the University of Wisconsin, drafted a bill providing for the establishment of unemployment reserves by employers and for the payment of the money thus accumulated in the account of each employer to unemployed workmen. Although the Wisconsin Federation of Labor and the Progressive party both endorsed the measure, it took ten years of vigorous campaigning to secure passage.

Enactment of the legislation in Wisconsin during the depression when the nation had become thoroughly unemployment conscious created a movement for enactment of similar legislation in other states. During 1932 bills were introduced in Massachusetts, Ohio, and California. In the same year the Democratic party endorsed the movement, and the A.F.L. announced itself in favor of state unemployment compensation legislation to be financed by employers under government supervision.

Another pressing problem was how to help men who were either too old to work or were considered too old to work. In agricultural and handicraft societies, which could readily make use of the lessened capacities of the aged, the problem had not been hard to solve. Old people worked as long as possible; when their strength declined, the family assumed the burden of their support. Church institutions, guilds, mechanics' societies, and state-erected poorhouses had supplemented this system. The rise of the factory system had slowly destroyed this time-honored method. In an industrial system men with lessened capacities often lost their jobs long before they were old. Simultaneously, family ties weakened; children left home more readily, and as they also grew insecure, they became less dependable as a support for aging parents.

Some labor elements had recognized this development soon after the factory became an important factor in the nation's economy. The consumer cooperative movement of New England in the fifties had tried to solve the problem by providing for private insurance funds. After the Civil War a feeling that support of the aged should become a charge on industry began to make headway. Although industry as a whole refused to recognize the obligation, various corporations set up old-age pension plans for their employees. The American Express Company created the first plan—paid for entirely by the employer. By 1929 there were 421 company pension plans in existence throughout the United States, covering 3,700,000 employees, most of whom worked for railroads, public utility companies, iron and steel corporations, or the oil industry. The company systems had two major faults. They required continuous service over a period of from fifteen to thirty years; because men constantly changed their employers within one industry, because of seasonal unemployment, and because of cyclical unemployment, only a small fraction of the employees covered by pension plans ever managed to achieve a long-enough service to become eligible. In addition the plans could be terminated at will by the company; during the years 1929–1932 ten per cent of the companies with pension plans abandoned their systems because the charge had become too great.

Although these weaknesses were recognized very early, little was done about the problem until after the First World War, when the Federal Government enacted a retirement law for its own civil servants and when the Fraternal Order of Eagles, a workingmen's social and benevolent organization with some 500,000 members, began a concerted drive for old-age pension laws. The Eagles' campaign had some success. Between 1923 and 1928 ten state legislatures passed pension laws, but since they were based on the idea that the cost should be borne by counties, and few counties accepted the obligation, the laws were ineffective. A change occurred in 1929 when the A.F.L. announced its support for pensions and California enacted a pension law mandatory upon all counties in the state. Between that year and 1932 nine others enacted similar legislation. This did not solve the problem: the overwhelming majority of the aged were not covered; many laws required a potential pensioner to be a near pauper; payments made were extremely low. Accordingly, in 1932, the Democratic party announced itself in favor of more adequate old-age legislation by states.

New Dealers began to give attention to the problem of unemployment compensation early in the Roosevelt administration. In 1933 Senator Wagner and Representative David J. Lewis introduced a measure for a Federal-state system of compensation supported by employer contributions. Although public response to the measure was encouraging enough to persuade the President to ask for enactment of the bill, the Senate committee which had the measure under consideration failed to reach an agreement after more than six months of deliberation. Meanwhile the problem of old-age pensions assumed political importance. During 1933 and 1934 Dr. Francis E. Townsend, a retired physician, organized a movement designed to solve both the financial problems of old age and the depression by the simple expedient of paying every person in the nation over sixty-five a monthly pension of $200 which had to be spent in thirty days. Simultaneously Huey Long, Governor of Louisiana, announced his "share-the-wealth" program which would guarantee to every citizen an annual income of $5,000. These movements, easily condemned as "crackpot" ventures, were nevertheless recognized as evidences of public concern with the problems. During 1933–1934 eighteen states enacted or rewrote old-age-pension laws; few, however, provided for more than the most meager of payments. Congress also responded to the pressure early in 1934 with the enactment of the Railroad Retirement Act which provided for the establishment of employer-supported old-age-pension systems on the nation's railroads, but this law only touched the surface of the problem.

In the summer of 1934 President Roosevelt appointed a cabinet Committee on Economic Security, which included Frances Perkins, Henry Wallace, and Harry Hopkins, to study the whole problem of unemployment insurance and old-age pensions. The committee made its report in January, 1935, and a bill, based on congressional taxing power, providing for a Federal-state system of unemployment insurance, a Federal system of old-age annuities for future aged, and a Federal-state system of assistance to those already aged, was introduced by Senator Pat Harrison and Congressman Robert L. Doughton. Almost the only opposition to the measure came from the Townsendites who argued that the benefits were too low. Congress, strongly New Dealish after the 1934 elections, revealed concern only with the questions of financing and constitutionality. The problem of finance raised the most difficulties. One group, which had a large support from the American Association for Old Age Security, argued that the money should come out of the Federal Government's general funds; another argued for a tax solely on employers; a third for a tax on both employees and employers. The question of constitutionality became important when the Supreme Court invalidated the Railroad Retirement Act, in the case of the *Railroad Retirement Board* v. *Alton Railroad Company*, because the act violated the due-process clause of the Fourth Amendment "by taking the property of one and bestowing it upon another." Alarming as it was, the decision did not hold up the bill. It became law in August, 1935.

The Social Security Act, as finally written, was something of a compromise and readily recognized as only a step toward solution. It set up an independent agency, the Social Security Board, to supervise the administration of the act which covered both the unemployed and the aged. The unemployed were to be handled by a Federal-state system whereby the Federal Government levied an excise tax on the payrolls of all employers except those in excluded categories—employers of agricultural, domestic service, shipping, government, charitable, and educational workers; and employers of less than eight workers. This exclusion limited unemployment coverage to about 22,000,000 workingmen, less than half of those gain-fully employed. The tax on employers was to start at 1 per cent in 1936 and rise to 3 per cent in 1938. To force the states to support the law, it was provided that wherever a state unemployment system was set up, 90 per cent of the taxes collected would be credited to the state fund. The remaining 10 per cent would be used to help defray the cost of administering the plan. The states, eager to keep this payroll money within their own borders, hastened to comply with the provision. Even before the Social Security bill became law, five states had enacted legislation to comply with the act. Every state in the union enacted satisfactory legislation by 1937. State laws were of several types. Most general was the creation of the "pooled fund" which required all employers to pay the same per-centage of their payroll; less frequent was the "merit-rating" fund which required smaller contributions from employers with less un-employment; a third plan provided for both employer and employee contributions. No benefits were to be extended under the act for two years. After that date a person who became unemployed was required to report to a public employment office or other approved agency—additional work for the USES—to record his condition. If during the next four weeks the employment agency failed to find him an acceptable job, he became eligible for unemployment compensa-tion. This compensation, amounting to one-half his pay, was to be paid for twelve weeks.

The aged were covered in a more complicated manner. The act provided for a Federal tax on the payrolls of all employers and on the wages of all employees except those in the exempted categories. The tax would start at 1 per cent and would gradually increase to 3 per cent in 1948. All money collected would be handled by the Federal Government; no benefits would be paid out of this fund until after January 1, 1942. When a worker reached the age of sixty-five, he became entitled to an annuity. If he quit his job he would receive an annuity as long as he lived, the amount depending upon the length of time he had worked and upon the amount of his earnings. But in no case was the amount to be less than $10 or more than $85 a month. The annuity provision of the act did not cover those who worked for employers in the exempted categories, those who reached the age of sixty-five before 1942, or those already over sixty-five. For this group the act provided a Federal-state pension system whereby the Federal Government agreed to pay 50 per cent of the monthly pension, or $20, whichever was less, to all persons over sixty-five in those states which erected tax-supported pension systems for the aged. All states soon adopted acceptable plans, though some in the South provided for pensions far too small to sustain life.

Enactment of the Social Security Act raised a storm of protest. Liberals criticized the law because it failed to cover all workers, because its unemployment benefits and annuities were small, because it permitted states to set up substandard pension payments, and because it was financed on "invalid" actuarial principles instead of out of regular taxes. Economists condemned it because the payroll taxes were deflationary. Employers complained of new tax burdens and increased accounting costs. The constitutionality of the taxes upon employers and of the state employment insurance laws were challenged. But general public reaction was highly favorable. During 1936 the Republicans attempted to turn workingmen against the act by an attack upon payroll deductions. The strategy failed. Laborers, pleased with the act and with its effect on future security, were solid in their approval. Within one year of its passage the act had become a fixed institution; the only threat it faced came from a possible unfavorable Supreme Court decision. In May, 1937, the court in a series of three decisions—*Steward Machine Co.* v. *Davis, Helvering* v. *Davis,* and *Carmichael* v. *Southern Coal Company*—upheld the constitutionality of the unemployment tax, the old-age benefit tax, and the state unemployment insurance laws.

The decisions gave impetus to a movement for liberalization of the law. In 1939 the act was amended to provide for benefit payments to widows and families of annuitants who died before they reached sixty-five and for dependent survivors of annuitants who died after they reached sixty-five. Meanwhile Congress extended the principles of the act to railways. In August, 1935, it enacted a new Railroad Retirement Act which provided for the creation of an annuity system for railway workers similar to that in the Social Security Act; in 1938 it enacted a Railroad Unemployment Insurance Act which extended to railway workers a plan of compulsory unemployment insurance similar to the system provided under the Social Security Act.

Thus, by the end of Roosevelt's second administration a huge step had been taken toward finding a permanent solution to the problems of unemployment and old age. Admittedly the solution was not perfect. It covered only 25,000,000 of the nation's working force. Agricultural laborers, Negroes who in the South were usually agricultural laborers, and women who were often found in domestic service or in small mercantile establishments were the largest groups without benefits. It was also easily recognized that unemployment insurance would give but slight benefit to labor in case of a prolonged depression and that old-age annuities and pensions were not always adequate. But the new system was a vast improvement over that of the twenties when the nation's workingmen had little or no protection against unemployment and when only 3,000,000 laborers were eligible for company pensions.

Simultaneously with the effort to find a permanent solution for the problem of unemployment, New Dealers also began working on those labor problems which they had hoped to solve by the inclusion of Section 7(a) in the National Industrial Recovery Act. The need for solution was more than obvious.

Invalidation of the N.R.A. had plunged labor into a period of decline; unemployment promptly increased, hours lengthened, and wages dropped. All labor did not lose protection; the Emergency Railroad Transportation Act of June, 1933, guaranteed railway workers the right of organization and collective bargaining and specifically recognized the regular railway unions as bargaining agents. Under the administration of Federal Coordinator Joseph B. Eastman these provisions had been applied and remained unchallenged. Railway workers, however, were only a small portion of the total labor world. Accordingly, after the election of 1934, a movement developed to reenact and strengthen the labor provisions of the N.R.A. in a new form. It centered upon a bill to outlaw company unions and force collective bargaining which Senator Wagner had introduced in 1934. President Roosevelt, who had originally revealed a somewhat hostile attitude toward it, now adopted the bill as his own; labor which had been urging its passage redoubled its pressure: William Green told a congressional committee that only the passage of Senator Wagner's bill would prevent a labor explosion.

The bill—known familiarly as the Wagner Act, known otherwise as the National Labor Relations Act—became law in July, 1935. Its enactment marked a major change in governmental policy. Although there had been several periods in the past when the Federal Government had revealed a favorable attitude toward labor, the passage of the Wagner Act revealed not only governmental favor but a willingness to form a partnership with labor. The New Deal, in short, had come to realize that labor's right to organize was only theoretical in the face of management's hostility. To ensure the right of organization, and the correlative right to bargain, governmental aid was needed. The New Deal announced itself ready to grant the aid.

The Wagner Act provided for the establishment of a new National Labor Relations Board of three experts empowered to supervise and enforce the principle that employees had the "right to self-organization, to form, join, or assist labor organizations to bargain collectively through representatives of their own choosing, and to engage in concerted activities for the purpose of collective bargaining or other mutual aid or protection." To carry out this principle the act stipulated that representatives of the majority of the workers in a bargaining unit should have the power to speak for the whole. The board was empowered to determine what was the appropriate bargaining unit through supervised elections. It was also given authority to prohibit "unfair" employer practices: interference with employees in the exercise of guaranteed rights; support of company unions; use of hiring or firing to encourage membership in a company union, or to discourage membership in an independent union; discrimination against a worker because he complained to the board; refusal to bargain collectively with the representatives of the employees. The board's power of enforcement was to be exercised through "cease and desist" orders and through use of the circuit courts.

While labor was pleased with the law, its expressions of approval were guarded. The caution was wise, for the act proved difficult to enforce. The President promptly named a board which established machinery for redressing grievances, but the machinery didn't always work: industry refused to cooperate. Although the reason for industry's attitude was more than obvious—the law could destroy management's control of its labor supply—the excuse most often advanced for refusing compliance was the charge that it was unconstitutional. The charge was given support by the Supreme Court's action upon the Guffey-Snyder Act, which had been enacted in August, 1935, as an attempt to reapply the principles of the N.R.A. to the bituminous coal industry. The act established a National Bituminous Coal Commission, promulgated a code, established minimum prices, and guaranteed labor the right of collective bargaining. Under the act producers of two-thirds of the nation's tonnage and representatives for more than half of the miners signed agreements providing for minimum wages and maximum hours. In 1936 the Supreme Court, in the case of *Carter* v. *Carter Coal Company*, invalidated the law on the ground that its labor provisions were an unconstitutional delegation of legislative powers. Thus, antiunion employers did not hesitate to violate the Wagner Act in all its provisions.

The attitude boomeranged. Perhaps the most important reason was the exposure of methods used by industry to combat unionism made by the La Follette Civil Liberties Committee during 1936 and 1937. The committee learned that many corporations commonly accumulated "industrial munitions," weapons especially adapted for use in industrial disputes such as submachine guns, tear gas, sickening gas, grenades, and shells. How these weapons were used became clear during the Little Steel Strike of 1937 when Youngstown Sheet and Tube and Republic Steel employed a uniformed police force of four hundred men equipped with revolvers, rifles, shotguns and tear gas, which they "loosed . . . to shoot down citizens on the streets and highways" during the strike. The arms, in short, were used to create "goon squads" whose job was to discourage unionization.

Another technique widely used by industry, first developed by the Remington Rand Company, was known as the Mohawk Valley formula. It provided for systematic denunciation of all labor organizers and leaders as dangerous radicals, use of local police to break up labor meetings, propaganda campaigns to align the citizenry behind law and order, organization of vigilante committees to protect plants which hired strikebreakers, back-to-work movements, and threats to remove the industry from the community if labor were not put in its place. In addition, almost every corporation of importance in the nation employed labor spies, which they hired from various agencies like Pinkerton, Burns, the Railway and Audit Inspection Company,

and the Corporations Auxiliary Company during times of labor up-
surgence. Their jobs were numerous: to corrupt union strength from
inside by sowing seeds of distrust and suspicion, to provoke strikes
before unions were strong enough to carry them to a successful conclusion, to report on labor activities, and to reveal the names of
strong figures so that employers could be rid of them. Committee
investigations revealed that between 1933 and 1937 industry had
hired 3,781 such agents; they had become affiliated with ninety-three
unions. Some had actually become union officials. There was some
evidence, moreover, that a labor spy or a stool pigeon could be found
in every one of labor's 41,000 locals—at a cost to industry of some
$80,000,000 annually.

Such revelations could not go unnoticed. The public was so loud
in its denunciations that even normally antilabor newspapers were
forced to admit that labor's civil liberties had been disregarded by
industry; many corporations, fearing greater reaction, abandoned
their practices. But the total effect was even larger. The public, which
had been showing considerable sympathy for labor's aims for many
years, now became convinced that labor needed not only sympathy
but protection. Industry's capacity for stifling labor's rights had to be
destroyed.

It was in this atmosphere that the Supreme Court began consideration of a number of cases designed to test the constitutionality of
the Wagner Act. During its deliberations the President, angered by
previous invalidation of ten New Deal laws, asked Congress for authority to reorganize the courts. In April, 1937, in the midst of the
uproar that followed the request, the Supreme Court handed down its
decision on the Wagner Act. Most important of the cases was that of
the *National Labor Relations Board* v. *Jones and Laughlin Steel Company*. The court pointed out that employees had as clear a right to
organize and select representatives "for lawful purposes" as employers had to organize a business and select officers and agents. It
likewise recognized that labor needed to organize because a single
employee was "helpless in dealing with an employer." The laborer
was dependent upon his daily wage for the maintenance of himself
and his family; since he could not easily leave his job, he was forced
to accept unfair treatment. Organization into unions gave laborers
the opportunity "to deal on an equality with their employer." Fur-

ther, it regarded employer discrimination and coercion to prevent the free exercise of the right of employees to self-organization and representation as a "proper subject for condemnation by competent legislative authority." Congress, it declared, had that kind of competence; it had the power to regulate labor conditions which affected interstate commerce.

The decision was a major victory both for the New Deal and for labor. The N.L.R.B., now freed of all shackles, proceeded to apply the law in full vigor. In the first five years of its life the board and its auxiliaries handled nearly 30,000 cases—two-thirds concerned with unfair practices and the remainder with elections. It settled 2,161 strikes and held nearly 3,500 elections. By 1945 the board had handled 36,000 cases involving unfair labor practices and 38,000 cases involving employee representation. It also held 24,000 elections to determine collective bargaining units involving some 6,000,-000 workers.

Out of these activities developed something of a revolution in labor-management relations. Through a long series of decisions interpreting the provision which declared employer attempts to interfere with, restrain, or coerce employees in the exercise of their rights as unfair practices, the board outlawed yellow-dog contracts, black lists, and other forms of discrimination; its decisions on these points resulted in the reinstatement of some 300,000 employees with back pay amounting to $9,000,000. It prohibited the use of labor spies and antiunion propaganda; it recognized the validity of peaceful picketing, the preferential union shop, and the closed shop. Through decisions and elections it practically destroyed company unionism. Although N.L.R.B. decisions of this nature were in a number of cases challenged, the Supreme Court consistently handed down opinions which supported N.L.R.B. rulings. Most significant were *Thornhill* v. *Alabama,* a case involving a state antipicketing law, in which the court declared peaceful picketing to be a legitimate exercise of free speech; and the two cases of the *United States* v. *Hutcheson* and *Hunt* v. *Cromboch,* both involving the Sherman Act, in which the court upheld the right of a union to impose a boycott that virtually drove a company out of business.

The Wagner Act and the Jones-Laughlin case climaxed a century-long struggle by labor for recognition of its right to organize and bargain collectively. Its previous theoretical rights on these points now became practical rights; all industry practices which transcended or thwarted the right to organize were outlawed. Labor, in short, had finally secured equality of position in the nation's economy.

24 ___

The Rise of the C.I.O.

The labor program of Franklin D. Roosevelt's first administration has been recognized in itself as the most important effort to advance labor welfare in the nation's history. It provided labor with relief from economic distress, assured it some security during periods of unemployment and in old age, and gave it an opportunity to help itself by guaranteeing its right to organize and bargain collectively. In addition, the program fostered an equally important by-product: it helped create a new labor organization—the Committee for Industrial Organization.

The movement that ultimately established the C.I.O. was motivated in part by a century-old recognition of the facts that American industry was no longer workshop industry, that the typical American laborer was no longer a skilled worker, and that industry was so organized that the craft union had ceased to be effective in the everlasting struggle of labor for just rewards. The movement was also a revolt against the casual attitude which the A.F.L. had assumed toward immigrant and noncraft labor. While the foreign born, the semiskilled, and the unskilled had accepted their lot in silence, in the twenties this docility began to change. The inferior workmen began to recognize that they constituted an overwhelming majority of the labor world and that they were a potential power. In addition, they had become Americanized. The First World War and the Immigration acts of 1921 and 1924 had nearly stopped the tide of incoming labor; the result was to create a semiskilled and unskilled element one or two generations removed from Europe, an element which had imbibed the American traditions of equality and organized protest. The movement also involved a reforming instinct. Criticism of the A.F.L.'s frequent refusal to recognize political action as a legitimate means of advancing labor's aims and of its apparent collaboration with employers through the National Civic Federation had left a heritage of suspicion in the labor world. The A.F.L.'s ineptitude during the twenties when it seemed to have no program with which to fight the American plan, company unionism, technological unemployment, or depression increased the suspicion. Collection of illicit contributions from union members in return for jobs, misappropriation of union funds, defense of officials whose criminal activities had been exposed, shaking down of employers, and friendship with crooked politicians and criminals made union men angry, ashamed, discontented, and open to suggestion for reform.

The N.R.A. was the catalytic agent that brought these forces together into a single movement. During 1933–1934 there was, as has been related, a strong upsurge of unionism in every trade; it was most spectacular among organizations not affiliated with the A.F.L. and among the neglected laborers in the great mass-production industries like steel, automobiles, lumber, rubber, and aluminum. A.F.L. leadership was delighted with this vast increase; it proceeded to organize these new members into Federal unions and made preparations to divide the membership among various crafts.

Leaders of the few industrial unions within the A.F.L. promptly protested against these plans. Contending that the old craft union was outdated, they urged that the new accessions to labor from the mass-producing industries be organized into industrial unions. The old craft-union leaders in turn argued that the granting of charters to industrial unions was contrary to A.F.L. traditions, and they reiterated the old claim that the craft union had proved itself to be the only successful type of labor organization. But during 1934, when employers inaugurated a strong campaign to roll back the tide of unionism, when the newly organized laboring men went down to defeat after defeat, when the rolls of the newly created Federal unions began to decline in an alarming manner, the demand for industrial charters reached a crescendo too great to ignore. At the San Francisco convention the A.F.L. agreed to charter unions in the automobile, rubber, cement, radio, and aluminum industries and to begin an intensive drive for the organization of steel.

The A.F.L. old guard did not keep its pledges. It had no sympathy for industrial unionism. No industrial charters were granted, and no organizing campaigns were developed. Industrial unionists were enraged by the failure. As they watched labor leave the ranks, muttering bitter imprecations upon unionism, they recognized that the undreamed-of opportunity for a tremendous union expansion which the N.R.A. had provided was slipping away, and all their deeply rooted hostility to the A.F.L.'s long established policies and tactics boiled to the surface.

The inevitable clash between the old guard and the industrial unionists broke out at the A.F.L.'s annual convention at Atlantic City in November, 1935. The senior officer of the old guard was A.F.L. president William Green, a former miner and member of the U.M.W., once an advocate of industrial unionism but now a cautious exponent of craft unionism. His career had been unspectacular, marked by few if any union successes. Tactical commander of the old guard was "Big Bill" Hutcheson, leader of the carpenters. A burly man, Hutcheson had lived a stormy career in his twenty years as president of the carpenters; he had destroyed all rivals and had made the carpenters one of the strongest unions in the nation. Yet a vast number of the rank and file hated him; they accused him of using dictatorial and illegal tactics to perpetuate his control and of making "sell out" deals with employers. Also included on the old-guard battle staff were Daniel Tobin, rough-and-tumble leader of the teamsters, who had publicly stated that in his opinion the men who worked in the mass-production industries were no better than "rubbish"; John P. Frey, head of the Metal Trades Departments; and Matthew Woll, head of the photoengravers and arch red baiter.

Leader of the industrial unionists, by both right of seniority and force of command, was John L. Lewis. The president of the U.M.W. was even then something of an enigma. Though head of the largest industrial union and one-time candidate of A.F.L. "progressives" for the organization's presidency, he had been a good trade unionist and would have made an excellent member of the old guard. But Lewis was the head of an organization which was trying to exist in a dying industry; in the twenties it had become riddled with dissension and had split into fragments. Lewis had learned something from this experience. He had acquired an economic advisor, W. Jett Lauck; under his tutelage he had given sufficient study to the coal industry to propose the passage of legislation which would permit operators to form combinations and adopt practices to control production and prices and which would specifically guarantee workers the right to organization. The N.R.A. and the Guffey Act embodied the idea. Lewis, moreover, had taken full advantage of the N.R.A. He had conducted a whirlwind organizing campaign in the coal fields that had more than restored the U.M.W.'s membership rolls; he had even begun organizing other industries through "District 50." He recognized, however, that his rebuilt U.M.W. was weak, particularly among the newly organized "captive mines" owned by big steel corporations. To protect the miners Lewis knew it was necessary to organize the steelworkers. Lewis was, therefore, an industrial unionist because his own union was industrial, because he had seen the success of an industrial organizing campaign in the coal fields, and because organization of the steel industry along industrial lines was necessary if his own union was to maintain its position.

Lewis' chief lieutenants among the industrial unionists included Philip Murray, quiet and effective U.M.W. vice president; Sidney Hillman, energetic and persuasive head of the Amalgamated Clothing Workers which had just returned to the A.F.L. fold; David Dubinsky, long an advocate of organization by industry and head of the radically tinged International Ladies' Garment Workers; and Charles Howard, head of the Typographical Union.

The clash between the craft and industrial unionists at the convention began when the A.F.L. Executive Council announced that it had not deemed it "advisable to launch an organizing campaign for the steel industry" in the previous year. The announcement was followed by a resolutions' committee report which reiterated the doctrine that the purpose of the A.F.L. was to protect the "jurisdictional rights of all trade unions organized upon craft lines." The implication was obvious: the old guard was opposed to industrial unionism and did not intend to encourage it. A bitter three-day debate followed. The climax was a floor scuffle between Lewis and Hutcheson and a speech by Lewis. In language for which he had become famous, he denounced the old guard for failing to act in the past year while the new unions established in the mass-production industries were disintegrating and for failing to carry out the pledges made at San Francisco. He admitted that he himself had been at fault because he had allowed himself to be "seduced" by promises. But having recognized his mistake, he was now ready to rend his seducers "limb from limb." He appealed to the convention to help the unorganized and to make the federation the greatest instrument ever forged on behalf of suffering humanity. Finally, he warned that another opportunity for expansion of unionism, supported as it might be by the new Wagner Act, would hardly arise in the near future; that if the opportunity were not seized, "high wassail" would prevail at the banquet tables of the mighty. The argument proved futile. The craft-union principle was upheld by a vote of 18,024 to 10,933.

The industrial unionists refused to admit defeat. Shortly after the Atlantic City convention, the presidents of eight unions or union divisions met to consider action. These included Lewis, Hillman, Dubinsky, and Howard, Thomas F. McMahon of the Textile Workers, Max Zaritsky of the cap and millinery department of the United Hatters, Harvey C. Flemming of the Oil Field, Gas Well and Refining Workers, and Thomas H. Brown of the Mine, Mill and Smelter Workers. The eight men organized a Committee for Industrial Organization to operate within the framework of the A.F.L. but intended, also, to promote industrial unionism.

The act was promptly denounced by Green as an attempt to establish dual unionism. He threatened dire consequences. The reply to Green's warning came from Lewis who resigned his position as vice president of the A.F.L. and continued to make plans for a huge organizing campaign. In January, 1936, as part of its preparations, the C.I.O. asked the A.F.L. Executive Council to grant industrial charters to steel, auto, rubber, and radio workers. The council reacted to this "effrontery" with a curt refusal and ordered the C.I.O. to dissolve. The C.I.O.'s reaction was to start collecting funds for a steel organizing campaign. During the next half-year the rift between the A.F.L. and the C.I.O. grew steadily wider. Green alternately threatened the recalcitrants with excommunication and pleaded for their return. Finally, in August, 1936, the Executive Council suspended the C.I.O. unions, now ten in number. The interdict had no effect. When the A.F.L. convention met at Tampa late in 1936, the

C.I.O. unions did not appear. The convention repronounced its anathema, and the break was complete.

Meanwhile, in June, 1936, the C.I.O. had begun a vigorous unionizing campaign in the steel industry. A Steel Workers Organizing Committee was set up under the leadership of Philip Murray, and four hundred organizers descended upon the nation's steel centers. The industry fought back but not with its old-time vigor and ruthlessness. It contented itself with a propaganda campaign which charged the whole movement to communist and radical influence, accused the C.I.O. of intimidating and coercing workers, and sought to prove that the industry's company unions were sufficient to care for labor's demands. The propaganda had little effect. Encouraged by the passage of the Wagner Act which seemed to be a guarantee of protection against employer reprisals, the steelworkers moved by thousands into the S.W.O.C.—sometimes in spite of company promises of wage increases. By the end of 1936 the S.W.O.C. had established 150 locals with 100,000 members. It had become strong enough for a showdown.

It never came. "Big Steel," as the United States Steel Corporation was known, side stepped. During the organizing campaign Lewis and Myron Taylor, chairman of United States Steel, began secret negotiations. In March, 1937, the results were announced: United States Steel's largest subsidiary, Carnegie-Illinois Steel, agreed to recognize the S.W.O.C. as a bargaining agent, granted a wage increase, the eight-hour day, and a forty-hour week. The nation was astounded. Here was a victory for unionism snatched from the very company which had once announced its unalterable opposition to unionism and had been in the forefront of a forty-year antiunion movement. But Big Steel wanted no labor trouble at the moment when business was good and getting better, when its whole carefully erected company union structure had fallen apart, and when the obvious trend throughout the nation was in the direction of new labor-management relations. Big Steel's action was quickly followed by similar recognition on the part of other United States Steel subsidiaries and of the nation's independent producers. By May, 1937, the S.W.O.C. had signed more than a hundred contracts, and its membership had reached 300,000.

The drive was not complete. The "Little Steel" companies—Bethlehem, Republic, Inland, and Youngstown Sheet and Tube—ranging from second to fifth in productive capacity, refused to surrender. Under the leadership of Thomas Girdler, president of Republic, the companies prepared for battle. In May, 1937, the S.W.O.C. called a strike; 75,000 workingmen responded, and an old-fashioned steel-labor conflict followed. The companies used every weapon: citizens' committees to support intimidation, back-to-work movements, special police which attacked picket lines and routed union leaders out of headquarters with tear gas, local police who made mass arrests, militia which protected strikebreakers. The most notable act of violence occurred on May 30th when Chicago police attacked three hundred men picketing the Republic plant. While the "Memorial Day Massacre" created widespread public sympathy for the strikers, "Little Steel" won the contest. It was the C.I.O.'s first defeat.

Meanwhile, the C.I.O. had begun another dramatic campaign in the automobile industry. Centered in the Detroit area, with far-flung outposts, the industry was one of the most crucial in the nation. Although many mass-production industries depended upon it for a large share of their sustenance, it was untouched by unionism as late as 1932. There were many reasons for this situation. The industry was almost wholly controlled by only three companies: General Motors, Chrysler, and Ford; each was strongly antiunion and big enough to keep unions out of its plants. A large proportion of the workers in the industry were immigrants or recent migrants from the South, inclined to be docile or antiunion. Labor in the plants, moreover, was unskilled and easily replaced.

Automobile workers had many grievances. In spite of their well publicized high hourly earnings, seasonal layoffs reduced their annual earnings to low levels; because of assembly line methods of manufacture they became the victims of the speed-up and worked under almost unendurable tension. In the early days of the N.R.A. they had become involved in a series of unorganized strikes; most of them were quickly defeated, for the automobile companies had excellent labor spy systems. Nevertheless the disorganized protest was not all in vain. Out of it developed about ten unions; though badly divided among themselves, they were indicative of the need for organization. It was at this point that the A.F.L. stepped in and, using the unions already established, reorganized them into federal unions. The act, which failed to meet automobile workers' needs, had its inevitable results: the unions, harried by company discrimination in hiring, melted away. In August, 1935, the A.F.L. sought to check the decline by merging the remaining federal unions into a single Automobile Workers Union, but the action came too late—membership had dropped to 20,000.

With the creation of the C.I.O. a new flush of enthusiasm stole through the automobile industry; men began to rejoin the union. Then, in the spring of 1936, the rank and file revolted against A.F.L. imposed leadership, elected a new president—Homer Martin, a former Baptist minister—adopted the name United Automobile Workers, and joined the C.I.O. During the remainder of the year Martin organized; it was a slow and painful process hampered by company spies and "goon squads." In December, 1936, U.A.W. officials decided that the union was strong enough to demand recognition from General Motors. The company, in defiance of the Wagner Act, refused to discuss either recognition or collective bargaining. The reply placed Martin in a quandary. On the one side, the C.I.O. was deeply involved in a steel strike and did not feel strong enough to support an automobile strike at the same time. On the other side, the rank and file, enraged by General Motors' attitude, were chafing for action. Since workers in glass and tire factories in the Midwest were winning concessions through strike action, automobile workers saw no reason for delay. "Quickie" strikes broke out in Cleveland, Toledo, and Flint. Martin surrendered to the pressure. In January, 1937, an official strike against General Motors began.

The strike was something new because workers instead of walking out of the plant just sat at their workbenches. Although women in the needle trades had engaged in at least one sit-down strike in the nineteenth century, and the technique had been used in Poland and France, these episodes had been forgotten. Rubber workers in Akron and automobile workers in Cleveland had used the weapon in 1936, but it was the Flint workers who made it famous. The sit-down proved highly effective. Unprepared, General Motors denounced the act as an unlawful invasion of property rights and demanded immediate ejection of the strikers. The workers countered with the terse statement that there was no more sacred property right than the right of a man to his job. A battle followed. G.M.C. cut off the heat in the Flint plants; the men stayed. Flint police rushed one of the plants and were driven off by a shower of coffee mugs, pop bottles, iron bolts, and hinges. Police attacked a second time with tear gas bombs, and the strikers retaliated by turning the plant's firehoses loose. The police retreated—an action which became known as the "Battle of the Running Bulls."

Meanwhile, General Motors demanded that the state militia be mobilized to remove the strikers: Governor Frank Murphy refused to take any action. Early in February, G.M.C. secured a court order setting February 3rd as the deadline for evacuation. The strikers announced their determination "to make General Motors Corporation obey the law and engage in collective bargaining." Governor Murphy suggested a conference between Knudsen and Lewis; no settlement resulted. As February 3rd dawned the nation prepared to hear news of a blood bath. But evacuation day came and went without event: Murphy had refused to call out the troops.

Murphy's stand was undoubtedly the turning point of the strike. On February 4th President Roosevelt requested that the Murphy-Knudsen-Lewis negotiations be resumed. A week of conferences finally produced an agreement. General Motors recognized the U. A.W. as bargaining agent for its members and agreed both to drop the injunction against strikebreakers and to make no discrimination against union members in its hiring policy. Although this was not a complete victory, it was the first step toward ultimate conquest of the industry. In April, 1937, the importance of the G.M.C. settlement became clear when a short sit-down strike forced Chrysler Corporation to come to terms.

In the meantime the U.A.W. campaign had created a problem. In revealing the efficacy of the sit-down strike, it induced imitation. Between September, 1936, and June, 1937, almost a half-million workers became involved in sit-down strikes in rubber, textiles, glass, and a myriad other trades and callings. So widespread was the enthusiasm for the new weapon that labor put the technique into a song:

When they tie the can to a union man, Sit down! Sit down!
When they give him the sack, they'll take him back, Sit down! Sit down!
When the speed-up comes, just twiddle your thumbs, Sit down! Sit down!
When the boss won't talk, don't take a walk, Sit down! Sit down!

The sit-down, however, had brought a public reaction. Employers who feared the effects of the weapon and their spokesmen among newspapers condemned it as an invasion of property rights. The United States Senate attacked it as "illegal and contrary to public policy." The widespread condemnation had its effect. During 1937 the public, which only a short while before had been demanding validation of the Wagner Act, began to make demands for new laws to curb labor. The A.F.L. also announced its disapproval. Such developments could not be ignored. After the summer of 1937 the C.I.O., which had used the technique primarily against employers who had failed to heed N.L.R.B. orders, decided that the sit-down was both unnecessary and impolitic. It was quietly abandoned. The Supreme Court's decision in the Fansteel case handed down in 1939, which virtually outlawed the sit-down as a trespass upon private property, ended the technique.

While C.I.O. victories in the steel and automobile industries during 1936–1937 were undoubtedly the most spectacular and most significant of its campaigns, they were only part of a much wider activity. During the same years strong organizing drives were also conducted in other mass-producing industries. In textiles the C.I.O. set up a Textile Workers Organizing Committee, headed by Sidney Hillman, with a huge war chest contributed mainly by Hillman's Amalgamated and Dubinsky's I.L.G.W.U. Despite bitter opposition from employers in mill towns, its campaign was a success. By the end of 1937 half the textile workers in the nation had been brought under contract; even southern plants had been infiltrated. Campaigns among rubber workers brought contracts with Goodyear, Goodrich, Firestone, and United States Rubber, covering 60 per cent of the workers in the industry. Strong drives were made among ladies' garment and clothing workers, among radio and electrical equipment workers, in oil fields, among longshoremen, among agricultural and packing-house workers, among telephone workers. No mass-production and large service industry was neglected. The effort paid. At the end of two years of activity, in December, 1937, the C.I.O. boasted a membership of 3,700,000—composed of 600,000 miners, 400,000 automobile workers, 375,000 steelworkers, 250,000 ladies' garment workers, 175,000 clothing workers, 100,000 agricultural and packing-house workers, 80,000 rubber workers. The day of labor giants had dawned.

25 —

Political Action and
Jurisdictional Warfare

In the midst of the C.I.O. drive for organization of the mass-producing industries, the presidential election of 1936 occurred, an election in which labor was destined to play an important role. It was inevitable that labor would become politically active during the New Deal period. Labor in general had recognized quite early that the New Deal was trying to solve a political and economic crisis in a way that would preserve both political democracy and capitalism and at the same time would spread the benefits of the nation's economic system over the entire population. Since labor had long revealed itself as one of the nation's leading exponents of political democracy, since it had likewise generally accepted the idea that its economic and social amelioration had to be worked out within the bounds of capitalism, it was natural that labor would support the whole New Deal program and that the support would extend politically. In addition labor had come to realize that its own status in industry was greatly dependent upon the government. Economic controls were needed to prevent a recurrence of the events of 1929. It was inevitable, likewise, that the political movement would be led by the C.I.O. Its leaders were eager to advance the fortunes of labor in any expedient manner. Since many of them were recruited from old-time socialist ranks, political action was often their only answer for solution of social problems. Members of C.I.O. unions, moreover, primarily semiskilled and unskilled, recognized that their ability to protect their position in industry was limited by the fact that they could be easily replaced; their position had to be bolstered by legislation.

The impulse for labor's political action in 1936 was largely a reaction against the American Liberty League which had emerged as a powerful force intent upon defeating Roosevelt for reelection. C.I.O. leaders, among them Lewis, whose past career had not revealed any strong political propensities, and Sidney Hillman, who had long regarded political action as an essential labor policy, revealed deep alarm over the possible consequences of a return of "economic royalists" to power. They began a campaign intended to unite both the C.I.O. and the A.F.L. into a single pressure group dedicated to the single program of reelecting Roosevelt, whom they now recognized as a firm friend. Two organizations were established: Labor's Non-Partisan League, headed by George L. Berry of the Printing Pressmen's Union with Sidney Hillman as treasurer, and the American Labor party in New York City.

The Non-Partisan League did not meet expectations. C.I.O. unions revealed a wild enthusiasm. Members of the unions forgot their exasperation with the New Deal's early relief program and the New Deal's handling of the N.R.A.; they recognized that Roosevelt's "heart was in the right place"; and they went overboard on his behalf. The A.F.L. was a different matter. While a large number of state federations and internationals cooperated with the league, William Green denounced the organization as a dual movement in politics. What part the league played in the Roosevelt landslide of 1936 is difficult to determine. It hardly built up a pro-Roosevelt sentiment; that already existed. Its chief contribution probably came in the form of getting out the vote. The American Labor party's contribution, some 250,000 votes, was obvious.

Both the C.I.O. and the Non-Partisan League expressed satisfaction with the results. The C.I.O. promptly indicated that it was in politics to stay; the Non-Partisan League announced that in the future it would cooperate "with every progressive group whose purpose is to secure the enactment of liberal and humanitarian legislation." Both organizations turned hopefully to President Roosevelt and an overwhelmingly New Deal Congress for further legislation designed to aid and permanently improve the condition of labor.

Their main objective, as Roosevelt's second administration began, was enactment of some measure dealing with wages, hours, and child labor. The objective coincided with the aims of New Dealers who had been preparing legislation on these points ever since the invalidation of the N.R.A. Their first measures had been peripheral. In the summer of 1935 Congress enacted the Walsh-Healy Act, which established a forty-hour week for contractors who were manufacturing supplies for the government, directed the secretary of labor to determine minimum-wage rates to be paid by manufacturers of such commodities, and forbade the employment of children by manufacturers on government contracts. Early the following year Congress, in the Air Transport Act, laid down the same provisions for air lines which received government subsidies.

By the spring of 1936 New Dealers appeared to be ready to introduce more generalized legislation. But the movement received a setback from a United States Supreme Court decision on state minimum-wage laws. Seven states had enacted such laws between November, 1932, and May, 1935. Although it was generally agreed that states had the right to enact such legislation, the New York law was challenged, and the Supreme Court, in the case of *Moorhead* v. *Tipaldo*, declared it illegal on the ground that it violated the equal-protection clause of the Fourteenth Amendment. The court's decision astonished the nation. It presented the spectacle of the nation's highest tribunal declaring Federal law unconstitutional because it invaded the powers reserved for the states, and at the same time declaring state law unconstitutional because in effect it transcended the Bill of Rights as applied by the Fourteenth Amendment to the states.

At this point President Roosevelt decided to delay further action. He was becoming sensitive to the oft-repeated charge that he had no respect for the Constitution. In addition A.F.L. leadership was once more blowing hot and cold on the question. Labor, it argued, had enough protection in the Wagner Act: hours and wages could be safely left to collective bargaining. But labor's rank and file, already in process of revolt against A.F.L. philosophy, demanded action. Wages and hours, therefore, became an issue of the election of 1936. Both major parties adopted planks concerning the issue. The Republicans proposed legislation by states—which had already been declared unconstitutional. The Democrats pledged that they would seek national legislation: President Roosevelt himself promised action.

Despite overwhelming victory in the election of 1936—readily interpreted as a mandate for action—New Dealers moved cautiously. The Supreme Court remained an obstacle. In the early spring of 1937, however, the Court approved a Washington State Minimum Wage Law in the case of the *West Coast Hotel Company* v. *Parrish*. It was an amazing decision; even the Court indirectly recognized its reversal by pointing out that the issue had not been properly presented when *Moorhead* v. *Tipaldo* had been argued.

New Dealers acted quickly. In May, 1937, Senator Hugo Black of Alabama and Congressman William P. Connery of Maryland introduced a bill providing for minimum wages, maximum hours, and for the abolition of child labor.

Little trouble was anticipated in securing the passage of the measure. Even industry confined its criticism to technical defects. Nevertheless, the bill encountered stiff opposition, some of it from unexpected sources. William Green refused to give the bill his unequivocal support; Matthew Woll, William Hutcheson, and John Frey came out in open opposition. Their objections to the bill were based on the oft-repeated charge that "minimum wages become maximum wages." John L. Lewis also revealed opposition. Southern and western legislators were critical. Southerners opposed because they recognized that the bill would equalize wages throughout the nation and would destroy the wage differential which attracted industry to the South; farm state representatives opposed because they feared that the measure would lure farm labor to the cities and complicate farm problems.

When the House Rules Committee, dominated by southerners, prevented the measure from coming up for a vote in the regular session, President Roosevelt called Congress back into special session in mid-November, 1937, and made a strong appeal for enactment on the ground that the bill was needed as a recovery measure to help maintain wages and to increase purchasing power. The plea proved ineffective. The A.F.L. threw the whole strength of its organization against the measure; the House sent it back to committee. The President persisted. When Congress met in January, 1938, he once more recommended passage of legislation "to end starvation wages and intolerable hours." A new bill was drawn, but the House Rules Committee checked the whole movement by refusing to send the bill to the floor. A petition to discharge was needed. While such a procedure was usually a drawn-out affair, political events in the South hastened the process. In Florida and Alabama Claude Pepper and Lister Hill,

campaigning for Senate nominations, were vigorously attacked for
their support of wage-hour legislation. When both were nominated
by spectacular majorities, congressmen rushed to sign the discharge
petition.

The bill—known as the Fair Labor Standards Act—became law in
June, 1938. As finally drawn, administration of the law was turned
over to the Department of Labor. It applied to employees engaged
in interstate commerce or in producing goods for interstate commerce—certain agricultural workers, seamen engaged in fishing, and
domestic servants were exempted. It provided for the establishment
of a minimum wage of twenty-five cents an hour, which wage would
be gradually increased over a period of seven years until a forty-cent
minimum was reached; it provided also for the establishment of a
forty-four-hour week which would be reduced in three years to forty
hours. Employees who worked more than the maximum were entitled
to time and a half pay for overtime. The act also forbade labor of
children under sixteen in most occupations and under eighteen in
hazardous occupations.

Enforcement of the Fair Labor Standards Act proved much easier
than enforcement of the Wagner Act. Almost immediately the wages
of some 300,000 persons who were receiving less than the twenty-
five-cent minimum were raised, and the hours of some 1,300,000 who
worked more than forty-four hours were shortened. As the standards
were raised over the next seven years more and more laborers benefited. Some 600,000 children were also affected. But the constitutionality of the measure remained in doubt for some time. Like all other
New Deal legislation its legality was questioned and a case was
brought to the Supreme Court. In 1941 the Court, in the case of the
United States v. *Darby Lumber Company*, approved the act in a
unanimous decision. The Darby case climaxed several labor movements. One, designed to secure wages adequate to maintain a decent
standard of living, had begun with the wholesale-order stage of the
eighteenth century. A second, designed to shorten hours and to give
labor more leisure, had begun in earnest with a Boston carpenters'
strike in 1825. A third movement, designed to regulate and abolish
child labor, had begun in the antebellum period. New Deal legislation had brought all three to near completion.

While the controversy over wages and hours was at its height in

Congress, the A.F.L.-C.I.O. split also reached a climax. A.F.L. leaders watched the C.I.O.'s spectacular organizing drive in the mass-production industries during 1936 and 1937 with amazement; they had not expected such rampant success. Their amazement then turned to trepidation, for they soon recognized that they would have to take equivalent action or disappear in the sound and fury of the greatest labor upheaval the nation had ever witnessed. The A.F.L. met the challenge. Long moribund internationals stirred into life and began campaigns to add to their numbers. While their drives, at first, were confined almost entirely to craftsmen, it became apparent that the number of craftsmen in the nation was limited and that such campaigns had fixed boundaries. With this recognition various A.F.L. affiliates led by machinists and teamsters, invaded the semiskilled and unskilled ranks to enroll thousands of workingmen whom they had once scorned. The action began the transformation of the A.F.L. A number of internationals ceased to be simple craft unions; called "amalgamated crafts," they became in reality multiple "craft" or semi-industrial unions. Hundreds of thousands joined A.F.L. ranks, enough to offset the loss of C.I.O. seceders and more. By the end of 1937 the A.F.L. had 3,400,000 members: a million more than it had boasted when the New Deal began, a half-million more than when the C.I.O. unions seceded.

The sudden upsurge awakened the hope that all labor could be organized into a single union. The rank and file expressed the hope most fervently. A majority of them had never belonged to a labor union and had never developed hard and fast prejudices against rival organizations; the same majority, since it lived cheek by jowl with laborers in every occupation known to the nation, recognized that all workingmen had the same common problems. One big union with a single program could do wonders in advancing the common cause. Some labor leaders responded quickly to the wish, among them Dubinsky of the I.L.G.W.U. By October, 1937, the movement developed enough strength to require action; thirteen delegates from the two organizations began consultations in Washington. They made progress but not enough. Craft-union consciousness and the problem of domination proved insurmountable. The A.F.L. conferees, fearful of the tremendous influence which the C.I.O.'s thirty-two industrial organizations could wield, would agree only to a return of the original twelve C.I.O. unions; they insisted that the other twenty would have to be divided among the existing internationals. Humiliating as these conditions were, some C.I.O. conferees were willing to accept, but the majority insisted upon admission of all C.I.O unions intact. The dream of labor ranks was pushed into the background.

Failure of the unity negotiations resulted in a logical step: in May, 1938, the Committee for Industrial Organization transformed itself into the Congress of Industrial Organizations. Structurally the new C.I.O. did not differ much from the A.F.L. At the top was an Executive Council, named by an annual convention, with powers similar to those of the A.F.L. Council. The convention was an annual meeting of delegates from the various industrial unions who were given voting power based on membership. Provision was also made for the creation of state and local industrial councils. In spirit this structure reflected the fact that some of its more powerful leaders, like Lewis, were exponents of craft-union policies: the main aim of the organization was to secure immediate bread-and-butter objectives through collective bargaining.

On the other hand, there were some obvious and some subtle differences. The C.I.O. was pledged, though not exclusively, to advance industrial unionism. It was, thus, not an organization of the élite but of the whole mass of workingmen. The C.I.O. Executive Council and convention proved, in practice, to be more powerful bodies than their A.F.L. counterparts. The basis of this difference lay primarily in the fact that there were fewer personal rivalries among industrial union leaders and fewer jurisdictional rivalries between industrial unions; the result was the development of a harmony of interest that permitted the Executive Council to interfere extensively in local affairs and to set broad policies—with little intransigence displayed by the industrial unions. The C.I.O., in addition, was not wedded to traditional policies; since it recognized that labor's welfare depended not only on wages and hours but on national trends as well, it developed both a keen interest in the nation's economic and social policies and a broad program of social reform intending to aid labor by aiding society as a whole. This awareness was illustrated after the election of 1936 when the C.I.O. endorsed measures intended to increase farm income and to destroy farm tenancy and legislation to increase the public works program, to extend the low-rent housing program, and to enlarge the T.V.A.

The failure of unity negotiations in 1937 had another result. It created a civil war in the "house of labor." Although the A.F.L. and the C.I.O. had already engaged in sharp conflicts, these dwindled into minor skirmishes in comparison with the battles that now developed. In the late months of 1937 war for control of the nation's labor force broke out in every industry and trade. Both sides threw off the shackles of tradition and principle. The A.F.L. forgot its craft unionism organization and began chartering industrial unions; the C.I.O. in turn chartered craft unions. All scruples were thrown aside. Both sides indulged in "raiding"; both used scabbing tactics; both aired their grievances before the public in loud, passionate denunciations. The struggle for power, in short, produced a tremendous jurisdictional strife which involved almost every union in the nation. It was a dog-eat-dog conflict: A.F.L. carpenters against C.I.O. woodworkers; A.F.L. meatcutters against C.I.O. packinghouse workers; A.F.L. machinists against the automobile workers; A.F.L. electricians against C.I.O. electrical workers; A.F.L. teamsters against C.I.O. retail and wholesale workers and C.I.O. food and agricultural workers; A.F.L. paper mill workers against C.I.O. paper workers; A.F.L. municipal employees against C.I.O. public workers. No aspect of the nation's industry except the railways escaped the strife. The government became involved through the N.L.R.B., which was inevitably called upon to settle the problem of proper bargaining units in industry after industry. Even under peaceful conditions its task was not an easy one since the C.I.O. claimed all employees regardless of what work they did and the A.F.L. claimed all men who accomplished any task however faintly it resembled a craft. In the midst of bitter conflict the work of the N.L.R.B. became much more difficult. As the impartial mediator it soon became the object of attacks by the A.F.L. and the C.I.O. Both accused it of favoritism and partiality.

In some respects the conflict proved beneficial. It forced both organizations to bend every energy toward unionization. Some notable victories were scored. The C.I.O. steelworkers' campaign, stopped short by Little Steel in 1937, was pushed quietly and relentlessly to victory in 1941 when N.L.R.B. ordered the companies to recognize the steelworkers, to reinstate all employees who had lost their jobs through participation in strikes, to pay back wages, and to accept collective bargaining. By that date the steelworkers had 600,000 members.

The C.I.O.'s automobile campaign was also carried to conclusion with a successful organization of the Ford empire. The U.A.W. drive in the Ford plants had begun in 1937 against almost insurmountable odds: Henry Ford had a reputation both as a genius and as a high-paying employer; Ford also had a highly efficient "service" department, captained by Harry Bennett and made up of spies and a goon squad of toughs who made a living keeping the union out of the plants. Nevertheless, the U.A.W. went to work on Ford's huge River Rouge plant, manned by some 85,000 workers. In the first year, it made little impression. On top of this failure came the recession of 1937–1938, which created large-scale unemployment. A crisis developed within the union; it came to a head in mid-1938 when the organization ousted Homer Martin and elected R. J. Thomas as president. The Martin forces, about one-fifth of the union, promptly joined the A.F.L., and for a few months jurisdictional conflicts threatened to shatter automobile unionism; ultimately the U.A.W. closed ranks and reengaged in conflict with Ford. In the spring of 1941, 200,000 Ford workers laid down their tools. The company surrendered; an election to determine the bargaining agent gave victory to the U.A.W. by a count of 51,000 to 20,000. Ford then signed an agreement which provided for a closed shop, retroactive wage increases, seniority rights, the checkoff, and the abolition of the "service department." Shortly afterward General Motors signed a similar contract for eighty-one plants and Chrysler for its entire empire.

Jurisdictional conflict also had a harmful effect upon labor. As the struggle between A.F.L. and C.I.O. advanced, it grew steadily more bitter; deep-seated enmities and hatreds developed among rival labor leaders, and even the rank and file became involved in personal feuds. In addition to making reconciliation improbable, the irrationality of the conflict had an adverse effect upon the public. Denunciations which sounded much like those charges which employers had often aimed at labor leaders made the public wonder if its sympathy for labor had not been misplaced. The veritable rash of strikes which broke out over jurisdiction in every industry, strikes which employers were helpless to check and which affected the whole economy, made the public wonder if it was not becoming the victim of irresponsible labor tactics. It began to grumble about "Big Labor" and its methods, to talk seriously about laws to regulate labor practices.

The reaction proved unfortunate. The growing hostility to labor tactics gave thousands of employers who had never been reconciled to the New Deal's labor program a foundation to begin a counter-attack on many fronts. A barrage of propaganda accusing labor of trying to rule or ruin the nation's economy heralded the campaign. Many employers began to disregard laws protecting labor. A drive to enact state legislation designed to check the effect of the New Deal's program was inaugurated. The campaign began in Oregon where a jurisdictional dispute which closed down the lumber industry for a great many months in 1937–1938 aroused public hostility to the point where the voters by referendum enacted a drastic antilabor law, severely limiting union activity. By 1940 four states had passed anti-union laws which variously outlawed sit-down strikes, jurisdictional strikes, some forms of picketing, secondary boycotts, and use of force, coercion, intimidation, or threat to compel persons to join labor unions or stop working.

Public reaction also formed the basis for a concerted employer attack upon the Wagner Act. Although employers had attacked it as one-sided from its introduction, such criticism had made little impression since the public and Congress had reasoned that the act had to be one-sided to redress the balance of power held by employers in their relations with employees. Once labor revealed its power, however, the public began to wonder if a balance was not more desirable. Employers used the sentiment to conduct a strong campaign for amending the act, proposing measures to favor the more conservative trade unions at the expense of the more aggressive industrial unions, to exclude agricultural and lumber workers, and to abolish the closed shop, the jurisdictional strike, boycotts, the check-off, and industry-wide bargaining. Employers also seized upon the A.F.L.-C.I.O. charges of favoritism and enlarged upon them in an attempt to discredit the N.L.R.B. Although a long investigation by Congress failed to reveal any indications of favoritism, the impression that the board was in fact pro-labor and anti-industry became general.

Employer campaigns for state laws to check labor and employer efforts to weaken the Wagner Act might have had a much greater success after 1937 if labor had not been so well organized, and particularly if labor had not been playing an important political role. Between the elections of 1936 and 1940 labor's political activity increased markedly. The American Labor party of New York City, made up primarily of socialistic needle trade workers, led the movement for reelection of Fiorello La Guardia as mayor. The Non-Partisan League worked closely with the Democratic party in New Jersey and Pennsylvania; conducted a vigorous, though unsuccessful, campaign to give Detroit a labor administration; and supported the Roosevelt purge in the congressional elections of 1938. In Washington the league's lobby supported Roosevelt's Supreme Court reform measures and worked assiduously for the enactment of a wage-hour law. The C.I.O., in addition, supported the Farm Tenant Act, the second Agricultural Adjustment Act, and the Wagner-Steagall Housing Act. Its most significant effort during the period was its campaign to fight off the employer drive to emasculate the Wagner Act and to discredit the N.L.R.B.

Its very success, however, gave rise to a stronger campaign to discredit labor through the charge that the C.I.O. was communist-led. In some respects the indictment had a real basis. During the N.R.A. period the communists had played only a minor role in the labor upheaval. In mid-decade, however, coincidentally with a change of party line in Moscow which began to preach support of a united Democratic front, the communists suddenly became active supporters of the new movement. Almost in a body they threw themselves into C.I.O. organizing campaigns and the Non-Partisan League's political activities.

The action created no crisis. Although C.I.O. leaders recognized that the communists were intent upon using "wooden horse" tactics to strengthen communism by placing party members in key positions, the organization could not afford to reject their help. What happened was well described by McAlister Coleman in *Men and Coal*:

Tight-lipped, humorless youngsters, burning with the hard flame of the class struggle, were soon displacing the easygoing, slapdash run of clerical help at union headquarters and making themselves invaluable by their diligence and willingness to take any job no matter how menial. They were indefatigable meeting-goers, caucusing before every gathering, acting as a group and bewildering the rank and file by their references to *Robert's Rules of Order*. No such disciplined, religious-minded zealots had appeared in the labor movement since the days of the Socialist Labor party, and while old-line unionists looked upon them with cold distaste, they had to admit that the Communists were "horses for work."

The communists, accordingly, were allowed to play a highly important role in the C.I.O.'s organizing drive; in the process they and their fellow travelers won many key positions in the new industrial unions and even secured seats upon the C.I.O. Executive Council. By 1940 it was generally known that they controlled locals in the electrical, radio, woodworking, fur, and leather industries, and the unions of the municipal, transport, and maritime workers. Early attacks upon communist influence in the C.I.O. and the Non-Partisan League had little effect. While C.I.O. leaders admitted to the danger in their midst, they also recognized that the vast bulk of union members were conservative and loyal to democracy and capitalism and that the rank and file of even communist-controlled unions could not be led too far along the party line. The C.I.O. continued to accept communist help. Its answer to criticism was, "The bosses hire them; why shouldn't we organize them."

In late 1939 the situation changed: Germany and Russia signed their infamous pact, Nazi Germany declared war on Poland and Soviet Russia seized Polish territory. The outbreak of the war immediately raised the possibility of American participation. A substantial majority of the people, including the leaders of the A.F.L. and the C.I.O., revealed themselves to be strongly opposed to entrance into the war. At the same time the leadership of the A.F.L. and the C.I.O. indicated that it was willing to use every energy to support the Roosevelt policy of building our own defenses and extending aid to the Allies. Labor, and particularly the C.I.O., was not united on this point. The communists in the organization, once the world's most virulent fighters against fascism, now became the bitter opponents of Roosevelt's "aid to the Allies" policy, and a large number of the rank and file followed their lead. It was quickly recognized that this split in labor ranks would have a marked effect upon the 1940 presidential campaign, already complicated by the question of a third term for Roosevelt. Labor in general was urging the President to run again, but whether he could command its united support as in the past was questionable. Communism had thus finally come to embarrass both the C.I.O. and the Non-Partisan League.

The communist issue did not come to a head during the campaign. Very early in 1940 it was replaced by the issue of John L. Lewis, who at the U.M.W. convention in January, 1940, suddenly announced his opposition to Roosevelt's renomination. There have been many explanations of the act. Often accepted is the charge that a break occurred when Roosevelt refused to accept C.I.O. dictation after the election of 1936. Lewis, the account runs, had assumed that he himself had been responsible for delivering the labor vote which gave such a sweeping victory to the Democratic party in 1936. During the General Motors sit-down in 1937 Lewis indicated what he expected as a *quid pro quo* by his now famous statement:

For six months the economic royalists represented by General Motors contributed their money and used their energy to drive this administration out of power. The administration asked labor for help and labor gave it. The same economic royalists now have their fangs in labor. The workers of this country expect the administration to help the workers in every legal way and to support the workers in General Motors plants.

Roosevelt remained silent, and Lewis began to nurse a grudge. During the "Little Steel" strike the breach was widened when Roosevelt, in a moment of exasperation, called down "a plague o' both your houses." Lewis promptly denounced the statement as a betrayal of labor: "It ill behooves one who has supped at labor's table and who has been sheltered in labor's house to curse with equal fervor and fine impartiality both labor and its adversaries when they become locked in deadly embrace." The final break came late in 1939 when objections to a third term became strong. According to Mrs. Perkins, Lewis approached Roosevelt with the suggestion that if he were Roosevelt's running mate in the 1940 campaign all objections to the third term would disappear; Roosevelt could then count upon the united support of labor and liberals. Roosevelt, however, brushed the suggestion aside and made the break permanent.

This explanation is hardly the whole story. Internal C.I.O. politics were also involved. While Lewis, in 1939, was undoubtedly the nation's outstanding labor leader, he was at odds with a number of his ablest lieutenants over many C.I.O. policies. They did not like his opposition to a rapprochement with the A.F.L.; they felt that he was responsible for much of the jurisdictional conflict which had aroused public hostility during the past year; they suspected that he was returning to the old trade unionist "public be damned" policy which had earned labor nothing but enemies; they objected to his too close association and support of communists and left-wingers in C.I.O. ranks at a time when expediency seemed to demand a purge; they likewise found themselves at odds with his isolationism, his opposition to granting any aid to the allies. Lewis, in short, needed some dramatic victory to regain his former domination.

Whatever the cause of the break, Lewis announced it when he told the U.M.W. convention in January, 1940: "Should the Democratic National Convention be coerced or dragooned into nominating him, I am convinced [that] his candidacy would result in ignominious defeat." In the months that followed Lewis continued his opposition, attacking the New Deal because it had failed to bring about economic recovery, because its policies had prolonged the depression. His position caused consternation both to Democrats and to labor. Democrats feared a major split in labor ranks; labor chieftains engaged in long heart searching concerning their course. Late in the campaign Lewis added to the perturbation with a radio speech. "I think the reelection of President Roosevelt for a third term," he announced, "would be a national evil of the first magnitude. He no longer hears the cries of the people. I think that the election of Mr. Wendell Willkie is imperative in relation to the country's needs. I commend him to the men and women of labor." It was obvious, he continued, that the President could not be reelected unless he had the overwhelming support of labor. "If he is, therefore, elected," Lewis declared, "it will mean that the members of the Congress of Industrial Organizations have rejected my advice and recommendation. I will accept the result as being the equivalent of a vote of no confidence and will retire as president of the Congress of Industrial Organizations in November."

Lewis' motive was not clear, for by the time he made his address labor leaders had chosen sides. William Green, a majority of A.F.L. leaders and unions, Lewis' lieutenants, and almost all C.I.O. organizations had announced their support of Roosevelt. Lewis may have felt that his announcement would influence enough of the C.I.O. rank and file to bring about Roosevelt's defeat, or he may have recognized that his days as C.I.O. president were numbered and was providing for retirement in a blaze of drama. Whatever the motive, the election made clear that Lewis had no control over labor's political opinions. The labor vote for Roosevelt was just as heavy as in the past. Even the miners voted for a third term. Lewis kept his pledge. At the next C.I.O. convention he resigned his office. There was little lamentation. Prepared for the event, the C.I.O. named Philip Murray as its new president.

Murray, born in Scotland, had joined the U.M.W. in 1902. His rise within the organization was not rapid; at thirty, he became president of District 5; four years later, in 1920, he became U.M.W. vice president. In that position, where he soon displayed his abilities as an administrator and organizer, he became Lewis' faithful alter ego. The public first became aware of him when he took over the leadership of the Steel Workers' Organizing Committee. His election ultimately brought a change in the C.I.O. A moderate, self-effacing man, he did not seek conflict unnecessarily. A man who to a large extent held to the old trade-unionist idea that organization and collective bargaining would solve much of labor's problems, he nevertheless developed a strong interest in social reform. Although many feared that Murray would become a Lewis mouthpiece, he promptly asserted his independence. He announced support for Roosevelt's aid to the Allies program; as a condition of his election he secured a resolution condemning communism and all foreign ideologies. The C.I.O. had begun to move out from under the Lewis shadow.

The nation had not heard the last of Lewis. The period between the reelection of Roosevelt and the attack upon Pearl Harbor was one in which aid to the Allies and the national defense programs created a tremendous industrial boom, which for the first time in more than a decade gave the nation a taste of prosperity and produced a strong demand for labor in all industries connected with war production. In some cases it produced a demand for workers difficult to find, for during the depression tens of thousands of workmen had lost their skills and apprentices had not been trained. A nationwide hunt followed for craftsmen engaged on emergency employment projects like the W.P.A., or who were engaged in industry at jobs that required little skill. Older men, regarded as unfit for industrial employment, were persuaded to return to work. The demand for skills was not met. It was necessary to resort to a training program. Between July, 1940, and December, 1941, some 2,500,000 people were given training to fit them for jobs in war plants—in vocational and trade schools, in colleges, in shops set up in public schools, and "on the job."

The demand for labor quickly reduced the unemployment rolls; between April, 1940, and December, 1941, the unemployed decreased from 8,800,000 to 3,800,000. At the same time the number of persons employed in nonagricultural pursuits increased 5,700,000, and the size of the armed forces, which stood at 882,000 in November, 1940, increased to 2,071,000 by November, 1941. Increase in employment was accompanied by higher wages. The payroll index advanced from 107.8 in 1940 to 195.4 by December, 1941; average weekly earnings increased from $29.88 to $38.62. Average weekly hours also increased with the reappearance of overtime from 39.2 in 1940 to 42.8 by December, 1941.

Labor unions, observing the vast influx of men and women into industry, determined to capture the new element. While, for the most part, they pursued a reasonable course, some unions, particularly newer ones, were unable to maintain discipline among their membership. These revealed a highly belligerent attitude toward employers and made excessive and unwarranted demands. The majority of industrial employers also pursued a moderate policy in their labor relations. There were some, however, who turned obdurate. They stubbornly refused to extend union recognition, refused new wage demands, and attacked the closed shop as un-American. Their policy followed the tactics that had developed since 1937 with one addition: they surrounded their antilabor position with a halo of patriotism; they were fighting labor in the interest of national defense. Irresponsible unions and obdurate employers made the year 1941 one of almost constant industrial strife. Large strikes occurred in the automobile industry, in the shipyards, in the building trades, in steel, coal, and textiles. Altogether nearly 4,300 strikes occurred, involving over 2,000,000 workmen, more than 8 per cent of the nation's industrial wage earners.

Because of their often harmful effect upon the national defense program, the strikes alarmed the Federal Government. Accordingly, in March, 1941, President Roosevelt, borrowing a page from the record of the First World War, created a National Defense Mediation Board, representing management, labor, and the public, with the right to attempt settlement of disputes in defense industries. The board was able in most cases to secure settlement, but since it had no power to enforce decisions it sometimes failed. In those instances more drastic action followed. In one case the War Department seized the strike-bound North American aviation plant at Inglewood, California; in another the Navy Department seized the Federal Shipbuilding and Dry Dock Company at Kearny, New Jersey, when the company refused to accept a Mediation Board proposal for maintenance of union membership.

But the biggest problem was Lewis. The one-time C.I.O. head remained quiet until the fall of 1941 when he leaped into prominence again with a demand that the steel industry recognize the union shop in its captive mines. Steel refused, and the dispute was referred to the Mediation Board. In spite of the government's long support of unionization, the board was doubtful of its right to insist upon a union shop in a government-sanctioned contract, and failed to include Lewis' demand in its suggestion for solution. Lewis immediately called a strike in the captive coal mines which threatened to shut down the entire steel industry. The act, roundly denounced by Roosevelt as "selfish obstruction," produced loud demands for anti-union legislation. Before any action was taken, Lewis and Myron C. Taylor, chairman of United States Steel, agreed to resubmit the controversy to the Mediation Board. Neither, however, agreed to be bound by the board's decisions. A truce was called and the miners returned to work. The board's decision went against the miners by a count of nine to two, only the C.I.O. members dissenting on the ground that the union shop was not a matter of government order but of collective bargaining. The strike was renewed—with the support of the C.I.O., whose convention upheld Lewis' position and whose members resigned from the Mediation Board—and soon spread from captive to other mines. In a short time 250,000 miners were idle and the steel industry began to show signs of strain. Lewis, however, suddenly called off the strike when Roosevelt suggested that the issue be arbitrated by a three-man tribunal made up of Lewis, Benjamin Fairless, president of United States Steel, and John R. Steelman of the United States Conciliation Service. The tribunal granted Lewis his demands.

His action was to prove costly to labor. During 1941 the public, influenced by the propaganda of antilabor newspapers and employers who constantly reiterated the charge that labor was setting its own selfish aims above national defense, and by the knowledge that a number of strikes that year were communist inspired, began to doubt labor's patriotism. During 1940 and 1941 some sixteen states in the South and Southwest passed antilabor laws of varying degrees of harshness; during 1941 some thirty antilabor bills were introduced into Congress. The coal strike served to intensify public hostility; demands for legislation to curb the power of labor unions and to protect the public welfare grew loud. All through the coal conflict Congress debated antilabor measures; on December 2nd the House approved by a vote of 252 to 136 a measure to prohibit all strikes in defense industries involving the closed shop or growing out of jurisdictional disputes, and any other strikes not approved by a majority of workers after a thirty-day cooling-off period. The measure, denounced by Murray as "subversive" and by Green as "oppressive," did not become law. Before it was given any consideration in the Senate, the attack upon Pearl Harbor occurred and the problem of labor was pushed into the background. As the war began, however, it was evident that the public no longer regarded labor's actions with full sympathy.

26 —

Labor and the Second World War

Fundamentally, labor's role in the Second World War was one of energetic cooperation with the government, with industry, and with itself. The spirit which labor was to display throughout the war was expressed by John L. Lewis shortly after Pearl Harbor: "When the nation is attacked, every American must rally to its defense. All other considerations become insignificant." Though Lewis himself was accused of disregarding this maxim, and labor was often similarly accused, the overwhelming majority of labor unions, labor leaders, and labor rank and file never forgot that the nation came first.

Labor's chief contribution to the war effort was made upon the production lines. The problem of production was highly complicated —involving conversion, utilization of existing plants, and allocation of materials. Even before the war the government had taken steps toward ultimate solution of these problems through the creation of the Council of National Defense, the Office of Production Management, the Office of Emergency Management, the Economic Defense Board, and the Supply Priorities and Allocations Board. These agencies hardly solved the problems involved since the nation was not at war during these years, and it was difficult to persuade industry to check its highly profitable production of peacetime goods.

Labor revealed a keen interest in this prewar conversion program throughout 1941. Early that year various labor leaders demanded that labor be given representation upon the governmental agencies that might be created to determine the nation's economic policy during the emergency. When the O.P.M. was established, Sidney Hillman was named codirector. Later, Walter Reuther, vice president of the U.A.W., offered government and industry a conversion program. Never adopted by the government, scorned by industry as impracticable, the Reuther plan nevertheless made an impression. Adopted as official policy by the C.I.O., the plan became a monument to labor's prewar interest in the nation's defense preparations.

The interest was rewarded. In December, 1941, Congress enacted a War Powers Act authorizing the President to redistribute the tasks of the various Federal agencies in order to achieve the most efficient prosecution of the war. Under this act President Roosevelt established the War Production Board containing a Man-Power Requirement and Labor Production Division, headed by a labor representative and assisted by labor advisory boards. Inclusion of these sections gave labor an opportunity to make an important contribution to the production drive with a program for establishment of labor-management committees in all defense plants to put into effect the suggestions of workmen for improving techniques and saving time. Denounced by industry as socialism and as a "foolish experiment," the W.P.B. nevertheless put the program into effect. In one year 1,900 plants had adopted the plan; by the end of the war some 5,000 plants were using labor-management committees and showing marked improvement in their efficiency.

War production also involved the problem of an adequate labor supply. The needs of the armed services during the Second World War were greater than at any time in the nation's history. During the course of the war some 11,000,000 men and women dropped their peacetime pursuits to enter the armed services. At least 60 per cent either were employed in industry and allied enterprises or would have become industrial workers under normal circumstances. The manpower needs of the fighting front thus created a very large gap in the nation's labor supply. In addition the need for war material increased the demand for industrial workers to hitherto unheard-of numbers. In 1938 nonagricultural enterprises used the services of 27,000,000 persons; by war's end the total of nonagricultural employees reached 38,000,000. This additional working force was recruited from many elements: the formerly unemployed, the normally unemployable, farmers, oldsters, women—of which there were 6,000,-000 employed—and children who were ordinarily barred from industry.

A most difficult problem to solve was that of an efficient distribution of the labor supply. Although the nation's industrial machinery was well distributed across the continent, the government's contract policy and war needs created a demand for labor in areas where sufficient manpower was not available or where it could be secured only by luring farmers from the neighboring agricultural areas. At first the government hoped that these geographical labor shortages would be solved through wage incentives. War plants were encouraged to increase pay rates and overtime. By September, 1942, the average durable goods plant paid $1.00 an hour and worked a 45-hour week, while the average nondurable goods plant paid 75 cents an hour and worked a 40-hour week. Though such incentives attracted men to war plants, it was not long before war plants began to lure workers from other similar plants. This activity was injurious to the war effort: it drained manpower from agriculture; it created a large turnover; it brought the loss of millions of man hours of labor; and it contributed to wartime inflationary tendencies.

To solve the problems of numbers and of distribution, bills to increase the work week to forty-eight hours were introduced into Congress. President Roosevelt, industry, and labor all opposed such action: Roosevelt and industry because it would create a demand for wage increases; labor because it feared a postwar return to a forty-eight-hour week. Labor, however, voluntarily agreed to abandon double pay for Sunday and holiday work. In April, 1942, President Roosevelt created the War Manpower Commission to coordinate the recruitment, placement, and training of manpower; both the A.F.L. and the C.I.O. were represented on the commission's Policy Committee. During most of the first year of its operation the W.M.C. made no striking contributions: it did no more than assume direction of the United States Employment Service which undertook the task of matching workers with essential jobs. In December, 1942, the War Manpower Commission took control of Selective Service with the idea that it could more thoroughly influence the allocation of manpower, and in February, 1943, it inaugurated a new policy of substituting "essentiality of employment" for dependency as the basis for draft deferment with the hope that it would induce married men to shift to more essential occupations. These measures did not solve either the problem of numbers or that of distribution. Many factories worked shifts of less than forty-eight hours, and war plants continued to lure workers from other essential employments. Turnover and consequent absenteeism remained high.

Further expedients were tried. In February, 1943, the President ordered defense industries to institute a forty-eight-hour week, with time and a half for more than forty hours. The W.M.C. was empowered to carry out the order. The commission immediately designated some thirty-two labor shortage areas in which the longer work week would be put into effect. In April, 1943, the W.M.C. issued an order "freezing" workers to their jobs; it forbade workers engaged in essential activity to shift to other jobs at higher pay rate except with the approval of the commission. All recruitment of labor, thereafter, was to be handled through the USES. These various orders and developments brought results. The work week increased; pirating of workers from essential industries, turnovers, and absenteeism decreased. Nevertheless, the problems of numbers and distribution remained so acute that late in the year the President recommended the passage of a national service act which would have empowered the W.M.C. to draft men and women for farm and factory work. Congress revealed a strong reluctance to enact such a measure. Labor opposition, some alleviation in the manpower problem in 1944 and 1945—in which union propaganda upon its members to stay on the job and to work the limit played a part—and the favorable military situation pushed the bill into the background.

In spite of shortages and maldistribution of manpower, production of war goods reached record proportions. By the war's end, man days of labor increased 50 per cent over 1939; output increased nearly 100 per cent. Industry and labor produced nearly 300,000 military aircraft, 71,000 naval vessels, 45,000,000 tons of merchant shipping, 17,000,000 small arms, 2,700,000 machine guns, 315,000 pieces of artillery, 165,000 naval guns, 86,000 tanks, 16,000 armored cars, 88,-000 scout cars, 2,500,000 trucks, 990,000 light vehicles, and 124,000 tractors. It was this production which was the greatest single factor in winning the war.

Labor's contribution to the war effort was revealed on several other fronts. Much of it appeared in the support it gave to governmental policies, in the aid extended toward the administration of those policies, and in the formulation of the policies themselves. Labor became a strong supporter of a heavy tax policy designed both to pay as large a proportion of the cost of war as possible and to retard inflation; it gave energetic support to the pay-as-you-go tax plan as proposed by Beardsley Ruml and adopted in modified form by the Treasury Department.

Labor also became the strong advocate of price control. As early as June, 1941, as the cost of living began a sharp rise, various labor leaders urged passage of price-control legislation. With the opening of the war, labor, remembering the inflation of the First World War, increased its demands. The Price Control Act which became law in January, 1942, was a partial answer; it authorized the establishment of an Office of Price Administration empowered to fix fair maximum prices, to stabilize or reduce rents in defense areas, and to ration scarce consumer goods. The interest of labor in the O.P.A. program was recognized with the establishment of a labor policy committee within the agency. The committee became labor's spokesman in demanding firm measures. It had considerable influence in securing the establishment of the General Maximum Price Regulation in April, 1942, and in establishing rent controls in October, 1942. It was tireless in its demand that the President's hold-the-line order of April, 1943, be rigorously enforced on all cost of living articles. The committee, in short, deserved considerable credit for the O.P.A.'s success in holding down the increase in the cost of living during the war to 29 per cent.

Labor cooperation with the war effort occurred in other areas. Scores enrolled in the Coast Guard Auxiliary; hundreds of labor leaders served on local draft boards. The Office of Civilian Defense, established five months before the war began, contained a labor policy committee; tens of thousands of laboring men offered their services to the O.C.D. as air raid wardens and auxiliary firemen; thousands took training to provide emergency medical service and thousands manned aircraft warning stations.

Labor's contribution was not without its accompanying conflict. The war began in the midst of a strong public reaction against labor. Friends of labor feared that this sentiment might result in the enactment of repressive legislation; on the other hand the antilabor element revealed some apprehension that labor might use the war emergency to advance its position at the expense of the nation. To prevent either event President Roosevelt called a conference of business and labor leaders to establish some basis for wartime cooperation. The conference agreed upon a program: no strikes or lockouts for the duration, peaceful settlement of industrial disputes, and the creation of a War Labor Board to handle all disputes which could not be solved through normal procedures. The agreement was highly important to labor since it not only provided for surrender of its most potent weapon but also suspended collective bargaining procedures for the duration. Labor, in brief, placed its fortunes in the lap of a commission. The action did not prove unduly injurious. In January, 1942, President Roosevelt appointed a War Labor Board with William H. Davis as chairman and made up of representatives of management, labor, and the public. The board was specifically authorized to assume responsibility for settlement of any industrial dispute which in the opinion of the secretary of labor might interrupt work contributing to the effective prosecution of the war. Decisions of the board were to be binding on both industry and labor.

The board was expected to keep production lines moving; it carried out the task conscientiously and fairly. One of its first problems was to find a solution for the union security issue, which had been involved in the captive mine strike and had wrecked the Mediation Board. Against the wishes of the management members, the board in 1942 found a compromise in the "maintenance of membership" program. This solution provided that union members or those who joined a union would remain members of the union during the life of the contract negotiated on their behalf; failure to maintain union standing would subject an employee to discharge. The solution, ultimately applied to some 3,000,000 workers, proved inspired. It assured labor that industry would not be able to take advantage of its no-strike policy to destroy labor unionism; it guaranteed labor that its membership rolls would not be depleted. Its chief result was a sharp decline in strikes during 1942.

The board was also faced with the even more perplexing problem of adjusting wages to the rising cost of living. At first it attempted individual solutions of granting increases where they seemed warranted. But after April, 1942, when the administration issued the General Maximum Price Regulation intended to stabilize both prices and wages, the board was handed the problem of promoting wage stabilization and at the same time making adjustments for inequalities and inflation. Its solution to this problem, announced in mid-1942, developed from a demand by employees of "Little Steel" for a dollar-a-day increase in wages. The board decided to limit the increase to the rise between January 1, 1941, and May, 1942, during which time the cost of living increased 15 per cent. The board granted the steelworkers an increase of forty-four cents a day. The action became known as the Little Steel formula.

Labor had no strong quarrel with the formula so long as prices were held down, but the cost of living continued to rise, making it difficult to reconcile the formula with realities. In October, 1942, Congress made the situation even more difficult with the Anti-Inflation Act, which directed the W.L.B. to limit all hourly wage increases, except where substandard or highly inequitable wages prevailed, to 15 per cent. By April, 1943, when the cost-of-living index reached

124, labor unions were complaining that they had been "sold down the river" for the benefit of farmers and industrialists and demanded revision of the formula. The government demurred; although it recognized the explosive qualities of the situation, it refused to permit any upward adjustment in wages. Instead President Roosevelt issued his hold-the-line order. A more vigorous enforcement of rent and price controls resulted; during the next twenty-one months the cost-of-living index rose only 1 per cent.

Labor was not satisfied. While a check on the rise in prices was desirable, such a check did not adjust existing discrepancies. Labor grew increasingly restless. A large number of strikes broke out during 1943. The vast majority were trivial—"quickies" and local affairs unauthorized by union leaders. They were caused by a number of factors: the strain of war, long hours, poor housing conditions in many industrial areas, failure to secure adjustment of minor grievances, long delay in settlement of disputes by the War Labor Board, resentment over the W.M.C. freeze order and over high prices. Often the strikes served a useful purpose, allowing men to let off steam and to take a vacation. Usually this was all that was needed to bring about quick adjustment. In and of themselves, such actions caused little interruption of production. But the sum total of interruptions had some effect. During the year 2,000,000 workers became involved in strikes; 13,000,000 man days of labor were lost, as compared to 4,800,-000 in 1942—one-seventh of 1 per cent of the total working time.

Not all strikes were trivial. During 1943 Lewis and the U.M.W. involved the nation in a serious situation. It began in April when Lewis asked for a new contract with a $2.00 a day increase and pay for travel time underground—the so-called "portal to portal" wage. He argued that the increase was necessary to adjust wages to the increased cost of living. Since the operators refused to negotiate on these terms the dispute was referred to the War Labor Board. Lewis announced that he did not recognize the board's authority. Reminded that he was a party to labor's no-strike pledge, Lewis announced that he would call no strike, but, he added, the miners would be reluctant to "trespass" upon mine property if they had no contract. On April 30th U.M.W. members stopped working and the nation was confronted with a potential crisis: if the strike lasted long enough war production would be seriously injured.

President Roosevelt acted quickly; he ordered government seizure of the coal mines and appealed to the miners to return to work under the old contract, promising that every effort would be made to adjust grievances. The miners returned when Lewis announced a thirty-day truce. Six months of controversy followed, during which time Secretary of Interior Ickes, who had been placed in charge of the mines, and Lewis conducted negotiations which the War Labor Board refused to approve because they violated the Little Steel formula. Twice during the summer work was stopped. The climax came in October when for a fourth time the miners quit work. This time Ickes and Lewis reached an agreement which satisfied the War Labor Board. Through a very complicated formula—which included vacation pay, portal-to-portal pay, and an increase in the length of the working day—miners received an increase of $1.50 a day. Since the hourly wage increase was within the Little Steel formula the War Labor Board approved. Lewis and the miners were satisfied.

As with other Lewis victories, labor paid a penalty. During 1943 public disapproval of labor policies increased. A fear that labor had secured a power which would enable it to choke off the nation's entire war effort appeared in many quarters. The nation's metropolitan newspapers, which had long been antilabor, and most of the rural press, which took its tone from its urban contemporaries, lost no opportunity to exploit this feeling. They gave wide publicity to every strike, no matter how trivial; continually accused labor of breaking its no-strike pledge; and exaggerated the menace of labor's policies to war efforts. At the same time they made no effort to present labor's grievances or to reveal how quickly most strikes were ended. Newspaper columnists and radio commentators aided the campaign. The coal conflict climaxed this presentation. Lewis was portrayed as Hitler's ally, and it was easy to transform this charge of unpatriotic behavior from Lewis to the entire U.M.W. and to labor itself. Antilabor employers also took advantage of the situation to remind the public of unpopular union practices, like featherbedding, which were injuring the war effort, to accuse unions of irresponsibility, and to enlarge on the dangers of industry-wide strikes.

The propaganda had its effect. President Roosevelt proposed raising the draft age for noncombatant service so that strikers could be brought into the army and then be assigned to work; five states enacted legislation prohibiting the closed shop or union security agreements; a large number of antilabor bills were introduced into Congress. Of all these measures the most important was introduced by two notorious antilabor congressmen, Howard W. Smith of Virginia and Tom Connally of Texas. It provided for the calling of strikes only after a strike vote was taken by the N.L.R.B. during a thirty-day "cooling off" period; for governmental seizure of any plant where a halt in production threatened the war effort, and for criminal penalties to be imposed on any person who instigated or promoted a strike. In addition it prohibited all union contributions to political campaign funds. The Smith-Connally bill went through both houses of Congress by decisive majorities. Although the President vetoed the measure because it ran contrary to labor's no-strike pledge and because it would create labor unrest, Congress paid no attention. The bill was enacted over his veto.

The Smith-Connally Act did not wholly repress labor. Union men were still angry over the fact that the Little Steel formula was working to their disadvantage; they saw the nation basking in prosperity while their own economic advances had been strait-jacketed. Their demand for modification of the formula became more acute. Early in 1944 the President himself recognized the justice of the demand, when railway workers threatened a rail tie-up if their wages were not increased, by approving rail wage increases beyond the Little Steel formula. The award gave the War Labor Board its clue. It began to meet labor demands by resorting to so-called "fringe benefits." It approved vacations and holidays with pay and allowances for travel time and lunch periods, permitted bonus and incentive payments and higher wages for night work. It also opened the way for further increases by ruling that the establishment of health and insurance funds was a legitimate subject for collective bargaining and that women deserved equal pay for equal work. Although these decisions were frequently criticized by management because they nullified the spirit of the Little Steel formula and by labor because they did not take into account the increase in prices since May, 1942, the decisions served their purpose. To a remarkable degree they quieted labor unrest in the last two years of the war, reducing strikes to less than one-third the prewar average.

How thoroughly the board's decisions met the nation's needs could be judged from the fact that out of 20,000 settlements which it imposed and out of 415,000 wage agreements which it approved, involving altogether some 20,000,000 workers, only fifty were disputed after the enactment of the Smith-Connally Act. In those cases the board recommended seizure. The President followed the recommendation in every case: twenty-six times because a union defied the board's decisions, twenty-three times because employers defied decisions, and once because neither management nor labor could agree.

The board's actions, moreover, proved of great significance to labor. During previous wars labor had generally lost some of the status and power it had enjoyed on the eve of the war. In the Second World War, in spite of tremendous pressure, the War Labor Board resisted all efforts that threatened to bring a deterioration in labor's position. It strongly supported the right to organize and bargain collectively through the maintenance-of-union-membership formula, which to a large degree enabled labor to continue "business as usual." Unions did not neglect the opportunity. By the end of the war they could boast 14,000,000 members: 6,800,000 in the A.F.L., which recovered the allegiance of both the I.L.G.W.U. and the U.M.W.; 6,000,000 in the C.I.O. Within the limits imposed upon it the board also maintained labor's right to an adequate wage. In attempting to maintain that right, it actually gave approval to, and in a sense created, additional institutions which would in time improve labor welfare.

While the board could protect labor's position in relation to industry, it could do nothing in regard to labor's internal problems. During the war the constant wrangling which had occurred between the A.F.L. and the C.I.O. abated markedly. At the same time division appeared within the C.I.O. Shortly after the war began, Lewis, who was still chairman of the committee to negotiate peace with the A. F.L., issued an invitation to Green and Murray to resume negotiations. The act marked the beginning of a new labor cleavage. Murray announced angrily that any negotiations with the A.F.L. would be initiated through his office. The differences between Murray and Lewis were further emphasized in May, 1942, when Murray attacked Lewis as a man "hell bent on creating national confusion and national disunity." Simultaneously the C.I.O. Executive Council reminded the U.M.W. that it alone of all affiliates had failed to announce a program for "gearing the nation's economy to the needs of the war." Lewis promptly demanded an apology. When none was offered, the U.M.W. demanded that the C.I.O. return $1,665,000 which the miners had loaned it. The C.I.O. disavowed the debt. In October, 1942, the mine union seceded from the organization it had helped to create.

With this break Lewis appeared to be declaring war against all organized labor, for the U.M.W. also announced that it would now seek to extend its jurisdiction over all unorganized workers. Its campaign in fact had already begun through catch-all District 50, which had been organizing coal by-product and chemical workers since 1934. The secession worried both the A.F.L. and the C.I.O. Green was inclined to condemn it as a campaign to create triunionism. Murray interpreted the act as the first step in a campaign to capture control of the A.F.L. The interpretation led the C.I.O. to move in two directions at once: to place firmer control over policies in the hands of the Executive Council and to negotiate a small rapprochement with the A.F.L. whereby the two organizations agreed to arbitrate jurisdictional disputes.

The question of Lewis' aims was soon forgotten in the outbreak of the 1943 coal conflict. That strike put the C.I.O. in a dilemma. On the one hand many of its members sympathized with Lewis' argument that the Little Steel formula was forcing labor to make sacrifices which no other element was obliged to make. On the other hand many C.I.O. leaders feared that Lewis' defiance of the government would be harmful to labor; they denounced him as a producer of discord. In the midst of the argument Lewis asked for readmission to the A.F.L. Reactions were mixed. Green waxed ecstatic even though he recognized that the Progressive Miners Union of Illinois, recently admitted to the A.F.L., would object and that there would be trouble over U.M.W. District 50. The C.I.O. was suspicious; its leaders reasoned that Lewis was joining men like Woll and Hutcheson with the intention of taking over the A.F.L. and of using it to line up all disaffected elements in the nation—Negroes, dirt farmers, workers in low-paid industries—in order to create disunity in labor ranks and to deliver the whole to whomever the Republican party nominated for the Presidency in 1944.

In October, 1943, the federation readmitted the miners. The act was a logical one. It ended, at least temporarily, the A.F.L.'s fears of triunionism. More important, it brought Lewis back into the fold where he seemed to belong. In the past Lewis had found fault with craft unionism and had engaged vigorously in politics; nevertheless most of his career revealed that, like the A.F.L. old guard, he was an exponent of craft-union tactics and suspicious of the efficacy of political action and alliance with the government. The act also helped to bring a large measure of harmony to the labor world. During the last two years of the war, wrangling among labor leaders died down—partly because of military and naval victories which brought some lightness of heart to the rank and file, and partly because of War Labor Board policies which placated labor tempers.

Peace in the labor world gave labor a better opportunity to engage in political activity. In the first year after the attack on Pearl Harbor, the Non-Partisan League, with its attention centered upon conversion and intralabor quarrels, relaxed some of its vigilance. As a result many liberal and prolabor legislators, congressmen, senators, and governors lost their seats in 1942. That jolt, together with the subsequent passage of the Smith-Connally Act, forced C.I.O. leaders to cast accounts; they began to recognize that a repetition of the employer attack upon unionism in the era of normalcy was being made possible. Accordingly, in the summer of 1943, the Executive Council decided on a vigorous campaign to renominate Roosevelt and a Congress favorable to labor. To carry out its program it created a Political Action Committee, headed by Sidney Hillman as chairman and R. J. Thomas as treasurer.

The P.A.C. campaign proved highly effective—as was revealed on the eve of the Democratic National Convention when an effort was made to nullify P.A.C. influence by the circulation of a fabricated story to the effect that Roosevelt had given orders to all New Dealers at the convention "to clear everything with Sidney [Hillman]." The P.A.C.'s first choice for Roosevelt's running mate was Henry Wallace, but it soon became clear that southern Democrats and city machine politicians would not accept him. Dixiecrats suggested James F. Byrnes, whose name was anathema to labor. Machine politicians advanced the name of Senator Harry Truman of Missouri, member of the Pendergast machine. In the backstage maneuvering that followed, the P.A.C. finally threw its support to Truman, to whom labor had been favorably attracted by his conduct as chairman of the Senate War Investigating Committee.

Once the nominations were made, the P.A.C. threw all its strength into the campaign to reelect Roosevelt; local branches, left free to make their own campaigns for congressional and senatorial candidates, also supported Democratic nominees in the overwhelming majority of contests. Although the P.A.C. campaign was handicapped by the Smith-Connally Act which forbade union contributions to campaign funds, the handicap was hardly apparent. Its aim was to make labor politically conscious and to encourage heavy registration and a full vote on election day, which would ensure victory for the liberal forces. The main feature of its campaign was a door-to-door canvass to bring out voters. In addition it published and distributed thousands of pamphlets, leaflets, and broadsides which urged labor to accept political responsibility, publicized the records of congressmen, and urged voters to elect men who favored a P.A.C.-sponsored program of social reform: protection for the right of labor and the farmer, full employment, fair wages, extension of social security, adequate housing, and help for veterans. The program won wide support. Every C.I.O. union endorsed Roosevelt. While the A.F.L. maintained its traditional policy of nonpartisanship, its constituent elements were almost unanimous in support of the President. A poll of 140 labor newspapers with a circulation of six million revealed that 128 supported Roosevelt, eleven were neutral, and only one supported Thomas E. Dewey.

The effectiveness of the P.A.C. campaign was indicated by the violence of the attacks made upon it. Anti-Roosevelt and anti-labor forces, enrolled in Republican and southern Democratic ranks, used every weapon known to politics to villify and disparage the movement. Typical was the action taken by the House Committee on Un-American Activities, headed by Martin Dies, which charged that the P.A.C. was radical and un-American, "a subversive Communist organization," whose aim it was to bring totalitarianism to the United States. John Bricker, Governor of Ohio, charged that the P.A.C. was "trying to dominate our government with radical and communistic schemes." All efforts to nullify the P.A.C. campaign proved vain. Since no Lewis-led anti-Roosevelt move materialized, the P.A.C. was able to shape labor into a fairly united front; and when the votes were counted in November, Roosevelt had won another victory. The P.A.C. also claimed it was responsible for the election of six governors, seventeen senators, and 120 congressmen. Thus, in late 1944 and all through the following year labor generally could look confidently to the future. Its confidence was reasonable. It was weathering a war, when it might have expected major setbacks, with most of its New Deal advances intact and in some cases pushed ahead, with its membership and organizational strength increased, and with a political organization tested and not found wanting in several campaigns. Never at the close of any war in the nation's history had labor appeared so powerful.

27 ——

The Truman Administration

Labor emerged from the Second World War into a "reconversion" period for which the nation was inadequately prepared. The Truman administration had given serious attention to the problem of converting the nation's economy from war to peacetime production. After V-E day, in May, 1945, it had developed a plan for reconversion based upon the assumption that the war in Asia would last another year. The plan anticipated a reduction of war production, a slow increase in the production of civilian goods, and a gradual lifting of wage and price controls. Although the government recognized that inflation would follow, it concluded that concentration on the achievement of a full-employment economy would compensate for the trend. It likewise expected that the machinery designed to assure industrial peace would remain in operation long enough to moderate labor-management conflicts that would develop during the period of transition.

While the government made a small start toward reconversion in the summer of 1945, its well laid plans were totally upset by the blasts that destroyed Nagasaki and Hiroshima. During the two-day holiday that followed the surrender of Japan, President Truman ordered the immediate inauguration of a reconversion policy. He authorized employers and unions to negotiate wage increases that would not affect prices and appealed to both management and labor to continue to accept War Labor Board decisions until a labor-management conference that he planned to call could formulate new methods to minimize industrial strife.

Labor was plunged into a situation which the A.F.L. and the C.I.O. had long anticipated with dread. Their main fear was that the number of jobs available would be inadequate. With twelve million men and women in the armed forces and eight million more engaged directly in the production of war goods, the task of relocating manpower after the war seemed almost impossible to solve. Ultimately, both organizations concluded that postwar prosperity depended fundamentally upon the amount of purchasing power in the hands of the lower-income labor groups. They differed in their attitude toward government involvement. The A.F.L., made up of skilled workers in a strong bargaining position, proposed an early removal of governmental controls; the C.I.O., whose members were more easily replaced mass-production workers, advocated a more gradual abandonment of governmental aids.

During 1945 labor had a small taste of what might be in store as the government began to cut back war production. When the factory at Willow Run, Michigan, was shut down in the spring of 1945, only 41 per cent of the men and 3 per cent of the women employed were able to get other jobs—at an average pay cut of 25 per cent. Between V-E Day and V-J Day unemployment figures increased from 500,000 to 1,000,000. With the confirmation of Japanese surrender the situation became worse. The War and Navy departments canceled 100,-000 contracts totaling over $20,000,000,000, and unemployment promptly leaped to 3,000,000.

The government's reconversion policy did not meet the situation. Although it enacted the Full Employment Act of 1946, accepting responsibility for creating conditions under which "there will be afforded useful employment opportunities . . . for those able, willing, and seeking to work," it had no program to effectuate. Moreover, there were too many unanticipated developments and too many conflicting interests to satisfy. The resignations of experienced directors of various control agencies and the incorporation of the War

Labor Board into the Department of Labor weakened the government's position. Employers' objections to continued operation under governmental restrictions and labor's desire for a return to free collective bargaining through which it could secure wage increases worked against the policy. Inability to decide on the standards to be followed in determining wage increases made mockery of the whole plan.

In November, 1945, President Truman's National Labor-Management Conference met in Washington to find a way to resolve the differences between management and labor without stopping production. The conference agreed that grievances under existing contracts could be settled by voluntary arbitration rather than by strikes and lockouts, that the United States Conciliation Service should be strengthened, and that strikes should be postponed until all peaceful procedures had been exhausted. But the conference failed to provide any machinery to minimize strikes during the reconversion period and it failed to come to any agreement concerning the all-important problem of how to raise wages without affecting prices. After the conference, the job of solving this problem was turned over to a newly created Wage Stabilization Board.

Meanwhile a wave of strikes provided newspapers with headlines. The actions were based on labor's contention that employers could afford substantial wage increases without increasing prices and that increases were necessary to sustain purchasing power to avoid large-scale unemployment. The contention was given support by the Office of War Mobilization and Reconversion which estimated that industry in general could maintain its prewar profit level and raise wages 24 per cent without affecting prices. While the number of strikes did not increase in comparison to the number before the end of the war, more workingmen were involved and the conflicts lasted longer. Between V-E and V-J days the number of man days of idleness averaged much less than 2,000,000 a month; in September the figure jumped to 4,300,000; in October, to nearly 9,000,000.

The outburst was only the beginning. In November, 180,000 workers in General Motors plants throughout the nation went on a strike. In the next three months other huge C.I.O. organizations joined the U.A.W. in conflict with industry. By January, 1946, the number of man days of idleness due to strikes reached a total of nearly 20,000,-

000—3 per cent of working time; in February, 1946, the figure reached 23,000,000—more than in the years 1943 and 1944 combined.

In many ways the strike wave was unique. For all its size there was little violence; plants were closed in orderly fashion and remained closed throughout the course of the strike. Both sides appealed to the public with pamphlets, press releases, and radio talks. Statistical evidence of industry's ability to pay higher wages became the focus of argument in all the controversies. Government intervention in the form of fact-finding boards and through the N.L.R.B. occurred in every conflict.

The General Motors Strike, which lasted 113 days, set the pattern. In September Walter P. Reuther, head of the U.A.W., asked for a 30 per cent increase in wages to increase purchasing power while prices were kept at the same level. He challenged the company to open its books for inspection to determine whether or not it could pay. General Motors countered with an offer of 10 per cent and refused to discuss ability to pay on the ground that no one could determine future earnings. After the strike began, President Truman announced that he was appointing a board to determine the facts in the situation and to make a recommendation. The dispute became an "ideological" battle as much as a quarrel over wages. As such it revolved around the question of whether or not the company should open its books, a controversy which ended when the company representatives refused further cooperation and walked out of the hearings. The board then recommended a 19½-cent hourly increase, asserting its opinion that General Motors could raise wages without increasing prices. General Motors rejected the recommendation.

Meanwhile other conflicts threatened to tie up production. Some were settled peaceably by fact-finding boards and negotiation. Notable were the settlements at Ford and Chrysler which involved not only hourly wage increases but the problem of management security. The issue, raised by Ford, involved payment of penalties by unions for unauthorized work stoppages. Ultimately Ford and Chrysler signed agreements providing for 18- and 18½-cent increases and for disciplinary measures against employees who participated in unauthorized strikes. Other efforts to secure prestrike settlements failed. Unions in the meat-packing, and in the electrical and steel industries went on strike in mid-January, 1946.

In February, 1946, the first postwar strike wave began to break up when the Wage Stabilization Board assured United States Steel of a $5 per ton increase in steel prices; agreement on an 18½-cent wage increase for workers in the entire steel industry quickly followed. Almost simultaneously President Truman issued an executive order permitting price rises to compensate industry for wage increases. In March General Motors and the U.A.W. settled their dispute on the general lines of the steel agreement, and the 18½-cent pattern was quickly adopted by most of the nation's industries.

Peace was not long enduring. In the spring of 1946, John L. Lewis appeared upon the scene with new demands. With coal contracts ready to expire, Lewis asked for new agreements which would not only incorporate the normal wage demands but which would also provide for the financing of health and welfare services in the mine fields, for more adequate safety provisions, and for the right of the miners to close any mine they considered unsafe. While operators were willing to grant wage increases, they refused to recognize health and medical issues as proper subjects for collective bargaining. On the mine safety issue they were silent. The usual deadlock began on April 1, 1946. The dwindling of coal supplies caused a nation-wide "brown out," and fear that industry would be brought to a standstill was expressed. In May a two-week truce was declared, and miners returned to work. Shortly before the truce expired, the Federal Government seized the mines, placing them under the administration of Secretary of the Interior Julius A. Krug, who promptly began new negotiations with Lewis. In a short time the two men reached an agreement whereby miners were granted the normal 18½-cent increase in wages and an increase in vacation pay. The welfare dispute was settled with the establishment of two funds—a welfare and retirement fund to be administered jointly by the union and management and a medical and hospital fund to be controlled by the union.

Before the mine dispute ended, another serious disagreement, involving the railways, partially paralyzed the nation's more important carriers. Months earlier the railway brotherhoods and shop crafts, twenty in number, had demanded wage increases and changes in working rules. After some negotiation all but two unions agreed to drop their demand for changes in rules and to submit the wage dispute to arbitration by the Railway Labor Board. Since the engineers and the trainmen insisted on the rule changes, their dispute went to an emergency board. Both boards proposed a 16-cent increase in salary. All the unions rejected the award; on May 23rd a nation-wide strike began as engineers and trainmen finished their runs.

A period of frantic negotiations followed. President Truman simultaneously appealed to the strikers to return to work and threatened to operate the roads, which the government had already seized, under military protection. On May 25th he appeared before a joint session of Congress to ask for emergency power to break strikes in any industry held by the Federal Government. His proposal included induction of strikers into the army and imprisonment of officers of striking unions who failed to obey a return-to-work order. Although the railway dispute was settled a few minutes before the President began to deliver his message, Congress proceeded to act. A bill embodying Truman's proposal passed the House by a heavy majority within a few hours. Organized labor, shocked by the vote, used all its resources to check the rising antilabor tide. The Senate deleted the labor-draft provision but passed the bill. It never became law. After the emergency was relieved, employer opposition to the measure also appeared, and the bill was allowed to die in conference. Labor had won its first postwar legislative victory.

It was the last that workingmen were to win for many years. While the coal and rail disputes had been reaching crisis proportions, a battle had been developing over extension of price controls. Wartime legislation, which had checked spectacular price increases, would expire on June 30, 1946. When the administration requested continuation for another year, most of organized labor—the major exception was John L. Lewis—recognized that the proposal was in labor's interest. Realizing that failure to continue controls would result in an inflation that would quickly nullify recent wage gains, the A.F.L. and the C.I.O. gave the President's proposal strong backing in Congress. Business groups, led by the National Association of Manufacturers and the Chamber of Commerce, organized an intensive campaign against the measure. Using newspaper advertisements they tried to convince the public that price controls themselves were the cause of shortages and inflation; they argued that removal of controls would bring a vast increase in production and reasonable prices. In the spring of 1946 an irritating shortage of meat convinced much of the public that business arguments were well founded. Congress responded with a measure so weak and ineffective that President Truman vetoed it, leaving the nation without controls. In two weeks the price of basic commodities increased 25 per cent and threatened to go even higher. Alarmed, Congress enacted a new measure which continued price controls but provided for establishment of new price ceilings; the measure also continued rent controls. The President accepted the measure as the best obtainable; he predicted that inflation would not be checked.

His prediction was accurate. Between June and December, 1946, consumer prices rose 15 per cent, with food prices rising 28 per cent. The rise more than canceled the wage increases labor had secured from the 1945–1946 strikes; real wages dropped from $32.50 a week in July to less than $30.00 a week in September, the lowest figure since American entry into the war. In the meantime corporate net profits soared to the highest point in history, reaching $12,500,000,000—20 per cent higher than in the best war year.

In the labor world the situation produced a steadily rising demand for a second round of wage increases. Most labor leaders responded cautiously, since the long conflicts of the previous year had depleted workers' wartime savings and had lessened enthusiasm for strikes. The exception was John L. Lewis who, in October, 1946, accused the government of violating the vacation pay and welfare clauses of the coal contract and threatened another strike unless a settlement was reached by November 20th. The government refused to reopen the contract on the ground that the Krug-Lewis agreement was in effect until the government lifted its control of the mines. When Lewis insisted that he was acting under the provisions of his 1945 contract which was still in effect, the government turned to the courts, requesting a restraining order against the officials of the U.M.W. on the ground that the union had no right to terminate the Krug-Lewis agreement and because the termination was a violation of the Smith-Connally Act. On November 18th Federal Judge Alan Goldsborough issued a temporary order restraining the union from continuing the contract termination notice. Lewis refused to surrender and the coal mines closed.

On December 3rd Judge Goldsborough found Lewis and the U.M.W. guilty of civil and criminal contempt for disregarding his order. Denouncing the strike as "evil" and "monstrous," he fined the union $3,500,000 and Lewis $10,000. The U.M.W. promptly appealed on the ground that the Goldsborough order was a violation of both the Clayton and Norris-La Guardia acts; the miners, meanwhile, returned to work. In March the United States Supreme Court upheld the conviction in a 7–2 decision; at the same time it reduced the fine against the U.M.W. to $700,000. Lewis could only obey; nevertheless at the end of June, 1947, when the Smith-Connally Act expired, Lewis secured a new contract raising wages from $11.85 for nine hours to $13.05 for eight hours and increasing the royalty payments to the miners' retirement and welfare fund.

Meanwhile C.I.O. unions, led by the U.A.W., the Steelworkers, and the United Electrical Workers, were working out a pattern for a second round of wage increases. The movement was preceded by a barrage of statistics, issued by the C.I.O., intending to show that industry could well afford a 23 per cent wage increase, which was necessary to bring purchasing power back to 1945 levels, without increasing prices. Unlike the previous year, negotiations developed with very little conflict; neither side wanted a strike, and industry, free of any price restraint, was willing to make concessions. The first major decision was made in mid-April, 1947, when General Motors agreed with its electrical workers on a wage boost of 15 cents an hour, of which 11½ cents was to be a direct wage increase and the remaining 3½ cents was to be used to provide for paid holidays and to correct wage inequalities. After the Steelworkers and the U.A.W. secured similar agreements, the pattern became general throughout the nation.

Any jubilation which labor might have felt because of its wage victories was soon dampened by the successful conclusion of a long-term, antilabor movement in Congress. The movement, as has been indicated, had begun to develop among antiunion employers during the period of jurisdictional warfare before the outbreak of the Second World War. It had continued during the war with some success—the Smith-Connally Act was the best example. But it reached even greater vigor after V-J Day. The postwar antilabor movement had its foundations in the widespread and large-scale strikes of 1945–1946 and the wage drives of 1946–1947 which irritated a public —far too busy converting itself to peacetime living to bother with the relevancy of issues raised by unions—which assumed, as the press constantly reiterated, that most of its economic problems were caused by labor. In 1946 the temper of the nation was reflected in a Congress, angered over some of the methods used by James C. Petrillo of the American Federation of Musicians to provide musicians with an income from the canned music they created, which passed the Lea Act prescribing penalties for trying to force broadcasters to hire more employees than needed, to pay for services not performed, to pay unions for the use of phonograph records, or to pay for broadcasting the transcripts of a previous program. Congress also gave sympathetic attention to the measure introduced by Francis Case of South Dakota which provided for notice of strikes, a sixty-day "cooling off" period, outlawed secondary boycotts, permitted unions to be sued for breach of contract, excluded supervisory employees from the protection of the Wagner Act, outlawed interference with interstate commerce by "robbery" or extortion, and made welfare funds illegal unless set up under employer-union administration. The Case bill came up for vote at the height of the railway strike of May, 1946. Although labor condemned the measure as an "ill assorted conglomeration of provisions" which would destroy sound labor relations, Congress passed it by heavy majorities. Only President Truman's veto saved the situation.

The antilabor movement, nevertheless, continued to grow. The development became clear three months after the veto of the Case bill when Congress enacted and the President approved a portion of the measure in the form of the Hobbs Act, which made it a felony to obstruct, delay, or interfere by robbery or extortion with the movement of goods in interstate commerce. It became forcefully evident during the congressional election of 1946. Since the electorate was far more interested in the immediate problem of living, and since labor was wrapped up in the problem of securing wage increases, little effort was made to secure a large vote. The C.I.O.-P.A.C. conducted a token campaign. A mere 33,000,000 people voted, and labor suffered its worst defeat since the inauguration of the New Deal. Only 73 out of 318 congressional candidates and 5 out of 21 senatorial candidates endorsed by the P.A.C. were elected.

For labor the full tragedy of the election of 1946 became evident in the following year when state legislatures enacted the largest

number of antiunion laws since the Haymarket Riot. While most of
the legislation, as during the war, was produced by states of the
South, the Great Plains, the Rockies, the Southwest, and the Pacific
Coast, industrialized states also contributed a portion of the total.
Sixteen states passed laws prohibiting union security agreements or
the closed shop. Twenty-one states—including Pennsylvania, Ohio,
Indiana, Michigan, Missouri, Wisconsin, and Minnesota—provided
for strike notices and cooling-off periods. Eleven states—including
Connecticut, Pennsylvania, and Michigan—restricted picketing.
Twelve states—among them Pennsylvania, Missouri, and Minnesota—
prohibited secondary boycotts. Ten states—including Massachusetts,
Michigan, and Minnesota—directed unions to file accounts of their
finances or otherwise regulated internal affairs. Six states lowered the
bars against the use of injunctions in labor disputes.

Congressional action in 1947 was even more serious. From the
opening session of the Eightieth Congress the antilabor sentiment was
obvious. It appeared first in the form of indignation over the Mount
Clemens case in which the Supreme Court expanded its definition of
portal-to-portal time to include preparatory work on equipment and
person as well as travel time. The decision upset the traditional concepts of working time held by both employers and unions; both had
more or less agreed that preparatory time was compensated by wage
rates for working time. Nevertheless, thousands of unions or groups
of employees, the bulk of them in the C.I.O., filed suit for billions of
dollars of back pay. Employers protested that they would be ruined,
and Congress responded with the Portal-to-Portal Act intended to
relieve employers from liability under the Supreme Court ruling.
But the act went further; it provided that employees were to be
paid portal-to-portal wages only if contracts or the tradition of the
job specifically provided for such compensation. This meant that
unions could secure portal-to-portal pay for their members, but the
unorganized who received protection only from the law were deprived of compensation.

Meanwhile a strong movement to revise the nation's basic Labor
Relations Act had been started by antilabor forces, who made three
criticisms of the legislation: The Wagner Act made unions too strong
and thereby increased industrial strife; to reduce conflicts it was
necessary to reduce the bargaining power of labor and increase that

of employers. The Wagner Act permitted such unreasonable actions as jurisdictional strikes and boycotts, violation of contracts, union refusal to bargain, and union coercion of individual employees; to redress the situation the law should be rewritten to give greater consideration to the public and employers who were seriously injured by union practices and to the individual employee whose freedom was crushed by unionism. The Wagner Act also permitted unions to encroach on management prerogatives through collective bargaining; preservation of the free enterprise system depended upon restoration of management control over all members of management, including supervisors.

By the time the Eightieth Congress met, the movement for drastic revision was so strong that President Truman tried to check it with a program of his own. He proposed that practices such as jurisdictional strikes, secondary boycotts in pursuit of improper objectives, and strikes or lockouts intended to produce specific interpretations of contracts be outlawed; that facilities for assisting collective bargaining be enlarged; that legislation covering social security, minimum wages, medicine, and housing be broadened to alleviate labor's sense of insecurity; and that a commission be appointed to inquire into the underlying causes of labor-management disputes.

Congress brushed the suggestion aside. Instead, it turned its attention to more than one hundred bills intended to curb unionism. For several months it listened to the impassioned arguments of representatives of the A.F.L., who admitted that the Wagner Act needed some minor amendments but who otherwise opposed any change; to members of the C.I.O. who opposed any change; to representatives of the National Association of Manufacturers who proposed sweeping revisions; to spokesmen for the United States Chamber of Commerce and the Committee for Economic Development who proposed changes less drastic than those of the N.A.M. but intended to reduce the power of labor unions in collective bargaining. Finally, after the usual House-Senate disagreements and conferences, it produced a measure which was adopted by overwhelming votes in both houses. President Truman vetoed the measure on the ground that "it would contribute neither to industrial peace nor to economic stability and progress," and because it contained "seeds of discord which would plague this nation for years to come." Congress promptly overrode the veto.

The new law, known officially as the Labor-Management Relations Act and popularly as the Taft-Hartley Act, followed in large degree the suggestions made by the National Association of Manufacturers. Like the earlier Case bill, it was made up of a "conglomeration" of provisions, whose only unity lay in the fact that they "corrected" labor practices which employers regarded as unfavorable to their own position. It was an act difficult to analyze and assess.

The purpose of the act, as the preamble explained, was to assist the free flow of commerce through support of collective bargaining. Since, however, action by unions might restrict the free flow of commerce, the act was also intended to restrain such behavior. While the act approved bona fide collective bargaining and assured employees that they had the right to organize and bargain collectively, it also asserted that individuals had the right to refuse to join unions under certain circumstances. The act restrained employers from committing the same unfair labor practices enumerated in the Wagner Act, but it also forbade unions from engaging in specific unfair labor practices. These included (1) the closed shop; (2) inducing an employer to discriminate against an employee who had been discharged from a union for any reason other than the failure to pay dues; (3) restraint or coercion of employees in their right to organize into trade unions; (4) refusal to bargain collectively with any employer; (5) inducing a strike or boycott with the purpose of forcing an employer to institute a closed shop or recognize a union not certified by the N.L.R.B., or to force management into recognizing a union when another had been certified by the board, or to force management to assign work to members of a certain union or craft when the employer was already complying with an N.L.R.B. certification order; (6) charging excessive initiation fees when a union shop was in existence; and (7) attempting to cause an employer to pay for work not actually performed.

To administer the act, the National Labor Relations Board was enlarged to five members and a General Counsel, who was to have sole authority to determine whether or not a complaint would be prosecuted or a restraining order issued against management or a trade union. Each union desiring to use the N.L.R.B. had to file reports with the secretary of labor showing the union's internal structure and finances and also had to provide annual financial information to its own members. In addition each union official of a national or international had to file an affidavit assuring the government that he was not affiliated with communism or the Communist party; failure to comply would cause the union to lose the protection and privileges of the law.

As under the Wagner Act, the N.L.R.B. was authorized to conduct elections to determine certification of unions to act as bargaining agents for employees, and to hold run-off elections where the election was inconclusive. In addition the N.L.R.B. could hold decertification elections to determine whether or not a union should lose its bargaining rights. Management was permitted to discuss with its employees and to publicize its views on trade unions provided it did not coerce or threaten individuals who planned to become or were union members. Supervising employees (foremen) were permitted to organize and bargain collectively but not under the protection of the act.

To make unions responsible for their behavior the act provided that they could be sued in district courts for breaches of contract, illegal boycotts, and strikes; the personal resources of individual members of the union could not be placed in jeopardy by such suits. To protect the individual further, the act permitted use of the check-off (whereby management withheld union dues and paid them to the union) only when the employee agreed in writing and for only one year at a time. Employers were permitted to contribute to welfare funds only if the funds were held in trust for specified purposes and if employers and employees were represented equally as trustees. Trust funds had to be audited annually.

In case of a strike which affected the welfare of the whole nation, the attorney general was authorized to secure an injunction prohibiting the strike. These injunctions were to run for eighty days during which time the Federal Government was to attempt settlement through the Mediation and Conciliation Service, which was removed from the sympathetic jurisdiction of the Department of Labor and made an independent agency. At the end of that period the N.L.R.B. was required to take a poll of the employees on the employer's last offer. If the vote was to accept, the strike was called off. If the vote was to reject, the strike could occur. The act prohibited contributions and expenditures by unions in elections, including primary elections, which were national in scope. Finally, it prohibited strikes by Federal employees.

Organized labor reacted to the Taft-Hartley Act with bitter and concentrated fury. Philip Murray castigated the measure as a bill "conceived in sin," and its promoters as "diabolical men who, seething with hatred, designed . . . this ugly measure for the purpose of imposing their wrath upon the millions of organized and unorganized workers throughout the United States." William Green charged that the bill was "conceived in a spirit of vindictiveness against unions." Specifically, labor objected most to the provision requiring anti-Communist affidavits which, they claimed, made labor leaders into second-class citizens; to the clauses permitting use of injunctions and requiring strike polls at the end of cooling-off periods which, they charged, would hamper collective bargaining; to the sections prohibiting a closed shop and employer discrimination against employees who were dropped from unions for reasons other than non-payment of dues which, they claimed, would make it difficult to maintain union discipline; and finally to Section 14(b) which permitted states to outlaw union shops even though the Taft-Hartley Act approved of them, which, they alleged, was an open invitation to engage in "union busting" by law.

The act produced a change of degree in the labor movement. After the first shock had worn off, organized labor turned to politics with a vengeance. "Repeal of the Taft-Hartley Slave Labor Act" became a watchword which brought about the revival or the creation of labor political agencies. The C.I.O. threw new effort into its Political Action Committee; the A.F.L., which had long practiced the policy of rewarding friends and punishing enemies and which now found its old methods prohibited, created its first political arm—Labor's League for Political Education—under the chairmanship of George Meany. The independent machinists and the telephone employees created political action groups; even the conservative railway workers who were not affected by Taft-Hartley organized a political agency.

Organized labor's campaign for repeal began in the winter of 1947–1948 and continued without faltering for eighteen months; during that time it learned that labor had lost the right to refuse to work on materials produced under substandard conditions; that states could enact legislation prohibiting any form of union security agreement; and that states might also require a two-thirds vote of employees as a condition precedent to entering a union security agreement. In addition labor claimed that events had revealed that elimination of the secondary boycott encouraged the "runaway" shop and that the Taft-Hartley Act made collective bargaining procedures more costly and time consuming.

Using pamphlets and union newspapers, radio and television, labor's political agencies entered the 1948 primaries with impassioned pleas to union members, farmers, housewives, and citizens in general to "get out and vote." Thousands of union members entered the race for office; nearly a hundred were elected as delegates to the national conventions. As the time for nomination approached, both the A.F.L. and the C.I.O. prepared platforms for consideration of the major parties, with a demand for repeal of the Taft-Hartley Act at the top of the list. Rejection of the demand by the Republican convention, which nominated Thomas E. Dewey, concentrated labor's attention upon the Democratic convention, which not only endorsed the demand but adopted the whole labor platform and nominated Harry S. Truman for the Presidency.

Although not all labor was satisfied with the Truman nomination—there were some rail leaders who hadn't forgiven the President his proposal to conscript them into the army, and there were others who feared that the President would be a weak candidate—labor on the whole threw all its strength behind the Democratic party. They recognized, particularly after the Dixiecrats made their own nominations, that the party was sincere in its friendship for labor and that the President was no exception. As the campaign progressed and the President revealed himself to be a tough, hard-hitting campaigner, labor's enthusiasm increased. But its campaign was not confined to the Presidency. Most of its efforts, in fact, went into the campaign to elect senatorial and congressional candidates who were opposed to the Taft-Hartley Act. Its drive was a repetition and an intensification of the primary campaign, with the strongest effort being made to get out the labor vote on election day.

The effort succeeded. Labor, as *The Federationist* exclaimed, "went to the polls as never before" and contributed greatly to the President's "upset" victory. Equally important, it claimed credit for the election of sixteen prolabor senators and the defeat of nine Taft-Hartley senators, for the election of 172 prolabor congressmen and the defeat of 57 Taft-Hartley congressmen. To labor the election was a clear mandate for repeal.

For a time the confidence seemed warranted. In his message to Congress the President asked for outright repeal, and the suggestion met with such enthusiastic response from the House and Senate committees that the A.F.L. predicted that "Taft-Hartley was on its way to the scrap heap." By April, however, labor confidence began to abate as it became evident that a coalition of Republicans and Southern Democrats was determined through delay and through amendment to keep the law on the books substantially as it was. In the House the coalition succeeded in substituting the Wood bill, which was the Taft-Hartley Act under another name, for the labor-favored Lesinski bill by a vote of 217 to 203, and then recommitted the measure to committee. In the Senate Taft succeeded in adding a provision permitting use of the injunction to the measure reported out of committee by a vote of 48–47. Organized labor promptly lost interest; the movement for repeal was checked.

During the remainder of the Truman administration, labor's drive against Taft-Hartley never again reached the intensity of the 1948–1949 campaign. Resentment against the act continued to develop. The A.F.L. grew bitter over rulings which, it charged, denied building trades the right to make contracts with employers before workmen reported to the job—a traditional practice; and labor, in general, became convinced that the act worsened labor-management relations where they were already bad.

During the congressional campaign of 1950 labor's political agencies made another effort to elect a Congress favorable to repeal. Although they did not neglect any election district, they aimed their campaign in large measure against Senator Taft, who was running for reelection in Ohio. The election was a disappointment. Not only did labor fail to reelect many of its friends but it failed to defeat a number of antilabor congressmen and senators, among them Taft. The failure, together with the involvement of the nation in the Korean War, made any drive for repeal almost futile. Nevertheless labor secured a concession from Congress in October, 1951, with the elimination of the provision for an election to approve a union shop.

Labor's concentration upon the drive to repeal the Taft-Hartley Act after August, 1947, did not blind it to other political issues. It gave an almost equal amount of attention to inflation and price control, wages, unemployment insurance, old-age insurance, health insurance, and fair employment practices.

Labor's interest in the rising cost of living after President Truman's decontrol order of December, 1946, remained very strong. In 1947 both the A.F.L. and the C.I.O. pointed to the inflationary trend as one of the two or three most important problems facing the nation; both were loud in their denunciation of Congress for passing legislation permitting rent increases. In 1948 organized labor, pointing to the fact that the average factory worker earned $2,652 a year and needed $3,600 to maintain a minimum standard of living, began to advance a program intended to check the trend; it demanded investigation to determine the cause of the price spread between the farmer and consumer, the imposition of excess profits taxes, and the extension of rent control. After the election of 1948, Congress partially responded to labor pressure with a measure which assured landlords of a "fair net operating income" but which extended rent control into 1950 and permitted recontrol.

Both the A.F.L. and the C.I.O. raised the wage issue with a demand for an increase in the minimum wage immediately after the war ended. While President Truman supported the demand, the bill to raise wage minimums to 65 cents an hour was stifled by the House Rules Committee, dominated by southern Democrats. In 1947 and again in 1948 the President recommended an increase of minimums to 75 cents an hour and an extension of the law to seamen and to employees in the agricultural- and seafood-processing industries. It was not until after the election of 1948, however, that Congress responded to the request with a new law providing for a 75-cents-an-hour minimum and time and a half for overtime for employees engaged in the production of goods for interstate commerce or in any closely related process or occupation "directly essential" to production of such goods. The law affected 1,500,000 employees, most of them unorganized.

Labor's concern with the problem of unemployment began during the war. Although the concern led it to the conclusion that the only answer to the problem was full employment, it recognized that a better cushion for unemployment had to be provided. During the war labor supported legislation for creation of a Federal Loan Fund, from which states might borrow if their unemployment insurance funds ran low, and the unsuccessful Wagner-Murray-Dingell proposals for nationalizing and broadening the coverage of unemployment insurance. After the war labor continued to press for the development of greater national control and for more adequate coverage. It supported proposals which resulted in legislation providing unemployment insurance for maritime workers and disability benefits for railroad workers in 1946.

Labor's greatest concern with the problem developed in 1949 when unemployment rose suddenly from a little more than 2,000,000 to more than 4,000,000 and average weekly hours of work dropped from 40.2 to 38.8. Large pockets of unemployment developed in New England, New York, New Jersey, Maryland, the Carolinas, Kentucky, Tennessee, Illinois, and California. Fear of a general depression became common enough to persuade labor to make an extra effort to advance unemployment compensation rates. About two-thirds of the states responded with laws providing more adequate protection for the unemployed by improving the amount and duration of benefits; Congress responded, in 1950, with legislation liberalizing disability benefits.

Increased cost of living after the war prompted labor to demand increases in payments made to the aged under the programs established by the prewar Social Security and Railway Retirement Acts. No major changes had been made in either act during the war. Labor agitation led to a small revision of the Railway Retirement Act in 1946 involving survivors' benefits. More important, it brought a change in the Social Security Act in 1950, extending the benefits of the Old-Age and Survivors Insurance program to more than 10,000,-000 additional workers, including the self-employed, regularly employed farm and domestic workers, outside salesmen, Federal civilian employees, and Americans employed abroad. Monthly benefits were increased about 90 per cent. In 1952 monthly benefits were increased another 12½ per cent.

Health insurance and Federal aid to increase available medical facilities also became a major concern to organized labor. Suggestions for the establishment of a national health insurance program which would include hospital and medical care had been made during the war. Labor's interest, based on the highly successful group health program of the International Ladies Garment Workers and other citizens' organizations, had been instantaneous. Accordingly, it pushed hard for enactment of President Truman's suggestion for a national medical insurance program. Although Congress failed to respond, both the A.F.L. and the C.I.O. continued to agitate for enactment of legislation to provide "a nationwide system of health insurance"; for Federal aid in the form of scholarships for schools of medicine, dentistry, and nursing; and for extension of the public health service to the 40,000,000 people who were without such service.

Legislation concerning fair employment practices received considerable labor attention. In 1947 President Truman suggested an amendment to the Fair Labor Standards Act intended to prohibit discrimination in employment by making it unlawful to refuse to hire or to discharge a person because of sex, race, religion, color, national origin, or ancestry. The proposal, which raised a storm of protest from southern Democrats and which was responsible in part for the Dixiecrat movement of 1948, was strongly supported by the C.I.O. No law was enacted either by the Eightieth or by the Eighty-first Congress; President Truman was able to apply the philosophy only to the Federal establishment. Labor, however, did secure legislation on the same subject in about ten states and thirty cities in the nation's industrial area.

Political action was only one of labor's reactions to the Taft-Hartley Act. It also turned its attention, as *The Federationist* announced, to "a revival of trade unionism." The announcement revealed that labor —the C.I.O. adopted the same attitude—was uncertain of its ability to gain its ends through political action and, therefore, found it necessary to develop its economic power. In practice this meant reinvigoration of organizational campaigns and the strengthening of internal structure.

At the close of the war the nation's labor unions had about 15,000,-000 members; of these the A.F.L. claimed a little less than 7,000,000; the C.I.O. claimed about 6,000,000—a figure which most observers

regarded as an exaggeration; and independent unions claimed 2,000,-
000, the bulk of which belonged to the railway brotherhoods and the
600,000-member U.M.W. During the winter of 1945–1946 this picture
changed only slightly. The International Association of Machinists
withdrew from the A.F.L. because of a jurisdictional quarrel with
the carpenters; their withdrawal, however, caused only a temporary
drop in A.F.L. rolls since it was almost immediately matched by the
reaffiliation of the U.M.W.

In the spring of 1946 both the A.F.L. and the C.I.O. began new
organizing drives in the South. The greatest prize was the oft-as-
saulted but only slightly infiltrated textile industry; in addition there
were large numbers of unorganized workers in the lumber, furniture,
chemical, and food-processing industries. The campaigns were not
easy; the race problem, the isolation of many southern industrial
towns, the violent antiunion attitude of employers, and the ruthless
determination of local officials "to keep unionism out of the south-
land" produced situations of violence reminiscent of the period before the New Deal. Nevertheless the A.F.L. and the C.I.O. reported
progress, claiming over 700,000 new members in 1947.

After the passage of the Taft-Hartley Act, the organizing drive
intensified. The southern campaign continued, spreading to workers
in aircraft and atomic energy plants. Equally important, strong
campaigns were begun among the nation's white-collar workers. In
1947 there were 11,000,000 white-collar workers; about 1,400,000
were organized with the strongest unions among telephone workers,
railway clerks, postal employees, musicians, and actors; and small
organizations among office workers, government employees, engineers, draftsmen, salesmen, newspapermen, and teachers. In addition
campaigns to organize farm labor were revived. The drives had some
success, particularly in 1951 when about 1,500,000 members were
added to union rolls. By 1952 the A.F.L., which had once more lost
the U.M.W. but had regained the machinists, claimed over 8,000,000
members and the C.I.O. claimed nearly 7,000,000. For both organizations the increase came largely from the South.

Strengthening of the internal structure of unions between 1947 and
1952 revolved primarily around two factors: communism and labor
education. Communism as an issue within the trade-union movement
developed with the deterioration of Russian-American relations fol-

lowing the war. To the A.F.L., with its long public history of opposition to the recognition of the Soviet Union and its record of warfare against communists within the organization, the issue did not present a major problem. As early as the fall of 1946 it renewed its old position with a denunciation of Soviet designs and a refusal to join with any international organization which admitted Soviet trade-union delegates. In 1947 it enthusiastically endorsed the Truman Doctrine and the Marshall Plan as means of combating the "red threats" to peace and to the freedom of labor—the only greater threats to labor being the Taft-Hartley Act and the high cost of living. The A.F.L.'s chief problem with the communist issue developed over the communist affidavit required by the Taft-Hartley Act. Because the A.F.L. contained about 1,300 "federal unions," General Counsel Robert Denham ruled that federation officials would have to file the affidavit as officials of the federal unions. The issue caused a battle between Daniel Tobin of the teamsters and John L. Lewis of the U.M.W. Tobin insisted that A.F.L. officials file the affidavit, and threatened to take his teamsters out of the A.F.L. if the organization did not comply. Lewis refused to "grovel," urging that no one comply to force a test of the law. The A.F.L. compromised by amending its constitution to designate only the president and secretary-treasurer as officers, which meant that the vice presidents would not have to file an affidavit. The compromise satisfied everyone but Lewis. In December, 1947, he sent a curt note to Green: "We disaffiliate." The U.M.W. was once more on its own.

For the C.I.O. the communist issue was more serious. From the days of its earliest organization it had enrolled, in fact welcomed, the communists. By the end of the war, many of its locals and some of its internationals were communist dominated, a matter of acute embarrassment that threatened to divide the organization over the issue of supporting the Marshall Plan. The Taft-Hartley Act increased the problem. To the C.I.O. itself the issue was not important. Since C.I.O. locals were all directly responsible to a C.I.O. affiliate, Murray announced that he would not sign the affidavit and instructed each union to decide for itself. To international officers and to the rank and file the problem became a grave one because the refusal of the officers of an international or a local to sign the affidavit would deprive members of the protection of the law.

Several C.I.O. unions became centers of a struggle over the question of whether officials who were communists should be purged. The biggest struggles, among automobile and maritime workers, resulted in the victory of Walter Reuther and Joseph Curran. Reuther then enlarged the conflict when he began to raid noncommunist locals affiliated with communist-dominated internationals. The raids led the United Electrical Workers and the Farm Equipment Workers to withdraw from the C.I.O., which promptly organized a competing organization, the International Union of Electrical, Radio, and Machine Workers to campaign for recruits. Within three years the "I.E." recovered half of the "U.E." members. The ready success of the movement was probably responsible for the next action. In 1950 the C.I.O. convention expelled seven communist-dominated unions: the Mine, Mill and Smelter Workers; the Fur and Leather Workers; the Food, Tobacco, and Allied Workers; the Marine Cooks and Stewards' Association; the Fishermen's Union; the International Longshoremen's and Warehousemen's Union; and the American Communication Association. As the Korean War reached its critical stage, the C.I.O. could claim a purity equal to that of the A.F.L. and was able, thereby, to escape public indictment during the years when the anti-communist hysteria in the nation reached its height.

Both the A.F.L. and the C.I.O. sought to strengthen their internal structure through the development of education programs for their own members. Pioneered by Mark Starr of the I.L.G.W.U., the movement had begun before the war with simple intentions: to develop larger attendance at union meetings, to inform members concerning the operations of a local, and to develop knowledge of grievance procedure and legislation involving the rights and welfare of labor. Although the Department of Labor encouraged the movement, its growth was slow until after the war when internationals, state federations, and industrial union councils began to recognize the value of labor education as a means of strengthening the whole labor movement: knowledge of labor history gave workers a feeling of loyalty and dignity; knowledge of parliamentary procedure and public speaking encouraged participation in union affairs; knowledge of protective labor and social security legislation gave greater assurance that the workingman would secure the rights and benefits he deserved; knowledge of political party methods and platforms, of pressure groups, of community problems, of the operation of government, of civil rights, of international problems gave workers a desire to participate in community affairs; knowledge of consumer problems helped workers to a better economic living.

Labor education increased as more and more labor units with the aid of sympathetic institutions of higher learning and of adult education services inaugurated programs to meet the needs of labor. By 1951 more than fifty A.F.L., C.I.O., and railway labor unions and an equal number of colleges and universities were carrying out educational programs. The effect was evident in larger attendance at union meetings, greater participation of rank and file in union affairs, in higher labor registration, in much greater participation of workingmen in community service and welfare organizations, and in local elections. The development of even wider participation of labor seemed inevitable.

Revival of trade unionism, finally, meant a continuation of efforts to improve labor's share of the benefits of American industrialization through collective bargaining. Failure of the Federal Government to check the continued rise in prices after the second round of postwar wage increases, together with the continued rise in corporate profits, led to a renewal of union efforts to keep labor abreast of the cost of living during the winter and spring of 1947–1948. Since labor was not sure how the Taft-Hartley Act would be applied, its movement was cautious. The number of strikes for higher wages and other benefits dropped 40 per cent and the amount of time lost declined by 47 per cent. The number of strikes involving at least 10,000 workers dropped to 14—compared to 45 in 1945–1946, and 26 in 1946–1947. Only the meat packers and the bituminous-coal miners engaged in industry-wide strikes. For the most part the push for increases stressed immediate gains and resulted in an average boost in hourly wages of about ten cents. Two major exceptions to the formula developed. The U.A.W. secured the first contract with a major industry tying wages to cost of living; the U.M.W. secured contracts providing for payment of $100-a-month pensions, over and above social security payments, to retired miners over sixty-two.

The third round of postwar wage boosts did not solve labor's economic problems. Even before increases had been won, labor began to point out that between January, 1945, and June, 1948, wages had increased only 14 per cent in comparison to a price rise of 33 per cent. A fourth attempt to raise wages in 1948–1949 was inevitable. The effort, handicapped by a decline in production and an increase in unemployment, met with a more adamant attitude on the part of employers. Negotiations over contracts, which involved pensions as often as wages, were more protracted, and the results were less satisfying. Wage increases, when granted, averaged about seven cents an hour.

The fourth postwar round became only a preliminary for another push by labor in 1949–1950. The drive began earlier than usual. For the A.F.L. the major issue was increases in wages; for the C.I.O. pensions and wages became important. Since industrial production improved, employers took a more favorable attitude toward demands. Both the number of strikes and the number of large strikes decreased, the latter to the lowest number since the war. Nevertheless, several large-scale and long strikes occurred. Most important were those in coal and in steel. The coal stoppage was intermittent and began with Lewis' order to miners to reduce their work week to three days in July, 1949; this was followed by a walkout in September that lasted seven weeks. A month of full production was in turn followed by a return to a three-day week, a series of wildcat strikes, and another walkout in February, 1950. At this point the government asked for an injunction; it brought no change. Lewis ordered the strikers to return to work; the strikers refused until a new contract was signed, increasing wages and welfare-fund royalty payments. The steel conflict in the fall of 1949 was shorter, but it had more far-reaching results. It brought the adoption of a plan to provide pensions of $100 a month, including social security payments, to retired workers; and it encouraged other C.I.O. unions in their own negotiations for equal benefits. By the end of the year 8,500,000 workers had similar pension contracts.

The fifth postwar effort to secure wage increases ended about the same time as the troops of the "People's Democracy of Korea" crossed the thirty-eighth parallel. The outbreak of the Korean War brought labor new problems. From the start of the conflict, labor expected that it would be asked to participate. Both the A.F.L. and the C.I.O. announced that its abilities were at the service of the nation. Both, moreover, urged the adoption of a program of economic controls to meet the crisis; the program included standby power for the President to ration consumer goods and allocate scarce materials necessary to war production, control of prices, and increases in taxes to prevent inflation and profiteering. Since wages were lagging behind the cost of living, labor suggested that wage controls were not immediately necessary.

Labor's suggestions were met only in part by the Defense Production Act of September, 1950, which granted the President power to institute allocations and priorities and to impose sweeping credit controls but gave only limited controls over prices and wages. The President named Charles E. Wilson, president of General Electric, as Defense Mobilization Director and under him established an Economic Stabilization Agency with two divisions, one for wages and one for prices. Although union representatives were appointed to the wage- and price-stabilization agencies, labor immediately pointed out that the law was too weak to check the inflationary trend—prices rose 15 per cent between June and September. At the same time it feared that the administrators of the law would be sympathetic to a "wage freeze." Accordingly unions everywhere moved to "beat the freeze." New wage and pension demands were made, even by unions which had long-term contracts. Employers, especially in those industries where it was obvious that manpower shortages would develop, did not resist the demands too strongly. Nevertheless a large number of strikes, most of them of the wildcat variety, involving 4,800,000 workers, broke out in almost every industry and on the railroads. Most were quickly settled with a ten-cent increase.

Inadequacy of the Defense Production Act also led the A.F.L. and the C.I.O. to a most portentous step; early in 1951 the two organizations created a United Labor Policy Committee. Its aim was to assure active participation of labor on all levels of the war effort and to develop a common approach to problems arising out of the mobilization and stabilization programs. The committee took its job seriously. In February, 1951, when the Economic Stabilization Agency issued an over-all wage and price order, it charged that Defense Mobilizer Wilson was operating his agency on behalf of big business, and that he had no desire to give labor a real voice in the formulation of defense policy. Specifically, it objected because the wage order limited wage increases to 10 per cent of the January 15, 1950, figures and in-

cluded in wages such funds as were set aside for pensions, health and
welfare programs, and vacation and holiday pay; because it made no
provision for adjustment of inequities due to industrial change and
growth; and because the formula was to be substituted for collective
bargaining. It also objected because the price order permitted increases in agricultural prices. Accordingly, it asked labor representatives serving on defense agencies to resign their posts, and called a
"grass roots" conference of representatives of all labor groups to
consider future policy.

Labor representatives resigned, and the grass-roots conference,
seven hundred delegates, met to demand real price ceilings, tighter
rent controls, and the plugging of tax loopholes. Although the adamant stand was roundly condemned as a strike against the government, it brought some results. President Truman created a new National Advisory Board, on which labor secured four of seventeen
seats, and appointed labor representatives as deputies to Defense
Mobilizer Wilson, Economic Stabilizer Eric Johnston, and Price
Stabilizer Michael V. DiSalle. He also reconstituted the Wage Stabilization Board, to include six labor members, with power to handle
all disputes which substantially affected defense production.

Labor, however, continued to protest the inadequacy of the nation's economic mobilization for war. While it found some satisfaction
in the effort of the Price Stabilization Agency to hold back meat
prices in 1951 and in the tighter rent control provisions of the Defense
Production Act of 1951, it also found much to criticize; failure of
Congress to strengthen the President's power to enforce price ceilings,
failure to close tax loopholes in 1951, and the even more complete
abandonment of controls in 1952 provoked the greatest criticism.

Meanwhile unions continued to press for increases in wages and
other benefits to match the continued rise in the cost of living under
the formulas provided by the Wage Stabilization Board. While controversies for the most part were settled relatively easily either by
collective bargaining or by the W.S.B., the disputes on the railroads
and in steel had separate and spectacular settlements. The railway
conflict began in November, 1950, when both operating and non-
operating railworkers demanded increases in wages, a forty-hour
week and, in some cases, a union shop. When operators refused to
negotiate the union shop, the government seized the roads, placing

them under the nominal control of the army. Negotiations between railworkers and operators continued peaceably for months, punctuated only by a short wildcat trainmen's strike. In November, 1951, the President appointed an Emergency Board to make recommendations. Its reports the following year granted operating workers a 37-cent increase and nonoperating workers an increase in wages, the union shop, and the checkoff. The steel conflict began in April, 1952, when the Wage Stabilization Board recommended a 15-cent wage increase, to enable steelworkers to catch up with other labor, and a union shop. Although the steel companies were assured of a price increase to cover increased wages, they rejected the recommendation. When steelworkers issued a strike call, President Truman ordered the mills seized. The government put into effect the W.S.B. recommendation. In May, however, the whole situation was upset by a ruling of David A. Pine of the District of Columbia Court to the effect that the President had no statutory power to seize the steel mills. When the Supreme Court upheld the decision, the President withdrew government control. After a 53-day strike, the steelworkers and the companies came to an agreement on a wage increase of 16 cents and a "union shop" compromise.

28 ——

The Eisenhower Years

The steel conflict ended on the eve of the 1952 presidential campaign. A year earlier labor had begun "training" for the event. Pointing out that "fighting back" had enabled labor to check the antilabor tide, both the Political Action Committee under the leadership of Jack Kroll and Labor's League for Political Education under the leadership of James McDevitt began to exhort labor forces to ready themselves for another battle. In the first months of the training period

labor's political agencies concentrated their efforts on contributions
and registration—only about two-thirds of union members were registered to vote. Both the A.F.L. and the C.I.O. produced platforms
to present to the Republican and Democratic parties. Demands for
repeal of the Taft-Hartley Act, for enactment of a strong anti-inflation program, and for strengthening the defenses of the free world
against communist aggression headed the list. Others included
Federal aid to education, more low-cost housing, liberalization of
social security to include medical care insurance, adoption of a $1.00
minimum wage, an F.E.P.C. law, and higher wages for Federal
employees.

As labor expected, the Republican convention, which nominated
General Dwight D. Eisenhower, rejected or ignored most of the platform. Its hope and attention, accordingly, was fastened upon the
Democratic party, which had a number of candidates for nomination, among them Estes Kefauver of Tennessee, who scored a number
of spectacular primary victories; Richard B. Russell of Georgia; W.
Averell Harriman of New York; Vice President Alben W. Barkley,
who had secured the support of President Truman; and, in spite of
his insistence that he was not a candidate, Adlai E. Stevenson of
Illinois. Before the convention opened, old Democrats were confident
that Barkley would be the party nominee; but the labor delegation
at the convention, about one hundred strong, informed him that they
regarded him as too old to run and asked him to withdraw. The
contest then narrowed to Kefauver, Harriman, and Stevenson, all of
whom had labor support. While Stevenson's victory and the Democratic party's almost complete adoption of labor's platform made it
obvious what course organized labor would take in the campaign,
neither organization made an open commitment until after Stevenson
and Eisenhower had addressed their annual conventions—an un-
precedented action. When Stevenson endorsed outright repeal of
the Taft-Hartley Act, while Eisenhower would only endorse amendments, both organizations gave unanimous approval to the Democratic candidates.

Labor's political agencies threw the full force of their organizations
into the campaign. Collection of campaign funds, widespread dissemination of the records of candidates for office, registration drives,
use of radio, and doorbell-ringing campaigns marked labor's efforts

to elect its friends. To an extent the effort was successful. Although deeply disappointed by Stevenson's defeat, labor could take much of the credit for preserving a strong Democratic party which in spite of the overwhelming Eisenhower victory still had 47 senators and 213 congressmen. Organized labor began the Eisenhower administration with new top leadership. On November 9, 1952, Philip Murray, president of the C.I.O. for twelve years, died at the age of sixty-six. Less than two weeks later, William Green, president of the A.F.L. for twenty-seven years, died at the age of seventy-two. The C.I.O. promptly elected Walter P. Reuther, one-time socialist who had risen to prominence as a member of the United Automobile Workers during the war and who had become president of the U.A.W. after a bitter intraunion fight only six years earlier. The A.F.L. elevated George Meany, who had entered the world of labor unionism as a plumber, had become president of the New York Federation of Labor in 1933, and secretary-treasurer of the A.F.L. in 1939, and had been quietly assuming many of the wearing duties of the aging Green for the previous five years. Meany was succeeded as secretary-treasurer by William Schnitzler, president of the Bakery and Confectionery Workers International Union.

Although rank-and-file labor speculated over the effect that the change of leadership might have on the labor movement, its main attention soon turned to the activities of the Eisenhower administration. It is doubtful that labor expected much from President Eisenhower or the new Congress, dominated as it was by a coalition of Republicans and southern Democrats. Some reminded themselves that the President had declared that he had "no use for those . . . who had some vain and foolish dream of spinning the clock back to days when unorganized labor was a huddled, almost helpless mass." Others took hope from the appointment of Martin P. Durkin as Secretary of Labor. Durkin, a Stevenson Democrat, had been Director of Labor in Illinois under two governors, and was currently president of the United Association of Journeymen and Apprentices of the Plumbing and Pipefitting Industry.

Hopes rose even higher when the President, in his first message to Congress, suggested that the Taft-Hartley Act needed amendments that would minimize government interference with collective bargaining. Both the A.F.L. and the C.I.O. prepared extensive lists of reforms intended to accomplish that purpose and buttressed the suggestions with arguments indicating the ways in which the Taft-Hartley Act had produced bad industrial relations and had hindered collective bargaining.

If labor expected its suggestions to be heard, it was soon disillusioned. The President, after his original proposals, left the problem of amending the Taft-Hartley Act to antiunion congressional committees. Instead of securing a favorable hearing, labor was forced to fight against proposals intending to return all labor relations to the states, prohibiting industry-wide bargaining, and providing for compulsory arbitration of labor disputes. Two months after Congress adjourned, any hope that labor had left was destroyed by the resignation of Secretary of Labor Durkin because the President had withdrawn his approval of Durkin's suggestions for Taft-Hartley amendments. To labor, Durkin's resignation was proof that "big business" had full control of the administration.

Additional proof came in 1954 when Senator H. Alexander Smith of New Jersey introduced an "administration" measure which, among other amendments, provided for a government-supervised strike vote before union leaders could call a strike. Charging that the provision would drive a wedge between union leaders and rank and file, both the A.F.L. and the C.I.O. adopted the slogan "We like this even less than Taft-Hartley" and threw all their strength into a campaign to stop the bill. They succeeded but only because Senate Democrats, including antilabor Southerners, became angry over Republican "steamroller" tactics and voted to return the bill to committee.

The Eisenhower administration's attitude on Taft-Hartley amendments was only one factor in labor's disillusionment. Failure of the administration to do anything about unemployment was equally important. With the end of the Korean War industrial productivity, influenced by cancellation of government contracts, fell off. As early as February, 1953, there were indications that extensive unemployment was inevitable. By April both the A.F.L. and the C.I.O. were urging the President to take action under the Full Employment Act of 1946, and received assurances that the government would respond. When unemployment reached 3,000,000 in January, 1954, labor began to urge specific remedies: tax reduction for people with the lowest incomes, an increase in unemployment benefits, a socially useful public works program, increased Federal aid for housing, slum clearance and urban redevelopment, and government allocation of defense contracts to industries in "distress" areas. Instead of action, labor was treated to the spectacle of a quarrel between the Department of Commerce and the Bureau of Labor Statistics over the actual number of unemployed, or what the *C.I.O. News* called, "a barrage of phony government figures." The depth of the recession came in April when the official count of unemployed was recorded at 3,725,-000, to which labor added another 9,000,000 who were only partially employed. Thereafter the number of unemployed dropped to about 3,250,000, at which point the figure remained for the rest of the year.

Meanwhile other administration and congressional actions and failures had completed labor's disillusionment: appointment of the "enemies" of governmental aid and regulation to agencies like the Housing and Finance Agency and the National Labor Relations Board; enactment of the Tidelands bill turning over offshore oil resources to states or, as labor charged, to already wealthy oil interests without any return provided for the nation; a new income-tax measure which granted considerable tax relief to stockholders and persons with upper-bracket incomes and only minor relief to persons with low incomes; a rise in interest rates which increased the cost of living and particularly the cost of housing; N.L.R.B. rulings which turned over "lesser" labor disputes to the jurisdiction of the states; removal of rent controls; reduction in funds for the Department of Labor, making necessary the closing of employment offices; failure to provide for adequate housing, for Federal aid to education, and for increases in unemployment benefits; and the veto of measures to increase the salaries of Federal civil servants and post-office employees.

In small part these "inequities" were balanced by a few prolabor events: a Supreme Court decision, in *Garner* v. *Teamsters' Union*, which held that states had no right to regulate or interfere with labor conduct in interstate commerce when that conduct was already controlled by Federal law; an act extending unemployment-insurance coverage to Federal employees; an amendment to the Social Security Act extending OASI coverage to an additional ten million persons, including employees of public and charitable institutions, and providing for disability benefits; an amendment to the Railway Unemployment Insurance Act liberalizing unemployment compensation; and an amendment to the Railway Retirement Act increasing the credit base, lowering the eligibility age of surviving dependents, and increasing disability payments.

Months before the Eisenhower administration had completed its first year in office labor made known its attitude by once more turning to politics. The P.A.C. and the L.L.P.E. began their drives to elect prolabor candidates in the off-year election in August, 1953. Labor's attention was centered primarily upon the gubernatorial and congressional election in New Jersey, and upon mayoralty elections in a score of major cities. Its apparent success, particularly in aiding the election of Governor Meyner in New Jersey and Mayor Robert A. Wagner in New York City, whetted its appetite for more. In the early spring of 1954 both organizations and the railway brotherhood political agencies went into action again. Reminding themselves that there would be little "coat-tail riding" in 1954, they set out with obvious determination to defeat the Republican party. They attacked the administration as a "government of postponement," a "government of drift," a "government by press agents," and played heavily upon the administration's "callous disregard for the unemployed." They adopted the usual campaign techniques to secure funds—"Give a Buck to the P.A.C. The Job You Save May Be Your Own"—and to bring out the vote. Two factors were emphasized more thoroughly than in the past: greater attention was given to gubernatorial and legislative races and stronger efforts were made to "educate" women voters, whom many observers regarded as the decisive factor in the 1952 election.

Labor's efforts—aided by Defense Secretary Charles E. Wilson's unfortunate reference to the unemployed as "kennel dogs," and by falling farm prices—produced favorable results. In a contest in which few Republican senators were up for reelection, the Democrats increased their membership from 46 to 49; all the prolabor senators were reelected. In the House, Democrats increased their membership from 212 to 232, which enabled them to organize the chamber in 1955. Democratic governors were elected in six of ten states outside the South, including New York, Connecticut, and Pennsylvania which had been Republican.

The effect of the election of 1954 was visible in the actions of both the Federal and state governments in the following year. Although the Eisenhower administration did little about unemployment, which stabilized at about 3,000,000, and although Congress was dominated by a conservative coalition, labor counted some gains. Most important was the partial success of its effort to increase minimum wages. After the President suggested an increase in minimums from $0.75 to $0.90, both the A.F.L. and the C.I.O. undertook strenuous lobbying campaigns for a $1.25 minimum. Despite administration pressure for a lower figure, Congress ultimately enacted a $1.00 minimum, bringing automatic increases to more than 2,000,000 workers.

In the states labor had additional success. When the year began, seventeen states had "right to work" laws, the term applied by anti-labor forces to legislation prohibiting union security agreements. With most state legislatures in session, new or stronger laws were introduced in thirty-three states. Except in Utah and in Kansas the A.F.L. and the C.I.O., sometimes separately and sometimes in combination, managed to pressure enough legislators to prevent passage. Labor also defeated an effort by Republican-dominated legislatures in several Midwestern states to "muzzle" the P.A.C. and the L.L.P.E. On the positive side labor secured changes in existing unemployment insurance legislation. Increases in maximum benefits, from $20–$33 a week to $25–$36 a week, were provided by thirty-two states; lengthening of duration of benefits was provided by twenty states.

All of labor's attention was not concentrated on politics during the first three years of the Eisenhower administration. An equal if not a greater amount of its energy was spent on trade-union affairs. Both the A.F.L. and the C.I.O. continued their organizing campaigns among southern and white-collar workers, reporting small gains which put the combined total of the two organizations at about 16,000,000 by 1955. In addition both organizations became involved in special organizing drives developing out of the actions taken against affiliates.

A.F.L. involvement grew out of exposures of the fact that gangsters were using Joseph P. Ryan's International Longshoreman's Union as a vehicle for extortion and exploitation on the New York waterfront. A.F.L. action in January, 1953, was without precedent. The Executive Council ordered the I.L.A. to remove all international and local officers who had accepted gifts or bribes, to remove all union representatives with criminal records, to abolish the notorious "shape up," and to establish democratic practices, or face expulsion. When the I.L.A. failed to act, the A.F.L. convention broke relations with its affiliate, created a new organization, the I.L.A.-A.F.L., and began a campaign to win over the I.L.A. locals. By mid-November the I.L.A.-A.F.L. had won over 121 locals, including all those on the Pacific Coast and the bulk of those on the Great Lakes and in the river ports. New York and New Jersey locals proved more difficult. Employer opposition, terrorism, and use of injunctions hampered activity. An N.L.R.B. election, held in December, 1953, revealed a plurality for the I.L.A. When the returns were voided because of charges of terror, a second election was held. The I.L.A. again secured a plurality. In spite of the loss, the A.F.L. refused to make concessions. When teamsters suggested that they be given jurisdiction over longshore work, a request which the A.F.L. regarded as a move to bring back ousted longshoremen, the convention curtly refused and established the International Brotherhood of Longshoremen. By 1955 the I.B.L. reported that it had won over the majority of former I.L.A. members.

C.I.O. involvement in special organizing drives grew out of the expulsion of communist-dominated unions. The biggest campaign was conducted by the International Union of Electrical Workers, which recovered 80 per cent of the old U.E. membership by 1955 and had asserted its position as bargaining agent for electrical workers in over 90 per cent of the U.E.'s former plants. Meanwhile steelworkers and glassworkers made inroads upon the former members of the Mine and Millworkers Union, and the U.A.W. invaded the jurisdiction of the Farm Equipment Workers. In 1954 the C.I.O. created the Leather Workers Organizing Committee and invaded the jurisdiction of the ousted Fur and Leather Workers.

Along with the organizing campaign the A.F.L. and the C.I.O. continued to strengthen their internal structure. Affiliates of both extended their labor education programs and expanded research departments. The A.F.L. adopted a new and comprehensive auditing system. Most important, both organizations adopted codes of ethical practices to govern administration of health and welfare funds. The step was taken as a result of exposure of malpractices by officers controlling funds of several C.I.O. retail clerks' locals in New York City. Both codes were similar, revealing the long experience of clothing workers' unions with such funds. They recommended that union officials who acted as trustees of funds be paid no extra compensation; that union officials or employees who administered funds have no ties with insurance companies; that insurance companies handling the funds should be chosen by competitive bidding; that investment of funds in any enterprise in which a trustee had an interest be forbidden; that a record be kept of all claims and payments made; that funds be audited annually; and that internationals approve plans of locals before they became effective.

Labor efforts to keep pace with the cost of living also continued throughout the first three years of the Eisenhower administration. For the most part the efforts were quiet. The number of strikes and the amount of man days of labor lost remained fairly constant at the 1947–1952 level. There were few big strikes during the period. Rubber workers, East Coast maritime workers, southwestern telephone workers, and Pacific Coast logging, lumbering, and plywood workers engaged in the most widely publicized conflicts. In 1953 and 1954 average wage increases were about six cents an hour, with not too much attention given to fringe benefits. In 1955 the situation changed. Although the number and size of strikes remained fairly stable, labor demands increased. Wage increases were slightly larger, about eight cents an hour, and the pension and welfare programs were strengthened and expanded. The most spectacular development involved the United Automobile Workers' drive for a guaranteed annual wage.

The movement for a guaranteed annual wage ran back to the 1890's when the National Wallpaper Company and the Machine Printers and Color Mixers Union had reached an agreement guaranteeing eleven months' employment. By 1946 nearly two hundred companies had adopted similar plans covering 60,000 workers. The postwar movement for a guaranteed annual wage was headed by the steelworkers who made a request for such a program during negotiations with the steel industry in the latter months of 1943. When industry refused to consider the suggestions, the problem was taken up by the National War Labor Board which in turn recommended a study. In 1951 the steelworkers renewed their demand, but the Wage

Stabilization Board refused to recommend negotiation on the subject.

The U.A.W. campaign began in 1953 and reached consummation, amid a barrage of analysis and criticism, in June, 1955, when Ford agreed to a contract. Within a short time General Motors, Chrysler, and various farm-machinery and airplane manufacturers signed similar contracts covering 900,000 workers. The agreement, which actually guaranteed a semiannual wage, provided that qualified workers, when unemployed, would receive from 60 to 65 per cent of their normal earnings, the company paying the difference between unemployment compensation and the guaranteed wage over a six-month period. Payment would begin when it was ascertained that two-thirds of a company's covered employees lived in states which permitted unemployment compensation to be drawn at the same time as supplementary benefits.

The most significant action of labor in the first three years of the Eisenhower administration was the reunion of the A.F.L. and the C.I.O. The postwar movement for unity began shortly after the election of 1946, motivated by recognition that the Republican triumph boded no good for labor. Murray made the initial overture to both Green and the railway brotherhoods, calling for reunion as "protection against the ferocious attacks . . . being made upon labor." In the spring of 1947, when passage of unfavorable legislation appeared imminent, ten men from the A.F.L. and the C.I.O. met in conference. The C.I.O. proposed that certain steps be taken before organic unity was achieved: establishment of joint committees to direct the fight against antilabor legislation, elimination of raiding, submission of jurisdictional disputes to arbitration, recognition of industrial unionism as an integral part of any new structure, preservation of the integrity of existing unions, and establishment of effective machinery for political action. In short, the C.I.O. wanted a period of joint action to precede efforts at unification. The A.F.L. proposed that the C.I.O. unions enter the A.F.L. with their full membership and that negotiating committees be appointed to "adjust details," make recommendations, and combine the resources of both organizations to fight antilabor legislation. The A.F.L., in short, felt that all issues were incidental to the fundamental one of unity. The conference ended without complete understanding. Although both groups of conferees agreed that organic unity was necessary, the A.F.L. delegates went away with the idea that unity would be established before any other actions would be taken and the C.I.O. delegates retired with the idea that a joint program of action would be started before organic unity was achieved. The differing conceptions led Murray and Green to an exchange of caustic letters in which Murray charged that the A.F.L. Executive Council was opposed to unity, and Green charged that communists in the C.I.O. were the real opponents of unity.

For the next several years the two organizations continued to issue statements concerning the desirability of unity, but neither made a positive step in that direction until after the outbreak of the Korean War and the congressional election of 1950. Then the fear that labor's interest might be "sold down the river" led the two organizations to form the United Labor Policy Committee as a watchdog over governmental policy. For a time cooperation was extensive, as evidenced by the "grass roots" conference of leaders of all labor groups in March, 1951, and by joint action in securing reform of the Economic Stabilization agencies. In August, 1951, however, the A.F.L. withdrew from the United Labor Policy Committee because the job of the committee had been completed and because there was "no substitute for organic unity." To the C.I.O. the action was highly discouraging. Once more Murray charged that the A.F.L. was opposed to unity and that the crafts were still trying to break up industrial unions. Green in reply indicated that the A.F.L. was not opposed to unity, that Murray in raising the issue of craft against industrial unionism was "resurrecting a dead cat," and that with "organized labor's stock . . . at low ebb in Congress and in the state legislatures" it was time for all trade unionists to take "a broader view of the problem."

Despite the obvious invitation to further negotiation nothing significant was accomplished until after the election of 1952 when the final movement for reunion began. A large number of factors made the movement successful: the gradual disappearance of old antagonists culminating in the death of Green and Murray, both of whom had become overly sensitive and suspicious; the recognition that the old craft versus industrial unionism was a dead issue since more than half of the A.F.L.'s members were in industrial unions; and the victory of the Republicans in 1952 which seemed to presage another antilabor drive. Both Meany and Reuther announced their intention of seeking labor unity in their inaugural addresses, and both responded to suggestions for a meeting by naming conferees. Both groups entered their first meeting "without prior commitments" and promptly appointed a subcommittee to draw up a program for elimination of one of the major sources of trouble between the two organizations: raiding.

In June, 1953, the subcommittee reported a proposal whereby each organization would agree not to conduct organizational raids against the other in every case where a union had been certified as a collective bargaining agent or had been recognized by the employer as a collective bargaining agent; it also suggested the appointment of an impartial umpire to make final and binding decisions in cases where a dispute could not be solved in other ways. Quickly approved by the Executive Councils of the A.F.L. and the C.I.O., the agreement was sent on to affiliates. Along with the agreement the Executive Councils sent the information that out of 1,245 cases of raiding, involving 350,000 workers, in 1951–1952 only 8,000 union members had changed affiliation. Approval of the agreement by the Executive Councils created a small crisis within the A.F.L. when the carpenters withdrew from the organization because the A.F.L. had made no effort to settle the problem of raiding, a major issue between carpenters and machinists, within the A.F.L. Quick negotiations soon settled the issue; the carpenters reaffiliated, and ratification of the agreement proceeded relatively smoothly, punctuated only occasionally by denunciations of notorious raiding unions like the teamsters and by announcements which indicated that not all suspicions of rivals had been allayed. In the fall of 1953 with the approval of sixty-five A.F.L. affiliates and twenty-nine C.I.O. affiliates, representing 10,000,000 workers, the A.F.L. and C.I.O. conventions ratified the pact. The no-raiding agreement became effective in July, 1954.

Almost immediately plans for total merger began to develop. The Unity Committee met in October, 1954, and announced a determination to create "a single trade union center . . . which will preserve the integrity of each affiliated national and international union." In February, 1955, the Unity Committee agreed upon terms of merger. Promptly ratified by the A.F.L. and C.I.O. executive bodies, with only Michael Quill of the C.I.O. Transport Workers dissenting, the terms, as before, were sent to affiliates. Meanwhile the Unity Committee continued its work on a constitution which was published in May, 1955. Without giving the new organization a name, the constitution announced that the organization would have twelve "objects and principles": (1) to aid workers in securing improved wages, hours, and working conditions with due regard for the autonomy and integrity of affiliated unions; (2) to promote the organization of the unorganized into unions of their own choosing, giving recognition to both craft and industrial unionism; (3) to encourage formation of locals, state and local central bodies, and nationals, and the affiliation of such organizations with the new federation; (4) to encourage all workers without regard to race, creed, or national origin to share in full benefits of unionism; (5) to secure legislation which would safeguard and promote the principle of free collective bargaining; (6) to protect and strengthen the nation's democratic institutions; (7) to give constructive aid in promoting the cause of peace and freedom in the world; (8) to preserve and maintain the integrity of each affiliated union in the organization; (9) to encourage the sale and use of union-made goods and union services and to promote the labor press; (10) to protect the labor movement from any and all corrupt influences and from the undermining efforts of communist agencies and all others who were opposed to the basic principles of democracy; (11) to safeguard the democratic character of the labor movement; (12) to encourage workers to register and vote and to exercise their full rights and responsibilities as citizens, at the same time preserving the independence of the labor movement from political control.

The constitution granted membership to all affiliates, including organizing committees currently chartered by the A.F.L. and the C.I.O. While it assured nationals and internationals that they would enjoy their current organizing jurisdiction, it encouraged them to eliminate duplication in organization and jurisdiction through merger or other voluntary agreement. It also gave membership to all state federations and industrial union councils and to local central bodies, all of which were ordered to merge in two years. It empowered the Executive Council to issue new charters or certificates of affiliation, authorized the convention to suspend any affiliate by majority vote and revoke a charter by a two-thirds vote, and barred organizations dominated by communists, fascists, or other totalitarians from membership.

The instrument declared that the convention, which would meet every two years, would be the supreme governing body of the organization. Nationals, internationals and organizing committees would be represented in the convention on a pro-rata basis: 1 delegate for any number of members; 2 delegates for more than 4,000 members; 3 delegates for more than 8,000 members; 4 delegates for more than 12,000 members; 5 delegates for more than 25,000 members; 6 delegates for more than 50,000 members; 7 delegates for more than 75,000 members; 8 delegates for more than 125,000 members; 9 delegates for more than 175,000 members; additional delegates for every 75,000 members over 175,000. Trade departments, state and local councils, and directly affiliated locals were entitled to one delegate.

The constitution provided for a president, a secretary-treasurer, and twenty-seven vice presidents. It established an Executive Committee—the president, secretary, and six vice presidents—which would meet and consult on policy matters every two months. It provided for an Executive Council—the president, secretary, and the vice presidents—which was to be the governing body between conventions. The constitution gave the Executive Council extensive power: to watch legislative measures and to initiate legislation; to investigate affiliates dominated in the conduct of their affairs by any corrupt influence or by a totalitarian movement and to suspend any affiliate under such domination; to assist organizing activity; to file charges against and conduct hearings of any executive officer of the organization suspected of malfeasance or maladministration and to make recommendations concerning him to the convention; to remove any member of the Executive Council who was tainted with totalitarianism. The constitution also provided for a "General Board" to consist of all members of the Executive Council and a principal officer of each national or international. The board would meet once a year to decide policy questions referred to it by the Executive Council.

The instrument recognized the old departmental structure of the A.F.L. by providing for departments involving building and construction trades, metal trades, union-label trades, railway employees, and maritime employees. It also recognized the C.I.O. pattern with a provision for a department of industrial organizations.

Finally the instrument set up rules and regulations to govern state and local central bodies, unions directly affiliated with the organization, organizing committees, and national councils (embryo nationals); provided for per capita taxes and for amendments; and for continuation of the A.F.L.-C.I.O. No Raiding Pact, the A.F.L. Internal Disputes Plan, and for the C.I.O. Organizational Disputes Agreement.

A.F.L. and C.I.O. Executive Committees ratified the new instrument with a speed that amazed the nation. Although much of the public, long accustomed to the reports of warfare between A.F.L. and C.I.O. leaders and unions, expected to see a bitter fight develop over unity in both the A.F.L. and the C.I.O., the reunion movement continued smoothly. In July the Unity Committee solved the last knotty problem with the suggestion that the new organization be called the American Federation of Labor and the Congress of Industrial Organizations. Early in December the A.F.L. convention, representing over 10,200,000 workers—after noting minor reservations from the typographers and sleeping-car porters—voted unanimously for unity. Simultaneously the C.I.O. convention voted 5,712,077 to 120,002 for merger, the only dissent coming from Michael Quill's Transport Workers Union and two industrial councils. A few days later under the bright lights of the cavernous Seventy-first Regimental Armory in New York the A.F.L.-C.I.O. became a reality.

The new organization elected George Meany president and William F. Schnitzler secretary-treasurer. It named seventeen A.F.L. vice presidents and ten C.I.O. vice presidents. It also approved creation of an industrial union department, headed by Reuther and Carey. All former C.I.O. unions, except the Transport Workers, and thirty-five former A.F.L. unions affiliated, giving the department some 7,000,000 members.

The A.F.L.-C.I.O. merger did not bring any miraculous change. The new organization, in fact, was confronted with some new problems. Shortly after the Unity Convention, the Eighty-fourth Congress met in its second session, and labor was immediately faced with a new threat presented by Senators Barry Goldwater of Arizona and Carl Curtis of Nebraska who, publicly fearful of the influence that the new A.F.L.-C.I.O. might bring to bear upon the nation's voters, proposed legislation to prohibit unions from contributing "directly or indirectly" to any political party or any "committee" that contributed funds "directly or indirectly" to parties or candidates. Although the measure was buried in committee, it seemed to forbode renewed efforts to clip labor influence.

Meanwhile, the A.F.L.-C.I.O. urged Congress to revise the Taft-Hartley Act on behalf of the building trades who were calling for amendments to permit certification of bargaining units before elections and to permit negotiations with multiple employers, both traditional practices forbidden by current N.L.R.B. rulings. The new organization also urged extension of minimum-wage laws to 21,-000,000 workers not covered by the Fair Labor Standards Act. Although neither effort succeeded, labor secured some satisfaction from the passage of amendments to the Social Security Act—providing for pensions to the permanently and totally disabled at the age of fifty and retirement benefits for women and wives at the age of sixty-two —and from the passage of amendments raising benefits for injured workers under the Longshoremen's and Harbor Workers' Compensation Act, which applied not only to longshore workmen but to all persons employed by private industry in the District of Columbia and to all citizens working for government contractors outside the United States. Labor was also gratified by its success in checking further enactment of "right to work" laws in fifteen states and in securing repeal of a Louisiana statute forbidding union security agreements.

The new organization also became involved as thoroughly as ever in the 1956 political campaign. Shortly after unity was achieved, a new political agency, the Committee on Political Education, directed by Jack Kroll and James McDevitt, was established and promptly began a drive for funds to make labor's influence felt at the next election. C.O.P.E. activity throughout the spring and early summer of 1956 was more vigorous than that usually revealed by labor's earlier political agencies. In addition to normal activities, C.O.P.E. directors and supporters scheduled scores of regional and union conferences to build up enthusiasm for the coming campaign. In the summer the A.F.L.-C.I.O. Executive Council prepared a labor platform for consideration of the two major parties. It contained five generalized demands: improvement of national defense and the unity of the free world; strengthening of the national economy by broadening purchasing power; legislation guaranteeing civil rights; "overhaul" of the Taft-Hartley Act; legislation protecting employee pension and welfare funds.

Although A.F.L.-C.I.O. officials announced that the organization would not be "tied to the coat-tail of any political party," labor was obviously more interested in the Democratic convention at which a large number of union members appeared as delegates. The party responded well, adopting planks on foreign policy, on economic policy, on welfare and housing, on the Taft-Hartley Act, minimum wages, and social security, which were entirely acceptable to labor. It also nominated Stevenson and Kefauver, candidates whom labor trusted. The Republicans also responded with a labor plank, but its wording was "hazy" and its coverage incomplete.

As the nation expected, labor "supported" the Democratic nominees. The Executive Council endorsed Stevenson almost unanimously; the General Board endorsed Stevenson with only slight dissent from the carpenters who objected to any endorsements. Nationals and internationals which held conventions during the election campaign enthusiastically endorsed Stevenson. Only four labor leaders—Dave Beck of the teamsters, Maurice A. Hutcheson of the carpenters, Richard Gray of the Building and Construction Trades Department, and Harry Lundeberg of the seafarers—publicly supported Eisenhower. Meanwhile C.O.P.E. engaged in one of the most vigorous political campaigns in labor history on behalf of candidates favorable to labor. Its greatest effort, occasioned by a knowledge that only five out of eight union members were voters, was used to secure a high registration.

While labor was deeply disappointed with the results of the presidential race, it did secure some gratification out of the fact that both houses of Congress were captured by the Democratic party. Of the 288 candidates for the House of Representatives endorsed by C.O.P.E., 159 were successful; of the 29 Senate candidates endorsed, 15 were successful. Labor was also gratified by the fact that Democrats had won 11 gubernatorial contests in the North and West and had made some gains in state legislatures. Nevertheless it began to anticipate another hard struggle to check passage of antilabor legislation.

Although much of labor's attention during 1956 was centered on Congress, state legislatures, and the political campaign, the A.F.L.-C.I.O. reunion also provided the spark for a new organizing drive. The new organization appointed John W. Livingston of the United Automobile Workers as Director of Organization, established an entirely new district organizing structure, and renewed its campaign to win over white-collar, textile, oil and chemical, and furniture workers. In its first two years the campaign showed only slight results. Some progress was registered by old organizing movements. The New Jersey district of the communist-dominated electrical workers, composed of 80,000 workers, severed its affiliation, reducing the once proud U.E. to less than 30,000 members. The meatcutters, moreover, were allowed to absorb the untainted former C.I.O. fur workers' locals. At the same time the International Brotherhood of Longshoremen made no further progress on the New York waterfront. In an election held in 1957 the I.L.A. defeated the I.B.L. for a third time, 11,800 to 7,400.

The problem of unemployment abated in 1956. While labor continued to point to certain industrial regions as "distress areas" and to demand action for alleviating misery in those areas, over-all employment figures reached new highs in both 1956 and 1957. At the same time the cost of living continued to mount month after month to new record highs. The inevitable result was a new drive for wage increases in 1956. As before, the efforts were quiet, provoking only a moderate number of strikes and few large ones. Most widely known was the strike of 55,000 I.E. workers against Westinghouse, which began on the eve of merger and continued for five months over management breach of contract concerning time and motion studies. Others included the strike of the Newspaper Guild against Detroit newspapers; the strike of hotel and restaurant workers against Miami hotels; and the strike of 650,000 steelworkers against 172 companies for guaranteed wages—or for supplementary unemployment benefits, as labor now described the institution—in the summer of 1956. For the most part labor was successful, securing wage concessions of 11 to 13 cents. Steel, aluminum, rubber, and maritime workers, among others, secured contracts providing for S.U.P. benefits.

Problems connected with the internal structure of the New A.F.L.-C.I.O. also engaged much of labor's attention. Some were relatively easy to solve. Integration of high-level committee structures, of administrative departments like labor education and research, and of the labor press associations provided personnel problems but no major policy decisions. Progress toward expansion of the organization was also satisfactory; the Brotherhood of Locomotive Firemen and Enginemen and the Brotherhood of Railway Trainmen, two of the nation's oldest independent unions, joined the new organization, and the metal engravers, another old independent union, affiliated by merging with the machinists. Various nationals also united. The movement toward unity, in fact, had started before the A.F.L.-C.I.O. had been created. Within the A.F.L. the boilermakers and the blacksmiths had merged before the final unity conferences had begun. In the C.I.O. the Retail, Wholesale and Department Store Union, the Distributive, Processing and Office Workers of America, and the Playthings, Jewelry and Novelty Workers had merged in 1954. Oil and chemical workers had formed a new international in the same year; Transport Workers and United Railway Workers had merged during the next year. After the A.F.L.-C.I.O. was formed, A.F.L. State, County and Municipal Employees and the C.I.O. Government and Civic Employees Organizing Committee formed a new union. A.F.L. Papermakers and C.I.O. Paperworkers also merged and celebrated the occasion by winning several N.L.R.B. elections from their old enemy, the U.M.W.'s District 50. In the summer and fall of 1957 the A.F.L. Meatcutters and the C.I.O. Packinghouse Workers and various barber, shoemaking, glassworking, and marine-engineering unions began to consider unification.

There was evidence of other harmonious actions. The number of unions in the Industrial Union Department increased from sixty-six to seventy-seven in the first year. More important was the pact between the Building Trades Department and the Industrial Union Department concerning working jurisdiction. Borrowing extensively from an earlier carpenters-machinists contract, the new agreement gave jurisdiction over new construction to the building trades, over production and running maintenance to industrial unions, and provided that jurisdiction over alterations, major repairs, relocation of existing facilities and changeovers would be governed by existing local practices. The agreement constituted a big step in the direction of interunion peace.

Less satisfactory progress was made in the movement to merge state federations and industrial union councils. By the time of the second A.F.L.-C.I.O. convention thirty-three state organizations had united. The bulk of the mergers, however, occurred among the weaker organizations of the South, trans-Mississippi West, and Southwest; included in the fifteen unmerged groups were those of Massachusetts, Rhode Island, New York, New Jersey, Pennsylvania, Ohio, Indiana, Michigan, Illinois, Wisconsin, and California.

The most pressing problem which the A.F.L.-C.I.O. encountered in its first two years of life involved the scandals that developed around administration of health and welfare funds. Since both the A.F.L. and the C.I.O. were well aware of the problem, it was inevitable that the new organization should give the situation much attention, particularly since labor leaders feared that exposure of corruption in the labor movement would give antilabor forces an opportunity to press for more "union busting" legislation. During its first year the A.F.L.-C.I.O. proceeded cautiously and quietly. It asked Congress to enact legislation requiring registration of, and annual reports from, all employee welfare and pension plans. Congress did not respond. The A.F.L.-C.I.O. then requested both the Democratic and Republican parties to adopt planks on the subject; neither complied. Meanwhile, the organization pushed investigations into the affairs of affiliates. In the spring of 1956 it ordered the teamsters to sever financial relations with the International Longshoremen's Association which had been ousted by the A.F.L. for corruption. In September, 1956, it warned the Allied Industrial Workers (formerly the A.F.L.'s automobile workers), the distillery workers, and the laundry workers that they were under suspicion.

In January, 1957, the whole problem of corruption in the labor unions suddenly became acute when the Senate established a special committee, headed by Senator John L. McClellan of Arkansas, to investigate racketeering in the field of labor-management relations. The McClellan committee promptly turned the spotlight on Dave Beck and other officers of the Teamsters Union. Although the union attempted to deny Senate jurisdiction and Beck pleaded the Fifth Amendment, the committee exposed a sordid story of misappropriation of union funds and of connections between West Coast racketeers and teamster officials. Further probing by the committee revealed misuse of funds in the Bakers Union and in the United Textile Workers.

Senate investigation undoubtedly prodded the A.F.L.-C.I.O. into more drastic action. In January, 1957, the Executive Council, adopting the position that labor must "keep its own house in order," announced that union officials had the responsibility of cooperating with the government and other public agencies who were seeking "fairly and objectively" to root out corruption. It also announced that a union official had no right to hold office in his union if he resorted to the Fifth Amendment on all relevant questions "for his personal protection and to avoid scrutiny by proper legislative committees, law enforcement agencies or other public bodies into alleged corruption on his part."

Then it turned its wrath and concern on Dave Beck. Charging him with malfeasance and maladministration, the council suspended him from his A.F.L.-C.I.O. vice presidential office and ordered an investigation of teamster affairs. A few months later the Ethical Practices Committee, using the evidence presented before the McClellan Committee, made a formal indictment of Beck and other teamster officials. Almost simultaneously it ordered an investigation into the affairs of the Bakers Union and the United Textile Workers; and suspended the Allied Industrial Workers, the distillery workers, and the laundry workers for failure to comply with "clean up" directives. Meanwhile, it continued to urge Congress to pass adequate legislation to govern welfare and pension funds. Although President Eisenhower and the Secretary of Labor announced their support, the request encountered unexpected opposition from industry. The National Association of Manufacturers asked that management-directed funds, about 90 per cent of the total, be exempted from the proposed law. Congress took no action.

Congressional adjournment did not end the problem of ethical practices. The McClellan committee, in fact, once more turned its attention to the teamsters and particularly to the activities of James R. Hoffa, vice president of the organization, revealing further misuse of funds and a connection with East Coast racketeers. The investigation of Hoffa became particularly significant when Beck, who

was indicted both for larceny and for income-tax evasion, announced
that he would retire as president of the teamsters and Hoffa announced that he was a candidate for the position. Obviously alarmed
by the development, the A.F.L.-C.I.O. president publicly declared
that election of corrupt leaders by any affiliate would mean expulsion from the federation. To give force to his words the Executive
Council, in late September, ordered the teamsters, the bakers, and
the textile workers to clean up in thirty days or face expulsion. The
order, coming as it did on the eve of the teamsters' convention at
Miami, was obviously intended to influence the convention's actions. It failed in its intention. The Beck-Hoffa forces, with a firm
grip on convention machinery, expunged the findings of the A.F.L.-
C.I.O. Ethical Practices Committee from the record and elected
Hoffa by an overwhelming majority.

To the public the significance of the teamsters' action was immediately apparent; they were challenging the A.F.L.-C.I.O. to battle.
Whether this was the intention or not, the A.F.L.-C.I.O. leadership
did not hesitate. The Executive Council ordered the immediate suspension of the teamsters. Meanwhile, the Federal courts became involved; in New York President-Elect Hoffa was indicted for wire-
tapping and perjury; in Washington Judge F. Dickinson Letts issued
an injunction, on application of thirteen New York City teamsters,
barring Hoffa's inauguration until the charge that he was elected by
a "rigged" convention could be investigated.

Simultaneously with the suspension of the teamsters, the Executive Council suspended the United Textile Workers, ordered the
bakers to call a clean-up convention in ninety days, and restored the
Allied Industrial Workers to good standing. At the A.F.L.-C.I.O.
convention of December, 1957, the council's efforts to clean up unionism were thoroughly reviewed. The convention expelled the teamsters by a 5–1 vote, expelled the bakers by a 7–1 vote (an action followed by the creation of a new affiliate, the American Bakery and
Confectionery Workers Union), and the laundry workers by an almost unanimous vote. It kept the distillery workers on probation and
restored the textile workers to good standing. Most significant was
the expulsion of the teamsters, the nation's largest union. Although
leaders on both sides disclaimed any desire to wage an internecine
war, such an event appeared possible in the winter of 1957–1958.

If the A.F.L.-C.I.O. expected that its housecleaning activities would check the McClellan committee's investigations, it was doomed to disappointment. Over the next two years the committee dug deeper into the activities of the teamsters—and particularly those of Hoffa, who in January, 1958, was allowed by the courts to assume his office as president of the union under the supervision of a three-man board of monitors. Although not conclusive, the investigations suggested that teamster officials were guilty of such previously unrevealed forms of misconduct as acceptance of payoffs by management. The committee also broadened its investigations to include inquiries into the allegedly unethical activities of various officials, national and local, of the operating engineers, the hotel and restaurant employees, the meat cutters, and the carpenters. It also inquired into the U.A.W.'s conduct during its four-year strike against the Kohler Company, a plumbing-fixture manufacturer.

As a result of the investigations, Congress enacted two measures: the Welfare and Pension Plans Disclosure Act in 1958—which the A.F.L.-C.I.O. had suggested and supported and which required that administrators make available descriptions of their plans to participants and file copies with the Secretary of Labor—and the Labor Management Reporting and Disclosure Act in September, 1959.

The latter measure, incorrectly but persistently called the Landrum-Griffin Act, was the product of a long wrangle in congressional committee rooms, a wrangle that was in turn the product of conflicting attitudes within the labor world and conflicting and contradictory forces in Congress. In part, it contained amendments to the Taft-Hartley Act urged by organized labor; the most important removed the prohibition against voting by economic strikers in representation elections and granted unions and employers in the building trades permission to conclude pre-hiring agreements. The Act also contained provisions designed to make the Taft-Hartley Act more severe. It extended secondary-boycott provisions to cover efforts to coerce an employer to cease doing business with another; it prohibited hot-cargo agreements except in certain specified circumstances in the construction and clothing industries; it defined organizational and recognition picketing as unfair labor practices in some instances.

Otherwise, the measure contained two major sets of provisions. One was the product of the A.F.L.-C.I.O.'s request for legislation to combat abuses in the handling of union funds and of the McClellan committee's exposure of misuse of funds. The Act established elaborate provisions to safeguard union funds and property and to limit use of such money and property to normal and traditional union activities—a provision that promptly led to a Federal court case in Georgia, which raised the question of whether or not political activity by labor was normal and traditional. The other set was the result of the McClellan committee's findings that some union officials had violated the rights of some union members, a finding that led much of the public to conclude that labor leaders were not reflecting the opinions and aspirations of the rank and file —which opinions and aspirations the public erroneously equated with its own interests. The findings also encouraged anti-union forces to seek to drive a wedge between union officers and members. Consequently, the Act contained extensive provisions for governing union elections and for protecting the rights of individual members.

Although the meaning of the L.M.R.D. Act was not clear at the time of its passage, it appeared that it might become a milestone in the history of labor. Before 1959 Federal enactments dealing with labor had usually been protective—in the nature of social-welfare legislation—or had attempted to regulate relations between organized labor and management. The latter laws had given labor and management quasi-legislative power to regulate their own relations within the limitations imposed by the "public interest." The new law assumed that the trade union had become a kind of public utility, that its actions so affected the nation that its internal organization, which governed its actions, could be regulated in much the same way as the internal organization of a political party. Passage of the Act raised the questions of whether or not trade unions were still voluntary and free associations and of whether or not the Federal government had the power to impose further regulations that might entirely destroy the trade-union movement as it had developed since colonial days. The raising of such questions understandably plunged organized labor into a state of gloom.

In some ways the L.M.R.D. Act, which contained some provisions supported by labor and some opposed by labor and which, on balance, appeared to be an anti-union measure, was symbolic of the whole of the A.F.L.-C.I.O.'s political-legislative activities and programs during the second half of the Eisenhower administration. In those years some welfare legislation that labor had suggested, supported, or approved was enacted by Congress; most of it took the form of amendments to or extensions of New Deal legislation. Congress twice provided increases in salaries for 1,500,000 Federal employees, including organized postal workers, whose importance in the A.F.L.-C.I.O. was growing; the second increase was enacted over the President's veto. Congress also provided small increases in O.A.S.I. benefits and 10–20 per cent increases in railway workers' unemployment benefits and pensions. The pension increase provided higher incomes to 700,000 retired workers and survivors.

In the states, legislatures made improvements all through the period in workingmen's compensation laws, in the form of increased benefits and extended coverage, and in unemployment compensation laws, in the form of extended duration of payments (a development aided by Federal loans) and increased payments to keep pace with rising living costs. By 1960 seven states paid maximum weekly unemployment benefits of $45 or more; twenty-three paid between $35 and $45; twenty paid less than $35. A number of states also began to give attention to two other problems in which trade unions were interested: job discrimination and migrant labor. California and Ohio enacted F.E.P.C. laws; Massachusetts, New York, Delaware, Colorado, and Nevada either strengthened old laws or enacted new laws intended to improve the conditions of migrant agricultural workers.

Organized labor also scored some victories during the elections of 1958. In addition to undertaking successful campaigns on behalf of the "friends" of labor, which increased Democratic majorities in both houses of Congress, it also defeated most efforts to enact right-to-work laws prohibiting union security agreements. In Ohio, Colorado, Idaho, California, and Washington it persuaded voters to reject such laws in state referendums—a clear indication that it might be able to sell its case to the public if it used the right tactics.

But such advances and victories were counterbalanced—even overbalanced—by failures and defeats. Organized labor was unable to secure legislation increasing minimum wages, to secure "adequate" Federal aid to education, or to secure a program of hospital and surgical care for aged recipients of Federal Social Security benefits. The best it could obtain for the medical care of the aged was the Kerr-Mills Act, which provided for a limited voluntary program in which states with approved plans could receive Federal grants to help meet the cost of aid to those who were on old-age assistance rolls or who could pass a means test—a measure that the A.F.L.-C.I.O. recognized as entirely inadequate. Nor could organized labor persuade Congress to repeal Section 14(b) of the Taft-Hartley Act, which permitted states to enact right-to-work laws, or prevent enactment of such laws in three additional states: Indiana, Kansas, and Utah.

More important were the problems of slackening economic developments and growing unemployment. The economy, which had been relatively stable in 1955–1956, began to feel the effects of a decline in business investments in plants and equipment and of a cutback in Federal defense outlays in mid-1957. The decline almost immediately revealed itself in the rise of unemployment by 750,000 (most of it in manufacturing industries) and by a drop in the length of the factory work week and in spendable income. In 1958 expenditures by state and local governments and an increase in construction, aided by an easing of mortgage rates, brought considerable revival in economic activity—a revival that continued into 1959 and 1960. Unemployment, however, continued to grow, reaching more than 5,000,000 in December, 1960. Continued reduction of the factory work week and a constant rise in consumer prices, furthermore, reduced the purchasing power of those employed. By the end of 1960, 51 of the nation's 149 major industrial areas and 123 smaller areas had substantial numbers (above 6 per cent) unemployed. Although organized labor renewed its often reiterated suggestions for alleviating the problem, it could not persuade anyone to listen.

As in the earlier Eisenhower years, not all of labor's efforts were concentrated on political matters. During 1958–1959, while the McClellan committee was continuing its investigations, the A.F.L.-C.I.O. accorded considerable attention to the problem of ethical practices. It continued its supervision of the distillery and textile

workers, investigated, and on threat of suspension ordered cleanups
in the unions of the operating engineers, the meat cutters, the hotel
and restaurant employees, and the jewelry workers. At the same
time, it took no action against Maurice A. Hutchinson, president
of the carpenters union, despite the McClellan committee's suggestion that he had misused union funds and his conviction in
Indiana for bribing highway officials.

The teamsters also gave the A.F.L.-C.I.O. some uncomfortable
moments. Although the anticipated conflict between the A.F.L.-
C.I.O. and the teamsters did not materialize, the former did have
to face the problem of long-standing good relationships that the
teamsters had developed with other unions. These relationships,
written into agreements, were renegotiated in 1958 with unions
covering nearly two-thirds of the A.F.L.-C.I.O. membership. The
situation, which appeared to make the expulsion of the teamsters
an empty gesture, was aggravated by Hoffa's efforts to create a
conference on transportation unity. The A.F.L.-C.I.O. Executive
Council ordered all such agreements dissolved.

In the meantime the teamsters' union was having problems of its
own. It engaged in extensive controversy over the legality, the
membership, and the powers of the monitors appointed to supervise
its affairs—which the courts seemed unable to resolve. It faced
several local revolts. Hoffa found himself embroiled in litigations
involving his own activities.

The A.F.L.-C.I.O. was also occupied with jurisdictional conflicts.
Despite earlier agreements, conflicts developed between the steelworkers and sheet-metal workers, between the airline pilots and
the flight engineers, and among building trades unions engaged on
missile sites. A.F.L.-C.I.O. efforts to establish arbitration procedures
to solve such problems failed.

On the brighter side was the continuing merger and affiliation
movement. Although the process seemed extraordinarily desultory,
47 state federations and industrial congresses had completed their
mergers by the end of 1958. Pennsylvania completed its process in
1960; New Jersey, in 1961. The wallpaper workers and the pulp,
sulphite, and paper mill workers united in 1958; postal clerks and
independent post-office craftsmen, in 1960. Negotiations among
seven airline unions, which resulted in a mutual-aid pact, and be-

tween the typographers and the Newspaper Guild, which proclaimed a goal of one union in the printing and publishing field, seemed to foretell additional mergers.

The A.F.L.-C.I.O. also added a major affiliate; the International Longshoremen's Association, which the A.F.L. had expelled in 1953 on charges of racketeering, was admitted on a two-year probationary basis on condition that it merge or develop a working agreement with its A.F.L.-created and generally impotent rival, the International Brotherhood of Longshoremen, and that it make no formal agreement with the teamsters. The I.L.A. and I.B.L. merged in 1959. This addition to the ranks, however, was partially counterbalanced by some losses. A splinter group of the American Federation of Musicians on the West Coast formed a rival union, the Musicians' Guild of America, and in 1958 displaced the A.F.M. as representative of the musicians in Hollywood; the Radio and Television Directors' Guild merged with the Screen Directors' Guild of America to form an independent union.

Organized labor's collective bargaining activities during the second half of the Eisenhower administration were fundamentally a continuation of the well-patterned developments of the earlier postwar years. They were an effort to secure higher wages to keep pace with the continuously rising cost of living and to secure fringe benefits giving the worker more leisure time and greater protection against ill health and old age. To a marked degree this kind of bargaining was successful. In each of the four years, wages and fringe benefits in manufacturing, construction, transportation, and mining increased in varying degrees.

Important in this development, particularly as far as wages were concerned, were contracts that had been negotiated to provide for deferred increases or cost-of-living escalator adjustments. During 1957 more than 5,000,000 workers received increases in wages of five to sixteen cents an hour under such arrangements; in 1958, despite a recession, nearly 4,000,000 received increases of seven to ten cents. The relative stability of prices in 1959 and 1960 reduced the number of workers receiving increases in both years to less than 3,000,000 and also reduced the average amount of increases to less than seven cents.

Not all workingmen were covered by such contracts, but for the most part those who were not conducted peaceful negotiations with their employers resulting in wage increases and fringe benefits somewhat above those provided by long-term contracts. Few negotiations resulted in strikes; except in 1959 man days of labor lost as a result of strikes were lower in each of the last four Eisenhower years than at any time since the end of the Second World War.

Although unions introduced no major innovations into the collective bargaining processes of those years, a number of problems that had appeared earlier became acute. At the root of these problems was the automation of manufacturing industries (and in some cases of distribution and service industries), which occurred very rapidly throughout the Fifties and created a number of issues. Automation destroyed jobs. It in turn raised the questions of severance pay for men thrown out of work, of the rights of workingmen to transfer to other plants of a company, of retraining for new jobs, of the rights of workers to new jobs, and of the regulations to be followed concerning seniority. On these issues—sometimes lumped under the term "working rules"—a sharp difference of opinion between management and labor had begun to appear as early as 1955. Management insisted on its right to make its own rules of employment when it changed its production methods; organized labor in turn insisted upon the worker's right to a job, upon the need to adopt a humanitarian attitude toward the problem, and upon negotiating rule changes.

Problems resulting from automation became an issue in the drawn-out negotiations (September, 1958—October, 1960) between the International Union of Electrical Workers and the Westinghouse and General Electric Companies. The negotiations were climaxed by a three-week strike of I.U. against G.E. in October, 1960. Similar problems became an issue in the negotiations between the packinghouse workers-meat cutters and Armour and Company and between the longshoremen and West Coast shippers in 1959. Both negotiations ended in notable agreements: The packers' contract provided for establishment of a $500,000 fund to finance a study of problems relating to technological unemployment, to develop a program to retrain workers idled by automation, and to relocate idle workers; the shipping agreement, finally approved in late 1960, provided for development of a fund to be used to pay each registered worker

$7,920 on retirement at age 65 (higher payments were to be made for compulsory earlier retirement), guaranteed minimum weekly earnings, and no layoffs as a result of decreased work opportunities, in return for provisions relaxing work rules and permitting use of labor-saving equipment on the waterfront.

The negotiations that attracted the most public attention occurred in the steel and railroad industries. In steel the negotiations started as a simple effort by steelworkers to increase wages, improve fringe benefits, and continue the escalator clauses of the previous contract. When the companies insisted upon changes in working rules as the price of any improvement, the whole situation changed into a struggle for survival of the steel union. A strike—which began on July 14 and gave David McDonald, president of the union since the death of Murray, his first great test as a labor leader—ended after 120 days, when President Eisenhower invoked the emergency provisions of the Taft-Hartley Act. Steelworkers returned to their jobs with firm determination to renew the contest when the eighty-day injunction expired. That determination and the Kaiser Steel Company's desertion of the steel corporations' united front undoubtedly produced the solution. Kaiser agreed to a contract providing for improvements in wages and fringe benefits and for appointment of a committee to study and settle problems resulting from automation and technological change and local working conditions. The steel agreement, which followed the pattern of the Kaiser-union settlement, was signed in January, 1960, before the expiration of the injunction.

Because of the nature of the procedure for settling management-labor problems on the railroads, negotiations between operators and rail unions became much more complex. Discussions between the parties began early in 1959. In September the five operating and eleven non-operating unions, representing about 840,000 workers, demanded wage and welfare-benefit improvements; the operators countered with a demand for pay cuts and then with a demand for changes in working rules intended to eliminate "featherbedding." Although the Federal government entered the dispute in October, 1959, it was not until June, 1960, that any agreement was reached. At that time an arbitration board awarded a wage increase to operating brotherhoods, and a Presidential Emergency Board offered a wage increase to non-operating workers. All but the switch-men accepted. But the work-rules issue had not been resolved.

Labor's organizing activities in the second Eisenhower administration could hardly be characterized as successful. The A.F.L.-C.I.O. continued its earlier efforts among white-collar, textile, oil, chemical, and furniture workers. But its task had become harder. Unfavorable, restrictive legislation and adverse public reaction to disclosures of union racketeering hindered organizing everywhere; in some industries rivalry of affiliates with similar jurisdictions proved a handicap; in the South labor support for racial integration also hindered organizers' efforts. Although the A.F.L.-C.I.O. reported small increases in areas where organizing drives were conducted, over-all membership of the organization slipped in the traditional areas of unionism among workers in manufacturing, railways, and mining. Such reductions, together with losses of affiliates like the teamsters, produced a decline. At the end of the Eisenhower years the Department of Labor reported that A.F.L.-C.I.O. membership numbered about 15,000,000 and unaffiliated membership about 3,000,000.

29 ——

Since 1960

Organized labor's deep and bitter disappointment with the Eisenhower administration made its support of the Democratic party and most of its candidates in the election of 1960 almost inevitable. The party developed a number of prominent candidates for the presidential nomination: Adlai E. Stevenson; John F. Kennedy, Senator from Massachusetts and one of the authors of the L.M.R.D. Act; Stuart Symington, Senator from Missouri; and Hubert H. Humphrey, Senator from Minnesota. Each won support from labor leaders and labor rank and file in the contest for delegates. Ultimately the greater proportion of labor delegates at the Democratic party convention cast its votes for Kennedy.

Although many workingmen remained slightly suspicious of Kennedy's devotion to civil rights and to labor's aspirations and although most workingmen found it difficult to accept Lyndon B. Johnson as the party's vice-presidential candidate, organized labor gave Kennedy and Democratic nominees for major offices its vigorous and enthusiastic support. In Kennedy the A.F.L.-C.I.O. saw an "intelligent, articulate and forceful" young man who had revealed "a keen and growing understanding of the labor movement . . . and a warm appreciation of the problems and aspirations of the working people." It also thought it saw in him a quality it had not seen in Eisenhower: a willingness "to use the powers of the Presidency" to carry out the Democratic platform, which in large measure coincided with its own. It was particularly attracted by Kennedy's insistence that Federal stimulation of economic growth—which labor believed would solve the frustrating problem of unemployment—was the major issue of the campaign.

The efforts of labor's political arm to elect Kennedy and other Democratic candidates were a repetition of its previous campaigns: a drive to persuade laboring men to register, large-scale dissemination of political literature comparing the records of candidates, political rallies, and a drive to get out the vote on Election Day. On the whole it was a satisfactory campaign. Although the Democratic majority in the Senate was reduced by two and in the House by twenty-two and the "liberal" strength in most state legislatures declined, Kennedy was elected by a narrow popular plurality of 34,227,000 over Richard E. Nixon's 34,109,000; minor candidates received another 600,000 votes. Kennedy's electoral majority—303 to 234 for all other candidates—was based fundamentally on the voters in the southern states and in the metropolitan areas. Although many factors were responsible for the size of Kennedy's urban vote —his religion won over Roman Catholics at all economic levels— there was little doubt that laboring men contributed a large share to his victory in most industrial states.

When the Kennedy administration began, the A.F.L.-C.I.O. confidently expected that a "turning point" in its period of frustration, relative impotence, and decline was at hand. As the new leadership was "pledged to end the spiritual and economic stagnation, the indifference and self-satisfaction" into which the nation had "drifted," the A.F.L.-C.I.O. prepared an extensive program, which it later elaborated, to accomplish necessary changes. Because it was more concerned with unemployment—which by its own calculations affected 7.5 per cent of the labor force—than with any other problem, much of its program was aimed at economic growth "at a rate fast enough to absorb . . . rapid population growth and workers displaced by technological changes; fast enough to wipe out poverty and insecurity."

Its own program for economic development included vast expansion of public works, particularly in distressed areas; aid to distressed areas in the form of grants and loans intended to encourage the establishment of new plants; "bold action in the field of housing and urban renewal"; retraining of men displaced by technological change; the grant to the President of authority to adjust personal income taxes in case of economic need—an obvious plea to reduce taxes on people with low incomes; intensive public development of land, mineral, and water resources and of atomic energy; and a new trade law that would "maximize opportunities for expanding trade and contain safeguards to ease the impact of change through a trade adjustment mechanism." The last plank was a compromise between those trade unionists who recognized the growing importance of foreign exports to the American economy and others, like the garment workers and steelworkers, who were feeling the impact of foreign imports on jobs.

In the area of labor legislation the A.F.L.-C.I.O. program was largely a repetition of earlier programs. It called for changes in the Taft-Hartley Act, which limited the freedom of workers to organize and bargain collectively—primarily the elimination of Section 14 (b)—and changes in the Labor-Management Reporting and Disclosure Act, which "shackled" honest unions in their legitimate activities, an oblique reference to the A.F.L.-C.I.O. belief that the Act did not limit the activities of teamsters. In addition it called for an increase of minimum wages to $1.25 an hour in order to permit the workingman to "catch up and keep pace with fast-rising national productive power." For the less fortunate it demanded extension or restoration of unemployment benefits to those whose benefits had been exhausted. For Federal employees it asked legislation recognizing the rights of organization and collective bargaining and increases in salaries. Reflecting its growing interest in migrant workers, it requested that Congress "end the disgraceful exploitation of the nation's migratory workers in the areas of wages, housing, education, social security, and public health."

In line with its long interest in political and social reform, the A.F.L.-C.I.O. called for "enforceable" Federal and state fair-employment practices and action to prohibit discrimination in housing, in educational institutions, and in hospitals; Federal aid to education in the form of funds to improve schools (which would also "provide jobs for thousands") and to increase teachers' salaries; and hospitalization insurance under the Social Security system for retired workers and their families. The program also contained proposals to liberalize and "humanize" the immigration program—something of a reversal of attitude—to lift the income of the small farmer, to strengthen national defense, and to extend aid to the underdeveloped nations of the world in the interest of promoting a more democratic and peaceful world society.

Although President Kennedy showed less vigorous executive leadership in persuading Congress to enact his domestic program than had been expected, organized labor was satisfied with a number of measures he proposed—some taken directly from the A.F.L.-C.I.O. program—and Congress, prodded by labor lobbies, enacted. The most important advances were in the field of economic growth. Congress not only increased public works appropriations but also included a $900,000,000 emergency program for distressed areas. It provided additional aid to depressed areas by providing a $390,-000,000 program to help both urban and rural areas with persistently high unemployment to attract new industries. It also enacted an expanded public- and private-housing program as the basis for urban renewal. In the Area Redevelopment Act of 1961 it provided that areas meeting the criteria (there were more than 800 such localities) could receive grants or loans for the purchase or development of property for industrial or commercial use; for purchase, development, or improvement of property for public facilities; for help in evaluating skill of the labor force; and for assistance in occupational training. In the Manpower Development and Training

Act of 1962 Congress provided for upgrading the skills of unemployed heads of families who had been employed at least three years. A year later Congress, as a result of studies revealing that most unemployed were underskilled and undereducated, extended the measure to encourage the underemployed to pursue training courses, to permit training of youth under the age of nineteen, and to allow teaching of basic subjects like reading, writing, and arithmetic as part of vocational training for those who lacked rudimentary education. Congress also enacted a Trade Expansion Act, which granted the President broader powers to reduce tariffs —expected to be used to stimulate American exports—and provided for assistance to industries injured by increased imports.

The President also suggested and Congress enacted a number of other measures lifted from the A.F.L.-C.I.O. program: progressive increases in minimum wages to $1.25 an hour and the extension of these minimums to 3,600,000 workingmen, increases in retirement benefits under social security and a lowering of the retirement age of males to 62, extension of unemployment compensation to workers who had exhausted their benefits under state laws, extension of the aid-to-dependent-children program to families whose chief wage earners were unemployed, and increases in the salaries of Federal employees. By executive order the President provided for recognition of the right of Federal employees to organize.

The amount of state labor legislation enacted during the Kennedy administration showed some decline from the earlier post-war period. Some of it followed previous patterns: Pressured by labor federations a number of states increased workingmen's compensation benefits; most states increased unemployment benefits, although some raised eligibility requirements; more states amended or enacted laws dealing with discrimination in employment—prohibition of discrimination against the aged became more frequent—and a large number of states provided laws to protect migrant workers, bringing to 28 the number that had some such kind of legislation. Other legislation reflected new Federal policies: In conformity with the current trend toward training and retraining, a score of states amended their unemployment compensation laws to permit payment of benefits to trainees; in line with new Federal minimums, several states raised minimum-wage levels for employees not covered by Federal laws.

As the "Kennedy Congresses" and the states had enacted a large portion of the legislation that organized labor had suggested at the opening of the administration, the A.F.L.-C.I.O. could hardly criticize the results; it was the best showing in more than a decade. Nevertheless, the A.F.L.-C.I.O. was still partly frustrated.

Efforts to attain economic growth achieved considerable success, particularly in larger cities where "downtown" reconstruction and renewal proceeded rapidly. Evidence of this growth was revealed in a constant increment in the gross national product, which reached a high point of 5 per cent in 1964; in the increase in employment; in the increase in hourly earnings of factory workers from $2.29 in 1961 to $2.53 in 1964. Nevertheless the problem of unemployment remained acute. Although the amount of unemployment diminished steadily from 6.8 per cent of the labor force in early 1961 to 5.1 per cent in late 1964, the number of unemployed—particularly among youth, Negroes, and the older workers—remained distressingly high. The statistics, furthermore, did not reflect underemployment or the number of women who wanted jobs.

In addition organized labor had failed to secure some of its high-priority social reforms. All efforts to provide adequate Federal aid for education were defeated in Congress by a coalition of Republicans, southerners who were fearful of integration, and Roman Catholics who were unwilling to see Federal support limited to public institutions. The attempt to provide hospital care to the aged under the Social Security system was defeated by strong lobbies led by the American Medical Association.

Even though it sometimes appeared to be the case, organized labor did not rest all its hopes for advancement of its welfare on the Kennedy administration and Congress. The A.F.L.-C.I.O. and its affiliates and independent labor unions also became extensively engaged in solving internal problems, in collective bargaining activities, and in organizing. Such engagements in fact seemed to occupy more of labor's efforts during the Kennedy administration and in the first part of the Johnson administration than at any comparable period in the previous two decades.

While the A.F.L.-C.I.O. gave less attention to the problems raised by unethical practices, primarily because the number and extent of such problems were diminishing, it gave far greater attention to jurisdictional conflicts. In an effort to provide machinery for settlement of interunion disputes that previous agreements had not been able to solve, the A.F.L.-C.I.O., at its fourth convention in 1961, adopted a new plan. It provided for handling of disputes first by mediators appointed from within the labor movement. If mediation failed, the dispute was then to be sent to an impartial umpire, who would base his decision on established collective bargaining procedures and work relationships. His decision could be appealed to the President of the A.F.L.-C.I.O., who had to refer it to a subcommittee of the Executive Council, which could either disallow the appeal, thus confirming the umpire's decision, or refer it to the whole Council. The Council could confirm or overturn the decision. The plan prohibited recourse to the courts and limited decisions to specific disputes. The need for such machinery became clearly evident. During the first year of its operation, 142 cases were started through the procedure. Quick settlement of the majority of them seemed to foretell a lessening of time-consuming conflicts.

The merger and affiliation movements, which had started after the creation of the A.F.L.-C.I.O., continued at their former pace. In 1961 the National Postal Transport Association joined the postal clerks, the Amalgamated Clothing Workers' Union absorbed the tiny Glove Workers' Union, and the independent railway conductors and brakemen agreed to unite with the railroad trainmen. In 1962 the independent lithographers and the photoengravers agreed to a merger. But, as before, these movements were counterbalanced by opposing developments. A previously created entente between the National Maritime Union and the Seafarers' International Union to organize "runaway" shipping broke down; hostilities developed among railway firemen, the unaffiliated locomotive engineers, and railroad trainmen. In 1964, 21,000 workers, members of two A.F.L.-C.I.O. paper makers' unions, broke away to form the independent Association of Western Pulp and Paper Workers' Union.

The A.F.L.-C.I.O. also encountered a problem that had helped to destroy the National Labor Union nearly 100 years before: the position of the Negro in the trade-union movement. That such a problem, engendered by the growing demand by Negroes for equal rights, would develop had been indicated in 1960, when Negro trade unionists formed the Negro American Labor Council, with a platform demanding removal of all union color bars to membership or job progress, reform of apprenticeship systems, elimination of racially segregated unions, and greater participation by Negroes at all union levels.

A. Philip Randolph, President of the Negro Council, presented its demands to the fourth A.F.L.-C.I.O. convention. After an altercation between Randolph and President Meany, who inquired testily concerning Randolph's right to speak for all Negroes, the convention recommended faster action to advance Negroes to positions of full equality within the labor movement; it refused, however, to provide for sanctions against unions that lagged in implementing this policy. The significance of the problem became apparent when in 1962 the National Association for the Advancement of Colored People, charging that the unions had not moved fast enough in their efforts to end discrimination against Negroes in the labor movement, took action in the courts and before the National Labor Relations Board. Specific charges of discrimination were made against a steelworkers' local in Atlanta, against seafarers on the West Coast, and against the railway trainmen.

In some ways the major problem that the A.F.L.-C.I.O. encountered during the Kennedy and Johnson administrations was presented by the expelled teamsters. In this period, teamster president Hoffa continued to find himself involved in litigations over his alleged illegal activities. The legal action came to a climax in two trials in early 1964. In one, at Nashville, Hoffa was convicted on some rather dubious evidence of jury tampering; in the other, at Chicago, Hoffa and six associates were convicted on charges of defrauding the teamster pension fund and of diverting $1,000,000 from the fund for their own use. Both convictions were promptly appealed.

If this involvement in legal action had any effect on the teamsters, it was hardly apparent. The board of monitors appointed to supervise teamster affairs was dissolved in early 1961. The teamster convention that followed promptly re-elected Hoffa and his slate of officers and made changes in the constitution increasing the powers of officers and decreasing those of the membership both in internal affairs and in collective bargaining. Although the meaning of the action was not immediately apparent, some of its significance may have been revealed in early 1964, when after extensive maneuvering the teamsters secured a long-sought national contract with 1,000 large trucking firms—an action that some observers concluded placed the teamsters in a position to paralyze a large part of the American economy.

For the A.F.L.-C.I.O. the problems raised by the teamsters, in addition to the feeling that the organization was giving the labor movement a bad reputation, grew out of the continued close relationship that the teamsters enjoyed with many affiliated unions. At both the fourth and fifth conventions of the A.F.L.-C.I.O., there were undercover movements for reaffiliation with the teamsters. All through the period the teamsters flirted with A.F.L.-C.I.O. affiliates like the National Maritime Union and the longshoremen, holding out mutual-assistance pacts as means of strengthening the positions of the weaker unions; simultaneously it formed mutual-assistance pacts with independent unions like the mine, mill and smelter workers, who were at war with A.F.L.-C.I.O. unions, and conducted fairly successful raids on the members of A.F.L.-C.I.O. affiliates like the I.U. and the communication workers. What made this situation serious was the fact that it sapped the energies of A.F.L.-C.I.O. officers, who should have been directing their attention to other matters.

Another area in which organized labor's problems increased was in collective bargaining. The increase was not apparent in all situations. All through the period effective long-term contracts were signed, which reduced considerably the amount of year-by-year negotiations. Such contracts provided average increases in wages of eight cents an hour in 1961 (covering about 2,500,000 workers), slightly less in 1962, and about the same amount in 1963 and 1964. For those workingmen not under such contracts (a greater number) most negotiations proceeded peacefully. The number of strikes and of man hours lost in the period 1961–1965 remained at approximately the same comparatively low level as in the previous four years.

The collective bargaining procedure took on a somewhat different character from that of previous years. There were several reasons.

The problems raised by automation began to affect more and more industries; solutions to these problems were in themselves complex enough and became more complex when management and labor approached the bargaining table with diametrically opposed views on the subject. The result was a noticeable lengthening in the time consumed in the bargaining process. Another factor was the increased interposition of the Federal government, either directly or indirectly, in many negotiations.

Early in his administration President Kennedy appointed an Advisory Committee on Labor-Management Relations. The committee, representing the government, business, unions, and the public, was charged with the task of studying and making policy proposals concerning collective bargaining, economic growth and unemployment, automation and higher standards of living, foreign trade, and wage and price policies. The committee did yeoman work in analyzing and preparing reports on the condition of the American economy, reports that led to presidential proposals for legislation. It also made general recommendations concerning collective bargaining, suggesting that such bargaining should be "responsive to the public, or common interest," that the problems created by automation should be solved "without sacrifice of human values," and that "use of third party assistance" was desirable. The result of these recommendations was an increase in the already apparent policy of the government to intervene in industrial disputes. Secretaries of Labor Arthur J. Goldberg and W. Willard Wirtz and numerous members of the Federal mediation services began to appear more and more frequently at bargaining sessions to speak for the public. Although they often were able to suggest formulas that resolved conflicts, their fundamental message revolved around the suggestion that increases in labor's wages and fringe benefits should be limited to the current economic growth in order to prevent an inflationary trend and to stimulate foreign trade. Although organized labor disagreed with the concept, grumbled over government pressure, and audibly wondered whether or not it still possessed the right of free collective bargaining, it accepted the formula because the results were generally favorable.

A number of negotiations, some of which were punctuated or climaxed by strikes, attracted extensive public attention during the period. Steel negotiations were almost continual; in 1962 a contract for increased wages had a startling aftermath: When steel companies raised prices to meet increased wages, President Kennedy sharply rebuked them for action contrary to public interest, and prices were reduced. A 1963 contract produced a job-saving agreement by creating extended vacations for long-term employees. In the auto industry there were two protracted negotiations: in 1961, when new contracts were written to provide for improvements in supplementary unemployment benefits and an extension of S.U.B. payments to a year, and in late 1964, when a strike threatened to affect the results of the presidential election. Maritime workers and longshoremen were almost perpetually in the news with their efforts to stay the advance of automation; their strikes were regularly checked by Taft-Hartley injunctions. In 1962 long negotiations over a complex set of issues in the aircraft industry involving Douglas, North American, Ryan, Convair, Aerojet, Boeing and the machinists were settled by government intervention. Much attention was also accorded to some strikes because they inconvenienced the public and not because they had a major effect on the economy. Among them were the strike of flight engineers in 1961 and the strikes in the newspaper industry in New York, Cleveland, and Detroit in 1963–1964.

The most significant and most protracted negotiations during the period occurred in the railroad industry. As has been indicated, the issue between rail managers and rail unions had become a major conflict in the fall of 1959, when managers demanded elimination of what they called "featherbedding" practices and alteration of working rules. They proposed alteration of pay standards to reflect greater train speeds—which no passenger had yet recognized—elimination of rules prohibiting crews from operating through "crew change" points, and definition of management's right to determine when firemen should be used on diesel locomotives (management insisted that none was necessary). Had the stakes not been so important, the negotiations that followed might have provided material for a comic opera. The issues, which gradually reduced themselves to the primary question of eliminating firemen, went through a presidential commission, three emergency boards, a Federal circuit court, the United States Supreme Court, a super emergency board, Congress, and a super arbitration board. Throughout the whole four-year period, rail managers constantly threatened to impose new working rules unilaterally, and rail unions alternately threatened to strike. Not until President Johnson called a White House conference of rail managers and operating unions in the spring of 1964 was any settlement made concerning firemen. The settlement appeared to be a milestone, for which the President assumed considerable credit, but it did not solve the whole rail problem; the issues, which involved the whole future of the railway industry, were too complex for easy solution. In early 1965 it was obvious that the nation could look forward to additional, even more bitter, railway disputes.

As with other aspects of organized labor's non-political activities in the Kennedy and Johnson administrations, the A.F.L.-C.I.O. adopted some new techniques in its drive for new members—a campaign made imperative by the continuing decline of membership rolls. In 1960 four affiliates of the Industrial Union Department—auto workers, steelworkers, machinists, and electrical workers—formulated a plan that called for a joint campaign to secure members and bargaining rights for any one of the unions in 25 factories in the Philadelphia area. A similar campaign was mounted in North Carolina.

The apparent success of these efforts led the fourth A.F.L.-C.I.O. convention to increase per capita taxes to extend the campaign. In 1962, 75 affiliates began a quiet but united campaign to unionize 750,000 workers of every type, including white-collar and technical workers, in 5,000 non-union plants in the Los Angeles area. According to reports made in 1963, this campaign resulted in the winning of representation rights in 38 establishments, a campaign successful enough to lead the A.F.L.-C.I.O. to make plans for a similar effort in the Washington-Baltimore area. Meanwhile the Industrial Union Department had extended its Philadelphia campaign to Boston, Chicago, North and South Carolina, and Houston, Dallas, and Fort Worth, Texas—with particular attention to furniture, wood, and textile industries and to office, technical, and professional occupations. It reported that these drives had won bargaining rights in 80 plants during the year. In 1964, however, the Los Angeles campaign was suddenly abandoned because of "meager results."

Over-all union membership to some extent reflected these efforts. Between 1960 and 1963 total A.F.L.-C.I.O. membership, in spite of some gains from organizing drives, dropped by a half-million— most of it in the United States; membership in 52 unaffiliated organizations also declined in spite of some increases in teamster rolls. Over-all international union membership thus stood at about 17,400,000 with about 16,500,000 in the United States. The decline had one major cause: reduction in the number of employees in manufacturing, mining, and railways because of automation; this reduction was greater than the number of newly organized members. In 1964, however, there was some sign that the trend might be reversed; as the economy continued to grow and employment in the traditional union areas stabilized, the organizing campaigns began to show greater results. In the first half of the year, for the first time in a decade, the A.F.L.-C.I.O. rolls showed an increase as more than 250,000 new members began to pay dues.

This upturn in the early months of 1964 was matched almost simultaneously by an apparent new rise in labor's political and legislative fortunes. It was doubtful that organized labor expected such developments. For one thing, the Kennedy administration changed its direction; for another, the Kennedy administration ended abruptly in November, 1963.

The main thrust of the Kennedy administration after 1962 was directed toward tax reform and civil-rights legislation on behalf of Negroes. Suggestions for a major revision of the nation's complex patchwork of income taxes had been made many times before Kennedy took office. Most such suggestions had aimed at a more simple and equitable tax structure, which would have meant drastic changes in definitions of income, exemptions, and deductions. In 1962, however, another reason for revision developed as it became apparent that Kennedy policies were not stimulating the economy to the extent expected; accordingly, advisers suggested that economic growth could be stimulated by tax reduction, a reduction that would add to consumer purchasing power and that by a process of dispersion would increase national income and tax revenues as well.

In 1962 American civil-rights policies and programs as they affected Negroes were a miscellany of Federal legislation, presidential orders, Supreme Court decisions, state laws, and municipal ordinances. Although these legal foundations had given Negroes an opportunity to make some advances toward full equality, they were obviously insufficient in the face of official hostility in the South and prejudice in the North. Negroes, furthermore, were becoming impatient—as a large number of demonstrations in the summer and fall of 1962 attested. Both idealism and practical politics demanded some action.

Accordingly, President Kennedy proposed that the 88th Congress enact legislation providing for both tax reform and tax reduction and legislation designed to assure that Negroes would secure those civil rights over which the Federal government had authority.

Although they recognized that this shift meant less attention to other programs, leaders of organized labor promptly announced their enthusiastic support of both proposals. They were particularly pleased with the possibility of tax revisions that would reduce the excessive burdens of low-income families and would also contribute to economic growth. Their comments concerning civil-rights legislation were more cautious—perhaps because they recognized that many trade unions were discriminating against Negroes—but they threw the full force of their organizations behind the composite measure, which included provisions designed to halt discrimination in employment.

John F. Kennedy did not live to see the enactment of his proposed legislation. But the goals that he had established before his tragic death in November, 1963, which seemed far from achievement at the time, were accepted and vigorously pushed forward by his successor. New tax legislation, which provided for little tax reform and for somewhat less tax reduction than over-enthusiastic supporters proclaimed, became effective in March, 1964. The civil-rights measure, bitterly opposed by Southern Senators, became law after cloture stopped a long filibuster in July, 1964. The measure included establishment of an Equal Employment Opportunity Commission to police enforcement of provisions prohibiting discrimination by employers, employment agencies, or unions in their employment practices—hiring, firing, promotion, and pay scales—against any person because of race, color, religion, national origin, or sex.

To labor these developments were more than satisfying. It had been profoundly shocked by the assassination of President Kennedy; its shock, furthermore, had been increased by its fear that his successor had little sympathy for labor's objectives. President Johnson's obvious determination "to continue" the Kennedy program on taxes and civil rights and his successful drive to push the measures through Congress made a deep and favorable impression. Other developments heightened this impression: his handling of negotiations in the rail conflict, his support for amendments to the Social Security Act to provide medicare for the aged, and his support of a law providing for a nation-wide food-stamp program to aid needy families.

But most important was his proposal for a "war on poverty." Although some of his proposals had been suggested by labor and some had been suggested during the Kennedy administration, the composite program was his own. As ultimately passed by Congress, the Economic Opportunities Act was aimed essentially at eliminating some of the causes of poverty and at increasing the incomes of the poor.

The Act set up several basic programs: two separate plans for aiding needy young people of high-school and college age to continue their educations; a Job Corps to train youth in the skills needed in land, water, and timber development and industrial crafts; job training for those on relief; a domestic Peace Corps to work on public-service projects; funds for community programs intended to develop jobs, offer health and social services, improve living conditions, and educate the illiterate; and loans to low-income farmers and small businessmen.

With so impressive a record of achievement few laboring men could disagree. Accordingly, long before either the Republican or Democratic convention was held it became obvious that organized labor would support the President's candidacy. And, when the Republican party nominated Senator Barry Goldwater and Representative William Miller as its candidates, it became certain that organized labor would support the President and his running mate (ultimately revealed as Hubert H. Humphrey, a long-time favorite of labor) with greater unanimity and vigor than it had revealed before.

It would have been difficult to find a presidential candidate whom labor detested and feared more thoroughly than Barry Goldwater. On every single current issue, ranging from an atomic test-ban treaty through civil rights to a food-stamp plan, the Republican candidate and organized labor stood on totally opposite sides. Furthermore, Barry Goldwater had a completely anti-labor record. In labor's opinion he had voted wrong on every labor measure since he had ridden into the Senate on Eisenhower's coattails in 1952. He had no redeeming qualities: He was even opposed to Social Security benefits.

To make matters worse, his candidacy threatened to create a "backlash" among laboring men over the civil-rights issue. The possibility that some laboring men, organized or otherwise, might desert their traditional Democratic allegiance in the election because of resentment over the civil-rights measure was first raised in the spring of 1964, when George Wallace, Governor of Alabama and the most vocal of the major segregationist leaders in the nation, entered his name in the primaries of Wisconsin and Indiana. In both states he received unexpectedly heavy votes in predominantly labor areas: South Milwaukee and Gary. The labor population of these areas was primarily of late immigrant stock, not more than one generation removed from central, eastern, and southern Europe. These voters had apparently become convinced that enactment of the civil-rights measure would destroy seniority rights and impose racial quotas on employers, that it would destroy the neighborhood school and force their children to associate with undesirable Negroes, that it would compel integration of white neighborhoods and lower property values. Labor feared that Goldwater forces would seek to exploit these sentiments in industrial states like Wisconsin, Illinois, Indiana, Michigan, Ohio, and Pennsylvania and that there would be enough defection in labor ranks to defeat Johnson.

Labor's drive to elect the Johnson-Humphrey ticket was spearheaded by the A.F.L.-C.I.O.'s Committee on Political Education, headed by Alexander E. Barkan. Greatly aided by "educational" funds from the treasuries of the big internationals and by thousands of paid union organizers and volunteer members, C.O.P.E. conducted an intensive registration campaign, distributed tens of millions of pieces of literature by hand and by mail to homes and factories, and organized a highly efficient "get out the labor vote" campaign on election day. Along with the campaign to elect Johnson and Humphrey—which was supported even by the normally Republican presidents of the retail clerks, the carpenters, and the glass-bottle blowers unions—labor also conducted a campaign to elect "friendly" senatorial, congressional, and state legislative candidates. Most of its efforts were concentrated in 90 "marginal" districts where incumbents had been elected by narrow majorities in the previous election; most of those whom it endorsed were Democrats.

The results were more than satisfactory. If there had ever been any danger of a backlash vote among laboring men—a potential threat that C.O.P.E. arguments countered with a constant iteration of Goldwater's anti-labor record—it did not reveal itself in the vote. The Johnson-Humphrey ticket secured more than 43,000,000 votes out of more than 70,000,000 cast, 61 per cent of the total. The electoral count was 486 to 52. Of the 31 senatorial candidates endorsed by the A.F.L.-C.I.O., 25 were elected; of the 351 congressional candidates endorsed, 234 were elected. In the 89th Congress labor counted 60 senators and 248 House members as friendly.

With the election of 1964 over the A.F.L.-C.I.O. once more turned its attention to future legislation. Late in November the organization's Executive Council met to endorse the concept of a "Great Society," which the President had indicated as his goal throughout the presidential campaign. Its own interpretation of this society included legislation designed to accomplish its own long-standing goals: hospital care for the aged under Social Security; Federal aid to education, housing, and poverty-stricken areas; and appropriations for public works to create more jobs.

The Council also announced some purely labor goals: repeal of Section 14 (b) of the Taft-Hartley Act in order to invalidate the anti-union security laws of states—a demand also contained in the Democratic platform; legislation to permit greater freedom to picket, strike, and engage in secondary boycotts—actions limited by the Landrum-Griffin Act; an increase in the minimum wage from $1.25 to $2 an hour and extension of the wage law to additional workers; reduction of the 40-hour week with time and a half for overtime to a 35-hour week with double time for overtime as a means of spreading work; higher unemployment benefits, extension of the period during which unemployment benefits could be collected, and the adoption of more rigorous standards for state unemployment compensation practices; and increased Social Security benefits for retired workers.

The A.F.L.-C.I.O. did not expect rapid achievement of this program. In spite of its yeoman service in the campaign, it recognized that the President did not owe labor any special debt of gratitude; in spite of the "liberal" majority in Congress, it recognized that much of the legislation it wanted could be enacted only with the support of the President.

But whatever the A.F.L.-C.I.O. expected, much was accomplished in the early months of 1965. The anti-poverty legislation enacted in the previous year was quickly implemented. Although there were charges that the program was a "political football"— charges that were partially substantiated by the fact that local politicians fought vigorously to secure more control—there was evidence that it would show results ultimately (perhaps in a generation) among the perpetually poor, the undereducated, and the underskilled. As part of the war against poverty and in line with organized labor's demand for aid to poverty-stricken areas, President Johnson suggested and Congress enacted the Appalachia Development Act for the expenditure of more than a billion dollars in the eleven-state Appalachian region centering on West Virginia (where the measure started to show quick results) and stretching through 360 counties from Pennsylvania and Ohio to Alabama. As the area's poverty was largely based on a mountainous terrain (without the highways needed to attract new industries to provide jobs for those who had been automated out of the coal mines) and on soil depletion, most of the funds provided were to be spent on highway building, land improvement, and water-resources development.

At the President's suggestion Congress also enacted a large-scale aid-to-education measure, which provided more than a billion dollars to be used for improvement of education among the "city and rural poor." The measure provided that the funds be used primarily in the public-school systems to provide more teachers, to help in building new schools, and to provide libraries and equipment. It also furnished aid to private-school pupils (not schools), most of them Roman Catholic, in the form of shared time in the use of vocational-training facilities, laboratories, and libraries.

These measures were followed a few months later by a reduction of excise taxes, designed like the previous reduction in income taxes to provide financial stimulus to the economy.

Most important perhaps, Congress finally enacted a measure which President Truman had suggested and for which labor had long agitated: the medicare bill to provide hospital care, nursing-home care, and nursing service at home for the aged under Social Security. The measure also provided for voluntary low-cost health insurance to pay physicians' and surgeons' bills. The measure, as labor recognized, struck at two problems: It was a step toward adequate health care for the aged, and it alleviated the financial problems that so many of the aged had faced in securing hospital care—a problem that surveys revealed had been largely responsible for the vast increases in relief rolls since 1950. The measure, in short, would increase Social Security payments but at the same time would reduce the need for public assistance.

There were other measures before Congress in mid-1965 that labor had long suggested. One was a presidential proposal for a housing and urban-renewal measure to include provisions for subsidies to help families of low and moderate income to pay rent and to buy houses, for development of "new communities on the rim of the city," for aid in developing water and sewage systems, and for renewal of downtown areas. Observers suggested that the proposal would ultimately be enacted. In addition, the President had requested repeal of Section 14(b) of the Taft-Hartley Act, extension of existing minimum wage laws to more than 4,000,000 workers, increases in overtime pay, and extension of unemployment insurance to more than 5,000,000 workers. Although the prospect for enactment of such measures was given only an even chance, it appeared that organized labor's long campaigns for the social and labor reforms developed since the passage of the Taft-Hartley Act were nearing their conclusion. In mid-1965 the fortunes of workingmen looked brighter than at any time in more than fifteen years.

Bibliography

GENERAL WORKS

There have been few general histories of American labor published. Most important is the four-volume work known generally as John R. Commons, *History of Labour in the United States.* It should be consulted for all phases of labor history from the colonial period to 1932. Single-volume works include Richard T. Ely, *Labor Movement in America* (1890); Frank T. Carlton, *Organized Labor in American History* (1920); Mary Beard, *A Short History of the American Labor Movement* (1927); and Foster R. Dulles, *Labor in America* (1949). A left-wing interpretation of the labor movement to the year 1890 will be found in Philip S. Foner, *History of the Labor Movement in the United States* (1947). There are also several general studies of the role of women in the labor movement: notably Edith Abbott, *Women in Industry* (1910); and two books by Alice Henry, *Trade Union Woman* (1915) and *Women and the Labor Movement* (1927).

THE COLONIAL AND REVOLUTIONARY ERA

The most extensive analysis of the history of labor in the colonial and revolutionary era is Richard B. Morris, *Government and Labor in Early America* (1946). The volume covers mercantilism and its effect on the colonies, the status and condition of indentured and free labor, and the effect of the Revolution on labor. It is the only book with an easily understandable account of seagoing labor. Works that follow should also be consulted for the subjects indicated:

MERCANTILISM: P. W. Buck, *Politics in Mercantilism* (1942); E. S. Furniss, *The Position of the Laborer in a System of Nationalism* (1920).

COLONIAL ECONOMY: Harold U. Faulkner, *American Economic His-*

tory (1954); Edward Channing, *A History of the United States* (1937), II; Thomas J. Wertenbaker, *First Americans, 1607–1690* (1927); James T. Adams, *Provincial Society, 1690–1763* (1936); and Evarts B. Greene, *The Revolutionary Generation, 1763–1790* (1943).

COLONIAL POPULATION: Evarts B. Greene and Virginia D. Harrington, *American Population before the Federal Census of 1790* (1932).

INDENTURED SERVITUDE: Abbot E. Smith, *Colonists in Bondage* (1947) is the best general work, but see also Marcus W. Jernegan, *Laboring and Dependent Classes in Colonial America, 1607–1783* (1931); Samuel McKee, *Labor in Colonial New York, 1664–1776* (1935); C. A. Herrick, *White Servitude in Pennsylvania* (1926); E. I. McCormac, *White Servitude in Maryland, 1634–1820* (1904); James C. Ballagh, *White Servitude in the Colony of Virginia* (1895); and John S. Bassett, *Slavery and Servitude in the Colony of North Carolina* (1896).

FREE LABOR: In addition to the books by Adams, Greene, McKee, and Wertenbaker cited above, see also Carl Bridenbaugh, *Cities in the Wilderness* (1938), *The Colonial Craftsman* (1950), and *Cities in Revolt* (1955); Thomas J. Wertenbaker, *Norfolk: History of a Southern Port* (1931); "High Wages in Colonial America," and "Salaries of School Teachers in Colonial America," *Monthly Labor Review*, XXVIII (1939).

COLONIAL POLITICS: Allan Nevins, *American States During and After the Revolution* (1924); Arthur M. Schlesinger, *Colonial Merchants and the American Revolution* (1918); Edmund S. and Helen M. Morgan, *The Stamp Act Crisis* (1953); John C. Miller, *Sam Adams: Pioneer in Propaganda* (1936); Esther Forbes, *Paul Revere and the World He Lived In* (1942); George P. Anderson, "Ebenezer Mackintosh: Stamp Act Rioter and Patriot" and "A Note on Ebenezer Mackintosh," *Publications of the Colonial Society of Massachusetts*, XXVI (1927); F. Kidder, *History of the Boston Massacre, March 5, 1770* (1870); H. B. Dawson, *The Sons of Liberty in New York* (1859); Carl L. Becker, *History of Political Parties in the Province of New York, 1760–1776* (1909); Herbert M. Morais, "The Sons of Liberty in New York," *Era of the Revolution*, ed. by Richard B. Morris (1939); C. H. Lincoln, *Revolutionary Movement in Pennsylvania, 1760–1776* (1901); Philip Davidson, "Sons of Liberty and Stamp Men," *North Carolina Historical Review*, IX (1932); and Leila Sellers, *Charleston Business on the Eve of the Revolution* (1934).

REVOLUTIONARY WAR DEVELOPMENTS: The aforementioned books by Becker, Greene, Herrick, Lincoln, McCormac, and Nevins, and William Miller, "Effects of the American Revolution on Indentured Servitude," *Pennsylvania History*, VII (1940).

THE TRANSITIONAL ERA

Aside from the first two volumes of Commons, *History of Labour,* and the single-volume histories mentioned at the beginning of this bibliography, there are no general works covering the history of American labor in the nineteenth century. The following should be consulted for the subjects indicated:

AMERICAN ECONOMY: The volume by Faulkner cited above and John A. Krout and Dixon R. Fox, *The Completion of Independence, 1790– 1830* (1944); Carl R. Fish, *The Rise of the Common Man, 1830–1850* (1927); Arthur C. Cole, *Irrepressible Conflict, 1850–1865* (1934), Allan Nevins, *Emergence of Modern America, 1865–1878* (1927); and Arthur M. Schlesinger, *Rise of the City, 1878–1898* (1933).

FIRST TRADE UNIONS: Ethelbert Stewart, "Two Forgotten Decades in the History of Labor Organization, 1820–1840," *American Federationist,* XX (1913); William Sullivan, *Industrial Worker in Pennsylvania* (1955); Louis Arky, "The Mechanics' Union of Trade Associations and the Formation of the Philadelphia Working Men's Movement," *Pennsylvania Magazine of History and Biography,* LXXVI (1952); Theodore W. Glocker, *Trade Unionism in Baltimore Before the War of 1812* (1907); and George A. Stevens, *New York Typographical Union No. 6* (1903).

EARLY POLITICAL ATTACHMENTS: Charles A. Beard, *An Economic Interpretation of the Constitution of the United States* (1948), and *Economic Origins of Jeffersonian Democracy* (1943); Robert E. Brown, *Charles Beard and the Constitution* (1956); Merrill Jensen, *The New Nation* (1950); and Eugene P. Link, *Democratic-Republican Societies* (1942).

WORKINGMEN'S PARTIES: The book by Sullivan, mentioned above, and Robert T. Bower, "Notes on 'Did Labor Support Jackson? The Boston Story,'" *Political Science Quarterly,* LXV (1950); Frank T. Carlton, "Economic Influence Upon Education Progress in the United States, 1820–1850," University of Wisconsin *Bulletin* No. 221 (1908), and "The Workingmen's Party of New York," *Political Science Quarterly,* XXII (1907); Joseph Dorfman, *The Economic Mind in Modern America* (1946), II, and "The Jackson Wage-Earner Thesis," *American Historical Review,* LIV (1949); Dixon R. Fox, *Decline of the Aristocracy in the Politics of New York* (1909); Herman Hailperin, "Pro-Jackson Sentiment in Pennsylvania," *Pennsylvania Magazine of History and Biography,* L (1926); Richard Hofstadter, *American Political Tradition and the Men Who Made It* (1948); Richard W. Leopold, *Robert Dale Owen* (1940); John B. McMaster, *History of the People of the United States* (1900),

V; A. J. G. Perkins and Theresa Wolfson, *Frances Wright: Free Enquirer* (1939); Edward Pessen, "Did Labor Support Andrew Jackson?: The Boston Story," *Political Science Quarterly*, LXIV (1949), and "Ideology of Stephen Simpson, Upper-Class Champion of the Early Philadelphia Workingmen's Movement," *Pennsylvania History*, XXII (1955); Arthur M. Schlesinger, Jr., *Age of Jackson* (1945); and William R. Waterman, *Frances Wright* (1924).

JACKSON PERIOD—LOCOFOCOISM: The books by Dorfman, Fox, Arthur M. Schlesinger, Jr., and Stevens, cited above, and Fitzwilliam Byrdsall, *History of the Loco Foco or Equal Rights Party* (1842); Arthur B. Darling, "The Workingmen's Party of Massachusetts, 1833–34," *American Historical Review*, XXIX (1923); Carl N. Degler, "The Locofocos: Urban 'Agrarians,'" *Journal of Economic History*, XVI (1956); Walter Hugens, "Ely Moore: The Case History of a Jacksonian Labor Leader," *Political Science Quarterly*, LXV (1950); Richard B. Morris, "Andrew Jackson: Strikebreaker," *American Historical Review*, LV (1949); Edward Pessen, "Workingmen's Movements of the Jackson Period," *Mississippi Valley Historical Review*, XLII (1956); and William Trimble, "Diverging Tendencies in New York Democracy in the Period of the Locofocos," *American Historical Review*, XXIV (1919), and "Social Philosophy of the Locofoco Democracy," *American Journal of Sociology*, XXVI (1921).

THE TEN-HOUR DAY AND SOCIAL REFORM: In addition to books by Dorfman and Leopold, cited above, consult particularly Norman J. Ware, *Industrial Worker, 1840–1860* (1924). For the role of women see Hannah Josephson, *Golden Threads* (1949); for utopian socialism and producers' cooperative movements see William A. Hinds, *American Communities and Co-operative Colonies* (1908), and John H. Noyes, *History of American Socialism* (1870). For land reform see Carter Goodrich and Sol Davison, "The Wage Earner and the Westward Movement," *Political Science Quarterly*, L (1935) and LI (1936); Murray Kane, "Some Considerations on the Safety Valve Doctrine," *Mississippi Valley Historical Review*, XXIII (1936); Joseph Schafer, "Was the West a Safety-Valve for Labor?" *Mississippi Valley Historical Review*, XXIV (1937); Fred A. Shannon, "The Homestead Law and the Labor Surplus," *American Historical Review*, XLI (1936). For workingmen and slavery see Joseph G. Rayback, "The American Workingman and the Antislavery Crusade," *Journal of Economic History*, III (1943).

"PURE AND SIMPLE" UNIONISM—NATIONAL LABOR UNION: Chester M. Destler, "Influence of Edward Kellogg upon American Radicalism," *Journal of Political Economy*, XL (1932); Emerson D. Fite, *Social and Economic Conditions in the North during the Civil War* (1930); Gerald N. Grob,

"Reform Unionism: The National Labor Union," *Journal of Economic History*, XIV (1954); Jonathan Grossman, *William Sylvis, Pioneer of American Labor* (1945); and D. D. Lescohier, *Knights of St. Crispin* (1910).

DEPRESSION OF 1873: For the Molly Maguire Riots consult particularly J. Walter Coleman, *The Molly Maguire Riots* (1936). See also William A. Itter, "Early Labor Troubles in the Schuylkill Anthracite District," *Pennsylvania History*, I (1934); and Anthony Bimba, *Molly Maguires* (1932). For the Railway Strike of 1877 see Arthur E. Holder, "Railway Strikes since 1877," *American Federationist*, XIX (1912); and Samuel Yellen, *American Labor Struggles* (1956). Spectacular accounts of both the Molly Maguires and the Railway Strike are in Louis Adamic, *Dynamite* (1931). For political activities see Harry J. Carman, *et al.*, eds., *The Path I Trod* (1940); and Edward B. Mittelman, "Chicago Labor in Politics, 1877–1897," *Journal of Political Economy*, XXVIII (1920). For the coolie labor problem see Mary R. Coolidge, "Chinese Labor Competition on the Pacific Coast," *Annals of the American Academy of Political Science*, XXXIV (1909).

THE KNIGHTS OF LABOR: In addition to Terence Powderly's autobiography, *The Path I Trod*, and the articles by Holder and Mittelman, cited above, consult particularly Norman J. Ware, *Labor Movement in the United States, 1860–1895* (1929), which is generally regarded as the most definitive on the whole subject. See also C. D. Wright, "An Historical Sketch of the Knights of Labor," *Quarterly Journal of Economics*, I (1887); Joseph R. Buchanan, *Story of a Labor Agitator* (1903); Ruth A. Allen, *Great Southwest Strike* (1942); J. B. S. Hardman and Maurice F. Neufeld, eds., *The House of Labor* (1951); David Creamer, "Recruiting Contract Laborers for the Amoskeag Mills," *Journal of Economic History*, I (1941); Charlotte Erickson, *American Industry and the European Immigrant, 1860–1885* (1957); Blake McKelvey, "The Prison Labor Problem, 1875–1900," *Journal of the American Institute of Criminal Law and Criminology*, XXV (1934), and Vidkunn Ulricksson, *The Telegraphers* (1953).

RIVALS OF THE KNIGHTS: The most thorough account of the early Marxian socialist movement in the United States is Howard H. Quint, *The Forging of American Socialism* (1953). See also Morris Hillquit, *History of Socialism in the United States* (1910), and Emma Goldman, "Johann Most," *American Mercury*, VIII (1926). For short-lived labor movements of the eighties see Frank T. Carlton, "Ephemeral Labor Movements, 1866–1889," *Popular Science Monthly*, LXXXV (1914). The development of the Federation of Organized Trades and Labor Unions of the

United States and Canada is related in Alfred P. James, "First Convention of the American Federation of Labor," *Western Pennsylvania Magazine of History,* VI (1923), and in the references to the American Federation of Labor below.

HAYMARKET: The definitive work on the subject is Henry David, *History of the Haymarket Affair* (1936). See also the books of Adamic and Yellen, mentioned above, and Marion C. Cahill, *Shorter Hours* (1932); Harry Barnard, *Eagle Forgotten* (1938); and Waldo R. Browne, *Altgeld of Illinois* (1924).

UNITED FRONT CAMPAIGN: The best and most complete account is Nathan Fine, *Labor and Farmer Parties in the United States, 1828–1928* (1928).

THE MODERN ERA

Aside from the fourth volume of Commons, *History of Labour,* and the single-volume histories mentioned at the beginning of this bibliography there are two other works covering substantial parts of the history of American labor since 1886. These are Selig Perlman, *History of Trade Unionism in the United States* (1922), and Norman J. Ware's most provocative volume, *Labor in Modern Industrial Society* (1935). Both should be consulted. In addition there are a number of books which deal with large portions of the history of the American Federation of Labor to which reference should be made on any phase of labor history involving that organization. These include: Samuel Gompers, *Seventy Years of Life and Labor* (1948); Rowland H. Harvey, *Samuel Gompers* (1935); Lewis Lorwin and J. A. Flexner, *The American Federation of Labor* (1933), and Philip Taft, *The A.F. of L. in the Time of Gompers* (1957).

TRIUMPH OF THE MACHINE: In addition to the book by Faulkner, mentioned above, see the same author's *Quest for Social Justice, 1898–1914* (1931); and Preston W. Slosson, *Great Crusade and After, 1914–1928* (1935).

STATISTICAL INFORMATION: Daniel J. Ahearn, *Wages of Farm and Factory Laborers, 1914–1944* (1945); Whitney Coombs, *Wages of Unskilled Labor in Manufacturing Industries in the United States, 1890–1924* (1926); Paul H. Douglas, *Real Wages in the United States, 1890–1926* (1930); Harold Barger, *Transportation Industries, 1889–1946* (1951), and *Distribution's Place in the American Economy since 1869* (1955); Harold Barger and Sam H. Schurr, *Mining Industries, 1899–1939* (1944); Solomon Fabricant, *Output of Manufacturing Industries,*

1899–1937 (1940), *Employment in Manufacturing, 1899–1939* (1942), and *Labor Savings in American Industry, 1899–1939* (1945); George J. Stigler, *Trends in Output and Employment* (1947), and *Trends in Employment in the Service Industries* (1956); Leo Wolman, *Growth of American Trade Unions, 1880–1923* (1924), *Ebb and Flow in Trade Unionism* (1936), and *Wages and Living Costs, 1939–1947* (1948).

EIGHT-HOUR CAMPAIGN: Sidney Fine, "Eight-Hour Day Movement in the United States, 1881–1891," *Mississippi Valley Historical Review*, XL (1953).

HOMESTEAD STRIKE: There is no definitive study of the Homestead strike. For varying accounts see the books by Adamic and Yellen, cited above, and the following: Barnard Alderson, *Andrew Carnegie* (1902); *Autobiography of Andrew Carnegie* (1920); James H. Bridge, *Inside History of the Carnegie Steel Company* (1903); John A. Fitch, "Unionism in the Iron and Steel Industry," *Political Science Quarterly*, XXIV (1909); George Harvey, *Henry Clay Frick* (1928); Burton J. Hendrick, *Life of Andrew Carnegie*, I (1932); and John K. Winkler, *Incredible Carnegie* (1931).

RAILWAY UNIONISM: In addition to the material in the articles by Holder, cited above, see D. W. Hertel, *History of the Brotherhood of Maintenance of Way Employees* (1955); Walter F. McCaleb, *Brotherhood of Railroad Trainmen* (1936); Archibald M. McIsaac, *Order of Railroad Telegraphers* (1933); E. C. Robbins, *Railway Conductors* (1914); and Donald L. McMurry's definitive work, *The Great Burlington Strike of 1888* (1956).

DEPRESSION OF 1893: Donald L. McMurry, *Coxey's Army* (1929), is the most thorough study.

PULLMAN STRIKE: The definitive study on the subject is Almont Lindsey, *Pullman Strike* (1942). The work may be supplemented by the previously mentioned books by Barnard and Browne on Governor Altgeld, and by McAlister Coleman, *Eugene V. Debs* (1930); Raymond Ginger, *Bending Cross* (1949); Donald L. McMurry, "Labor Policies of the General Managers Association of Chicago, 1886–1894," *Journal of Economic History*, XIII (1953); Allan Nevins, *Grover Cleveland* (1932); Dennis T. Lynch, *Grover Cleveland* (1932); Henry James, *Richard Olney and His Public Service* (1923); Clarence Darrow, *The Story of My Life* (1932); and Irving Stone, *Clarence Darrow for the Defense* (1943).

A.F.L.: ADVANCE AND REGRESSION: Analyses of the structure and problems of trade unions in the early part of the twentieth century may be found in Jacob Loft, *Printing Trades* (1944); Robert A. Christie, *Empire in Wood* (1956); Frank T. Carlton, *History and Problems of Organized*

Labor (1911); Theodore W. Glocker, *Government of American Trade Unions* (1913); and French E. Wolfe, *Admission to American Trade Unions* (1912). For two of the strikes of the period see Ernest L. Bogart, "Machinists' Strike of 1901," *Yale Review*, X (1901); and Russell A. Bauder, "National Collective Bargaining in the Foundry Industry," *American Economic Review*, XXIV (1934). For labor racketeering see Harold Seidman, *Labor Czars* (1938). For the MacNamara case see the previously mentioned books by Adamic, Darrow, and Stone. For legal problems faced by labor see James Boyle, "Organized Labor and Court Decisions," *Forum*, XLII (1909); George G. Groat, *Attitude of American Courts in American Labor Cases* (1911); Edward Berman, *Labor and the Sherman Act* (1930); and Donald B. Robinson, *Spotlight on a Union* (1948), a history of the hatters.

ANTHRACITE STRIKES: The most thorough study of the anthracite conflicts is Robert J. Cornell, *The Anthracite Coal Strike of 1902* (1957). But see also McAlister Coleman, *Men and Coal* (1943); Elsie Gluck, *John Mitchell* (1929); and Henry F. Pringle, *Theodore Roosevelt* (1931). For the activities of the National Civic Federation consult Marguerite Green, *The National Civic Federation and the American Labor Movement* (1956).

THE SOCIALISTS, 1889–1917: A complete history of American socialism from the United Front campaign to the First World War may be secured from three works: the previously mentioned book by Quint; Ira Kipnis, *American Socialist Movement, 1897–1912* (1952), and David A. Shannon, *The Socialist Party of America: A History* (1955). Reference should also be made to the previously cited older work by Hillquit, and to the books of McAlister Coleman and Ginger on Debs.

WESTERN FEDERATION OF MINERS: There is no definitive study of the Western Federation of Miners. See *Bill Haywood's Book* (1929); Benjamin Rastall, *Labor History of the Cripple Creek District* (1908), and the books by Darrow and Stone, mentioned above.

INDUSTRIAL WORKERS OF THE WORLD: The most thorough account is Paul F. Brissenden, *The I. W. W.* (1920). Supplementary material will be found in Haywood's autobiography, cited above, and in Louis Levine, "The Development of Syndicalism in America," *Political Science Quarterly*, XXVIII (1913); John G. Brooks, *American Syndicalism* (1913); David J. Saposs, *Left-Wing Unionism* (1926); Paul U. Kellogg, "The McKee Rocks Strike," *Survey*, XXII (1909); *Report on the Textile Strike in Lawrence, Massachusetts*, Senate Document 870, 62nd Congress, 1st Session; Mary H. Vorse, *Footnote to Folly* (1935); and Vernon H. Jensen, *Lumber and Labor* (1944).

FEDERATION'S REVIVAL: For the A.F.L.'s resort to politics see Mollie R. Carroll, *Labor and Politics* (1923). For the developments in the needle trades see Joel Seidman, *Needle Trades* (1942); Matthew Josephson, *Sidney Hillman* (1952); Benjamin Stolberg, *Tailor's Progress* (1944); Hyman H. Bookbinder, *To Promote the General Welfare* (1950); and Charles E. Zaretz, *Amalgamated Clothing Workers of America* (1934). For developments in the coal industry see the previously cited works by Yellen, and Coleman, *Men and Coal.*

PROGRESSIVE LABOR LEGISLATION: The third volume of Commons, *History of Labour,* is by far the most complete account of the labor legislation enacted in the early part of the twentieth century. For additional information concerning workingmen's compensation see Frank Lang, *Workingmen's Compensation Insurance* (1947); for more material on hour legislation see the previously cited book by Cahill. Seagoing labor and its problems are briefly explained in Elmo P. Hohman, *History of American Merchant Seamen* (1956). For railway developments and the Adamson Act see the previously cited books by McCaleb and Robbins, and Edwin C. Robbins, "The Trainmen's Eight-Hour Law," *Political Science Quarterly,* XXXI (1916); Frank H. Dixon, "Public Regulation of Railway Wages," *American Economic Review,* V (1915), supplement; Leonard A. Lecht, *Experience under Railway Labor Legislation* (1955). Additional material on the Clayton Act is in Charles O. Gregory, *Labor and the Law* (1949).

FIRST WORLD WAR: A concise and lucid summary of the organization of the war economy will be found in George Soule, *Prosperity Decade* (1947). An excellent account of labor and the war effort is Gordon S. Watkins, *Labor Problems and Administration during the World War* (1919).

POSTWAR DEVELOPMENTS: In addition to the book by Josephson, cited above, see George S. Mitchell, *Textile Unionism and the South* (1931); and George G. Groat, *Introduction to the Study of Organized Labor in America* (1921). For more material on labor's attitude toward immigration see Isaac A. Hourwich, *Immigration and Labor* (1912).

ATTACK ON THE RADICALS: For the wartime attack on the socialists and Wobblies, which has not been thoroughly explored, see the previously cited books by McAlister Coleman, Fine, Ginger, and David A. Shannon, and John S. Gambs, *Decline of the I.W.W.* (1932), which also covers the subject through the twenties. The definitive work on the "Red Scare" is Robert K. Murray, *Red Scare* (1955). The most thorough study of postwar socialism is in the previously cited work by David A. Shannon. See also Louis Waldman, *Labor Lawyer* (1945). Material on the communist movement may be found in James Oneal and G. A. Werner, *American Communism* (1947), and William Z. Foster, *History of the Communist Party of the United States* (1952). For the great strikes of 1919 see Interchurch World Movement of North America, *Report on the Steel Strike of 1919* (1920); William Z. Foster, *The Great Steel Strike and Its Lessons* (1920); Randolph Bartlett, "Anarchy in Boston," *American Mercury*, XXXVI (1935), and the previously mentioned books by Adamic (which also contains material on the Centralia incident), Vorse, and Yellen. Some further information on the postwar Wobblies is in Carleton H. Parker, *Casual Laborer* (1920).

PROGRESSIVE MOVEMENT: In addition to the account in Fine, previously cited, see Kenneth C. McKay, *The Progressive Movement of 1924* (1947).

DECADE OF DECLINE: See the previously cited books by Berman, McAlister Coleman on the coal industry, Lecht, Mitchell, Harold Seidman, Joel Seidman on the needle trades, and Soule, and the following: Savel Zimand, *Open Shop Drive* (1921); Lyle W. Cooper, "American Labor Movement in Prosperity and Depression," *American Economic Review*, XXII (1932); David J. Saposs, "American Labor Movement since the War," *Quarterly Journal of Economics*, XLIX (1935); Elizabeth F. Baker, *Displacement of Men by Machines* (1933); Robert W. Dunn, *Company Unions* (1927); Robert F. Hoxie, *Trade Unionism in the United States* (1931); Sterling D. Spero and Abram L. Harris, *The Black Worker* (1930); James A. Wechsler, *Labor Baron* (1944), on the coal industry; Paul M. Angle, *Resort to Violence* (1954), on the Herrin Massacre; Alpheus T. Mason, *Organized Labor and the Law* (1925); John B. Andrews, *Labor Problems and Labor Legislation* (1932); Alfred Harding, *Revolt of the Actors* (1929); and Murray Ross, *Stars and Strikes* (1941). The last two are on the organization of Actors Equity.

THE DEPRESSION OF 1929: Brief and clear accounts of the causes and course of the depression may be found in Soule, previously cited, and Broadus Mitchell, *Depression Decade* (1947). See also William S. Myers and Walter H. Newton, *The Hoover Administration: A Documented Narrative* (1936); and Ray L. Wilbur and Arthur M. Hyde, *The Hoover Policies* (1937). For communism see the previously cited books by Oneal and Werner, and Foster, and Thomas Tippett, *When Southern Labor Stirs* (1931).

NORRIS-LA GUARDIA ACT: For a background and analysis see the previously cited book by Gregory, and Felix Frankfurter and Nathan Greene, *The Labor Injunction* (1930); Edwin E. Witte, *Government in Labor Disputes* (1932); and Joel Seidman, *Yellow Dog Contract* (1932).

NEW DEAL: For a general view consult Charles A. Beard and George H. E. Smith, *The Old Deal and the New* (1940); Louis M. Hacker, *Short History of the New Deal* (1934); Basil Rauch, *The History of the New Deal, 1933–1938* (1944); and Arthur M. Schlesinger, *New Deal in Action, 1933–39* (1940).

THE NEW DEAL AND LABOR: The only over-all revelation of the New Dealer's concern with the problems of labor is Frances Perkins, *The Roosevelt I Knew* (1946). The previously cited book by Broadus Mitchell should also be consulted. For the relief program see E. W. Bakke, *Unemployed Worker* (1940); Donald S. Howard, *WPA and Federal Relief Policy* (1943); Arthur MacMahon et al., *Administration of Federal Work Relief* (1941); and Lewis Meriam, *Relief and Social Security* (1946). The general effect of the N.R.A. on labor may be studied in Lois Mac-Donald et al., *Labor and the N.R.A.* (1934); Carroll R. Daugherty, *Labor under the N.R.A.* (1934); and Irving Bernstein, *New Deal Collective Bargaining Policy* (1950). Specific influences of the N.R.A. may be found in the previously cited books by McAlister Coleman on the coal industry and Yellen, and in Charles L. Franklin, *Negro Labor Unionist of New York* (1936). The classic account of the problem of security is Abraham Epstein, *Insecurity* (1933). Analyses of the Social Security law may be found in the book by Meriam, cited above, and in Paul H. Douglas, *Social Security in the United States* (1939). For studies of two aspects of the La Follette Civil Liberties Committee investigations see Leo Huberman, *Labor Spy Racket* (1937), and Clinch Calkins, *Spy Overhead* (1937). The history of the Wagner Act may be found in Joseph Rosenfarb, *National Labor Policy and How It Works* (1940); Louis G. Silverberg, *The Wagner Act, After Ten Years* (1945); and in Harry A. Millis and Emily C. Brown, *From the Wagner Act to Taft-Hartley* (1950).

THE RISE OF THE C.I.O.: For general studies see Robert R. R. Brooks, *When Labor Organizes* (1937), and *Unions of Their Own Choosing* (1939); Bruce Minton and John Stuart, *Men Who Lead Labor* (1937); J. Raymond Walsh, *C.I.O. Industrial Unionism in Action* (1937); Edward Levinson, *Labor on the March* (1938); Mary H. Vorse, *Labor's New Millions* (1938); and Benjamin Stolberg, *Story of the CIO* (1938). For information concerning specific groups of workers consult previously cited books by Bookbinder, McAlister Coleman, Hohman, Josephson, Robinson, Joel Seidman, Stolberg, Wechsler, and Zarets, and Robert R. R. Brooks, *As Steel Goes . . .* (1940); Henry Kraus, *The Many and the Few* (1947); Clayton W. Fountain, *Union Guy* (1949); Carl Raushenbush, *Fordism* (1937); Vernon H. Jensen, *Nonferrous Metals Industry Unionism, 1932–1954* (1954); and Harold S. Roberts, *Rubber Workers* (1944).

POLITICAL ACTION AND JURISDICTIONAL WARFARE: Most of the best
material on the subject will be found in the works cited on the previous
subject. In addition consult previously cited works by Christie, Hardman
and Neufeld, Oneal and Werner, and Waldman. See also Orme W. Phelps,
Legislative Background of the Fair Labor Standards Act (1939); Herbert
Harris, *American Labor* (1938), and *Labor's Civil War* (1940); Horace
R. Cayton and George S. Mitchell, *Black Workers and the New Unions*
(1939); Lucy R. Mason, *To Win These Rights* (1952); Harold U. Faulkner and Mark Starr, *Labor in America* (1944); Florence Peterson, *American Labor Unions* (1945); and Wellington Roe, *Juggernaut* (1948).

SECOND WORLD WAR: The most thorough study is Joel Seidman, *American Labor from Defense to Reconversion* (1953). Reference should also
be made to previously cited books by Hohman, Josephson, Lecht, Wechsler, and Jane C. Record, "The War Labor Board: an Experiment in Wage
Stabilization," *American Economic Review*, XXXIV (1944); and Julius
Hirsch, *Price Control in the War Economy* (1943).

THE POSTWAR PERIOD: Published material on the history of American
labor since the Second World War is scarce. It is necessary to use the
sources to secure a clear picture of developments. See *Monthly Labor
Review;* the *American Federationist;* the *A.F.L. News Reporter;* the
C.I.O. News; the *A.F.L.-C.I.O. News;* and *Labor.* Among books, Eric
F. Goldman, *Crucial Decade* (1956), provides an over-all review, and
Joel Seidman's book, mentioned in the previous section, covers developments from the end of the Second World War to Taft-Hartley. In addi-
tion consult the previously cited works of Hardman and Neufeld, Hoh-
man, Millis and Brown, and the following: Sidney C. Sufrin and Robert
C. Sedgewick, *Labor Economics and Problems at Mid-Century* (1956);
Colston E. Warne *et al., Labor in Post-War America* (1949); Philip Taft,
Structure and Government of Labor Unions (1954); Lloyd Ulman, *Rise
of the National Trade Union* (1955); Sanford Cohen, *State Labor Legislation, 1937–1947* (1948); Charles P. Larrowe, *Shape-Up and Hiring
Hall* (1955); Commission on Educational Reconstruction, *Organizing the
Teaching Profession* (1955); Robert D. Leiter, *The Musicians and Pe-
trillo* (1953); Irving Howe and R. J. Widick, *The UAW and Walter
Reuther* (1949); James Nelson, *Mine Workers' District 50* (1955); Alvin
W. Gouldner, *Wildcat Strike* (1954); and Frank McCullough, *Strike!*
(1954).

BIBLIOGRAPHICAL ADDENDA

Since the original preparation of this work for publication, a considerable number of books and articles has been published in the field of labor history. Among GENERAL WORKS Foster R. Dulles has issued a revised edition of his *Labor in America* (1960); Henry Pelling, well-known in the British labor field, has presented an Englishman's view of the, American labor movement in *American Labor* (1960); and Philip Taft has published a long account, *Organized Labor in American History* (1964). Excerpts from original manuscripts describing labor conditions since 1864 have been published by Leon Litwalk in *American Labor Movement* (1962); and autobiographical accounts describing working conditions since 1900 have been published by Eli Ginzberg and Hyman Berman in *The American Worker in the Twentieth Century* (1963). An interesting effort to relate British and American trade-union movements is Clifton K. Yearley's *Britons in American Labor: A History of the Influence of the United Kingdom Immigrants on American Labor, 1820–1914* (1957).

New publications have also appeared in the following specific fields:
WORKINGMEN'S PARTIES IN THE JACKSON PERIOD: Walter Hugins, *Jacksonian Democracy and the Working Class* (1960), which provides significant information on New York City.

SOCIAL REFORM IN THE ANTEBELLUM PERIOD: Benjamin J. Klebaner, "Poor Relief and Public Works during the Depression of 1857," *Historian*, XXII (1960).

DEPRESSION OF 1873: Wayne J. Broehl, Jr., *The Molly Maguires* (1964), which makes revision of the commonly held concepts of that organization imperative; Herbert G. Gutman, "Trouble on the Railroads in 1873–1874: a Prelude to the 1877 Crisis," *Labor History*, II (1960); and Robert V. Bruce, *1877: Year of Violence* (1859).

KNIGHTS OF LABOR AND THEIR RIVALS: Gerald N. Grob, *Workers and Utopia: A Study of the Ideological Conflict in the American Labor Movement, 1865–1900* (1960) provides a new interpretation.

AMERICAN FEDERATION OF LABOR: Bernard Mandel, *Samuel Gompers: A Biography* (1963), provides the most complete account of the A.F.L. leader's life to date; James O. Morris, *Conflict within the A.F.L.: A Study of Craft versus Industrial Unionism, 1901–1938* (1958), is in many ways the most significant book in labor history in the last decade; and Marc Karson, *American Labor Unions in Politics, 1900–1918* (1958), not only relates the A.F.L.'s involvement in politics but also contains a significant and unfortunately neglected chapter on the influence of the Roman Catholic church on the early twentieth-century labor movement. An illustration of local labor problems is Robert E. L. Knight, *Industrial Relations in the San Francisco Bay Area, 1900–1918* (1960).

HOMESTEAD STRIKE: Leon Wolff, *Lockout* (1965), the first popular book-length account.

ANTHRACITE STRIKES: Robert H. Wiebe, "The Anthracite Strike of 1902: A Record of Confusion," *Mississippi Valley Historical Review,* XLVIII (1961).

PROGRESSIVE LABOR LEGISLATION: Jerold S. Auerbach, "Progressives at Sea: The Lafollette Act of 1915," *Labor History,* II (1961). Conflicting interpretations of the labor portions of the Clayton Act are provided in Robert K. Murray, "Public Opinion, Labor, and the Clayton Act," *Historian,* XXI (1959), and in Stanley I. Cutler, "Labor, the Clayton Act, and the Supreme Court," *Labor History,* III (1962).

ATTACK ON THE RADICALS: A major event of the post-First World War period is recorded in Robert L. Friedheim, *The Seattle General Strike* (1964).

DECADE OF DECLINE: A somewhat episodic account of the 1920s is provided in Irving Bernstein, *The Lean Years: A History of the American Worker, 1920–1933* (1960). Specific activities and problems in the Twenties are provided in Allen M. Wakstien, "The Origins of the Open Shop Movement, 1919–1920," *Journal of American History,* LI (1964); Stanley I. Cutler, "Chief Justice Taft, Judicial Unanimity, and Labor: the Coronado Case," *Historian,* XXIV (1961); and Milton J. Nadwerny, *Scientific Management and the Unions, 1900–1932: A Historical Analysis* (1955). The last years of the decade are thoroughly covered in Philip Taft, *The A.F. of L. from the Death of Gompers to the Merger* (1959).

TRADE UNIONS: A biography of one union leader prominent in the early twentieth century has been provided in Hyman Weintraub, *Andrew Furuseth: Emancipator of the Seamen* (1959). David Brody has written monographs on the early iron and steel workers in *Steelworkers in America: The Nonunion Era* (1960) and on butchers in *Butcher Workmen: A Study in Unionization* (1964). Reed C. Richardson has provided an especially timely study of the railway problem in *The Locomotive Engineer, 1863–1963: A Century of Railway Labor Relations and Work Rules* (1963).

LABOR DURING THE NEW DEAL: Although no attempt has yet been made to study the whole of labor's history during the New Deal, the previously mentioned volume by Taft on the post-Gompers A.F.L. should be consulted. In addition, Milton Derber and Edwin Young have edited a volume of essays by specialists to illuminate various issues in *Labor and the New Deal* (1957), and Walter Galenson has published *The CIO Challenge to the AFL: A History of the American Labor Movement, 1935–1941* (1960), which is primarily a history of individual trade unions. Jerold S. Auerbach has published an article on one specific New Deal event in "The LaFollette Committee: Labor and Civil Liberties in the New Deal," *Journal of American History,* LI (1964).

THE POST-WAR PERIOD: The only new books touching on this period are the aforementioned volumes by Dulles and Taft. Information on this period must still be secured from sources mentioned in the original bibliography. One provocative pamphlet is Solomon Barkin's, *The Decline of the Labor Movement* (1961).

Index

abolition of slavery, 100, 103
Adams, Deacon, 24
Adams, Sam, 30
Adamson Act, 271
Air Transport Act, 358
Allen, Samuel C., 82
Allied Industrial Workers, 432, 433
Altgeld, John P., 168, 203
Amalgamated Association of Iron, Steel, and Tin Workers, 131, 195
Amalgamated Clothing Workers, 259, 306
Amalgamated Trades and Labor Assembly of Chicago, 166
American Confederation (of socialists), 150
AMERICAN FEDERATION OF LABOR: war with the Knights, 175–178; origin,194; attempt to convert to political action, 197–198; growth between 1896–1904, 207–213; open shop campaign against, 213–223; corruption within, in early twentieth century, 221–222; internal divisions in early twentieth century, 222; revival after open-shop campaign, 250–260; departmentalization policy, 251; during World War I, 273–275; development between 1918 and 1921, 275; support of Progressive party, 299; effort to convert to industrial unionism, 301; campaign against communists in 1920's, 302; campaign in South during 1920's, 303; causes of decline after 1924, 303–307; attitude toward "dole," 323; opposition to minimum wages, 327, 359; attitude toward W.P.A., 333; revival after 1937, 361. *See also* AMERICAN FEDERATION OF LABOR AND CONGRESS OF INDUSTRIAL ORGANIZATIONS; jurisdictional conflicts; MEMBERSHIP; POLITICAL ACTIVITY

AMERICAN FEDERATION OF LABOR AND CONGRESS OF INDUSTRIAL ORGANIZATIONS: unity negotiations, 361, 383, 422–427; constitution, 425–427; organizing activity, 430; internal strengthening, 431; action against corruption, 432–434. *See also* AMERICAN FEDERATION OF LABOR; MEMBERSHIP; POLITICAL ACTIVITY

American Labor party, 297
American Labor party (of New York), 357, 366
American Labor Union, 237
American Liberty League, 356
American Railway Union, 200–201, 229, 230
Ammon, Robert H., 134
anarcho-syndicalism, 153–154, 166
antiextension movement, 101–102
Anti-Inflation Act of 1942, 379
anti-intimidation legislation, 113
ANTILABOR CAMPAIGNS: during nineteenth century, 56–57, 59, 81, 113–114, 168–169; open shop movement, 213–223; "American Plan" movement, 291–294; after 1937, 365; during New Deal, 373;

Executive Development Center
U. S. Department of Labor
14th & Constitution Ave., N.W.
Room 6148, Main Labor
Washington, D.C.   20210